# Contrast and Connection

# Contrast
# and Connection

*Bicentennial Essays in
Anglo-American History*

EDITED BY
H. C. ALLEN and ROGER THOMPSON
*of the University of East Anglia*

OHIO UNIVERSITY PRESS
Athens, Ohio
1976

© G. Bell & Sons Ltd. 1976

ISBN 0-8214-0355-9
Library of Congress Catalog
Number LC 76-7095

Printed by offset and bound
in the United States of America
for Ohio University Press, Athens, Ohio
by Oberlin Printing Co., Inc.

# Contents

v

# Foreword

For the erstwhile Mother Country of the 'revolting' colonies officially to celebrate two hundred years later the anniversary of the American Revolution is an exercise fraught with ambiguities. However, for a group of historians to signal this Bicentennial by publishing a set of essays is both felicitous and natural. Here is a *Festschrift*, but a *Festschrift* with a difference, in honour, not of a distinguished scholar and master but of an historical event, an event so momentous as to have exerted its own mastery upon a whole tradition of historical scholarship and scholars. The historiography of the American Revolution is almost as old as the event itself: and in ever more sophisticated and revisionist forms it continues to inform, if not the whole span of American history, certainly of Anglo-American relations. Only three of the essays in this volume deal with topics directly bearing on the Revolution itself, but they are all, without exception, concerned with the complex tissue of Anglo-American relationships, from the Puritan Migration to the Cold War, of which the events of 1776 were but a tear in the web.

There is a sense in which this *Festschrift* also celebrates a new coming-of-age in Anglo-American scholarship. For too long, from Henry Adams to the generation of Samuel Bemis, Anglo-American history was predominantly written by Americans; but with the growth in the last twenty years of interest in American history in Britain there has come to maturity a new generation of British scholars with professional concern in the Anglo-American field, in which by nature, nurture and access to sources they have become eminently qualified. This has not in any sense induced rivalry let alone separate national schools. On the contrary, the scholars of this British generation are almost as much the alumni of the great American graduate schools as their American counterparts, and certainly the accepted critical standards of research owe most of their rigour to our American colleagues if writing itself is still cherished as a native British talent.

At the same time most of our American colleagues have worked at British universities and on British archives. The result has been the emergence of a genuine Anglo-American temper of collaborative study. In this sphere of historical scholarship at any rate a 'special relationship' lives and is taken for granted. And so it is natural and not in the least surprising that this volume, which is an English gesture of homage to the Revolutionary Bicentennial, should include in its baker's dozen of essays, two by sympathetic American colleagues and friends. The rest are, with two Welsh exceptions, by Englishmen, and help justify the traditional description of the field as 'Anglo' and not 'British'-American.

This, then, is the spirit in which our thirteen authors offer this volume to celebrate the Bicentennial. Like almost all *Festschriften* this is a collection of distinct offerings by scholars mostly writing about their own special interests. They make a varied bundle, and this itself is also a reflection of the range of topics, the complex and sophisticated techniques, that modern scholarship may bring to bear upon the Anglo-American relationship. Three of the essays deal with traditional, orthodox, topics in diplomacy and international relations; Professor Maldwyn Jones on the diplomatic problems of transatlantic emigration, Professor Campbell on the ludicrous Edward J. Phelps as American Minister to London under Cleveland, and Mr Garson on the Anglo-American alliance during the second world war. But for the most part the essays are concerned with transatlantic connections of an institutional, social or ideological kind which take one far beyond the formal relations between the two States. In the two essays bearing on the Revolution itself Mr Bonwick analyses the role of English Dissenters and Professor Wright suggestively assesses the riches of archival material about the Loyalists, still to be explored. Anglo-American origins in the colonial period are strongly represented, in a study of the Massachusetts Charter of 1691 by Mr Simmons, some curiously revealing aspects of the reading tastes of Puritan Divines through the colonial book trade by Mr Thompson, and a stimulating account by Mr D. G. Allen of the migration from Hingham, Norfolk, to Hingham, Massachusetts: an essay in that rewarding contemporary *genre* of institutional studies, the result of marrying New England use of sources with the ideas of the Cambridge population group. Closer to the present and concerned with the early twentieth century there is original new work on the image of the American Trust in Britain, on the Anglo-American aspects of the Progressive movement and of Women's Suffrage. Each of these disparate themes in its own way is essentially related to the basic stuff of the Anglo-American connection as it has developed and altered over three centuries. In addition to these contributions on topics in specific historical periods two essays stand out for the widely ranging and speculative way in which their authors handle continuities and change in the Anglo-American relationships from the detonation of 1776 to the present, thereby giving an overt unity to the book as a whole. Mr Temperley applies new perceptions derived from modern mass psychology concerning images and image-makers to ideas about the image of America in Britain and vice versa, first explored by Allan Nevins and others a generation ago and there carried forward with a new seriousness of purpose. And finally, Professor Allen, in his historical perspective of Anglo-American relations, distills from his immense knowledge and experience the quintessential ideas and power relationships and he concludes by recording important compass readings for the present. It is a strong contribution in itself, but in addition, picking out as it does the dominant colours and patterns of the whole grand tapestry, it serves to inform the volume as a whole and to draw it into a more overt unity than would otherwise be readily apparent to the general reader from the individual chapters. This book does indeed possess an organic intellectual unity derived from the grandeur of its basic theme, and it permits a rich sequence of variations within it, and from its group of authors, colleagues of a generation who have grown to maturity in the professional study of Anglo-American history.

*University of East Anglia*                    FRANK THISTLETHWAITE
*Norwich*

# A Tale of Two Towns: Persistent English Localism in Seventeenth-Century Massachusetts

## DAVID GRAYSON ALLEN

With all the studies of early New England town development during the past decade, the English background of the early New England immigrants still remains a mystery. We still have little specific knowledge of conditions under which men lived in the decades before the Great Migration. Furthermore, not enough is known to be able to distinguish those who left from others who remained behind. And finally, we have seen only glimpses of how men of New England differed from their former neighbours once they had settled in the New World.

The matter is further compounded by the slim, though absorbing literature that is available. Even with the fine sensitivity for English local history that Sumner Chilton Powell displays in *Puritan Village*, one quickly senses his whiggish bias. The continuity of local English society with seventeenth-century New England is denied in important areas. 'To emigrate from accustomed social institutions and relationships to a set of unfamiliar communities . . . meant a startling transformation', he argues. 'The townsmen had to change or abandon almost every formal institution which they had taken for granted.' 'Life in Sudbury [Massachusetts] was indeed a "new" England.'[1] Certainly life in the New World was simpler and much of the institutional complexity of England waited until the following century under provincial arrangements. The significant question, however, was whether institutional behaviour had changed drastically after arrival in Massachusetts or whether the old, familiar ways of doing things were merely channelled through different or more simplified institutions. 'Gone were the courts-baron, courts-leet, vestries, out hundred courts' and countless other institutions, it might be argued, but did town and selectmen's meetings and local governmental business in New England, ranging from agricultural regulations to the types of men elected to town office, change drastically? More recently T. H. Breen and Stephen Foster have attempted to generalize about early seventeenth-century migration to New England from passenger lists of 1637. Taking their data of emigrants from primarily urban areas including a generous number from Norwich, the second largest city in the realm, they have postulated a migration of primarily urban artisans who upon arrival in the Bay Colony 'gave up their English callings to become farmers in New England'.[2] Did the transatlantic passage have such a disrupting effect on the lives of most emigrants, however? It will be some time, of course, before a figure for the actual number of urban emigrants can be made even from our incomplete data of the passenger lists of the Great Migration, and even longer before life-long residents can be distinguished from less permanent men who arrived in London, Norwich and other provincial capitals only years before embarkation to America. More likely a larger number of men came from small to medium sized English market towns where the shock of transition from Old to New England was less noticeable. Even so, seventeenth-century English urban centres were hardly comparable to their nineteenth- and twentieth-century counterparts. Borough officers spent time and energy in enforcing agricultural regulations and the occupational structure there and in market towns was much more fluid. Borough men in seventeenth-century England were never really far away from agriculture or the necessity and ability to shift from one trade to another. Tradesmen from less urban areas and weavers and spinners usually combined a number of pursuits in order to make their livelihood.[3]

Finally, there is John Waters's well-known study of early Hingham, Massachusetts. Unlike the other writers he describes how conservative the change from Old to New England was as men in new Hingham 'successfully preserved many features of traditional English life in the Massachusetts wilderness'.[4] But his yardstick of steadfastness to local ways actually extended to only two political issues between the town and the General Court, the familiar cases of the Child Petition and the Militia Dispute of 1645. In this regard Hingham was hardly unique; it was like many communities which either had local problems that were only reluctantly carried up to the county and General Court or asserted their own local rights in opposition to higher authority.[5]

Waters's concept of town conservatism was skilfully emphasized by the theme of a 'generation of rivalry' between East Anglian settlers who were principally from Hingham, Norfolk, and earlier arrivals in the New England community (which they called 'Bear Cove') from widely scattered places in the West Country. And yet with the possible exceptions of the Militia Dispute and the shift from West Country to East Anglian town officers in the late 1630s and early 1640s, Waters shows few demonstrable or potential signs of friction between the two English groups. Indeed, what is striking in the early Hingham town records is the lack of any conscious effort to institute West Country ways when these men were 'in power'. What they do suggest is how overwhelmingly East Anglian customs and local practices came to dominate daily life in the community. In matters ranging from land management and agricultural practices to leadership structure and town government, the habits of old Hingham carried over to the new even when social and economic reasons for doing so no longer existed. In calling a small promontory of land in their harbour 'World's End', the men of new Hingham may have seen themselves as that far-flung Christian outpost described in Psalms 23:27, but they seldom acted as men driven by circumstances to abandon familiar ways of doing things in the New England wilderness.

Hingham is unique among Massachusetts communities in having a sizeable number of its inhabitants originate from a single English community of the same name, but as such it also provides an unusual opportunity to compare basic features of pre-industrial community development. The purpose of this essay is to explore these two communities in some of their most important activities of daily living. Like most New England immigrants, Hingham men came from English agricultural towns where they pursued a life based on the soil with some small trades and crafts. The agricultural economies of both Old and New England towns were remarkably alike. Emphasis on agriculture meant preoccupation with landholdings and in this regard the Massachusetts community perpetuated with extraordinary detail the land system which characterized central Norfolk in the early seventeenth century. Both communities were also run by a small group of local families, yet both were founded upon a strong township organization where all power and approval of actions by local leaders ultimately had to come from the 'inhabitants' in the vestry or town meeting. Life in this Massachusetts community was more a new 'England' than a 'new' England.

In every direction from present-day Hingham, Norfolk, there are small villages with their omnipresent churches, often great monuments in now shrunken or nonexistent communities. From the bounds of Hingham alone probably as many as a dozen churches are visible, but now they are often isolated and deteriorating. Seventeenth-century sources indicate that the area encompassed by the Norwich and Norfolk dioceses contained a very large concentration of parishes, a considerable number more than most areas of the country of equivalent size.[6] The physical conspicuousness of the village church seems to have been matched by its equally important role in town affairs in Norfolk communities, or so appears to have been the case in Hingham. Based on strong notions of 'town' government through the parish organization, still dependent upon a need for some common agricultural regulations such as in the Midlands, yet living in a region in which the manor no longer functioned in activities essential to the local villager, a comparable set of relationships in law, government, economy and society was established in the New World Hingham. These, in fact, produced much less of a 'revolution in the systems of social and economic status' involving 'a staggering number of changes' than has been formerly thought.[7]

Hingham, itself, was not a very conspicuous English parish, though it was considerably larger than average. It was the head town of a deanery containing forty-three parishes, but this was of waning importance by the seventeenth century. Located about eighteen miles west of Norwich, its population at the beginning of the seventeenth century numbered 500 communicants, or about 800 inhabitants in all. Although major market towns were much larger, contemporary documents refer to Hingham as a marketing centre for the surrounding countryside and occasionally even call it a 'Borowe'.[8]

In addition to the numbers from old Hingham, the New England community was inhabited by others from the surrounding Norfolk towns of Wymondham, Attleborough, Bridgham and Hapton Hall.[9]

Although physical geography and soil varied widely throughout
Norfolk, Henry Spelman, a contemporary, explained that there were
basically only two regions where 'the parte of it toward the Sea &
mutch of the reste Westward is champian: the other parte toward
Suffolk, woodland & pasture grounde'. Hingham and surrounding
communities were on the fringe of these two agricultural regions
'betwixt the grazing & the Corn parts' sharing characteristics of both.
Like the woodland–pasture region it was 'susteined cheifely by
Grazinge, by Deyries, & by rearing of Cattell', while on the other
hand it normally produced sufficient quantities of grain, as in the
champion sheep and corn country to the north.[10]

Though usually self-sustaining, Hingham was susceptible to the
periodic 'vulnerability' of crop failure and other natural catastrophe
of the 'woody part of Norfolk'. This region supported many more
small husbandmen than did the champion country. Here the small
farmer possessed a larger holding than his counterpart in the open
fields of the north where large-scale capitalistic farming predominated.
Favourable as the size of his holding might be for him to secure his
livelihood, the wood–pasture country swelled in population creating
social instability and insecurity in times of scarcity. In Forehoe
Hundred, in which both Hingham and Wymondham lay, royal rates
collected in the late 1620s indicate that it was among the most populous
rural areas in the county.[11]

Swelling populations and increasingly smaller acreages devoted
primarily to animal raising allowed the time and encouraged the drive
for many woodland families to supplement their small incomes by
taking up home 'industries'. In some regions it might have been wood-
craft or iron production, but in the Norfolk woods where most
inhabitants were dairy and cattle men 'a greate many' were also 'hand
crafte men . . . [who] lyve by dressing & combinge of woolle, carding,
spinning, weaving &c'.[12]

The effects of this vulnerable subsistent life in old Hingham on
religion and migration in the decades before 1640 merit further discussion elsewhere.[13] Yet with all the uncertainties of this English
economy, it was reproduced intact in new Hingham. In Hingham,
Norfolk, it consisted primarily of dairying though supplemented with
some grain growing on limited arable land to feed their livestock and
for local consumption. Nearly all homes with inventories had a dairy

room or buttery, together with churns, pails and other equipment regardless of the size of the estate. The lack of agricultural equipment in many inventories suggests extensive sharing of needed items for production on arable land as in common-field areas. Cloth-making supplied the extra income and filled the spare hours which cattle tending provided. A great number of inventories refer to yarn, wool and hemp. Some state that there were '29 pounds yarne' at £20, or '34 grose of woolsy' for £25:10:00, but many estates list more humble entries averaging, as Margaret Beale's did, £3:01:00 in wool and yarn.[14]

The modest estate of John James, Yeoman, who died in 1662 with an inventory valued at only £45:16:00 reveals an outline of the agricultural structure of this Norfolk community. James's estate included 4 cows and 2 bullocks, 9 sheep, 1 mare, hay in the barn, a plow and cart, a cart harness, poultry, grain in a chamber valued at £3:10:00, and cheeses worth £3. Even estates valued at ten times as much, of men not primarily engaged in agriculture, were similarly proportioned. When Edmund Dey, clerk of the church, died in 1667, his goods included 80 cheeses, 1 horse and mare, 3 milch cows, 3 heifers, a calf, some swine, grain and hay worth £28, some wood in the yard, carts and a plow with furniture and some malt.[15]

A fairly distinct picture emerges, then, from seventeenth-century Hingham, Norfolk inventories. Most farmers in the area devoted their primary attentions to dairying and some rearing, though the largest herds in Hingham, as judged from extant records, were never over a dozen head. There was also some interest in horse breeding such as the ten John Cowper, Jr, was raising when his estate was proved in 1617. A number of farmers had some sheep, but they were never raised to the same extent as in the sheep–corn region in northern Norfolk. Pig-raising and poultry-keeping were very important sidelines in the area.[16]

Several grains were grown. The Hingham 'Town Book' of the late seventeenth century refers yearly to the prices of four crops, presumably the four grown there, but possibly the most commonly imported, or a combination of the two. These included barley, wheat, rye, peas (both grey and white), and oats as well as vetches, roughly in that order of importance. All are accounted for in local inventories of individuals who died during or just after the growing season.

Robert Constable had 1 coombe of wheat, 5 bushels of barley, and 10 coombes of malt worth £5 in his corn chamber, while Edward Lincoln, linen weaver, left 14 coombes of barley, 5 of wheat, rye, and of white peas all worth £11:15:00. Wealthy Francis Bubbin had in his corn chamber 4 coombes of wheat, 2 of 'mistlyn', 7 of malt, and 6 bushels of gray peas. Hay was a constant item in men's estates as well, a supplement to other winter feed for their dairy herds.[17]

By far the most arresting items were the individual listings of wood and timber. Even the lowliest of estates contained an entry of 'wood in yard' or 'timber in wood house'. There was a great variety of wood in the region including hazel and oak as well as the highly sought after ash used by coopers for herring barrels in the fishing industry off the Norfolk coast. The lumber was readily sold and easily transported to various points by river and coastal vessels. The river Yare which flows through Norwich on its way to Yarmouth has its headwaters near Cranworth, only several miles northwest of Hingham. Such commercial uses of wood became a central problem in the New England Hingham, one which created more town orders and controversy than any other single issue in the early years.[18]

Inventories filed in Massachusetts bear out an essential continuity of the structure of Norfolk agriculture in the New World. Hingham remained basically a dairying town. Oxen may have more often replaced Suffolk Punches as draft animals for the arable land. This was due in large part, no doubt, to the labour required to cultivate heavy virgin soils. Pig-raising and cattle-rearing were important secondary interests there, as they had been in Norfolk. Weaving remained a vital part-time occupation, and grain production included all those used in old Hingham except for Indian corn which was substituted for white and grey peas.[19]

Dairying and rearing activities became the basis for several town regulations in new Hingham. As early as 1640 the town ordered that 'there shall be no *Tree* or *Trees* cut, or felled upon the *Clay*, upon the *Payne* of *twenty shillings*, to be *levied* to the use of the Town, because all those Trees are to be preserved for the shading of *Cattle* in the summer time'. Several years earlier as land at Nantascus was being prepared for division among the proprietors, the method selected was 'according to the number of names—having some respect to men's stock—*that is to say*—three acres to a person—and of all other stock

of lesser cattle, or goods proportionable as it amounteth to a cow—
be it more or less, being a rule nearest the rule of the word of God,
as far as we are empowered'. Later on, cattle became a most significant
variable in the determination of town rates. At the same time all lands
improved for 'corn' or broken arable were rated at only thirty shillings
per acre, whereas improved salt or fresh water meadow used for livestock was valued twice as highly.[20]

Dairying was a significant part of the overall proportion and value
in new Hingham inventories, though it was supplemented by other
activities in much the same way as in Norfolk. Inventories of villagers
from the most important to the least significant all generally corre-
sponded to this pattern. John Farrow, whose estate was valued at only
£78:14:00, included one ox at £3, 3 cows at £7, 2 swine at £1:04:00,
some 'lynnen & wollen' cloth at £2:10:00, and lumber for £1:14:00.
Another smaller inventory, of Margaret Johnson lately widowed, contained 2 cows, 2 shoats, some flaxen yarne, along with pork, butter,
suet, wheat and cheese as provisions in the house. Thomas Thaxter's
larger inventory of £213:18:04 included 2 oxen, 4 cows, 2 three-year-
old steers, 1 two-year-old heifer, 4 calves, 8 'milch gootes', 2 fat hogs,
6 shoats, 20 bushels of wheat, '2 Remnants of woolen cloth', 3 bushels
of rye, 7 bushels of peas, some Indian corn and meal, and some
pork worth £3:10:00 which was for household consumption or for
sale.[21]

There may have been more 'corn land' or arable fields in new
Hingham than old, which made it easier for New World settlers to
supply their needs, but with the exceptions of some large open-field
areas granted to settlers in the first divisions, new Hingham did not
contain extensive arable areas. The early inhabitants were more interested in meadow land, or salt or fresh water marsh as the names of
most early grants indicate. Later, from the 1650s to the 1670s, the
grants of land were almost exclusively for timber rights of the territory,
and there never seems to have been a concerted effort among the proprietors to acquire additional acreage of arable land in the seventeenth
century.

Stephen Lincoln, who came from Wymondham in Norfolk, left an
inventory which typified this dairying economy. He had no arable,
neither plow nor oxen, but had raised 4 cows and a yearling, a mare
colt, 5 ewes, 1 ram and a lamb, 3 hogs and 2 pigs and must have just

purchased a £4:10:00 supply of salt marsh hay for the winter of 1658/9 when he died. In addition, he had a quantity of woollen cloth valued at £8, some sheep's wool, and cotton wool and yarn for his pursuit in the local handicraft, plus some stored cheese, and finally his valuable collection of carpenter's tools. Men like Lincoln balanced their dependence upon others for the products of the arable against their own independence and flexibility in various skills ranging from cheese and clothmaking to carpentry.[22]

Lincoln was not alone in retaining the weaving habits of the Norfolk woods where it only supplemented an essentially strong dairying and rearing economy. There was a rough parity between the Old and New World communities as to the number engaged in this part-time livelihood. One of the four Thomas Lincolns of new Hingham, designated by his neighbours as Thomas Lincoln, 'Weaver', was one of at least three such men who occupied most of their time in this pursuit and had spinning wheels, pairs of cards, and a supply of wool, cotton and sometimes flax along with finished cloth. Two out of every three other new Hingham inventories mentioned more modest supplies or equipment, particularly 'woolen & linnen yearne' as in Edward Wilder's, but some contained more ambitious lists such as Nicholas Jacobs's 14 pounds of wool or John Tucker's 4 yards of 'searge' and 12½ yards of 'holland'.[23]

As in Hingham, Norfolk, a significant aspect of the local economy was in selling wood and lumber. Samuel Maverick described Hingham principally as the supplier of Boston 'with wood, timber, leather and board' as well as trees for masts. Edward Johnson also visited Hingham in the early years and stated that its 'people have much profited themselves by transporting Timber, Plank and Mast for Shipping to the Town of Boston, as also Ceder and Pine-board to supply the wants of other Townes, and also to remote parts, even as far as Barbadoes'. Although inventories do not indicate the whole scope of this activity in Hingham, they do show some of its aspects. Thomas Andrew's estate mentions the wages due from the county for a load of cedar bolts of £12, while Nicholas Jacob had an entry referring to 'board wood & a boat of Barke' valued at £5:04:00. In addition, the town records show, for instance, that in 1638 Thomas Nichols sold 3 acres of land, 'planting land', to Ralph Smith 'for *five hundred* of merchantable Cedar *boards*'. The underlying significance of the timber and lumber trade in Hingham, as we shall see later, was more important than these commercial entries indicate.[24]

The position of Hingham, Norfolk, between two distinct forms of agricultural production also implied a land system reflecting this variation. In simplest terms the land pattern of central Norfolk contained elements of the Midland open-field system, but at the same time incorporated some characteristics of the enclosed consolidated farmsteads of the woodlands in Suffolk and Essex to the south. Village land surveys in many parts of central Norfolk reveal this characteristic pattern. In Horstead and Lessingham, Norfolk, for example, the field 'strips' of open-field agriculture had become in this system field blocks or 'pieces', as they were called, varying in size from 5 acres to 1 rood. In the wood–pasture country of Forncett as early as the fourteenth century 'the rolls contain no clear indications that there were within the vill three great fields', as in the Midland system; ' "campi" are mentioned, but they were numerous and small'. The pattern was typically of small blocks of land which were tiny and unconsolidated by the standards of farmsteads of Suffolk and Essex, yet small enough and often in roughly defined and scattered 'fields' to demand some sort of common regulation and supervision though not necessarily in the Midland open-field manner.[25]

The 1633 Hingham glebe terrier or listing of church lands highlights some important aspects of the central Norfolk land pattern of small holdings in 'fields'. The glebe contained twenty-three parcels of land, excluding the parsonage and its 6-acre lot, ranging in size from a plot of 3 roods to one of 3 acres. The average size of each lot was only about 7/6 of an acre. Some lands did lay in 'fields' such as Church field where several were 'newly enclosed' or in West field, but as the former holding suggests, the agricultural significance of the 'field' as such was diminishing here and undoubtedly it had been abandoned altogether in other parts of the town. In fact, the chief roads of the township appear to be the distinguishing factor in identifying the location of much glebe land rather than positions in 'fields'. In a great many instances, the small Hingham glebe plots were parcels, often 'pightles', in various closes or crofts—both enclosed areas—in such places as Woodcock, White and Shoemaker close. In addition, there was some apparent consolidation as a small number of parcels abutted each other, and several others were 'lyeing nyghe' one another in fields. Possibly individuals' lands were more consolidated than the church glebe since many of the closes were given the name of a contemporary rather than some predecessor on the land. Nevertheless, the lands of old Hingham men were also scattered. Peter Sharpe's lands bounded the glebe parcels throughout the village—at the Sharp Close, Dumes Close, 'Five Roodes', and three other unspecified locations—as did the lands of such men as Robert Cooper, Henry and Richard Lincoln and Robert Longe.[26]

Therefore, in seventeenth-century Hingham, Norfolk, there were a large number of small scattered enclosures each of which was probably further divided up into enclosed plots by a small group of men, giving the countryside, as contemporaries remarked, a distinctly wooded appearance. Quite likely men who owned land in each close got together from time to time to adopt regulatory orders for the land by private agreement. The manor or town could intervene in a general way upon the activities of these men in their enclosures if it became necessary, and they undoubtedly used their authority upon individual farmers in establishing regulations upon the common grazing lands and wastes used by their livestock. Since all commons and wastes were not enclosed until 1780, a century and a half after the Hingham emigrants left, there must have been some common regulation of grazing areas and arable fields in the 1630s.[27] This slowness to change was also reflected in the inactive state of land transactions in the town as judged by surviving feet of fines records.[28] Consequently Hingham's hybrid land system remained stable and unaffected throughout the seventeenth century.

From 18 June 1635, the first day land was formally granted and recorded in Hingham, New England, there was never a totally contemplated system of large open fields divided into strips where *all* proprietors could receive their appointed share. Except for the house lots, the original 'planting' lots, and the 'Great Lots' which were soon expended, no sizeable number of inhabitants received land from the same 'fields'. Even in these there was not an equitable division as in typical open fields. In the 'Great Lots', for instance, only eighteen men received grants on 4 June 1636, and not all of the original proprietors ever received land there or in comparable arable fields elsewhere.

Instead, most parcels of land came from small areas of land found haphazardly throughout the township and divided up among several to perhaps twenty settlers. The place names for these odd-sized enclosures convey some impression of how they were originally appropriated by the settlers. On 12 June 1637, several men received from the town the 'fresh meadow as you go to Weymouth myll' while others on the same day were given portions of 'a little meadow lying to the north west of the fresh meadow going to Weymouth Mill', or 'Salt marsh, at Lawford's Liking as you go up to the Strayts Pond, in the South side of the river, that run[s] east and west'. It would appear from these and other examples that Hingham men were expected to petition the town for scattered areas of land throughout the unclaimed portion of the township as they were found.

And so land division in Hingham took one of two forms: open fields or small scattered enclosures, and it was not surprising that these old Hingham patterns were followed in the new. After all, some of the initial land grants, such as Nantascus Division of 5 March 1637/8, were made under the direction of townsmen Anthony Eames, Edmund Hobart, Sr, Samuel Ward, Thomas Hammond, Edmund Hobart, Jr, and Joseph Andrews, all *deputed* by the Town, and *body* of *Freemen*. Two-thirds of these men were from old Hingham or other parts of East Anglia. By 1640 when 'Conyhasset' divisions were made only two of the nine man committee in charge of the task can be identified as having come from outside this eastern English region. The town, however, was never as careful in supervising divisions of land for individuals throughout the township. Townsmen were consequently encouraged by default to seek out small pockets of desirable land and petition the town for ownership. It was assumed that men entitled to land would receive it 'in a place convenient, as soon as a place can be discovered'.[29]

The size of landholdings in Hingham, New England, before 1670 varied widely. Some 146 individuals received lands in the original divisions and most of these grants were rather modest. The average holding in Hingham was $22\frac{1}{2}$ acres, while the median figure was 15 acres. The average grant in Hingham was about half again as large as the typical holding in central Norfolk in the early seventeenth century, but new Hingham was never overcrowded with small freeholders as was the Norfolk countryside during this period. Nevertheless, the size of holdings indicates that no 'revolution of status' accompanied the crossing of the Atlantic by Hingham townsmen.[30] Furthermore, study of land records reveals that these Massachusetts settlers, no different from their Norfolk counterparts, were only slightly more inclined to view the value of land as commercial potential or as a medium of exchange. Unlike men in other Massachusetts towns the movement toward consolidation of their scattered bits of land or the selling of unwanted or unused portions for more profitable parcels never became an absorbing ambition or a dedicated goal of the settlers of Hingham.[31]

In recreating the new Hingham economy and land practices from the old, this community also continued familiar patterns of leadership in town government. In the woodland–pasture region of Norfolk the manor never commanded the influence over men it did in the open-field country of the Midlands. The East Anglian woods harboured another institution, the town or parish, which increasingly directed the activities of local men there which four, six or twelve manors in the same geographical space could not provide. A fairly complete listing of parish officers for the period from 1660 to 1690 exists and this period coincides with available records of selectmen's elections in new Hingham. A comparison shows how closely men in the New World community were tied to Old World assumptions of leadership.

Two churchwardens were annually chosen in Hingham, Norfolk, so that in the period from 1660 to 1690 (excluding 1681), there were sixty positions (plus the one created at a resignation) to be filled. Forty-seven men served, 35 of them for only one year, 10 for two, and 2 for three years. About 25 per cent of the men controlled 40 per cent of the positions.

There were 129 positions to be filled among the overseers of the poor, the other important English parish office, during this period since four were generally chosen each year although the number was occasionally increased to six. Ninety-seven men served, 76 of them for only a year, 16 for two, 1 for three, 3 for four, and 1 for six years. Taken separately, the overseers, who were responsible for the largest share of the town finances each year, accounted for little consolidation of responsibility among townsmen. But when the names of overseers and churchwardens are matched, several patterns develop. The top 10 per cent of the most frequently elected individuals to both offices filled 48 out of 190 positions, or 25.3 per cent of the total. The top 25 per cent controlled 93 positions, or 48.9 per cent. If those men elected to constableships were also included as well as manorial positions which are extant after 1690, even greater consolidation of office-holding would be apparent.[32]

There was also a strong correlation between the number of terms an individual served and his economic position in this Norfolk community. Unfortunately, few tax records of seventeenth-century Hingham have survived, including the Hearth Tax returns of the 1660s and 1670s. However, one rate for 1689 does exist for the town and it lists 118 ratepayers.[33] Of course, the rate does not include all those who served in office between 1660 and 1690, but among those that are listed, nearly all of them are among the top per cent of the town in rated wealth (see Table 1).

TABLE 1

*Tax ranking of the most consistently elected churchwardens and overseers 1660–90, Hingham, Norfolk*

| Name | Terms served | Ranking in the 1689 Tax Assessment |
|------|------|------|
| Samuel Pyke | 6 | 14 |
| Barnaby Parlet | 5 | 17 |
| Isaac Fison | 4 | 11 |
| Samuel Gilman | 4 | 21 |
| John Amyas, Gentleman | 4 | 6 |
| John Duffield | 4 | 29 |
| Henry Andrews | 4 | 36 |

Rankings of these individuals would have been higher if those at the top of the rate list, such as the Lord of the Manor and the Rector, plus gentlemen of property who did not reside in Hingham were excluded. Nevertheless, these men and others who had been regularly elected but who had died previously to this rating represented a much more selective group than might otherwise have been chosen.

Hingham leadership patterns represented one final characteristic. To the men in this town and perhaps other towns of a similar size and function in seventeenth-century England, occupation in a town or parish position may have been almost as much a proprietary right as it was a vehicle to promote the common good. Fathers were replaced by their sons, and sons by their sons. Using last names alone, some fifty-one men related by name held eighty-eight positions as overseer or

churchwarden from 1660 to 1690, filling about 45 per cent of all
positions available for those offices.

This was one of the most clearly transmitted presumptions of local
leadership which was carried to new Hingham. In the years prior to
1686 there had been forty separate elections for selectmen in the new
town accounting for a total of 226 positions. Three families alone held
34.5 per cent of all the positions. These included the Hobarts (Edmund
Sr and Jr, Joshua, Josiah, David and Thomas), the Cushings (Matthew
I and II and Daniel), and the Beals (Joshua, Caleb, John Sr, Nathaniel
and Heremiah) who accounted for 78 positions. In all, 39 men of the
67 chosen as selectmen were related in name to each other as father,
son or grandson. This accounted for over 58 per cent of all men
chosen and 64.2 per cent of all the positions available.[34]

Even in other Massachusetts towns composed primarily of men
from nearby Suffolk or Essex, there was never such a close relationship
between family and office-holding. In both Ipswich and Watertown
there may have been a greater consolidation of office-holding by fewer
men, but fewer of them were known to be directly related or sharing a
common last name. In Watertown, for instance, only 28 of the 76 men
chosen as selectmen before 1686, or 36.8 per cent, were so related,
while in Ipswich the number was even lower, 18 out of 65, or 27.8 per
cent, during the same period.[35]

'Proprietary' ties to leadership certainly encouraged consolidation
of office-holding in new Hingham and may help to explain why it was
even more effective in the new community. This attitude may tell us
why men like Joshua Hobart (b. 1614), son of the town patriarch and
brother of the town minister, began his seventeen terms as selectman
in 1644 (and his twenty-four terms as town representative to the
General Court) at such an early age and was able to hold on to these
and other town positions through the consent of the inhabitants as
older leaders died off. Perhaps, too, Minister Peter Hobart's 'tendency
to Presbyterianism', so often commented upon by contemporaries,
reinforced or complemented ideas about local leadership from a
religious source.[36]

Whatever the reasons, Hingham, Massachusetts, had a considerably
tight-knit group of town leaders. The top 10 per cent of the most
frequently elected of them, some seven men, controlled 83 positions
for a total of 36.7 per cent. The top 25 per cent, or eighteen men, held

144 positions for 63.7 per cent of the total. As in Hingham, Norfolk, their social position was high. Eleven of these eighteen men had inventories recorded before 1692, and nearly half of those eleven were among the top 10 per cent of inventoried town wealth, while 90 per cent were among the top 25 per cent.[37] While there is no evidence that the leaders of new Hingham were 'the very families that had held positions of leadership in the old country', as Waters has stated,[38] they certainly did bring with them the essential presumptions of leadership from their Norfolk community.

The pattern of town government offers a final example of how Norfolk men carried over social institutions intact from their English setting. Hinghamites brought with them strong notions of 'townsmanship' not common to all other settlers in Massachusetts, and through their leaders and the town meeting, the men of this community were able to perpetuate a strong dairying economy, a land system and other local distinctions through the town by-laws and customs they enacted.

In viewing English local governmental institutions of the seventeenth century, it has already been suggested how little the manor seemed to affect the life of these Norfolk villagers. There were some specific reasons for manorial 'decay' here. In the first place, Hingham manor was not coterminous with Hingham parish. In all, there were at least three manors existing within Hingham bounds in the early seventeenth century—Hingham, Hingham Gurneys and Hingham Rectory—and possibly a fourth, Ellingham Hall Manor. Several centuries earlier and before some consolidation there may have been twice as many in the township. In Norfolk as a whole there had been a general consolidation of manors, so that by 1600 only one village in three had more than one manor. Hingham was in sharp contrast to this.[39]

In addition to the lack of effective territorial control over the expanse of the parish, records of the 'Hingham Rectory Manor' suggest that, for the most part, manorial government only periodically functioned here. During the reigns of James and Charles I, for instance, the manor court may have met on possibly three occasions but no more. The court may have governed with more detail in the time of Philip and Mary when the records began, or have met more regularly as it did in the later Stuart and early Hanoverian periods, but its institutional presence barely could have been known to future Hingham emigrants in the early seventeenth century. The same account could be made for 'Hingham' manor records which have only survived from the 1690s. Only basic manorial functions such as homage, jury selection and other routine matters fill its pages.[40]

Norfolk manors generally suffered from other weaknesses as well. Weak or 'open' manors could not control rapid growth of population where there was land to attract the landless. There seems to have been little effort to check the growth of such wanderers among the wood–pasture manors of central Norfolk. The region, too, was one in which there were few resident major gentry. The Woodhouse family, lords of Hingham manor, lived in nearby Kimberly. There were the Cranes in Woodrising and the Knevetts in Ashwellthorpe, both some distance away, but by and large if gentry resided in Norfolk in the early seventeenth century, they lived on the manors of the sheep–corn area to the north and east, and not in the wood–pasture region in the south. The Woodhouses' local presence never appeared to reflect particular interest in the management of Hingham manor, however. They were large landowners and controlled several manors in the region. More important, their interests were directed away from the locality to the county level. There they served as justices of the peace and busied themselves in and out of sessions in the administration of laws regulating social and economic affairs throughout the region such as those imposed during the critical harvest years of the 1620s and 1630s. The Woodhouses also served a very active role in the county militia, one member became deputy lieutenant of the county during the early seventeenth century.[41]

In addition to the decline of Hingham manors, the township had special characteristics which were uncommon to most parishes. For instance, Hingham enjoyed special royal privileges of which local inhabitants were probably keenly aware. Being an ancient demesne of the crown, Hingham inhabitants were exempted from jury service at the assizes or quarter sessions. Tenants were, in addition, excused from the payment of tolls while going into Norwich and travelling through-out the country. They were also exempt from contributing to the expenses of knights of the shire in Parliament. These privileges, most of which were granted in the fourteenth and fifteenth centuries, were repeatedly reconfirmed throughout the period in 1564, 1610 and 1703.

Special rights such as these were not the only provisions of which borough charters were made, but they did convey with periodic reconfirmation a sense of corporateness to Hingham inhabitants which many Englishmen did not possess.[42]

Hingham residents also must have felt this sense of municipality through the act of selecting parish officers and of requiring duties from them. Villagers expected to choose men representing them and providing service for their section of the town so that when four constables were chosen in 1656 and all were 'remote from Market Stead or Town Street', a complaint was made to quarter sessions that 'Hingham inhabitants' were 'accustomed to choose one or two constables' for that section of town. A 'List of suitable names' was submitted to the justices so that this void might be filled quickly.[43]

The meetings in which the parish officers were chosen were in a strict sense, vestry meetings, though inhabitants at the time simply referred to them as 'town' meetings much as some of them would call their periodic assemblages in New England. In addition to the election of churchwardens and overseers of the poor, this annual meeting in Hingham also selected the town constables. In Midland areas this would have normally been the function of the court leet, the manorial court charged with police power. But in Hingham, whether due to the decline of manorial government, the need for a more efficient tax collecting system, or a desire for more responsive control over local officials, constables were chosen for the year, listed in the 'Town Book', and were required at year's end to make an account of revenue and expenses to be 'yeilded up to ye Inhabitants then present' at the meeting.

In electing constables, churchwardens, surveyors or way wardens, and overseers each year and approving of their actions, Hingham inhabitants were giving their support to men levying rates on them which were abnormally high for English parish standards of this size during the seventeenth century. Table 2 lists all three accounts separately except for the years when several were combined. These rates were phenomenally high for a group of only 118 ratepayers, ranging from 12s. to £2 on the average for each individual. In many parishes, rates occurred only on special occasions, but they came with ceaseless regularity in Hingham. Churchwardens' rates fluctuated according to the needs of the parish, often being related to the current state of repair of church property. Even though Hingham's rate varied from year to year, it was, overall, higher than towns and boroughs much larger in size.

TABLE 2

*Hingham, Norfolk, Town Accounts, 1661–90*[44]

| Year | Constables' Accounts | Church-wardens' Accounts | | Overseers' Accounts |
|---|---|---|---|---|
| | (£:s:d) | (£:s:d) | | (£:s:d) |
| 1661 | 8:02:04 | | 85:02:07 | |
| 1662 | 11:11:08 | | 75:11:00 | |
| 1663 | 9:15:08 | | 74:18:00 | |
| 1664 | 9:17:00 | 178:06:04 | | 58:10:00 |
| 1665 | 10:18:04 | 99:14:02 | | 52:01:05 |
| 1666 | 13:00:04 | 18:15:00 | | 49:11:08 |
| 1667 | 13:00:00 | 25:19:00 | | 43:17:04 |
| 1668 | 12:11:00 | 8:12:00 | | 43:03:06 |
| 1669 | 8:08:08 | 9:15:00 | | 38:12:00 |
| 1670 | 8:15:00 | 22:06:01 | | 48:15:00 |
| 1671 | 6:10:06 | 23:07:00 | | 55:10:06 |
| 1672 | 5:10:00 | 12:03:04 | | 52:06:09 |
| 1673 | 6:10:00 | 8:12:00 | | 53:12:06 |
| 1674 | 8:11:04 | 29:07:00 | | 68:05:04 |
| 1675 | 19:08:07 | 20:10:05 | | 68:04:10 |
| 1676 | 9:10:00 | 17:18:00 | | 78:10:00 |
| 1677 | 9:08:06 | 41:11:00 | | 67:12:02 |
| 1678 | 5:04:06 | 13:10:04 | | 71:13:09 |
| 1679 | 8:07:04 | 28:16:06 | | 71:03:06 |
| 1680 | 6:05:05 | 22:02:03 | | 84:02:04 |
| 1681 | 12:13:02 | 12:03:00 | | 78:00:00 |
| 1682 | 6:06:10 | 18:16:04 | | 90:12:01 |
| 1683 | 9:09:05 | | 113:16:07 | |
| 1684 | | 18:08:00 | | 82:10:06 |
| 1685 | 16:18:08 | 15:04:00 | | 83:03:04 |
| 1686 | 10:04:10 | 8:17:03 | | 91:15:09 |
| 1687 | 10:01:00 | 59:14:06 | | 81:09:02 |
| 1688 | 9:05:07 | 20:03:00 | | 76:00:09 |
| 1689 | 14:02:08 | 22:16:04 | | 79:19:03 |
| 1690 | 8:01:05 | 17:15:02 | | 82:04:01 |

North of London in Berkhamsted, Herts, for instance, the borough churchwardens levied rates irregularly ranging in size from £5:05:01 to £35 over a period of twenty-five years. There was one rare £600 assessment in 1630 for which the ratepayer was to 'be rated as he has been up to £1' which was below Hingham's maximum rate. With few exceptions, however, the churchwardens of Berkhamsted seldom made assessments in excess of the small market town of Hingham. In Cottingham, Yorks, a parish more comparable in size to Hingham, the parish rates varied in size, but were generally much lower than Hingham. In the decade of the 1660s, for instance, there were three years where no assessment was made, and two years in which the rate was £56 and £34, respectively. Most other years it was nearer £10.[45]

The remarkable fact about the Hingham figures is, however, the consistently high level of funds devoted for disbursement among the poor by the overseers. With the enactment of poor law legislation in the closing years of Elizabeth's reign, the parish became the focal point of social change and policy at the expense of the manor, particularly in areas such as central Norfolk where conditions were crowded and harvests uncertain. However such large sums were given out by the overseers, the experience provided training in local government for many as well as fostering a closer relationship between inhabitants and leaders through a 'town' government.

Despite the heavy responsibility and wide power local leaders had through their taxing and disbursal functions as well as their close economic and family ties as a group, the wisdom of their decisions did not go unchallenged in Hingham. Whenever expenditures exceeded revenues, churchwardens would petition the town for reimbursement. In lieu of cash, the town would, often, 'by the consent of ye Inhabitants' allow them the use of the 'towne land' for a period of time. In 1667, for instance, the town's inhabitants granted to Francis Stacy the town land for one whole year, setting the rent of the land at £4, the cost of Stacy's bill. Such additional expenses were, however, not always so easily accepted by the town. In 1680, for example, the churchwardens delivered a bill of their disbursement amounting to £22:02:03 which was in excess of the rate set at £12:06:00. The deficit simply 'was not accepted by the Inhabitants that day'. Only after the churchwardens' constant 'Importunity' was the town 'prevailed upon' to allow them the following year's rent for the town land 'in Full satisfaction of all their disbursements'. They might have had to wait for some time before claiming the town land since the previous day the town had granted those lands to the overseers for half a year due to their deficit of £3:16:00 from their rates. Nevertheless, thirteen years before the rent on the town land amounted to less than half the churchwardens' deficit, so they undoubtedly had to settle for much less than they had expected. The same duality between responsibility of leaders and the power of townsmen was a constant theme in 'town' government in Hingham, New England, during the seventeenth century.[46]

The men who came from old Hingham had very definite ideas about townsmanship, and they incorporated them very early into their concepts and definitions of community life in Massachusetts. In some New England communities land proprietorship was the only definition of local citizenship, but in Hingham the relationship between the town and its inhabitants was established at the very beginning, on the day the town records were first recorded. On 18 September 1635 'It was agreed that upon *everie man*, that is admyted to be Townes man, and have Lots *graunted* them shall beare charges both to Church and Commonwealth proportionable to their abilities.' This reciprocal relationship was expressed a number of ways during the early years. In 1639, for instance, Henry Chamberlain, the smith, was 'recorded a Town's man—and is to have a House Lot' among other inhabitants. Three years later Edward Gould was 'admitted a townsman, and is to stand to the Town's *Curtisie* in any question—and to require anything of the Town, by vertue of his Township'.[47]

In the first decade the 'Freemen' decided upon such questions as division of lands and the selection of town officers like the selectmen, but any distinctions in wealth and church membership attached to freemanship did not remain for long in early Hingham. At a town meeting in January 1645/6 the town went one step further and ordered 'that the 7, or 9 men chosen to order the prudential affayers of the Town, shall be chosen out of the body of the Town, as well non-Freeman as Freemen'. Land divisions were becoming a matter of town consideration, too.[48] Apparently, then, the power to choose town selectmen had always resided in the town meeting since it assumed this power in passing the town order.

The variety of town business in town and selectmen's meetings typified the issues and problems associated with a Norfolk pastoral economy. By-laws were enacted by both bodies on a number of matters, but the most important issues centred around regulation of open fields, granting of private rights to several proprietors in small enclosures and the maintenance of various timber regulations. Several examples of the town's interest in and perpetuation of dairying have already been cited.[49]

Since Hingham did possess some open fields, certain men were appointed to field offices or duties from time to time. Town orders involving common field fencing occurred irregularly but when promulgated they were exacting and comprehensive. Fences, for instance, were established in three common field regions of the town in 1656, one involving the smaller fields of the plain neck, 'Old Planter's hill', and World's End; the second in Broad Cove field; and the third in the Great Lots and Hockley Fields. The men assigned to this task in these field areas were 'to set up, or cause to be set up and mayntayned—the sayd fences from time to time—and to levy their charge upon every person according to their several acres of land and meadow within the sayd field'. If persons refused to pay their proportion, it was 'lawfull' for these men along with the constable to take 'a distress upon the goods of such as shall refuse to pay'. Fences in these 'general fields' were maintained during the growing season, as one selectmen's order stated, so 'that no Cattle shall be kept in any *Common Field* from the first day of March, until Indian Harvest [corn or maize] be fully ended'.[50]

Much of the land in the two Hinghams was enclosed by a small number of proprietors, however. If some form of co-operation was required among the handful of men who occupied these pockets of land throughout the community, they consented to it and regulated matters by private agreement rather than by a general order of the town or selectmen. Occasionally one of these agreements was included in the town records such as the one involving Thomas Hammond, Stephen Gates, William Sprague and Samuel Ward. All four men held parcels of arable and meadow in 'Crooked meadow river'. By joint agreement they all fenced in the area according to the proportion of land each owned. The fences were 'to be sufficient agaynst *great* cattle —and so to be mayntayned from year to year, by the owners and possessors of these aforesayd lands'. They also did '*bind*' themselves to keep all livestock off the land from 1 March until the harvest of hay and corn and that after that date 'none [are] to put in any cattle, till there be notice given to either party'. Unlike some Massachusetts communities Hingham was able to work out and continue a system of land management neither wholly of common fields with a large group of cultivators holding separate strips in several large fields nor entirely composed of enclosed land on which individual farmers decided how best to use their own land on their separate farmsteads.[51]

The town meeting passed other forms of common regulation. At the first recorded assemblage all those present must have been aware of the vast potential in trade to other towns that the cedar, pine and oak trees of the township might possess. It was ordered then 'that all Cedar and Pine Swamps be in common and preserved for the Towne's use, although any should fall into any mans Lot'. Between this session and the year 1660, the town passed almost two dozen regulations on timber and lumber. Essentially most of the orders restricted the felling and transportation of timber from leaving the town, but it also fostered a stringent system of surveillance. At least seven men were fined for felling trees on 4 September 1641, for a sum of £2:12:08. The fine was 8d. per tree and the town warned others that unless 'every Tree that is now brought in and submitted to the fyne', they would be charged a penalty of 10d. Earlier in March the town had appointed three men to find the 'transgressors'. They, apparently, would hear the cases of the accused brought before them and then deal 'according to the nature of the offence'. The town inspectors were '*to stand for one whole year*—and they have the power to inquire into their [the transgressors'] offences which be *past*, as well as into such as shall come within their year following'. Even with such thorough enforcement, fines increased in time. By 1655 the town ordered a penalty of 20s., a thirty-fold increase since 1641, on the cutting or transportation of wood or timber for outside use.[52] As in Norfolk, the timber regulations, their enforcement and non-compliance, reflected the importance of this local industry in both town economies.

The role of the selectmen in town affairs seems analogous to that of the parish officers in old Hingham. We find the selectmen taking strong and firm direction in agricultural matters, for instance, in appointing subordinates and enacting many though often repetitious agricultural by-laws. Unlike the selectmen in such Massachusetts towns as Watertown and Dedham where these officers ran most functions of local government with the tacit approval of the town meeting, the Hingham selectmen were given only very limited discretion in matters handed them by the town. Certain areas of local administration were clearly

B

forbidden by the town such as making rates, though like parish officers in Norfolk they were allowed to collect and disburse them. Stinting the commons and giving away land were also too important to be left outside the purview of the meeting.[53]

The Hingham selectmen's agricultural duties were important and time-consuming. They were in charge of appointing perhaps over a dozen men each year as fence viewers, pound keepers and by-law enforcers. They infused their choices with specific *ad hoc* powers as in an order of 1644 for fence viewers who were provided with the 'power to strayne for the forfeiture' if it became necessary. In executing their own by-laws and the occasional ones enacted by the town, the selectmen implemented many measures. In 1649 alone, they appointed men to serve as fence viewers and fine takers, or agents to prohibit the 'felling [of] trees for goats', to execute the hog, oak timber and cedar swamp orders, and to regulate cattle in the general fields.[54] But although these officers were given more discretion than selectmen in open-field Massachusetts towns, the town really never granted them much authority to act. And just as in old Hingham where the 'inhabitants' had the upper hand in matters of difference with parish officers, the meeting in new Hingham always retained town authority.

Having said this much about the structural continuity of this Old World community's economic, legal and institutional systems into the New, little has been mentioned about the influence the transatlantic change had on this society of settlers or on individual inhabitants of this New England town. As the foregoing has suggested, for many there was little change at all.

Movement from one side of the Atlantic to the other afforded Hingham townsmen the opportunity to change the structure of the society they knew, but without hesitation they recreated one closely matching the Old World counterpart. Had these immigrants been well-off and influential, one might expect them to recreate a community like the one they knew, but the most arresting feature of this new community was the lack of any social prominence the new leaders had held in Hingham, Norfolk. In the subsidy lists that survive like the one in 1625, four dozen heads of households are listed, but only three of this number were among the many leaving Hingham in the 1630s. The three who were recorded—Adam Foulsham, Edward Gilman and Joseph Peck—all left new Hingham several years after they settled in Massachusetts. Though no parish poor relief lists for the period have survived, it appears likely that men of lesser means were also not a part of the exodus from central Norfolk. Even servants who came with families from old Hingham seldom remained for long.[55]

And so, even though the emigrants who stayed in new Hingham did not represent the social extremes of their native English village, they nevertheless fashioned a society in the wilderness typifying the dimensions of wealth and society to which they had been accustomed. A comparison of surviving inventories in both locations for approximately the same period reveals an astonishing level of consistency and retention of social class of the older community in the new (Table 3). This was in spite of the fact that the New World immigrants brought

TABLE 3

*A comparative analysis of seventeenth-century inventoried wealth in Hingham, Norfolk, and Hingham, Massachusetts*[56]

| Classification | Proportion of Total Wealth | |
| --- | --- | --- |
| | Hingham, Norfolk 1642–88 | Hingham, Massachusetts 1654–92 |
| Top 10% | 31.9% | 31.0% |
| Top 25% | 66.2% | 57.8% |
| Top 50% | 89.3% | 81.5% |
| Median inventory | £55:02:00 | £68:01:06* |
| Average inventory | £112:06:00 | £112:00:00* |

*Based on goods only (i.e. excluding land) as in English inventories.

with them neither an established ruling class nor a despised group of poor, and, therefore, even less reason to perpetuate such a social order.

The moulding of old Hingham society in the new community can be seen in the lives and backgrounds of the men who emigrated to the New England town. Edmund Hobart, for instance, was the patriarch of the Hobart family which came to dominate the town in civil and church affairs through his sons Joshua and Peter. A 1637 land conveyance shows that the elder Hobart was unable to write his name and, presumably, could not read either. When it came to the early decisions made by men like Hobart in the new Hingham in such matters as land granting, powers of town leaders and the types of laws to be made and enforced, he could only rely upon the past knowledge of living in an oral culture where most transactions went by word of mouth. The oral tradition, in effect, isolated village from village, confining men like Hobart to a world no larger than his Norfolk town—whether in England or Massachusetts.[57]

William Ludkin, the locksmith from Norwich with early ties to old Hingham, never, it seems, engaged in agriculture while living in new Hingham although it was primarily an agricultural community. Even though the town granted him 22 acres of land, none is mentioned in his inventory in 1652 nor is there reference to the simplest of agricultural implements. Shortly before his death, Ludkin moved his shop to Boston, probably in order to build up his business which only an urban setting, an American Norwich of sorts, might offer. Still, Ludkin typified his more agrarian new Hingham neighbours. Even though people from the wood–pasture country involved themselves in countless small industries and forms of agriculture, and were, therefore, probably more adaptable to the kinds of changes a new land might make them accept, there is very little evidence of widespread changes in livelihood for the new settlers.[58]

For others the town was so inflexibly conservative that the only hope of prospering was to assert that one significant element of seventeenth-century American freedom, the ability to move on. Although Stephen Gates arrived in 1638 on the ship *Diligent* with many others from Hingham, he seems never to have been given a home lot or subsequent land grants. His later inventory shows that he was a farmer, so he probably rented land from some other settler during his years in Hingham. In fact, he was a tenant on Samuel Ward's land in 1650. Gates's prospects did not improve in the decade after his arrival, and in the aftermath of the controversy between the General Court and the town in 1645 over the leadership in the town militia, Gates was excused, in 1646, from the payment of a fine imposed by the Court because he was 'so pore'. He finally decided to leave town and settled in Cambridge in 1652. In the following year he became one of the original proprietors of Lancaster, Massachusetts, where he was made a freeman in 1656 and constable in 1657. When he died in Cambridge five years later, Gates had a total wealth of at least £261:11:08, and if his Cambridge home had been included in the inventory, it might have exceeded £300, almost three times higher than the 'average' Hingham estate. Had he remained in Hingham, he probably would have died as poor as he had been in the 1640s. Only by leaving Hingham with its stringent Norfolk assumptions of wealth, status and opportunity could someone like Gates or the early servants ever hope to succeed in the New World.[59]

Hingham was, indeed, a unique community. No other town in Massachusetts Bay contained so many inhabitants from the same English community. But this was not an unusual Massachusetts township as many were composed of men from the same or similar English regions. Indeed, the characteristic feature of Hingham and other early towns was the geographical homogeneity of their populations which, in turn, helped perpetuate certain English regional and subregional social, economic, institutional and legal patterns in New England communities. Among the two and a half dozen communities founded in the Bay Colony before 1650, a great number were settled by groups of settlers who came from the same general locality in England. There were, of course, certain obvious exceptions to this statement. Boston, Charlestown and Salem were complex, transient communities with highly heterogeneous populations.[60] Occasionally there were communities like Sudbury and Reading which had from the very beginning a mixed or heterogeneous population representing various English areas and institutional experiences.[61] Yet even in transient communities like Cambridge and Dorchester there were distinctive population clusters from particular parts of England living together until they made way for new waves of immigrants which were also homogeneous.[62] When early town records have been well preserved and when the identification of the places of English origin for a large part of the town's inhabitants can be reliably traced, there was generally a community populated with men of similar English backgrounds.

Paradoxically, with all their internal homogeneity Massachusetts towns displayed a wide diversity of backgrounds from one another. This diversity was a product of local English insularity. Depending upon their North or West Country or East Anglian origins, for instance, each New England town operated its agricultural life, land management and local government in its own way, reflecting different English regional economic, social, legal and institutional arrangements. For the most part, these local English patterns in emigration centres remained little affected by national political forces or economic rationalization during the decades before migration in a countryside where most men knew little beyond their own locality except for the closest market town.[63] Coming from the same English region or sub-region and settling in the same Massachusetts township, it is therefore not surprising that the men of Hingham carried on their old Norfolk ways.

This emphasis of local distinctiveness within diversity was also perpetuated throughout the early years by the lack of centralized control by higher colonial authority over local matters. Part of the difficulty in recognizing differences among Massachusetts towns in the seventeenth century has been our unquestioned assumptions, for instance, regarding the role of the General Court. The Court may have regulated towns at a general level yet it allowed them considerable latitude in setting up and handling local affairs. The so-called Town Act of 1635[64] actually represented a recognition of existing practice rather than a delineation of rights and privileges from higher authority. Vital matters such as who should manage town affairs and the role that the town should play in the lives of individuals through local government were questions left to the communities themselves. It is significant, for example, that the selectmen who became the chief administrators (and in some towns the chief controllers) of town affairs were never officially designated or recognized by the colony until May 1642 when they were authorized to lay 'particular & private wayes' in their towns.[65] Such latitude allowed the towns to adapt their own particular views of governing to the broad outline of local affairs drawn up by the General Court.

The New World offered the migrants from Hingham, Norfolk, a chance to reproduce the ordering of life, from land system to local government, which had prevailed in their native village. By and large they succeeded though their efforts show no active and conscious desire to reclaim and preserve their customary way of life. Yet, ironically, these Englishmen could only reproduce English local institutions in an American environment, and, indeed, only in an American society. Unlike their native Norfolk there was extreme local control with little fear or expectation of intervention from outside higher authority. Unlike England, there was never a threat to this 'peasant utopia' from the very rich because they never migrated, nor from the very poor because they did not come either. Only by leaving

England and coming to America could these English villagers continue to live unfettered the lives they had led.

## NOTES

1. Sumner Chilton Powell, *Puritan Village: The Formation of a New England Town* (New York, Anchor Books Edition, 1965), pp. 181–183.

2. T. H. Breen and Stephen Foster, 'Moving to the New World: The Character of Early Massachusetts Immigration', *William and Mary Quarterly*, 3rd Series, XXX, no. 2 (April 1973), 220.

3. On these aspects, see, for examples: B. Howard Cunnington, compiler, *The Orders, Decrees, and Ordinances of the Borough and Town of Marlborough (Wilts.). Founded on the Charter of Queen Elizabeth 1575. Extracted from the Municipal Records of Marlborough* (Devizes, 1929), Ordinances XXVIII, XXIX, XXX, XXXI, XXXV, XXXXIV, XXXXVII, LVIII; Carl Bridenbaugh, *Vexed and Troubled Englishmen, 1500–1642* (New York, 1968), p. 253; Sidney and Beatrice Webb, *English Local Government from the Revolution to the Municipal Corporation Act: II The Manor and the Borough* (London, 1908), 303; John Patten, 'Village and Town: an Occupational Study', *Agricultural History Review*, 20, Part 1 (1972), 1–16; Archdeaconry of Sudbury, Probate Inventories, Ac. 592/6/82, 9/82, 9/29, Bury St Edmunds and West Suffolk Record Office, Bury St Edmunds, Suffolk.

4. John Waters, 'Hingham, Massachusetts, 1631–1661: An East Anglian Oligarchy in the New World', *Journal of Social History*, 1, no. 4 (Summer, 1968), 352.

5. For examples in Newbury, Ipswich and Watertown, Massachusetts, for instance, see, *Records of the Governor and Company of the Massachusetts Bay in New England*, Nathaniel B. Shurtleff, ed. (6 Volumes in 5; Boston, 1853–1854), I, 216–217; II, 115; IV, 487, 549, 521–524; *Records and Files of the Quarterly Courts of Essex County, Massachusetts* (3 Volumes; Salem, Massachusetts, 1916–20), IV, pp. 122, 122n.–124n., 143n., 232, 234, 232n.–234n., 350, 350n.–367n.; 'The Voting Rights of Freemen in 1658: A Petition from Some of the Inhabitants of Ipswich', *Essex Institute Historical Collections*, XXXXVI, no. 3 (July 1900), 245–247; James Kendall Hosmer, ed., *Winthrop's Journal: History of New England, 1630–1649* (2 vols; New York, 1908), I, 74, 79, 122–123; *Recs. G & C*, I, 95, 117–119.

6. Roland G. Usher, ed., *The Presbyterian Movement in the Reign of Queen Elizabeth as Illustrated by the Minute Book of the Dedham Classis 1562–*

*1589*, Camden Society, 3rd Series, VIII (1905), xxv; Tanner MSS., Bodleian Library, Oxford, Vol. 178, fols. 45–50. On the conspicuousness of the parish in Norfolk, see, Peter Laslett, *The World We have Lost* (New York, 1965) p. 58.

7. Powell, *Puritan Village*, p. 179.

8. Laslett, *The World We have Lost*, pp. 54–55; Francis Blomefield, *An Essay Towards a Topographical History of the County of Norfolk, containing a Description of the Towns, Villages, and Hamlets, with the Foundations of Monasteries, Churches, Chapels, Chantries, and other Religious Buildings:* . . . (11 Vols; London, 1805–10), II, 424; 'The Population of an English Village, 1086–1801: A Study of Wigston Magna', in W. G. Hoskins, *Provincial England Essays in Social and Economic History* (London, 1963), p. 187.

9. The English places of origin for Hingham, Massachusetts, settlers prior to 1640 are listed in Appendix III in David Grayson Allen, 'In English Ways: The Movement of Societies and the Transferal of English Local Law and Custom to Massachusetts Bay, 1600–1690', unpublished Ph.D. dissertation, University of Wisconsin, 1974, pp. 433–446.

10. T. S. Cogswell, 'Reasons agst a General Sending of Corne to ye Marketts in ye Champion parte of Norfolke', *Norfolk Archaeology: or Miscellaneous Tracts Relating to the Antiquities of the County of Norfolk*, XX (1921), 11. For a description of the champion region to the north of the Hingham district, see, K. J. Allison, 'The Sheep-Corn Husbandry of Norfolk in the Sixteenth and Seventeenth Centuries', *Agricultural History Review*, V, Part I (1957), 12–30.

11. Walter Rye, ed., *State Papers relating to Musters, Beacons, Shipmoney, &c. in Norfolk, from 1626 Chiefly to the Beginning of the Civil War* (Norwich, 1907), pp. 21, 131, 132, 205; Tanner MSS., Vol. 189, fol. 8b, 'Yearly Valuation of every town & Hundred', 1625/6. Unfortunately no ecclesiastical census survives for the area such as the one for 1603 in the British Museum, Harleian MSS., Vol. 595, or a 'Compton-like census' of 1676.

12. Spelman, 'Reasons', p. 11.

13. For a discussion of these factors, see David Grayson Allen, 'The Hingham, co. Norfolk Parish Register', forthcoming note and document in the *New England Historical and Genealogical Register*.

14. Eric Kerridge, *The Agricultural Revolution* (London, 1967), pp. 85–86; Norfolk Inventories, Norfolk and Norwich Record Office, Central Library, Norwich, Norfolk, Inventory Boxes 50A/4 and 51/71.

15. NNRO Inventories, 55A/122, 52B/74.

16. NNRO Inventories, 28/119.

17. NNRO Inventories, 36/119, 61A/76, 50A/4.
18. For a general description of Norfolk agriculture, see Joan Thirsk, 'The Farming Regions of England', in H. P. R. Finberg, gen. ed., *The Agrarian History of England and Wales*, Vol. IV, *1500–1640*, ed. by Joan Thirsk, 46–49.
19. See, generally, Suffolk County Probate Office, First Floor, Old Suffolk County Court House, Boston, Massachusetts, Suffolk County Probate Records, II, 117–119; IV, 29–31, 62–63; and VI, 277–278.
20. Hingham Town Records (originals), in two MS. Volumes (Vol. I, 1635–55, and Vol. II, 1657–1720), Town Clerk's Office, Hingham, Massachusetts, I, 20 February 1640/1; 5 March 1637/8; II, 16 October 1677. (Hereinafter cited as 'HMTR'.) In Norfolk's central region, too, pasture land generally rented for a higher price than plough land. See, J. Spratt, 'Agrarian Conditions in Norfolk and Suffolk 1600–1650', M.A. Thesis, University of London, 1935, p. 119.
21. Suffolk Probate Records, X, 83; III, 180; and II, 117–119.
22. Suffolk Probate Records, III, 131.
23. Suffolk Probate Records, V, 272–273; VIII, 199; III, 83–84; IV, 29–31.
24. Samuel Maverick, 'A Briefe Description of New England and the Several Townes therein, together with the Present Government thereof', Massachusetts Historical Society, *Proceedings*, 2nd Series, I (1884), 239; *Wonder-Working Providence*, J. Franklin Jameson, ed. (New York, 1910), p. 116; Suffolk Probate Records, VIII, 198, III, 83–84; HMTR, I, 1 February 1638/9.
25. W. J. Corbett, 'Elizabethan Village Surveys', Royal Historical Society, *Transactions*, New Series, XI (1897), 67–87; Howard Levi Gray, *English Field Systems* (Cambridge, Massachusetts, 1915), pp. 307–334; Kerridge, *The Agricultural Revolution*, pp. 84–85, 87–88; Frances Gardiner Davenport, *The Economic Development of a Norfolk Manor 1086–1565* (Cambridge, England, 1906), p. 27.
26. Hingham Terriers, 1633, nos. 35 and 104, NNRO, Norwich Diocesan Terriers—Hingham. Cf. also the Hingham Terrier for 1613, no. 105, which reveals a similar pattern.
27. 'An Act for Dividing and Inclosing the Commons and Waste Lands Within the Parish of Hingham, in the County of Norfolk', Private Acts, 21 George III, 1780–81. There was some local enclosure in the sixteenth century. See, I. S. Leadam, 'The Inquisition of 1517. Inclosures and Evictions', Royal Historical Society, *Transactions*, New Series, VII (1893), 127–218. For examples of the interest shown to livestock by the 'Town' or vestry meetings in Hingham, Norfolk, see the meetings

of 1680–82 in the Hingham Town Account Book, 1660–1752, NNRO, MS. 9935.

28. Rye Index to Norfolk Fines: Charles I to 1650, Colman and Rye Libraries, Central Library, Norwich, Norfolk.

29. HMTR, I, 6 July 1640; 14 August, 8 October 1637; 5 March 1637/8.

30. Compiled from HMTR, Vols. I and II, including all grants from the original houselots to the December 1670 division; Spratt, 'Agrarian Conditions in Norfolk and Suffolk', p. 198.

31. Examples are few and the size of Hingham land exchanges between Hingham men was small, but see for the years to 1662, *Suffolk Deeds*, Liber I (Boston, 1880), 70, 89, 103, 133, 221–222, Liber II (Boston, 1883), 103, 161–162, 255–256, Liber III (Boston, 1885), 63–64, 372–373, 376, 396, 400–401, 401–403, 403–405, 470–472.

32. Compiled from the Hingham [Norfolk] Town Account Book, 1660–1752. Hingham manor records after 1690 are located at Payne, Hicks, Beach & Co., Solicitors, 10 New Square, Lincoln's Inn, London, W.C.2. A rough check of manor officers elected in the decade after 1690 suggests that they were the same names which appear as parish officers in the Town Account Book.

33. Hingham [Norfolk] Town Account Book.

34. Compiled from Hingham [Massachusetts] Town Records, I and II, *passim*.

35. Compiled from Town Grants, Town Meetings, 1634, and Town Records, Land Grants, 1634–1757, Office of the Town Clerk, Ipswich, Massachusetts; *Watertown Records* (Six Vols in Five: Watertown, Massachusetts, 1894–1928), I and II, *passim*.

36. *Wonder-Working Providence*, pp. 116–117, 116n.; William Hubbard, *A General History of New England*, Massachusetts Historical Society, *Collections*, 2nd Series, VI (1819), 418–419.

37. Regrettably, inventories do not exist for important selectmen who died after 1692. These include: Daniel Cushing (d. 1700), Matthew Cushing II (d. 1700/01), Jeremiah Beals (d. 1716), Joshua Beals (d. 1717/8), and Nathaniel Beals (d. 1708). Two that have survived—that of John Smith (d. 1695) valued at £1106:18:00, and John Jacobs (d. 1693) at £1298:05:00—suggest that they may have been very wealthy as a group. Suffolk Probate Records, XIII, 295–296, 611–612.

Recently, Robert Wall, Jr has suggested that Dedham, Massachusetts, was similarly dominated by several families—the Lushers, Fishers and Alduses. Further research may reveal that *small* market towns such as Fressingfield, Suffolk, from where many Dedham settlers came may have had a similar social and leadership structure as in Hingham,

Norfolk. See Robert Emmet Wall, Jr, *Massachusetts Bay: The Crucial Decade, 1640–1650* (New Haven, 1972), pp. 28–29.

38. John J. Waters, Jr, *The Otis Family in Provincial and Revolutionary Massachusetts* (Chapel Hill, 1968), p.15.

39. Blomefield, *An Essay Towards a Topographical History of Norfolk*, II, 422–445; Spratt, 'Agrarian Conditions in Norfolk and Suffolk', p. 20.

40. Hingham Rectory Manor Court Book, 1553–1723, Parish Chest, St Andrew's Parish, Hingham, Norfolk; Hingham Manor Records, note 32; and cf. Henry Gurnay's 'common-place book, containing an account of courts held and leases of land at Ellingham, Hingham and Irstead', Tanner MSS. Vol. 175, *passim.*

41. B. A. Holderness, ' "Open" and "Close" Parishes in England in the Eighteenth and Nineteenth Centuries', *Agricultural History Review*, XX, Part II (1972), 126–139; Spratt, 'Agrarian Conditions in Norfolk and Suffolk', map adjacent to p. 101; J. H. Gleason, *The Justices of the Peace in England 1558 to 1640 A Later Eirenarcha* (Oxford, 1969), pp. 145–163; A. Hassell Smith, 'Justices at Work in Elizabethan Norfolk', *Norfolk Archaeology*, XXXIV, Part II (1969), 93–110; and Walter Rye, ed., *State Papers relating to Musters . . .* (Norwich, 1907), pp. 6, 31, 48, 78, 101, 102, 124, 125, 129, 130, 132, 140, 143, 156, 157, 165.

42. *History of Hingham, Norfolk, and its Church of St. Andrew* (East Dereham, Norfolk, 1921), p. 5; Blomefield, *Topographical History of Norfolk*, II, 439–440; PRO Patent Rolls, C.66/1000, membrane 27 (1564).

43. D. E. Howell James, *Norfolk Quarter Sessions Order Book 1650–1657*, Norfolk Record Society, *Publications*, XXVI (1955), 89.

44. Compiled from the Hingham [Norfolk] Town Account Book, 1660–1752. Tabulated figures indicate the amount distributed or disbursed rather than revenue or income.

45. Powell, *Puritan Village*, pp. 44–50; Cottingham Churchwardens' Accounts, 1660–1890, East Riding Record Office, Beverley, Yorks.

46. Hingham [Norfolk] Town Account Book, *passim.*

47. HMTR, I, 17 February 1638/9; 10 February 1641/2.

48. HMTR, I, 30 January 1645/6. See also, the election of officers and granting of land at the 24 May 1652 town meeting.

49. See note 20.

50. HMTR, I, 6 May 1656; Selectmen's Records, Town Clerk's Office, Hingham, Massachusetts, 2 December 1644.

51. HMTR, I, 10 March 1650/1.

52. HMTR, I, 18 September 1635; 4 September 1641; 10 March 1640/1.

53. HMTR, I, 12 March 1646/7; cf. Kenneth A. Lockridge and Alan Kreider, 'The Evolution of Massachusetts Town Government, 1640 to 1740', *William and Mary Quarterly*, 3rd Series, XXIII, no. 4 (October, 1966), 549–574.

54. Hingham Selectmen's Minutes, 2 December 1644; 13 February 1648/9.

55. PRO E179/153/586, 1 Charles I (1625), Forehoe Hundred, and cf. 153/556, 7 James I (1610), Mitford, Forehoe & Humbleyard Hundreds. There seems to have been little correlation between wealth and emigration in neighbouring Wymondham, Norfolk, either. Cf. William Hudson, 'Assessment of the Hundred of Forehoe, Norfolk, in 1621; A sidelight on the differences of National Taxation', *Norfolk Archaeology*, XXI, Part III (1923), 285–309.

56. Norfolk Inventories, NNRO, Inventory Boxes 47A, 49A, 50A, 51B, 52A, 52B, 55A, 55B, 56, 60A, 61A, 63, 64; Suffolk Probate Records, II-V, VII-X, XII-XIII, I and II, new series.

57. HMTR, Record of Land Sale of Nicholas Jacob to Ralph Woodward, 6 November 1637.

58. Percy Millican, ed., *The Register of the Freemen of Norwich 1548–1713 A Transcript with An Introduction, An Appendix, to Those Freemen Whose Apprenticeship Indentures are Enrolled in the City Records, and Indexes of Names and Places* (Norwich, 1934), p. 232; Suffolk Probate Records, II, 51–54.

59. HMTR, I, 10 March 1650/1; *Recs. G & C*, II, 164; Middlesex County Massachusetts Probate Office, First Floor, Deeds and Probate Building, East Cambridge, Massachusetts, Wills and Inventories, II, 53–57.

60. See, for examples, Darrett B. Rutman, *Winthrop's Boston Portrait of a Puritan Town, 1630–1649* (Chapel Hill, 1965), pp. 135–163; Richard Frothingham, Jr, *The History of Charlestown, Massachusetts* (Charlestown and Boston, 1845–49), pp. 78–88; and Donald Warner Koch, 'Income Distribution and Political Structure in Seventeenth-Century Salem, Massachusetts', *Essex Institute Historical Collections*, CV, no. 4 (October, 1970), 252–276.

In all cases the English origins of settlers has been determined from such sources as: James Savage, *A Genealogical Dictionary of the First Settlers of New England, showing Three Generations of Those who came before May, 1692, on the Basis of Farmer's Register* (Four Vols; Boston, 1860–62); Charles Henry Pope, *The Pioneers of Massachusetts, A Descriptive List, Drawn from Records of the Colonies, Towns and Churches, and other Contemporaneous Documents* (Boston, 1900); Henry F. Waters, *Genealogical Gleanings in England* (Two Vols; Boston, 1901); Charles E. Banks, *The Planters of the Commonwealth* (Boston, 1930) and

*Topographical Dictionary of 2885 English Emigrants to New England 1620–1650* (Philadelphia, 1937); *New England Historical and Genealogical Register*, Vols. I–to date (Boston, 1847–1975), and local English research.

61. Powell, *Puritan Village*, pp. 206–212; Lilly Eaton, *Genealogical History of the Town of Reading, Mass. including the Present Towns of Wakefield, Reading and North Reading, with Chronological and Historical Sketches, from 1634 to 1874* (Boston, 1874), pp. 1–16.

62. J. Gardner Bartlett, 'The English Ancestral Homes of the Founders of Cambridge', The Cambridge Historical Society, *Publications*, XIV (April, 1919), 79–103; Maude Pinney Kuhns, *The 'Mary and John' A Story of the Founding of Dorchester, Massachusetts, 1630* (Rutland, Vermont, 1943), pp. 7–87, *Annals of the Town of Dorchester by James Blake, 1750*, Dorchester Antiquarian and Historical Society, *Collections*, no. 2 (Boston, 1846), *Journal of Richard Mather, His Life and Death. 1635*, ibid., no. 3 (Boston, 1850).

63. Joan Thirsk, 'The Farming Regions of England', pp. 1–112; Alan Everitt, 'The Marketing of Agricultural Produce', ibid., pp. 466–595, and his *Change in the Provinces: The Seventeenth Century*, Department of English Local History *Occasional Papers*, Second Series, Number 1 (Leicester, 1969), especially pp. 22–23, 36, 38–39.

64. *Recs. G & C*, I, 172.

65. *Recs. G & C*, II, 4.

## 2

# The Puritans and Prurience:
# Aspects of the Restoration Book Trade

## ROGER THOMPSON

One of the least recognized and least recommended weapons in the historian's armoury is the fine art of browsing. Often Clio seems to take a wanton delight in withholding a vital clue or a fertile lead from the painful and methodical researcher, only to drop it before him in the most unlooked-for context after he has given up all hope of its existence. This piece of research, which is only the first stage of a larger project, began as I was idly flicking through the pages of the *New England Quarterly*, a diversion from more methodical reading. My eye fell on '*The London Jilt*, ordered specifically for [Increase] "Mather" on invoice No. 2, September 5, 1683, has raised some eyebrows . . .'[1] Yet, it soon transpired, precious few questions had been raised in succession to the eyebrows. As I digested this savoury morsel, four main lines of inquiry gradually opened up: (i) The dirty book trade in Restoration London; (ii) The book export trade to New England and the book trade there; (iii) The readership and authorship of such '*Pestilential Instruments of Wickedness*';[2] (iv) The relationship, if any, between the dirty book market and puritanism.

David Foxon, the doyen in this field, has pointed out the difficulties of this elusive topic. Many of these 'ugly ducklings' have not survived, or are extremely rare.[3] It is sometimes impossible to tell from a title whether the contents are disreputable or not: *The Nightwalker of Bloomsbury*, for instance, is a political tract about Lord Russell, whereas Sinibald's *Geneanthropeia* is a pseudo-medical piece of salacity.[4] The understandable furtiveness of readers of such works—the very secrecy may indeed be part of the thrill[5]—is only rarely counteracted by the survival of booksellers' records. Pious descendants may prefer family honour to historical completeness.[6] There is, moreover, the problem of gauging what people in different classes, sects and areas in the period from 1660 to 1720 regarded as obscene or scandalous. Public executions, mutilations or degradations, for instance, which would nowadays be regarded as 'morally obscene', were then a source of popular interest, even entertainment.

Sutton Nicholls's print, *The Compleat Auctioner*,[7] c. 1700, depicts a slightly seedy looking gent standing beneath a tree on which is fixed a placard advertising the sale of the library of 'The late unborn Doctor'. Before him, on a table, stand the rows of books; two ladies, possibly of easy virtue, and two gentlemen are about to browse. They would have found most ostentatiously displayed some unexceptionable works, like Heylin's *Life of Cosin* or various of Ogilby's works, but a second glance would have uncovered some very different quarries. In the front row are labelled: *Aretine's Post*, *Play of Sodom*, *Roch Poems*, *Eng Rogue*, *Tullia Oct* and *Sch of Venus*, all pornographic or obscene. Alongside these are various popular picaresque, quasi-medical, seditious and amorous works. In the second row are several bawdy jest books, and what may be *Venus in the Cloister* and *The Nuns Complaint Against the Fryers*.[8] For a certain type of reader, they are indeed 'A Choice Collection of Books'.

The (often surreptitious) publication of books of this kind seems to have occurred particularly in two periods in London: around the year 1660, and in the 1680s. From 1656 to 1663, there appeared: (i) *Choice Drollery* (1656); (ii) *Sportive Wit* (1656); (iii) *The Crafty Whore* (1658); (iv) Sinibald's *Rare Verities* (1658); (v) *The Practical Part of Love* (1660); (vi) *The Wits* (1662); and (vii) *The Wandering Whore*, an ephemeral periodical, published with continuations in 1660 and 1663.[9] The crop in the 1680s included: (i) *Poems on Several Occasions by the E of R* (1680); (ii) *The School of Venus* (1680); (iii) *The Whores Rhetorick* (1683); (iv) *Venus in the Cloister* (1683); (v) *The London Jilt* (1683); (vi) *Tullia Octavia* (1684); (vii) *Erotopolis, The Present State of Bettyland* (1684); and (viii) *Sodom* (1684).[10] The remainder of the Restoration period was by no means lily-white, but the increased output in these two periods is nonetheless marked.

Within the scope of this essay, we can only glance at the possible causes of this. A major reason is undoubtedly the fact that France was producing dirty books in both these periods, which quickly became available on the clandestine market in London, and were as quickly translated and adapted to an English readership. Both were times of great political insecurity, of censorship blunted, of authority distracted by other threats, as had been the occasion of the previous efflorescence, the early 1640s. Politico-religious controversies were inflamed, and the fashion of libel and satire could easily slide into obscenity. Other general reasons why demand should have increased will be discussed later.

Apart from these cultural circumstances, however, there were also particular conditions in the Restoration book trade which encouraged the publication of erotica and bawdy. In the first forty years of the seventeenth century, the average number of books published annually had risen from 259 to 577.[11] The onset of open political controversy after 1640 had accelerated even this rapid rise.[12] Richard Atkyns, writing in 1664, stated: 'There are at least 600 Booksellers that keep shops in and about *London* and Two or three Thousand free of the Company of Stationers; the Licensed Books of the Kingdome cannot imploy one third part of them: what shall the rest do? I have heard some of them openly at the *Committee* of the *House of Commons* say, They will rather hang than starve; and that a man is not hang'd for stealing, but being taken; *necessitas cogit ad turpia*.'[13] The Great Fire wrought havoc with the already over-manned trade. According to Clarendon, the booksellers, many of whom used the crypt of old St Paul's for storage, lost £200,000.[14] Two decades later, at the very summit of the 1680s boom, 1683, Roger North bemoaned the fact that Little Britain, which in 1666 had been 'a plentiful and perpetual Emporium of learned Authors. . . . And the booksellers themselves were knowing and conversible men', had, as such, 'vanished, and the trade contracted into the Hands of two or three Persons . . . The rest of the Trade are content to take their Refuse, with which, and the fresh scum of the Press, they furnish one Side of a Shop . . . They crack their brains to find out selling subjects, and keep hirelings in garrets, on hard meat, to write and correct by the grate.'[15]

There were those who had not far to seek to find selling subjects. Around 1660, a group centred around Henry Marsh, an unscrupulous pirate who received his just deserts in the Plague, was responsible for many of the pornographic books already mentioned. It included Nathaniel Brook, Thomas Johnson and Francis Kirkman. Both Marsh and Kirkman disingenuously admitted their main motive: 'The first

and chiefest was to gain ready money.'[16] John Crouch, who was probably the publisher of *The Wandering Whore*, had been behind such
scurrilous Royalist ephemera as *The Man in the Moon* and *Mercurius
Democritus* during the Interregnum.[17] Less is known of the smut-
pedlars of the 1680s. Henry Rhodes, responsible for *The London Jilt*
and *Venus in the Cloister*, had only become free of the Stationers'
Company on 26 March 1680. He may well, therefore, have been trying
to amass capital fast. He was a prolific publisher for four decades,
mainly in cheap, popular books, including some 'mild pornography',
though his list in the Term Catalogues does show higher pretensions
in the 1690s.[18] Of the others, men like Thomas Coxe, Thomas Fox,
William Cadman, Benjamin Crayle and Joseph Streater, whose names
often come to us through records of prosecutions, little is known,
except that they had a penchant for off-colour merchandise.[19]

The second line of research examines the export trade to New
England, brief descriptions of some of the saltier cargo, and a word
about the Boston book trade in the seventy years following the
Restoration.

The most detailed source on the export trade is the Jeffries Family
Papers in the Massachusetts Historical Society, partially and not
always accurately reprinted in W. C. Ford's *Boston Book Market*.[20]
Dotted chaotically around Volumes II, IV and XV are incoming letters
and invoices 1682–85, to John Usher, the second-generation Boston
bookseller and merchant, from his London agent John Ive and from
Richard Chiswell, a rising London publisher, who, by 1705 'well
deserves the title of metropolitan bookseller of England, if not of all
the world'.[21] There is also an invoice of 'Bookes sente by Robert
Boulter without ordre per Mar John Foy', c. 1682/83. The books which
Chiswell sent were all ordered from Boston, in response to circulars of
stock, which Chiswell sent, or to the Term Catalogues, which he
enclosed with the consignments, or to such periodicals as *Weekly
Memorials for the Ingeniose*. Occasionally, as with the 1683 invoice,
particular customers, like 'Mr Mather' are named; the original invoices
demonstrate that he did *not* order *The London Jilt*, although *The
Womans Advocate . . . With Satyrical Reflections on Whoring* was on
his list.[22] It is clear from correspondence and accounts that both
Chiswell and Boulter were already well-established exporters to New
England before the 1680s.

The total value of the books listed in the seven invoices, covering probably only two or three years, is £533.[23] Other correspondence adds at least another £251 for 1682–85.[24] In the year 1694, a letter from Ive to Usher states that Guy, the London bookseller, has sent £100 worth of books. Of course these figures only refer to portions of Usher's trade, and there were at least seventeen booksellers trading in Boston in the 1680s and fifteen in the 1690s.

T. G. Wright's *Cultural Life of Early New England* and G. E. Littlefield's *Early Boston Booksellers*[25] have ably analysed New England publishing, and both have stressed the reliance of the area on imports from England. There were four men in Boston in the seventeenth century who may well have engaged in clandestine importing of disreputable works into the wilderness Sion, two of whom brushed with the Massachusetts censors. Marmaduke Johnson, a printer in Cambridge from 1660 to 1674 was closely connected to the Marsh group in London, who probably sent him Henry Neville's proto-Crusoe *Isle of Pines*, with its one or two erotic passages and its amoral account of polygamy. He had already been convicted of attempted bigamy; he was now, in 1668, fined £5 for attempting to reprint Neville.[26] The second was Benjamin Harris, on the run from the Tory backlash. His *Publick Occurences*, a news sheet, was suppressed in 1690 partly because it contained a gratuitously titillating item about the rumoured incest of Louis XIV with his daughter-in-law.[27] The other two were John Dunton and Andrew Thorncomb;[28] in 1685 the latter had published the slightly bowdlerized but still obscene edition of Rochester's *Poems on Several Occasions*. Dunton does not tell us what titles were in his shipment in 1686. However, there is some reason to believe that he had already embarked on the publication of prurience under a transparent veil of pious cant.[29]

What we have so far lacked is an *overall* picture of the transatlantic book trade. From 1697 onwards, the great *Ledgers of Imports and Exports*[30] kept by the newly established Inspector General in London provide it. The figures, which have never been published before, are given in Table 1.

Three points need to be made about these figures. First, the years 1702–1706 were years of international war. Secondly, there is some reason to believe that the weights may be somewhat exaggerated.[35] Thirdly, however, the cargoes of books to New England would seem to have been grossly undervalued by Inspector General Culliford's rate of £4 per cwt. Unless the type of trade had changed drastically since the 1680s, the valuation should have been £12 per cwt at the very least, which would make an average annual total of nearly £800 for

TABLE 1

Book[31] exports from England to New England,
Michaelmas 1697 to Christmas 1706

A. FROM LONDON

| P.R.O. Customs 3 Vol. | Folio | Year | Weight cwt qr lb | Valuation per cwt | Value £ s. d. | |
|---|---|---|---|---|---|---|
| 1 | 44 | M97–M98 | 82 0 14 | £3–£5 | 164 10 0 | (should read |
| 2 | 85 | M98–X98[32] | 42 2 0 | £3–£5 | 170 0 0 | £329 0 0) |
| 3 | 123 | X98–X99 | 63 3 13 | £3–£5 | 255 9 3½ | |
| 4 | 105 | X99–X1700 | 129 0 6 | £3–£5 | 516 0 0 | |
| 5 | 80 | X00–X01 | 107 1 0 | £3–£5 | 429 0 0 | |
| 6 | 65 | X01–X02 | 27 0 7 | £3–£5 | 108 5 0 | |
| 7 | 64 | X02–X03 | 48 1 7 | £3–£5 | 193 5 0 | |
| 8 | 87 | X03–X04 | 38 1 7 | £3–£5 | 153 5 0 | |
| 9 | 76 | X05–X06[33] | 19 2 0 | £3–£5 | 78 0 0 | |
| Total | | | 557 3 26 | | £2067 14 3½ | (Amended £2232 4 3½) |

B. FROM OUTPORTS

| P.R.O. Customs 3 Vol. | Folio | Year | Weight cwt qr lb | Valuation per cwt | Value £ s. d. |
|---|---|---|---|---|---|
| 1 | 182 | M97–M98 | 2 0 0 | £3–£5 | 8 0 0 |
| 2 | 87 | M98–X98 | 0 0 7 | £3–£5 | 0 7 0 |
| 3 | 223 | X98–X99 | 5 0 0 | £3–£5 | 20 0 0 |
| 4 | 143 | X99–X1700 | 0 0 0 | £3–£5 | 0 0 0 |
| 5 | 194 | X00–X01 | 0 0 10 | £3–£5 | 0 7 1 |
| 6 | 160 | X01–X02 | 1 2 14 | £3–£5 | 6 10 0 |
| 7 | 161 | X02–X03 | 0 0 0 | £3–£5 | 0 0 0 |
| 8 | 163 | X03–X04 | 0 0 0 | £3–£5 | 0 0 0 |
| 9 | 104 | X05–X06 | 0 0 0 | £3–£5 | 0 0 0 |
| Total | | | 8 3 3 | | £35 4 1[34] |

Note: M = Michaelmas, X = Christmas

the eight and a quarter years, or £1220 for the three 'normal' inter-war years, Christmas 1698 to Christmas 1701.[35]

Some further information on book exports to New England in the early eighteenth century can be gleaned from the MS. Account Book of Daniel Henchman of Boston. From 15 March 1727 and 1 January 1729, he received £993:3:1½ worth of books from ships plying between London and Boston.[37]

These data suggest that from the 1670s there was a thriving export trade in books from London to New England. They make Dunton's claim that in 1686 he was owed £500 in bad debts there seem feasible.[38] Benjamin Franklin's famous response to the Commons question during the Stamp Act Crisis 'What used to be the pride of the Americas?', 'A. To indulge in the fashions and manufactures of Great Britain' could cover the whole of the preceding century as far as books were concerned.[39]

What sort of books did this tide flood westward across the North Atlantic? The Boulter–Chiswell invoices give the most detailed picture for the narrow period from 1682–85. Predictably, theology dominates, with school books, then as now a great book trade staple, coming second. W. C. Ford's comparative break-down of Boulter's speculative consignment and Chiswell's 1685 invoice is slanted against the normal light literature content of John Usher's orders.[40] Boulter sent 160 copies of various romances; Chiswell's first three lists give forty-seven, forty-three and thirty-one copies respectively. These titles have already been well surveyed.[41] It is highly improbable that the contents of later consignments changed markedly.

Here I propose to draw attention briefly to five titles, *all ordered from Boston*, which represent an element of New England's participation in the 1680s peak of English published prurience. The books are *The London Jilt* (1683), two copies sent in 1683, but Usher's re-order not met in May 1684, because 'London Gilt is out of print and not to be had'; *The Womans Advocate* (1683), one copy ordered 'For Mr. [?Cotton] Mather' in 1683, and two more copies sent in 1684; '2 *Erle of Rochesters Poems*' [*on Several Occasions*] (1680) sent in March 1684; six copies of *Nugae Venales* and three of *Venus in the Cloyster* in the same consignment.[42]

I have elsewhere discussed Rhodes's successful venture *The London Jilt, or, The Politick Whore. Shewing All the Artifices and Stratagems which the Ladies of Pleasure make use of for the Intreaguing and Decoying of Men; Interwoven with Several Pleasant Stories of the Misses Ingenious Performances.*[43] It is sufficient here to say that it belongs to that perennially popular branch of rogue literature, the whore story. The subtitle was borrowed from a droll acted before the

King at Newmarket in 1680,[44] and some of the ideas are taken from a penny broadsheet, *The Character of a Town Miss* (c. 1680).[45] The tone of this not very distinguished precursor to *Moll Flanders* is reminiscent of Mrs. Dorothy's story in *The English Rogue*[46] (invoiced, but apparently not sent to Boston about 1682), though the *Jilt*'s narrative and sense of process is far more coherent. Apart from the transparently hypocritical preface, the writer's stance is amoral and the subject's career is painted as adventurous and financially rewarding. There is no nemesis.[47] The jilt is utterly unsentimental about her life and profession. This realism is, however, slanted. There is, for instance, hardly any mention of disease, protection rackets or frequent pregnancies. A reader unacquainted with this branch of seventeenth-century literature might well find the sexual innuendoes, puns, situation comedy and general comments racy and amusing. Yet almost all the stratagems, 'cheats', dirty jokes and indirections are commonplace chestnuts of the period. *The London Jilt* is emphatically not pornographic, in the sense that it was written with the intention of arousing sexual excitement as a verbal aphrodisiac. Its descriptions are rarely explicit, nor are its imagery or situations erotic. Rather, it is bawdy, aimed at providing saucy entertainment.

Similar in tone, though a collection of jokes rather than a sustained narrative, is Richard Head's *Nugae Venales, or, Complaisant Companion, Being New Jests, Domestick and Forraign, Bulls, Rhodomontado's, Pleasant Novels and Miscellanies.* Many of the jokes, plots and farcical situations derive from Italian, Spanish and French sources.[48] Like the jest books in Pepys's collection of *Penny Merriments*,[49] it is a cross between the old music-hall comedian's patter, dirty stories told in pubs or schools, and the more inventive graffiti in public lavatories. Some of the farces or 'novels' run to half a dozen pages; the jests, bulls (gargantuan exaggerations) and rhodomontades, in verse or prose, are generally only a paragraph or two. Some of the material is lifted bodily from other compilations; the rest would be familiar fare to any ballad, chapbook or jestbook reader. There is conventionally frequent use of phallic symbolism,[50] and the language is often coarse. Again, however, though a surprising dish for New England palates, this four hundred page miscellany is not pornography. It demanded a guffaw or a snigger—or a supercilious 'We are not amused': the expected puritan reaction.

The two copies of *Poems on Several Occasions by the E of R* must have been from one of the full-blooded '1680' editions, not the slightly bowdlerized Thorncomb edition of 1685.[51] The false 'Antwerpen' imprint of 1680 was enormously popular, running to at least eleven reissues or piracies,[52] despite the family's attempts at suppression,[53] and despite the fact that less than half of the poems can be ascribed to Rochester.[54]

Wilmot's verse is too well known nowadays to demand extended comment here.[55] In pieces like 'A Ramble in St. James's Park', 'The Maim'd Debauchee', 'The Imperfect Enjoyment' and most of the songs, the man who symbolized not only the satiric wit and philosophical questioning, but also the savage wildness, destructiveness and lawlessness of Charles II's court, brazenly flouted all taboos. He rarely stoops to indirection and metaphor. It is, as the lady in 'Timon' complains, 'Unfit for modest ears'. Of course, none of the contributors to *Poems on Several Occasions* ever expected to see their efforts in print. Their verses were pirated by an enterprising publisher from manuscripts which circulated widely around the court, coffee-houses and *demi-monde*, helped along the gutters by such as Captain Robert Julian, self-styled 'Secretary of the Muses', and his copyists at Wills's.[56] As might be expected from such semi-private compositions, many have the kind of coterie allusions reminiscent of institutional satire.

Rowlandson depicted the *Poems* as pornographic.[57] Gershon Legman, on the other hand, writes: 'No book more verbally obscene exists in the English language . . . by far the most obscene examples of erotic poetry in English (or any other language).'[58] Basing, as we have, our definitions of types of prurience on author's intention, the epithet obscene seems nearer the mark. Rochester's main intention in the scabrous pieces—and it should be stressed that some of the contributions are charming lyrics, philosophical debates and verse essays in criticism—seems to be to shock or disgust or to pillory opponents with spiteful personal abuse rather than to arouse sexual fantasies. Often the author purposely intrudes his own personality. Similarly, there is frequent recourse to philosophical justification: follow nature, break free from senseless social restraints, from the tyranny of both reason and superstition.[59] There is wit. Finally, even the most obviously erotic verses, like 'The Imperfect Enjoyment', have an untainted realism and a sense of the author's own involvement.

None of these elements has a place in the obsessive, fantastic and perverted sexuality of pornography.

Of the disreputable books shipped by Ive to Usher, *Venus in the Cloyster, or, The Nun in her Smock*, is in a class by itself. The French author, Duprat according to the title-page, but more probably Jean Barrin,[60] seems plainly to have a pornographic intention, though his skill is not always equal to his aim. The book is cast in the conventional Aretine dialogue, between Sister Angelica, a professed nun of about twenty, and a novice to the closed order, Agnes, and harks back to the first day of the first part of the *Ragionamenti*. Like its model it is obsessed with sexual perversion, and the narrative has a voyeuristic quality. The titillating venue of the cloister and the projection on religious[61] are inevitably anti-clerical, a common sibling to the pornographic.[62] The Roman Catholic subject matter could well have helped to rationalize protestant reading of the book and others like it,[63] especially in the 1680s. For example, Angelica coaches Agnes in a vague, and therefore innocuous, confession, which would remind Englishmen of popish casuistry and the oft-trumpetted fact that fornication was 'but a venial sin' to Rome. Puritan prejudice would be similarly confirmed by prurient satire of prelates, spiritual directors and male orders, like the Jesuits, the Capuchins and the Carthusians. Yet the polemic is secondary in emphasis to the pornographic, unlike such Jansenist diatribes as *Le Moine Secularisé*, *Lettres d'un Clerc Tonsuré*, or *Profession de Foy de Monsieur L'Archevesque de Paris*.[64]

Barrin, again following Aretino, makes Angelica justify her scandalous behaviour in various ways. She is in the convent, like many others, without a genuine vocation. God does not give everyone the gift of chastity. Her most sustained rationale is libertinism. 'I am an enemy of Restraint . . . who would always act with Liberty . . . be guided by that pure and innocent Nature, by following entirely the inclinations which she gives us.' She condemns, paradoxically, the reading of such 'evil books' as *L'Escole des Filles* and *L'Academie des Dames*[65] as 'provocatives and incentives to concupiscence', distinguishing rather fuzzily between her obedience to 'Law, Nature and Prudence' and the debauchery of 'those who never taste any perfect pleasure'.

The rounded elegance of Barrin's style is in marked contrast both to the indigenous hacks' bawdy and to Rochester's blatant obscenity. There is little explicit imagery or coarse vulgarity. The author aspires to a more sophisticated erotic evocation, looking forward to the fastidious indirection of John Cleland.

*The Womans Advocate, or Fifteen Real Comforts of Matrimony*, invoiced in two consignments, was, according to its sub-title, written *in requital of the late Fifteen Sham Comforts*.[66] The publishers' names, Alsop and Malthus, would warn any half-knowledgeable reader against any possibility of a serious feminist defence, as would the rest of the sub-title *With Satyrical Reflections on Whoring, And the Debauchery of this Age*. The probable originator of the growing collection of XVs was Louis XI's romancier and retainer, Antoine de la Salle.[67]

The disdained 'sham comforts' view marriage from a rampant and ribald male outlook, cataloguing stock female plagues, like the nag, the shrew, the gossip, the hypochondriac, the unfaithful or the insatiable. The *Real Comforts* respond in kind. We meet familiar figures like the fortune-hunter, the impotent, the pervert and the cuckold. Like so much English bawdy, a spirited style cannot conceal the jaded uninventiveness of plot or unoriginality of wit. This guerilla war of the genders might raise a snicker, but hardly more.

*The Womans Advocate* is the only item in our group for which we have the name of an orderer: Mr Mather. Cotton Mather[68] was 20 in 1683, in a trauma of doubt and guilt about his vocation. Conceivably he might have been gathering material for *Ornaments for the Daughters of Sion* (1691), in which case he had been misled. The pious ejaculations in his *Diary*, later carefully edited by himself for posterity, would, however, bear the interpretation that his motives were less than scholarly.[69] He claimed in his letter to Chiswell to read 'the catalogue of books printed' which had the whole sub-title, including *Satyrical Reflections on Whoring*. Perhaps this is one of the 'lusts' he so frequently bewails.

This discussion of Mather's motives brings us to the third general topic of readership in England and America. Despite the plethora of experiments measuring reactions to pornography in recent years, virtually no systematic work has been done on contemporary habitual readership. The informed hunch is that regular customers are middle-aged and middle-class; that 'the man in the greasy raincoat' is largely myth.[70] Research is urgently needed, and might have an important bearing on studies such as this.

The seventeenth-century assumption that the main customers were whores, hacks, debauchees and gallants may also be wide of the mark.[71] The best sources are diaries, commonplace books and letters, and sometimes literary references, all of which can demonstrate the actual reading and even reaction to dirty books. The most famous is Pepys's typically conscience-stricken purchase and reading of *L'Escole des Filles* which led to involuntary ejaculation.[72] We know from letters that Donne and Jonson knew Aretino, that Sir Henry Wotton wanted to,[73] that the postures were surreptitiously printed in Oxford,[74] and that Halifax ordered works 'forbid' from Paris.[75] A letter of Pepys to Will Hewer in October 1680 admits to a hidden copy of Rochester's *Poems* 'written . . . in a style I thought unfit to mix with my other books'.[76] He also copied down the words of two 'very lewd songs' and knew *La Puttana Errante*.[77] Clarendon blamed *The Amours of Henri IV*, given to Charles II, which were 'too concernedly read by him and made that impression on his mind', for his initial involvement with 'the lady', Barbara Castlemain.[78]

Proof of ownership, though far less satisfactory, is rather more easily found in wills and inventories, booksellers' records, catalogues of private libraries, and of their sale, and most obviously from signatures or book plates in the offending books themselves. As with Burghley and the first edition of Aretino in England, so we have 'Nar[cissus] Luttrell his book' in the unique surviving copy of *The London Jilt*. Possession of *La Puttana Errante* by Thomas Barlow, calvinist Bishop of Lincoln, and *The Wandering Whore* by Anthony à Wood[79] are similarly authenticated, as is Henry Vaughan's purchase of Sinibald's *Geneanthropeia*, dated 1676.[80] The fact that the evangelical Robert Boyle made, in his youth, 'many copies of amatory, merry and devout (verses) in English', implies that he must have owned or had access to the originals.[81] Of course, just as ownership does not prove readership, so non-ownership does not prevent borrowing; nor are these the kinds of works many owners would admit to with a signature.

Contemporary library catalogues, where they exist, are reliable guides, though we must remember Pepys's Rochester in his scriptor drawer. The secretive but meticulous John Locke listed the following in his collection: Louis de Gaya, *Ceremonies Nuptials* (Paris, 1680); 'Machiavel', *L'assino d'oro* (1550); Ferrante Pallavicino, *Opera Scelte* (Villefranche, 1666, this edition included *La Retorica delle Puttane*); four editions of the *Satyricon*, and one of the *Priapeia*; Poggio, *Sales seu facetiae*; *Erotematica*; P. Aretino *Ragionamenti* (1660) and nine books, some prurient, on V.D. 'His favourite reading', we are told, 'was French romance, some of it salacious'.[82] In Blicking Hall, Norfolk, the library gathered by Sir Richard Ellys of Nocton, Lincs, with the advice of Michael Maittaire includes: *Il Putanismo Romano* (Holland, 1668); F. Pallavicino, *Opera Scelte* (1666); P. Aretino, *Pornodidasculas* (Frankfort, 1628); six editions of *Satyricon*; *La Puttana Errante* (Amsterdam, n.d.); and a 1740 edition of Brantôme including *The Lives of Amorous Ladies*.[83]

We turn to the largest, though least reliable, English source that I have so far had opportunity to consult: the sale catalogues of individuals' libraries. That it is large, even for the seventeenth century, a quick glance at the massive *British Museum List*[84] will show. Doubts about accuracy and usefulness for this study impinge more slowly. First, leading auctioneers like Edward Millington and William Cooper often combined two or more libraries in their catalogue without any indication of which books belonged to which man. They also tack 'aliis eruditorum virorum libris' or 'aliorum librorum' to a named owner; in some catalogues with a suspicious number of 'repeaters', especially of recently published books, they probably smuggled in slow-moving stock for the trade. Sometimes, the auctioneers, like some inventorists, lump unnamed duodecimi or 'pamphlets in bundles' in anonymous job lots, thereby possibly concealing our quarry. Then again it is impossible to tell whether older books were purchased or merely inherited, or what incriminating morsels have been removed by executors, heirs or auctioneers. It seems probable that the more important the collector, the less was this kind of interference. Despite these shortcomings, sale catalogues are too important a source of identification to be neglected.

My first analysis of seventy English catalogues, a third of which list collections made before the efflorescence of the 1680s, has turned up a surprisingly large number of disreputable books. Predictably Latin erotica, Apuleius, Ovid and Petronius, with their cleansing balm of antiquity, lead with forty-eight copies; Italian, Aretino, Pallavicino,

Poggio and Boccaccio follow with forty-five; there are only four copies of the much more recent French pornography, *Aloisia* and *L'Escole des Filles*, and three of Aristophanes' *Comedies*. The *English Rogue*, thirteen copies, is the most popular of the English publications, followed by *The London Jilt*, eight, *XV Comforts of Rash and Inconsiderate Marriage*, seven, and Rochester's *Poems*, five. In all, fifty copies of disreputable English books have been identified, excluding plays, gallantry and romances.

Within this essay, there is room only to mention owners of significant numbers of disreputable books who can be fairly safely identified. These are Elias Ashmole; Sir William Coventry; Thomas Britton, the polymathic small coal-man; the Revd Thomas Grey, late of Dedham, Essex; Edward Wray of Barling, Lincs, armiger; Dr Richard Smith; Walter Rea, armiger; John Dunton; John Parsons, barrister of the Middle Temple; John Warner, Bishop of Rochester; the Revd John Maynard, of Mayfield, Sussex; William Levinz, M.D., President of St John's College, Oxford; and Richard, Lord Maitland, who also owned a set of prints of 'Aretines Postures'.[85]

The most superficial analysis of readers and owners reveals that a marked number of them had puritan, calvinistic or low-church upbringings and backgrounds, as indeed had many of the known authors, like Rochester, Kirkman, Nashe, Oldham, Crowne, Marvell, Neville or Dunton. It begins to appear that Kirkman's slur that 'crop-eared fellows', believing 'stollen meat is sweetest', indulged in such 'private reading' may not be so outrageous.[86]

The sources for New England readership or ownership are sparser, but better worked. The few extant sale catalogues, library lists and inventories produce a very thin crop. Increase Mather owned Ovid's *Ars Amatoria* and the *Comedies* of Plautus and Terence;[87] the last two were also among John Harvard's gifts to the College,[88] which also owned by 1723 *Celestina*, Aristophanes' *Comedies*, the *Satyricon* and the *Erotikon*.[89] Significantly, the books listed in the College Library *Catalogus* of that year are overwhelmingly pre-Restoration. Yale was a trifle more catholic in taste; among the books drummed up by Dummer in England in 1713 were Boileau's *Historia Flagellantium*, Bayle's *Dictionary*, a complete Ovid, Aristophanes *Comoediae Undecim*, Works of Chaucer, 'Hudibras' and Jonson's *Works*.[90] By the time of Clap's *Catalogue* in 1743 these were supplemented by the *Plays* of

Wycherley and Otway, *The Dunciad*, Oldham's *Works*, Plautus, Terence, Juvenal and Martial.[91] Lots in the Revd Eleazer Pemberton's library sale in Boston in 1717 included *Monk Unvail'd*, *Hudibras* (two copies), *Night Adventures*, *Rehearsal Transprosed* and an infuriatingly vague 'Miscellanies'.[92] The Revd George Curwen had Cotton's coarse *Virgil Travestie* and five books from the *Rehearsal Transprosed* controversy, including *S'too him Bayes*.[93] Wright's investigations of inventories, so often too imprecise for our purposes, has thrown up nothing but a few romances among a dozen New England worthies.[94]

More has been gleaned from the careful sifting of diaries, sermons, commonplace books, letters and published works. Morison's majestic *History of Harvard College*, for instance, analyzes the light reading of Elnathan Chauncey and Seaborn Cotton, the son of John Cotton 'the unmitred Pope', both future ministers.[95] The latter was much taken with the bawdy *Wit's Recreations* (London, 1640). Some passages transcribed in his commonplace book Morison did not feel able to publish in 1935. Morison quotes many other transcriptions of erotic passages from Spenser, ballads and lyric poems, which he believes were made *after* Cotton was ordained. *Wit's Recreations*, which had far cruder pieces than those transcribed, was still in demand in 1696.[96] Chauncey quotes a few mildly exceptionable passages from Cleveland and *Wit's Recreations*. A contemporary of Chauncey's at Harvard was John Crowne, who, despite his puritan parents and the tutelage of John Norton, became a playwright protégé of Charles II and proponent of 'the most outrageous expression of libertine philosophy in Restoration comedy'. Unfortunately I have been unable to find any record of his undergraduate reading.[97] Edward Taylor was also familiar with Cleveland's erotic poetry.[98] Dunton's account of trading in Boston includes a character of 'Mrs. Ab——l [or Ab——t], (a Person of Quality) A well-wisher to the Mathematics: a young Proficient, but willing to learn, and therefore come to Enquire for the *School of Venus* . . . a book I cou'd not help her to'. If only Dunton were trustworthy![99] When Cotton Mather read 'The Wife of Bath's Tale', *Hudibras* and Rabelais is not known, but it must have been before 1700.[100]

The early eighteenth century brings a distinct change of tone in New England, including a marked secularization of reading material. Twice, Cotton Mather was driven to protest about undergraduate reading at

Harvard: in 1708 it was Ovid's Epistles in private; in 1723 the charges were expanded to '*Satan's Library* . . . plays, novels, empty and vicious pieces of poetry, and [again] even Ovid's Epistles . . .'[101] These vague charges were spelled out three years later in reference to 'such Pestilences . . . all those worse than Egyptian Toads; spawns of a Butler and a Brown and a Ward and company whose Name is legion . . . scribblers of . . . vile Rapsodies.'[102] As far as Tom Brown was concerned, several of whose works and translations were obscene or pornographic, he was right.[103] Ebenezer Turrell's (H.C. 1721) MS. Notebook betrays familiarity with the debauched hack 'of facetious memory'. The future minister also records an anal joke of profound unoriginality.[104] The most striking evidence of this change in reading habits is in the MS. list of 'all ye Authours in those Arts and Sciences wh. I intend to gain an insight into' compiled by Nathan Prince (H.C. 1718) the brilliant but unstable Harvard tutor,[105] and younger brother of Thomas Prince, who himself was not averse to low literature when safely out of Massachusetts.[106] Despite the hypocritical brotherly advice to 'Converse as little as possible in British authors, and hardly for anything else than to polish your Brittish language', Nathan planned to read Mrs Behn, Butler, Bergerac, Congreve, *History of the Whores and Whoredoms . . . of Rome*, Etherege, Farquhar, *The English Rogue*, Thomas Brown (the poet), Ovid on love, Otway, Lee, Oldham, *Pastime Royal*, Petronius, *Father Rock*, Rabelais, Sedley, Ned Ward, Wilmot, Wycherley, Poggio, and our old friend *The London Jilt or The Politick Whore*.

Meanwhile a Yale graduate, himself not averse to romances, 'if sound and moral',[107] was weathering a storm about stimulating reading in Northampton, Massachusetts. Jonathan Edwards's clumsy handling of the sexual scandal resulting from youthful perusal of quasi-medical and midwifery books in 1744 has been amusingly and fully recounted by Thomas H. Johnson.[108] One of the books which caused the obscene outbursts may well have been his own. About this time undergraduates at New Haven, understandably challenged by the name and humourlessness of the rector, Thomas Clap, were decorating certain library books with obscene graffiti. Later in the century one wit claimed familiarity with *Fanny Hill*.[109]

The press, after abortive attempts in the seventeenth century, was beginning to provide a comparatively innocuous, but for Increase

Mather God-provoking, home-grown bawdy. In 1712 John Green was fined £5 for publishing a profane mock sermon.[110] Perry Miller exaggerated wildly when he described *The Origin of the Whale bonepetticoat. A Satyr* (Boston 2 August 1712) as 'social pornography'.[111] The jaunty eight page squib is at worst voyeuristic. Josiah Franklin's *New England Courant*, 1720–26,[112] with its coarse-cum-titillating libels, its mild anti-clericalism, its fearless piracy of news and satirical items from the London press, would have tasted like weak tea in a London served by the hard core porn of the unspeakable Curll. Yet some hearts must have missed a beat in Boston when they saw Increase Mather described in print as 'The reverend scribbler'. The reprinting in London of the broadside *Father Abby's Will* (1731) and its sequel was for their quaintness rather than their faint suggestiveness.[113]

Even more than the English readership of disreputable books, Massachusetts owners and readers came from the inner puritan 'tribe'. The common herd there, as in England, seems to have had ample opportunity to feast its eyes on bawdy and scatological chap-books and ballads.[114]

Why, we must ask finally, was there this interest in the prurient among the devoutly and zealously raised? Edmund S. Morgan has argued in an influential article that the puritans were not squeamish about sex.[115] His argument, evidence and deductions fail to convince. Though puritans in old and New England may have been less obsessed with sex than post-Freudian man, they were certainly addicted to a sense of sin. Frequently their conviction of complete worthlessness and their adolescent sexual drives reached peaks of intensity concurrently. These dual traumas had to be endured in an often terrifying isolation. The incessant demands that the Old Adam must be slain, the truism that natural man could never achieve the liberating rebirth, resulted in an insistent need to repress or sublimate sexual drives or romantic desires to the primal and all-consuming relationship with God. Their ordeal on this spiritual assault course left many puritans, or ex-puritans, with a deeply branded sense of guilt, anxiety, fear and shame. For the zealous, the course never ended until they joined the saints triumphant.[116] In the process, they internalized rigid and authoritarian social controls exerted by their church communities.[117] Within this voluntarily repressive system there were few of the ritualistic safety valves which other contemporary societies provided: no *mardi gras* before a day of fasting and humiliation; no *terrae filius* at Harvard commencement; no apprentice riots; no carnival; no Book of Sports; no Christmas; no mystery at the altar or beauty of holiness. It has recently been suggested that the manic spree at Salem in 1692 was a folk necessity in a doldrum of passionate sobriety.[118]

Another side of this puritan mentality in England and America was their emphasis on 'verbalism', not only the preached but also the written word. They shared this passion for books with many middle-class Englishmen in the seventeenth century, with the crucial proviso that the reading matter should be at least useful, if not monitory or elevating.[119] Even purveyors of bawdy acknowledged this necessity with their fulsome rationalizations 'To the Reader': this whore story was to warn the young and their parents; that collection of dirty jokes was 'a pill to purge melancholy'. Given the puritan code, and a sense of self-righteous impunity for some, 'the book' could become a necessary vicarious experience for the self-denying.

For the Restoration period in England and New England, we must add the contextual ingredient of political stress, ulcerating the endemic sense of personal insecurity which anyone living in the capricious and unrelenting natural world of a pre-industrial society must have felt.[120] The world turned upside down too often from 1640 to 1700, both for Englishmen and New Englanders, for most thinking men to be able to preserve intact their scrupulous consciences. After 1660, they lived with the threat of catholicism and political autocracy on the one hand, and secularism, commercialism, materialism and libertinism on the other. Political uncertainty about the long-term future in both areas led inevitably to bitter divisions and factional strife, spawning in turn libels, satires and violence in deed as well as word.

These factors in the personal, social and political environment all had bearing on puritan attitudes to sexuality. Where men wallow morally rudderless, the voice of Jeremiah exhorts the more insistently for self-discipline. There is, for instance, the fearful, even morbid, need to castigate physical drives illustrated by the growing concern with masturbation,[121] the teaching that over-active marital sex is a form of adultery,[122] the warnings that the faculty of the imagination must be rigidly controlled by the reason and the will.[123] There is the surprising omission even in the most detailed personal records and diaries of any specific details about married sexual relations.[124] Or again, there is the reiterated horror at the dangerous effects of reading romances, let alone stage plays.[125]

We should expect such compulsive repressions to be compensated for in other forms of overt behaviour. Cotton Mather has habitually been lampooned, or pitied, for his neurotical excitability.[126] Yet recent research suggests that, though an extreme example, he was a not uncommon puritan type.[127] Examination of puritan devotional works, notably the ecstatic mysticism of Edward Taylor, reveals an almost abandoned use of erotic imagery in verses describing the relations of the believer and Christ.[128] Again, it is noticeable how the aroused puritan sprang to sexual imagery. John Demos has noted the prevalence of sexual insults in the not infrequent rows between neighbours in Plymouth,[129] and Archbishop Sheldon would have confirmed that this kind of slur was not confined to New England.[130] When puritans indulged their passion for 'censoriousness and detraction', not to mention railing and contention against their enemies, they spat out words like 'lust' (for long hair or worldly success), or 'whoring after' (toleration), or wantonness (of football), or, of the temptation not to give alms, 'the strange woman who flattereth with her lips . . . the WELL-FAVOURED HARLOT . . . holy Scripturian whore . . . her words being smoother than oile; and her lips dropping as the honey comb . . . my quondam Mistris . . .'[131] Unclean, wanton, carnal, filthy, naughty, corrupt, polluted, with their strong sexual overtones, were cliché epithets for *anything* reprehensible. When puritans attacked what they considered to be sexual licence, they could indulge so delightedly in their catalogues of vice as to be guilty of what David Frantz terms 'secret pornography', but which I can't resist calling 'purnography'.[132] Needless to say, the alleged debauchery of the Roman Catholic church could release all restraints. Here the pornograph and the purnograph almost touch hands. Yet along with this form of usage in polemic, there runs a distinct prudishness of expression in the calmer moods of counselling or consoling or recounting.[133] We know all too little about the puritan subconscious, their fantasy or dream life. The examples of Simon Forman or Samuel Pepys suggest that it may well have been rich in sexual symbolism.[134] It could be argued that graffiti are another emanation of the fantasy world, in which case the 1743 library at Yale is a spectacular example of sexual suppressions finding outlets.[135]

THE PURITANS AND PRURIENCE

There was no shadow of a doubt what the good puritan *should* do if he happened upon a dirty book: 'I went to the fire, and with my tongs I lifted out the best burning coal, and laid in this book [Petronius] in the place of it, laying on the burning coal above it.'[136] Yet I hope I have sketched in a scenario in which the reading of pornography, or bawdy, or obscenity by people of puritan persuasion becomes at least a plausible proposition. This study is still at the exploratory stage. Many sale catalogues, libraries, suspicious titles, individual backgrounds, diaries, letters and autobiographies remain to be searched— along, of course, with a little browsing.

## NOTES

1. Jules Paul Siegal, 'Puritan Light Reading', *New England Quarterly*, XXXVII (1964) 193–194. I later discovered that my interest had been spuriously excited. Mather did not order this book. See notes 20, 22.

2. The phrase is, predictably, Cotton Mather's: *Bonifacius: An Essay upon the Good that is to be Devised and Designed* (Boston, 1710) p. 69.

3. David Foxon, *Libertine Literature in England 1660–1745* (New Hyde Park, N.Y., 1965) *passim*; originally published under the same title in *The Book Collector*, XII, nos. 1, 2 and 3 (1963). Succeeding references, cited as Foxon, are from the book. Two of the books exported to Boston in the 1680s, *The London Jilt* and *Venus in the Cloister*, survive in unique copies, the latter only recently discovered in Bournemouth, of all places, by Foxon.

4. See Foxon, p. 40, on Tonson's 1681 'sucker-trap', *Aloisia, or the amours of Octavia*. Similarly, Alexander Smith purloined the title of *The School of Venus* (London, 1716) for his non-pornographic life of Mrs Anne Robinson.

5. Geoffrey Gorer, Ch. iii, in C. H. Rolph, ed., *Does Pornography Matter?* (London, 1961) p. 35.

6. For instance, the MS. Notebook of Ebenezer Turrell at Harvard has had several pages suspiciously cut out.

7. B.M. 1415. It is discussed, not very revealingly, in the *Catalogue of Prints and Drawings, Political and Personal Satires*, Vol. II, Part I 1689–1733 (London, 1873).

8. *Aretine's Postures, Sodom*, Nicolas Chorier's *Satyra Sotadica* (*Tullia and Octavia*) and Millot and L'Ange's *School of Venus* are all discussed

c

by Foxon. On the last, see also Donald Thomas, Introduction, *The School of Venus* (London, 1972). Rochester's *Poems on Several Occasions* and Duprat's or Barrin's *Venus in the Cloister* are described below. The *Complaint* (London, 1676) lists scandals, many sexual, in the 1660s at Provins.

9. For (i) see W. H. Hart, *Index Expurgatorius Anglicus* (London, 1872–78) p. 178. He includes Anthony à Wood's account of the Council's orders for its burning on 8 May. For (ii) see Bodleian Malone, 391; H. E. Rollins, '*Sportive Wit . . .*', *Studies in Philology*, XVIII (1921) 322; *Publick Intelligencer*, 21–28 April, 1656. It was published by Nathaniel Brook. (iii) This was an English adaptation of Aretino's *Ragionamenti*, published by Henry Marsh. (iv) Discussed in Donald Thomas, *A Long Time Burning* (London, 1969) pp. 18, 21. (v) Rechristened *Venus Undrest* in Marsh's advertisement at the end of *The Wits*. It is in the Thomason Collection in the B.M. (vi) A collection of 'drolls', or scenes acted in the popular theatres. Many are merely light-hearted bawdy, with occasional obscene jokes; one or two, like 'The Stallion', excerpted from Beaumont and Fletcher's *Custom of the Country* are distinctly lewd. Published by Marsh and Kirkman. (vii) See Foxon, pp. 8–9, 28. The title was an attempt to capitalize on the pseudo-Aretine *La Puttana Errante* (*c.* 1650). It was written by John Garfield; the 1663 continuation claimed John Johnson as publisher.

10. For (i), (ii), (iv), (vi) and (viii) see note 8. The publishing dates of (ii) and (iv) are derived from J. C. Jeaffreson, ed., *Middlesex County Records*, Vol. IV (London, 1892) pp. 145–46, 243, and bring forward the dates in Foxon, pp. 33–34, 40. (iii) This is an English adaptation of Ferrante Pallavicino's *La Retorica delle Puttane* (1642); there is a copy in B.M. (see Foxon, pp. 10, 25); (v) is discussed below; and (vii) was published for Thomas Fox, and possibly written by Charles Cotton; its Greek title was changed in the *Term Catalogue* for Michaelmas 1684 to *The Kingdom of Love*. As the title suggests, it is a bawdy sexual allegory, similar to Venus's famous description of herself in *Venus and Adonis* 229–240. There are several other titles, like *Eve Revived, or the Fair One Stark Naked* (1683), *The Adamite, or The Loves of Father Rock and his Intreagues with the Nuns* (1682), which have erotic passages and titles. That this appetite for titillation was widespread socially is suggested by G. Legman's statement that 'in the 1680s, it is unquestionable that bawdy song was particularly in demand'. *The Horn Book* (New Hyde Park, 1964) pp. 337–338. Furthermore there are two prosecutions for selling filthy pictures which might also

appeal to the less literate in the decade. Jeaffreson, *Mx. Records*, IV,
p. 239, Barnardi Case 1684; he was still at it in 1696, Foxon, p. 12. In
1688 a woman was indicted at the Guildhall Sessions for selling 'a
percell of cutts'; Foxon, p. 11.

11. H. S. Bennett, *English Books and Readers 1603–1640* (Cambridge,
1970), p. 230.

12. F. S. Siebert, *Freedom of the Press in England 1476–1776* (Urbana,
1952) p. 191. There are 22 pamphlets in the Thomason Collection for
1640, over 1000 for 1641, and 1966 for 1642.

13. *The Original and Growth of Printing* (London, 1664) p. 16.

14. George Kitchin, *Sir Roger L'Estrange* (London, 1913) p. 167.

15. Roger North, *Lives of the Norths*, ed. A. Jessopp, Vol. II (London,
1890) pp. 281–282.

16. 'Preface to the Reader', signed by Kirkman, in *The English Rogue*,
Part I (London, 1672). Marsh's Preface to *The Wits* (London, 1662)
stated: 'I intend to raise no other reputation to my self then that of
Ready Money.'

17. J. B. Williams, *A History of English Journalism to the Foundation of
the Gazette* (London, 1908) pp. 111, 145–147, 262.

18. His later career is briefly discussed by Cyprian Blagden, 'Memorandum
Book of Henry Rhodes 1695–1720', *Book Collector*, III (1954) 28–39,
103–117. He advertised regularly in the *Term Catalogues* from Easter
1681; among his other more or less risqué offerings were several
comedies of Mrs Behn, *Pastime Royal* (1681), *The Dutch Rogue* (1683),
*Confessions of a New Married Couple*, which was the second part of
*Ten Pleasures of Matrimony* (1683), and several bawdy jest books.
Rhodes was cited as the unscathed publisher of *Venus in the Cloister*
by Curll in 1727; Foxon, p. 14.

19. Coxe (*School of Venus*) and Cadman (*Tullia and Octavia*) are named
in Jeaffreson, *Mx. Records*, IV, pp. 145–146, 243. The latter also
published *The History of the Palais Royal: or The Amours of Mlle.
de la Valliere*, in partnership with Richard Bentley in 1680. Fox
(*Erotopolis*) advertised *Boccaces Tales*, *Grammatical Drollery*, *The
Ramble* and *French Intreagues* at the back of the first edition. On Crayle
and Streater, see Thomas, *Long Time Burning*, pp. 24–25, and
'Prosecutions of *Sodom . . . and Poems on Several Occasions by the
E of R . . .*', *The Library*, 5th Series, XXIV (1969) 51–55.

20. (Boston, 1917.) This was the source for Siegal's article, n.1.

21. John Dunton, *Life and Errors* (London, 1705) p. 280. The invoices
are located as follows: 5 September 1683, Vol. XV, fol. 87; 3 March
1683, i.e. 1684, Vol. IV, fols. 89, 90 (two copies); 29 May 1684, Vol. XV,

fol. 89; 13 April 1685, Vol. IV, fols. 91, 92 (two copies). I have discovered two other short invoices, one in Chiswell's hand dated 21 August 1685, Vol. XV, fol. 141; the other is of law books, hand unknown, Vol. IV, fol. 94.

22. A recently discovered letter to Chiswell, dated 27 November 1683, in the Rawlinson MSS. at the Bodleian strongly suggests that Cotton, not Increase, was the orderer. Kenneth Silverman, *Selected Letters of Cotton Mather* (Baton Rouge, 1971) p. 12.

23. Stationery and binding goods have been extracted.

24. Vol. II, fol. 116, £33:9:3d.; fol. 122, £128:1:9d. (includes stationery); Vol. XV, fol. 59ᵛ, £76:16:1d.; fol. 61ᵛ, £13:12:8d.; Vol. II, fol. 118, £149:16:4d. ('Bookes and other goods') might be a further consignment, but it could refer to the 1685 invoice; similarly Vol. XV, fol. 61 could be an amendment of Vol. II, fol. 122, but the £125 worth of books and stationery ware could be yet another consignment. The total value of books sent from 1682 to 1685 could therefore have exceeded £1000.

25. (New Haven, 1920); 2 vols. (Boston, 1907).

26. Littlefield, *Booksellers*, I, pp. 209–261; W. C. Ford, *The Isle of Pines* (Boston, 1920); C. A. Duniway, *Development of Freedom of the Press in Massachusetts* (New York, 1906) pp. 43–48; S. E. Morison, *Harvard College in the Seventeenth Century* (hereafter *Harvard*) Pt. I (Cambridge, 1936) p. 346. Licensing may well have been introduced because of Johnson's suspect presence.

27. Ford, *Boston Book Market*, pp. 40–42; Littlefield, *Booksellers*, II, pp. 1–48; Harris is mainly famed for his seditious publications. A whiff of scandal hung over his married life, but it is extremely difficult to trace his output because of its surreptitious nature. The one number of *Publick Occurrences* is reprinted in *The Historical Magazine*, I (1857) 228–231. Sewall's reaction, 'much distaste', is quoted by Duniway, *Freedom of Press*, p. 69.

28. Dunton, *Life and Errors*, p. 127; P. Gray, 'Rochester's *Poems* . . .', *Transactions of the Bibliographical Society*, New Series, III (1938) 185–197.

29. W. Graham, *The Beginning of English Literary Periodicals* (New York, 1926) pp. 41, 55; Dunton's advertisement at the end of *The Amazement of Future Ages* (London, 1684) is mainly of theological works. However, *The Amazement* itself, among its outlandish wonders, has several items on transvestism, sex changes and hermaphrodites. I am grateful to Dr Stephen Parks for help with this Heepish character.

30. P.R.O. Customs 3, 1–81.

31. Book sometimes seems to include stationery, but often this has a separate ledger entry.

32. This ledger for the three month period, Michaelmas Day, 29 September, to Christmas Day 1698, represents the change from the old Customs House to the new parliamentary financial year. G. N. Clark, *Guide to English Commercial Statistics* (London, 1938) pp. 11–12.

33. The ledger for Christmas 1704 to Christmas 1705 is missing.

34. Comparable figures for other colonies (London figures first) are: Virginia and Maryland, £1901:7:11, £267:11:9½; New York, £314:5:0, nil; Pennsylvania, £273:15:0, £6:14:3½.

35. Clark, *Guide*, pp. 15–16. The amount of exaggeration may have been about 4 per cent. T. S. Ashton, 'Introduction', p. 5, E. B. Schumpeter, *English Overseas Trade Statistics, 1697–1808* (Oxford, 1960).

36. On the assumption that the average folio weighs 1 lb 4 oz, quarto 12 oz, octavo 8 oz, and duodecimo 4 oz, the total weight of the 598 books in Chiswell's invoice of 5 September 1683 (see note 21) would be 210 lb, or just under 2 cwt. Their value is £48:0:0, or £24:0:0 per cwt. I have halved this, partly to take exaggerated weights into account, and partly to err, perhaps excessively, on the side of caution.

37. In the Boston Public Library, fols. 137, 144, 204, 276 and 292.

38. *Life and Errors*, p. 101.

39. Frank Donovan, ed., *Benjamin Franklin Papers* (New York, 1962) p. 12. In the second half of the eighteenth century, according to the London bookseller, Thomas Cadell, 'America . . . took off a vast number of Works'. S. B. Parks, 'Booksellers' Trade Sales', *The Library*, 5th Series, XXIV (1969) 241–242.

40. *Boston Book Market*, p. 44.

41. Siegal, 'Light Reading', 185–199; S. E. Morison, *The Intellectual Life of Colonial New England* (Ithaca, 1956) pp. 127–132; J. D. Hart, *The Popular Book* (New York, 1950) pp. 7–36; T. G. Wright, *Literary Culture in Early New England* (New Haven, 1920) pp. 120–126, and *passim*.

42. Space prevents discussion of *The London Bully* (London, 1683) which has some highly objectionable passages. I have not yet examined *Wonders of the Female World*, *A Ramble to Hackney*, *Popes Life* and *Informers Doom*. All these were in the 29 May 1684 consignment.

43. Wing o 264. His ascription to Alexander Oldys is an error. See my '*The London Jilt*', *Harvard Library Bulletin* (1975).

44. Here the connection ends.

45. Reprinted in Philip Pinkus, *Grub Street Stripped Bare* (London, 1968) pp. 280–285.

46. Richard Head and Francis Kirkman, *The English Rogue*, Parts III & IV (London, 1671) *passim*.

47. Cf. M. Katanka, 'Women of the Underworld', unpublished M.A. Thesis, Birmingham University, 1973, pp. 115–116.

48. F. W. Chandler, *The Literature of Roguery*, Vol. I (New York, 1907) p. 224. The 'second' edition of *Nugae* was published in 1675, a 'third' in 1686. Mr Hugh Amory tells me the first edition was *The Complaisant Companion* (London, 1674).

49. I have a checklist and descriptive article forthcoming on these.

50. Foxon, p. x, argues that the free use of these symbols suggests that the internal sexual censorship was less severe then than now. I rather doubt this. Head writes with a conscious naughtiness.

51. Cf. Ford, *Boston Book Market*, p. 121.

52. Thorpe correspondence, April 1953, in John Hayward Papers, Rochester Box II, King's College Library, Cambridge. I am much indebted to the late Dr A. N. L. Munby for directing me to this rich source.

53. Thomas, *Long Time Burning*, p. 76.

54. D. M. Vieth, *Attribution in Restoration Poetry* (New Haven, 1963).

55. D. M. Vieth, ed., *The Complete Poems of John Wilmot, Earl of Rochester* (New Haven, 1968); the Scolar Press has reproduced a facsimile of *Poems on Several Occasions* (Menston, Yorkshire and London, 1971) from the 1680 B.M. C. 131.b.4, with a brief informative introduction.

56. Brice Harris, 'Robert Julian', *E.L.H.*, X (1943) 304; G. de F. Lord, *Poems on Affairs of State*, Vol. I (New Haven, 1963) pp. xxxvii–viii; A. Beljame, *Men of Letters and the English Public in the Eighteenth Century* (London, 1948) p. 124. I am grateful to Dr Stephen Parks for showing me a collection of such manuscripts made for Lorenzo Magalotti, the Florentine virtuoso in England 1668–69, in the Osborn Collection at Yale.

57. Hayward Papers, Rochester Box II, has a photographic reprint of the drawing.

58. G. Legman, *The Horn Book* (New Hyde Park, 1964) p. 261.

59. On libertinism, and Hobbesian influences on the court writs, see Dale Underwood, *Etherege and the Seventeenth Century Comedy of Manners* (New Haven, 1957); Robert Jordan, 'The Extravagant Rake in Restoration Comedy', in H. Love, ed., *Restoration Literature: Critical Approaches* (London, 1972) pp. 69–90.

60. Foxon, p. 43.

61. Wayland Young, *Eros Denied* (London, 1968) p. 256.

62. 'Nunnery' was Shakespearean slang for a brothel. E. Partridge, *Shakespeare's Bawdy* (London, 1955) p. 226.

63. E.g. *The Nuns Complaint against the Friars* (London, 1676); *The Adamite, or the Loves of Father Rock and his Intreagues with the Nuns* (London, 1682); *Romes Rarities, or The Popes Cabinet Unlockt* (London, 1683). *The Amorous Abbess* (London, 1684) and the sets of love letters which passed between a nun and a cavalier are both purely sentimental.

64. I owe these titles to the kindness of Dr Neil MacMaster.

65. The title of the French translation of *Satyra Sotadica*, Englished as *Tullia and Octavia*.

66. *XV Comforts of Rash and Inconsiderate Marriage, or Select Animadversions upon the Miscarriages of the Wedded State*. Done out of French. Third edition with the 'Addition of Three Comforts' (London, 1683).

67. Noticed in *Biographie Universelle*, Tom. XL (Paris, 1825) pp. 141–142. The celebrated Read and Carter prosecution in 1707 was for *Fifteen Plagues of a Maidenhead*.

68. See note 22 above.

69. W. C. Ford, ed., *The Diary of Cotton Mather*, Vol. I (New York, n.d.) pp. 78–80.

70. I am indebted to Messrs Maurice Yaffé and David Foxon, the librarian of the Tavistock Centre, and certain psychiatrists for private communications on aspects of this question. *The Report of the Commission on Obscenity and Pornography* (New York, 1970) p. 25, describes some impressionistic investigations.

71. See e.g. G. Markham, *The Famous Whore* (London, 1609); Robert Anton, *Philosophers Satyrs* (London, 1616); Thomas Cranley, *Amanda, or The Reformed Whore* (London, 1635); Humphrey Mills, *A Night Search* (London, 1646); Sir John Davies, *A Scourge for Paper Persecutors* (London, n.d.); F. Kirkman, *The English Rogue*, Part II (London, 1671) p. 342. *A Session of the Poets* (London, 1696) pp. 6–7 has a long list of books allegedly owned by Tom Brown. See also references in Foxon, pp. 5–7. Buckingham's commonplace book, on the other hand, showed 'a singular absence of coarseness'. W. Burghclere, *George Villiers, Second Duke of Buckingham* (London, 1903) p. 84.

72. 13 January, 8 and 9 February 1668. Mr Robert Latham kindly allowed me to consult the proofs of the new edition of the Diary.

73. Thomas, *Long Time Burning*, p. 18.

74. E. M. Thompson, ed., Letters of Humphrey Prideaux to John Ellis, *Camden Society*, New Series, XV (1875) 30–31. This occurred in 1675.

75. W. D. Cooper, ed., *Savile Correspondence*, *Camden Society*, First Series, LXXI (1858) 68. The book could have been seditious.

76. A. Bryant, *The Years of Peril* (London, 1935) p. 340.

77. M. Emslie, 'Two of Pepys's "Very Lewd Songs" in Print', *The Library*, Fifth Series, XV (1960) 291–293.

78. G. Huehns, ed., *Selections from Clarendon* (London, 1955) p. 40.

79. Barlow's and Wood's books are both in the Bodleian.

80. Edwin Wolfe 2nd., 'Some Books of Early English Provenance in the Library Company of Philadelphia', *Studies in Bibliography*, IX (1960) 275–284.

81. Thomas Birch, *Robert Boyle* (London, 1744) p. 31.

82. J. Harrison and P. Laslett, *The Library of John Locke* (Oxford, 1965) *passim*, p. 29.

83. Mr Julian Gibbs kindly helped me over the Blickling books.

84. *A List of English Book Sales 1676–1900 now in the British Museum* (London, 1915). The late Dr A. N. L. Munby helped me greatly with this area.

85. Wray, Maynard, Maitland, Levinz, Ellys, Smith and Dunton definitely fit this pattern, as, of course, do Pepys, Barlow, Locke, Luttrell, Boyle and Vaughan. Other owners require further investigation.

86. Preface to the Reader, *English Rogue*, Pt. II (London, 1668). Cf. J. F. Ostervald, *The Nature of Uncleanness Consider'd* (London, 1708) p. 122.

87. J. H. Tuttle, 'Libraries of the Mathers', *Proceedings of the American Antiquarian Society*, IV (1910) 289, 343, 351. These lists are incomplete. There is no sign of *The Womans Advocate*.

88. A. C. Potter, 'John Harvard's Library Gift to Harvard College', *Proceedings of the Colonial Society of Massachusetts* (hereafter *PCSM*) XXI (1919) 190–230.

89. *Catalogus Librorum Bibliothecae Collegii Harvardini* (Boston, 1723). Less than one sixth of the holdings had been published since 1660.

90. Louise M. Bryant and Mary Patterson, 'List of Books Sent by Jeremiah Dummer', Mary C. Withington, ed., *Papers in Honor of Andrew Keogh* (New Haven, 1938) pp. 423–487.

91. *Catalogue of the Library of Yale College* (New London, 1743).

92. *Catalogue of Curious and Valuable Books* (Boston, 1717).

93. *Catalogue of Curious and Valuable Books* (Boston, 1718).

94. T. G. Wright, *Literary Culture*, and 1917 Yale Ph.D. thesis of the same title, reprints inventories, etc. of William Bradford, William Brewster, Thomas Dudley, Samuel Eaton, Cotton Mather, Increase Mather, Thomas Prince, Miles Standish, Edward Tench, Thomas Weld,

Senior, William Tyng and John Winthrop, Junior. For instance, Bradford's inventory lists '3 & fifty smale bookes'.

95. *Harvard*, Part I pp. 125–132. He gives extracts in greater detail in 'Revd. Seaborn Cotton's Commonplace Book', *PCSM*, XXXII (1935) 320–352.

96. Jeffries Family Papers, Vol. XV, fol. 108. Pembrooks Account. Cruder items in George Herbert's collection are nos. 98, 391, 407, 432, 435, 479 or 503.

97. Morison, p. 329; Jordan, 'Extravagant Rake', 88–89, citing *The Country Wit* (1675) pp. 22–23.

98. Donald E. Stanford, 'Edward Taylor and the Hermaphrodite Poems of John Cleveland', *Early American Literature*, VIII (1973) 59–61.

99. W. H. Whitemore, ed., *John Dunton's Letters from New England* (Boston, 1867) p. 112; C. N. Greenough, *John Dunton's Letters from New England* (Boston, 1912).

100. Wright, *Literary Culture*, records quotations from all of these in *Magnalia Christi Americana* (London, 1702) Vol. I, pp. 58, 107; Vol. II, p. 645.

101. *Corderius Americanus* (Boston, 1708) p. 24; letters to Overseers, in J. Quincy, *History of Harvard University*, Vol. I (Cambridge, Mass., 1840) p. 588.

102. *Manductio ad Ministerium* (Boston, 1726) p. 43.

103. B. Boyce, *Tom Brown of Facetious Memory* (Cambridge, Mass., 1939).

104. The MS. Notebook is in Harvard University Archives; see a recorded copy of Telltale, a student squib, of 21 October 1721.

105. Harvard University Archives. List compiled around the mid-1720s.

106. Such as Tom Brown, Shadwell's *The Squire of Alsatia*, and various satiric broadsides, *en voyage* for England in 1709. E. A. Evans, 'Literary References in New England Diaries 1700–1730', unpublished Harvard University Ph.D. Thesis (1940) pp. 33–35.

107. T. H. Johnson, 'Jonathan Edwards's Background of Reading', *PCSM*, XXVIII (1931) 193–222. He owned *An Essay on Midwifery*.

108. T. H. Johnson, 'Jonathan Edwards and the "Young Folks' Bible" ', *New England Quarterly*, V (1932) 37–54.

109. Richard Warch, 'Graffiti Olde and Bolde', *Yale Alumni Magazine* (Nov. 1969). I am grateful to Mr Warch for guiding me to his sources in the 1743 Library at Yale. The main problem for our purposes is dating. I am reasonably confident that two very obscene drawings, and comments about Clap and his black maid Juno (Churchill, *Collection of Voyages*, pp. 225, 508, 552) were the work of Richard Woodhull (Y.C. 1752). The obscene alteration of 'constable' in Kennett's *Com-*

*plete History of England*, p. 529, was probably the work of one of the Evans family, at Yale around 1740.

110. C. A. Duniway, *Development of Freedom of the Press in Massachusetts* (New York, 1906) p. 79.

111. *The New England Mind: From Colony to Province* (Cambridge, Mass., 1953) pp. 332–333. The unique copy is in the British Museum. I have never seen any validation of the imprint.

112. Cf. Miller, *Colony to Province*, pp. 334–337.

113. Reprinted in O. E. Winslow, ed., *American Broadside Verse* (New Haven, 1930) p. 162.

114. Cotton Mather mentions hawkers and pedlars touring New England with their wares, *Diary*, I, p. 65; II, p. 242. Chapbook and broadside characters are occasionally alluded to, e.g. *New England Courant*, no. 24, 15 January (1722).

115. 'The Puritans and Sex', *New England Quarterly*, XV (1942) 591–607.

116. Three fine recent studies are O. C. Watkins, *The Puritan Experience* (London, 1972); R. Middlekauf, *The Mathers* (New York, 1972); L. Ziff, *Puritanism in America* (New York, 1973). I have also learnt a lot from the graduate work on spiritual autobiographies of my former pupil, Sheila Gates.

117. Ziff, *Puritanism*, pp. 67–71, 144; A. Macfarlane, *The Family Life of Ralph Josselin* (Cambridge, 1970) p. 194.

118. Ziff, *Puritanism*, pp. 165, 245–246.

119. L. B. Wright, *Middle-Class Culture in Elizabethan England* (Chapel Hill, 1935) pp. 86, 100, 376; H. S. Bennett, *English Books*, pp. 2–9, 108; Watkins, *Experience*, pp. 1–2, 124–125.

120. K. V. Thomas, *Religion and the Decline of Magic* (London, 1971) pp. 3–24; Macfarlane, *Josselin*, pp. 170–174, 193–194.

121. Thomas Cobbet, *A Fruitful and Usefull Discourse* (London, 1656) pp. 173–177; C. Mather, *The Pure Nazarite* (Boston, 1723); C. Mather, *Manductio*, p. 20; *The Crime of Onan* (London, 1724); *Onania, or The Heinous Sin of Self-Pollution* went through fifteen editions from c. 1717 to 1730. The tenth edition, claiming 15,000 copies sold, was reprinted in Boston in 1724.

122. Robert Carr, *An Antidote against Lust* (London, 1690) p. 105; Morgan, 'Puritans and Sex', p. 593; S. Fender, 'Edward Taylor and the Sources of American Puritan Wit', unpublished Ph.D. Thesis, Manchester University, 1962, pp. 34, 154; Middlekauf, *Mathers*, pp. 202–204; A. D. J. Macfarlane, 'Regulation of Marital and Sexual Relationships in the Seventeenth Century', unpublished M.A. Thesis, London University, 1968, pp. 123, 124, 142–144.

123. Cecelia Tichi, 'Thespis and the Carnall Hipocrite', *Early American Literature*, IV (1969) 86–103; Watkins, *Experience*, p. 6.

124. E.g. Josselin, Sewall, Evelyn, Pepys. Pepys's use of a private code for sexual entries is suggestive.

125. See note 119, and C. Mather, *Manductio*, pp. 39, 42, 43, 64; *Bonifacius*, pp. 50, 58, 69, 110.

126. For two sensitive recent studies, see Middlekauf, *Mathers*, and D. Levin, ed., *Bonifacius, An Essay Upon the Good* (Cambridge, Mass., 1966) pp. vii–xxvii.

127. N. S. Grabo, 'The Veiled Vision', S. Bercovitch, ed., *The American Puritan Imagination* (Cambridge, 1974) pp. 19–33, instances comparable 'reeling and staggering' in Richard Baxter, Samuel Willard, Edward Taylor, Increase Mather, Anne Bradstreet and Jonathan Edwards.

128. W. T. Weathers, 'Edward Taylor and the Cambridge Platonists', *American Literature*, XXVI (1954) 1–31; K. Keller, 'Rev. Mr. Edward Taylor's Bawdry', *New England Quarterly*, XLIV (1970) 382–406; Fender, 'Edward Taylor', pp. 201, 210. Cf. Watkins, *Experience*, p. 213.

129. *A Little Commonwealth* (New York, 1970) pp. 50–51, 136–137, 153. Cf. A. L. Rowse, *Simon Forman* (London, 1974) pp. 67, 141, 144.

130. V. D. Sutch, *Gilbert Sheldon* (The Hague, 1973) p. 167.

131. Fender, 'Edward Taylor', p. 209; Roxbury Petition of 1672, in Morison, *Harvard*, Pt. I, p. 88; D. Minter, 'The Jeremiad as a Literary Form', Bercovitch, *Imagination*, p. 46; Watkins, *Experience*, pp. 145–150, 176; Middlekauf, *Mathers*, pp. 92, 191, 194. I have not been able to see D. J. Hibler, 'Sexual Rhetoric in Seventeenth Century American Literature', unpublished Ph.D. Thesis, Notre Dame University, 1970.

132. 'Leud Priapians and Renaissance Pornography', *Studies in English Literature*, XII (1972) p. 172, and, forthcoming, *Festum Voluptatis: A Study of Renaissance Pornography*.

133. E.g. C. Mather, *Pure Nazarite*; Dunton, *Life and Errors*, esp. p. 99; my colleagues D. Aers and R. Hodge kindly allowed me to read their provocative 'Rational Burning: John Milton on Sex and Marriage' in typescript.

134. Rowse, *Forman*, pp. 20, 59, 290. There is little sexual symbolism in Josselin's thirty-three recorded dreams.

135. See note 109. Morison has drawn attention to special punishments for 'filthy speaking' at Harvard, and to the prevalence in the latter part of the seventeenth century of window-smashing. *Harvard*, Pt. I, p. 121.

136. Robert Blair, a student at Glasgow University. Watkins, *Experience*, p. 209.

# 3

# *The Massachusetts Charter of 1691*

## R. C. SIMMONS

In October 1691 the Great Seal was applied to the charter of Massachusetts, the instrument which, with few amendments, served as the colony's constitution until and beyond the American Revolution. This was the second charter of the colony. The first, granted in 1629, had been vacated in 1684 in a Crown law suit in London, a move that brought anger and lamentations from the colony, where it was identified with civil and religious freedoms, successful progress and prosperity. Until 1691 Massachusetts was without a charter, governed successively under royal commission as part of the Dominion of New England or under the revolutionary bodies that resulted from the overthrow of the Dominion and its governor, Sir Edmond Andros, in April 1689 and were tolerated as temporary arrangements by the Crown. From the date of the April revolution calls had come from within Massachusetts for the restoration of the 1629 charter, while in England, where he had been living as an emissary from Massachusetts since May 1688, the Reverend Increase Mather took immediate advantage of the Glorious Revolution to step up his lobbying for the same end. The charter of 1691, therefore, emerged after a revolution in both New and old England. This essay examines the genesis of the charter, reassesses Increase Mather's role in that genesis, and suggests some of the intersections between events in England and Massachusetts relevant to the story.

First, Massachusetts. There, naturally, the question of the colony's charter was of vital concern. After the uprising of April 1689 there was substantial support in the colony for an immediate return to the old charter of 1629, without any reference to the wishes of the English government, an attitude which culminated in a resolution of a convention of towns that any orders from England for the alteration of government should be 'signified to the respective Towns of the colony

66

that they may be consulted with in order to their approbation and Compliance'. A second body of opinion supported a return to the old charter with the proviso that this be approved in England; persistent representations went to the English authorities for this. A third group seem to have had mixed feelings about the restoration of the charter of 1629; they gave their support to the revolutionary government on condition that it maintained lines of communication with England and promised the acceptance of a royal settlement of English affairs, with a satisfactory, even if new, charter.[1] Finally, a small but articulate number of displaced office holders or members of the Church of England, or both, friends to the overthrown Dominion of New England, hoped for a powerful royal government to be installed in Massachusetts.

The progress of events in Massachusetts indeed made it necessary for the government to appoint a second agent to join Mather in London, Elisha Cooke, an assistant since 1684, who was soon to become a leader of the opposition against royal authority. Yet at this stage he seems to have been identified not with the unyielding old charter group but with those who favoured the old charter and negotiations with England. Fifteen days after his appointment, the lower house put forward the name of another agent, Thomas Oakes, to accompany him to London. Oakes was speaker of the house and the facts of his appointment suggest that he was a leading spokesman for the resolute old charter men. Only after two requests from the house did the governor and assistants, apparently unwillingly, accede to the representatives' requests.[2]

Divisions of opinion in Massachusetts were reflected in a stream of documents sent to the English government. A petition from Charlestown condemned the revolutionary government as arbitrary and tyrannical; it contained no recommendations for the constitutional settlement of Massachusetts, leaving this to the King.[3] Another petition allegedly representing thousands of Massachusetts Anglicans —although signed by only three—condemned the tyranny of the congregational system under the old charter, condemned the overthrow of the Dominion, and appealed for a royal governor and a council appointed by the Crown, with an assembly acting 'in matters proper for their Cognizance as others your Majesties Plantacions are Ruled and Governed . . .'.[4] So although those critics of the

Massachusetts government referred to Andros's rule as well established and orderly, it is obvious that they too were hesitant about its unrepresentative nature. A third petition from Boston represented the position of moderates—many of them merchants—who had no necessary love either for the Dominion or for the old charter. It made no attack on Andros, no allegations against the Dominion government of tyranny or arbitrary proceedings but nor did it criticize the revolution of 1689 or the charter group. Its gist lay in the statement that the Dominion had lacked an assembly and was therefore a different kind of government from that found in England and most of the other plantations but that the revolution had created fresh distress rather than a solution to the colony's ills. The King should provide for a governor and council, and an assembly elected by the freeholders.[5] In addition to these petitions a constant stream of letters went from Massachusetts to London from the supporters of the Dominion, all of which were hostile to the revolutionary government. Edward Randolph, Secretary of the Dominion government, a constant critic of Massachusetts under the old charter, sent thousands of words to his contacts at Whitehall, representing the revolution as the return to power of the same disloyal and refractory 'faction' that had formerly controlled the colony.[6]

It is noticeable that in all the petitions and documents sent to England by the beginning of 1690, the only position not fully articulated was that of the extreme supporters of the charter. Obviously it would have been impolitic for them to send a manifesto to the English government expressing their deepest convictions about the necessity of virtual independence from English control. A letter does exist, from the General Court to the Queen, couched in language very unlike the business-like pleas of the governor and council for English favour. Its fulsome comparison of Mary with Isabella and Elizabeth as nursing mothers to the churches and its review of Massachusetts history in terms of its religious distinctiveness may be taken as the rhetoric of the traditional charter men. But it is uncertain if it was ever sent.[7] Presumably the old charter group relied on Oakes, perhaps on Cooke, to present its point of view; perhaps it realized that its claims were too extreme for written statements.

Political power in the colony now rested in an uneasy balance. On the one side, those who hoped for an unconditional return to the old charter controlled the lower house. And while many council members took a less inflexible position, several of those were defeated in the annual elections in 1690. John Pynchon, who had signed the Boston petition, and Samuel Shrimpton, a merchant moderate, were defeated, while Thomas Oakes was, for the first time, elected to the upper house.[8] John Nelson, a merchant moderate, who had signed the Boston petition was prevented from commanding a military expedition against Port Royal.[9] On the other side, many men of substance supported a compromise on a new charter. In 1691 a second petition was sent to England. Its main emphasis was on the ineffectiveness of the revolutionary government in conducting the war against the French and Indians, a matter likely to attract a soldier King's attention. New England was represented as near to total ruin, comparisons were implied with New York where the revolutionary leader, Jacob Leisler, had opposed royal troops, and William was once more asked to take the colony under his control. The total impression given was of governmental incapacity and military chaos.[10]

The petition had sixty-one signatures, a considerable number of which had also appeared on the Boston petition of early 1690. There is, however, some further indication of a growing opposition to the restoration of the old charter. Thirty-two of the men who signed had not before put their names to such documents. Nor were these men alone in their concern for the state of New England. A Salem petition to the governor and council, whose most important subscriber, Bartholomew Gedney, was a moderate and former member of the revolutionary Council of Safety, expressed apprehensions about the conduct of the war. Although Gedney and his co-signers were careful to indicate their support of the government, their loyalty was obviously strained.[11] Yet despite these strains, it is evident that the moderates never entered into outright opposition to the revolutionary government. A number of them did not sign any of the petitions calling for the dispatch of a royal governor. And those who did sign meant not to create internal difficulties for the Massachusetts authorities but to influence the English government in its future policy.

In Massachusetts during 1690 and 1691, therefore, two distinct opinions seem to have formed about the Massachusetts charter. The first called for a return, pure and simple, to the charter of 1629. The second would be content to accept a new charter from England that provided political liberties, including a representative assembly, even if the colony lost some of its former privileges.

What of events in England? Certainly the letters and petitions from Massachusetts to the government were received, sometimes read, and definitely filed by the Committee of Trade and Plantations, the body responsible for colonial affairs. Yet in 1689 and 1690, Increase Mather provided the mainspring of action. At this stage, he pressed hard and confidently for the restoration of the old charter. Since William of Orange had promised that English municipal charters previously vacated would be restored, his confidence seemed justified. Moreover, his closest contacts in England were naturally with prominent dissenters and their allies and he shared their early optimism that William's often-advertised Calvinism would favour dissenting fortunes. In fact the elder statesman of English dissent, Philip Lord Wharton, conducted the New Englander to his first audience with William on 9 January 1689. By this time Mather had also made contact with Sir Henry Ashurst, son of an influential London Presbyterian, son-in-law of the Presbyterian Lord Paget and brother-in-law of the dissenting politicians, Philip Foley and Richard Hampden.[12] At this meeting William, who probably knew and cared little about New England, although in the 1670s he had spoken, during unsuccessful periods in the war with France, of carrying on the struggle against Louis XIV from the other side of the Atlantic, promised an investigation of Mather's claims for the restoration of Massachusetts' ancient privileges. More immediately useful, through his nonconformist contacts, and through the goodwill of a Scot, William Carstares, the Prince's chaplain and agent, Mather was able to prevent the dispatch to Massachusetts of a letter then being sent to all colonial governors confirming them in office after the change of ruler in England.[13]

Mather now pressed hard the point that the Massachusetts charter had been illegally revoked; this submission, narrowed down to a claim that the writ of *scire facias* by which the charter had been condemned had been flawed, brought failure. An hitherto unused note of the meeting of the Lords of Trade on 22 February shows that Sir Robert Sawyer, who as Attorney General in 1684 had prosecuted the charter, convinced the committee of the validity of those proceedings.[14] The Committee's conclusion, that a new governor should be sent to the colony with a provisional commission until a new charter could be prepared, seemed to preclude all hope of the restoration of the old charter and government. And although the Committee specified that the new charter should 'preserve the rights and privileges of the people of New England,' it was not slow to add that it ought also to 'reserve such a Dependence on the Crown of England as shall be thought requisite'. The only relief these decisions brought to Mather was the confirmation of the removal of Andros and the implication that there would be no revival of the Dominion of New England.[15] On 14 March Mather again saw the King, obtaining a further promise for the removal of Governor Andros.[16]

Yet all was not lost. While an order-in-council endorsed the call of the Committee for the preparation of a new charter, two commissioners rather than a temporary governor were ordered to take over the colony's administration.[17] No action was ever taken on this command and no further mention of Massachusetts was made by the English government until April. Then the Secretary of State, the Earl of Shrewsbury, was asked to submit the names of governors for New York, for the Jersies and for New England.[18] This provoked a protest from unidentified parties—no doubt at Mather's instigation—who cited both the previous freedom of New England to choose its own governors and the parliamentary condemnation of the illegal revocation of charters including those of the colonies.[19] At about the same time there was a clash at the Committee of Trade between those who favoured the continuation of Andros and others who accepted the arguments for his removal. The Earl of Nottingham, a moderate Anglican, unsympathetic to the political claims of dissenters, is alleged to have led the defence of Andros while the Duke of Bolton, the eccentric Whig politician whose views often clashed with those of Nottingham, spoke against him.[20] Presumably the hostility of Anglican Tories and Whig dissenters underlay the dispute, the formers' support having been rallied to Andros as a loyal servant of the Crown and a member of the Church of England forced to preside over an unruly and seditious mob of colonial dissenters. But the whole discussion of the governorship and the new charter lacked urgency. The English government took no further action on either matter until February 1690 and no substantial measures to prepare a new charter until 1691.

Inactivity towards New England was, of course, a reflection of the relative unimportance of the region among the English colonies. Great care and attention was given by the Committee of Trade in these same months to the West Indian sugar islands.[21] Nor did the growing pressure of the war with France on the defective machinery of the English government leave much room for official consideration of New England. Although William and his advisers were later to become concerned about French military strength in North America, little was now made of it. Yet, as important, after his rebuff in February, Mather refrained from making further requests to the Committee about Massachusetts. Without this stimulus, it was happy to let the colony's affairs slide from view.

In fact, during the rest of 1689 and for much of 1690, Mather dealt with the Committee or saw the King only when forced to by some direct challenge to the interests of Massachusetts. This silence was part of an intentional strategy. Mather was continually busy elsewhere in almost daily meetings and lobbyings aimed at the restoration of the charter. His initial lack of success with the Committee in February 1689 pushed Mather towards the full development of a possibility that had been emerging since the beginning of the Convention Parliament. The idea of a parliamentary rather than a Crown remedy for the ills of Massachusetts directly contravened the usual view that the colonies were particularly the affair of the King. Any consideration by Parliament of their constitutional or political as opposed to their commercial relationship with England was highly unusual, perhaps unprecedented since the Restoration.[22] Yet as early as 2 February 1689, only 12 days after the opening of the Convention, a Commons committee reported that action was necessary to secure 'Cities, Universities, and Towns Corporate, and Boroughs and Plantations' against 'Quo Warrantos and Surrenders and Mandates' and to restore them to their 'Ancient Rights'. On the same day this recommendation was accepted by the House.[23]

Whether Mather or one of his Whig or dissenter friends first suggested the addition of the colonial charters to those of the English corporations is not known, although the connection could not have been a difficult one to make. But Mather had met with several members of the committee responsible for the 2 February resolution before that date; on 1 February he had seen Hugh Boscawen, a leading

Whig on the committee, and it is likely that this interview was responsible for the inclusion of the colonies in the report. It was of the greatest importance that many members of the same committee were Whigs or dissenters or otherwise sympathetic.[24] Among these, and already contacted by Mather, were not only Boscawen but William Jephson, the King's secretary (whom Mather had met through Lord Wharton), John Wildman, the famous former leveller and political agitator, and one of the Hampdens, John or Richard.[25]

In the days and weeks that followed, Mather continued and enlarged these parliamentary contacts, dining with Boscawen and the Hampdens, meeting with such London nonconformist notables as William Love, and discussing Massachusetts and New England with the Harleys, the Foleys and other House of Commons men.[26] In fact Mather's fortunes were now linked to those of the dissenters and the Whigs in their endeavour to return the English corporations to their old forms prior to Charles II's and James II's regulation of them in the Crown's search for electoral control. With the steady progress in the House of preliminaries for a bill to restore corporations, the hopes of Mather for the Massachusetts charter and of the English dissenters for their legal readmission to the parliamentary and civic life of the English cities and boroughs seemed assured.[27] But when, on 11 March, a Commons committee came to make a final report on the bill, the reference to the plantation charters was missing. It seems unlikely that any deliberate meaning can be attached to this, although there was agitation at the time and later about including the colonies in the bill.[28] But, given the composition of the committee, the omission was probably the result of the slip of a clerk's pen. An amendment was immediately proposed and carried, without comment, and the words 'New England and the Plantations' were included in the proposed bill.[29] Mather's contacts in the House were obviously well primed in his interests, evidence of his successful lobbyings.

This episode was even advantageous to Mather's cause. To the anonymous 'plantations' of the first proposals was now added the specific reference to New England. The text of the resulting bill is unfortunately lost. But there is no reason to think that in its passage through the Commons—the first reading was on 30 April, the second on 2 May and it was reported from committee on 23 July—there was any modification to the mention of New England.[30] By August,

Mather felt confident enough to think that he 'might with Joy and good Tidings in my mouth return home to New England'.[31]

In the event Mather remained in England, prevented from sailing by the illness of a son. By the time he could have set forth again, circumstances were less bright. Further progress on the Corporation bill was delayed by the Commons preoccupation with attacks on the ministry and the hindering of important fiscal legislation. The consequence was the prorogation of Parliament by William on 20 August. When it reassembled again, it was decided to reintroduce some uncompleted bills from the previous session. The Corporation bill was accordingly given new first and second readings. It was reported from committee on 2 January 1690. The committee included such dissenters as Paul Foley, Boscawen and John Birch. But the moderate and Anglican element on it was strong and, when the bill emerged, it contained clauses unacceptable to the Whig nonconformists.[32] They responded with their own amendments, including the famous Sacheverell clause, causing bitter debates and their subsequent defeat. But New England was not excluded and final triumph for Mather seemed near when the bill reached the Lords for its first reading on 11 January 1690.[33]

Contemporary evidence indicates that the inclusion of the colonies in the first and second Corporation bills caused more controversy than Mather ever admitted. During the first session William Blathwayt, Secretary to the Committee of Trade, wrote to Sir Robert Southwell to create ministerial concern over the clauses referring to the colonies and several tracts which were printed to influence the contents of either the first or second bills argued directly about the inclusion of Massachusetts.[34]

The colonial clauses in the second bill definitely provoked debate. The Earl of Halifax even took the trouble to explain to William the reference to New England which, he wrote, the King 'did not before fully apprehend'.[35] As we have seen, the first bill contained the words 'New England and the Plantations', a very broad category that would have meant the restoration of all the colonial charters vacated or surrendered in the reigns of Charles and James. The texts of the revived bill of the second session, prior to its engrossment for transmission to the Lords, are not extant. But the engrossed bill shows that, by this time, due notice was taken of potential dangers to the govern-

ment of the colonies that it represented. The enacting clauses provided
for the restoration of the charters of the 'several plantations and
Colonies in New England and other parts beyond the seas belonging
to the Crown of England', but in the body of the bill several para-
graphs specifically excluded the West Indian islands, 'the Bermudas,
Maryland, Pennsylvania, Carolina, New York or Long Island' from
its effects.[36] These clauses must have resulted from the intervention of
colonial officials who would also have sought to have New England
removed from the bill. The failure to exclude New England from
either the first or second bills in the House of Commons can probably
be attributed in part at least to Mather's powers of persuasion over
influential Members of Parliament.

Mather's own reaction to the progress of the bill in the Lords shows
that he was still not without fears for its possible fate. He recorded
with great jubilation his thankfulness that at its consideration by a
committee of the whole house on 18 January: 'The Lord did appear:
for New England was not (as some would have it) cast out of the Bill,
but that Bill for restoring charters was referred to a committee on
Wednesday next, and the chairman a friend. Blessed be God, and
blessed be Jesus Christ the son of God. Let him who knows what I
have committed to him please yet further to appear for his name
sake.'[37]

In fact, on 23 January, although in his diary and his other writings
justifying his agency, Mather nowhere mentions this, the committee
'After debate, Agreed, that the charters of the Plantations shall be
considered distinctly'.[38] This was a serious setback to Mather's plans
to link Massachusetts to the general restoration of the charters and it
is almost certain that, had the bill proceeded further, all his work of
the last year would have been destroyed. A contemporary, Thomas
Brinley, admittedly hostile to Mather, asserted that he was 'well
informed' by a 'Person of Quality that sitts in the house of Peers that
if the Corporation act had past, New England had been left out as
being in the forreigne Plantacions and so belonging more Immediately
to the king. . . .'[39] But since William, a few days later, prorogued and
then dissolved Parliament, the bill never was again discussed. Mather
could excuse his parliamentary failure on the grounds of the dissolution, the subsequent elections which were unfavourable to the
Whigs and the domination of the next Parliament by the Tories.[40]

Mather was to make one further attempt at a parliamentary restoration of the charter, in May 1690, when there was a chance that a new bill to restore corporations would be introduced. This led him 'to apply myself to five or six members of the House, to pray them to take effectual care the Bill might be so worded as to comprehend our N.E. charters; which they promised me they would do'. But the adjournment of Parliament in the same month and his accurate assumption that it would not be recalled until the winter finally turned Mather away from the House of Commons.[41] He also failed in a plan to bring before the courts his and the revolutionary government's frequently asserted view that the instrument by which the charter had been vacated was flawed in law.[42]

At about this time Mather must have decided that the quest to restore the old charter was unrealistic. At least he turned now away from Parliament and the law courts and back to the Crown, presenting a petition to the King by the hand of the Earl of Monmouth, the Whig friend of Wildman and Locke.[43] The petition, now lost, probably asked that 'you will be Graciously pleased by your Royal Charter to Incorporate your Subjects in the same Colony as formerly. . . .' Nor was the move at first unsuccessful. The petition was referred by the King not to the Committee of Trade but to the law officers, Sir George Treby, the Attorney-General, and Sir John Somers, the Solicitor-General, and to the two Lord Chief Justices, Sir John Holt and Sir Henry Pollexfen. Mather reported that this was done 'through the Intercession of a Great and Worthy Personage', and he was able to join these men, apparently at their every discussion of the colony's affairs. The original petition was later supplemented with additional documents, asking for provision to be made for practices that had grown up outside of the powers given in the old charter, and that the new charter should be confirmed by act of Parliament.[44] These points, however, were referred to the Committee of Trade.[45]

Treby had drafted a proposed new charter by May 1691 which virtually reincorporated the old Massachusetts Bay Company.[46] Yet Mather had experienced one vital defeat. On 30 April, after representations from the Committee of Trade, the Privy Council declared that Massachusetts should have 'a Governor of his [Majesty's] own nomination and appointment . . . as in Barbados and other Plantations'.[47] Mather would afterwards claim that this misrepresented the

King's own wishes, but since all his later efforts to obtain William's revocation of the order were fruitless it appears either that the King or Mather had not understood what had been promised, or that Mather embroidered his account of the episode to put himself in a favourable light.[48] Even so, a noteworthy feature of the Attorney-General's draft charter is that the royal governor is hardly anywhere given a power that he can exercise alone. The whole General Court was to appoint the colony's major non-elective officials and the members of the judiciary, to create courts of law including probate and admiralty courts, to commission military officers and to control the militia, to remove members of the council in case of 'mis-demeanors or defects'—a very generous power—to legislate ceremonies of government and to pass laws for the furtherance of civil and religious life.

The elections of the deputy-governor and assistants were to be by and from the freemen of the corporation, as in the 1629 charter. And although mechanisms were specified for ensuring that the General Court should meet annually, nothing was included about correspond-ing powers of prorogation or dissolution for the governor. With such grants of patronage and such possibilities for checking the executive, the position of the General Court was paramount. Well-suiting the proclivities for self-government free from English control and for a powerful representative assembly, already so strong in Massachusetts, the charter could also have won admiration for its limitations on executive power from an English radical Whig or Commonwealthman.[49]

The draft charter was then referred to the Committee of Trade. It is doubtful that its members ever carefully read it. On the day it was officially received, the Committee referred it directly to William Blathwayt.[50] Blathwayt showed his accustomed efficiency by bringing together an extensive and important series of documents on the history of Massachusetts and its relations with England.[51] He also demonstrated in his minute and devastating comments on the Attorney-General's draft that he had abandoned few of his beliefs in the necessity of firm English control of its colonies. Under thirty-seven different headings, he disposed of the most cherished hopes of the agents. Each time the draft made some extravagant or over-ambitious claim for the colony or granted some liberal power to the General Court, Blathwayt deflated it. By the time he had reached his final page, the Attorney-General's clauses had been raked with cogent and well-directed fire. The inevitable conclusion that the colony should have no more and no less privileges than any other English possession arose plainly and convincingly from his comments.[52] And from two other documents penned by him, there can be no doubt that Blathwayt would have liked Massachusetts to have been placed in the most severe and stringent dependence on the English Crown.[53]

His general arguments about colonial government and colonial relations with England could have been applied to any charter. Yet there is no doubt that Blathwayt, a bureaucrat thwarted for years by prevarications and delays emanating from Massachusetts, had a particular anger against the colony. For example, he severely criticized the part of the Attorney-General's charter that retold the story of the foundation and early history of Massachusetts, as it might have been recounted by an enthusiastic Puritan. He also suggested that the transfer of land from the original twenty-six grantees to the Massachusetts Bay Company might have been illegal. He held that the claim that England had gained economically by the growth of the colony was the opposite of the truth, as numerous breaches of the Acts of Trade attested. His caustic observations took in many other points, including the exclusiveness of the Massachusetts corporation which had always favoured church members, the colony's disdain for the writs of English courts and its long history of hostility to England.

Blathwayt's criticisms were received by the Committee of Trade late in June. In July, it began a detailed consideration of the charter. By the 17 July there was general agreement that the deputy governor as well as the governor should be a Crown appointment, and that the Crown through its Governor should appoint sheriffs, justices and judges. Similarly, control of probate would be vested in the governor and council. It was also decided that the governor should have a veto over the acts of the assembly and that he should be given several other powers previously awarded by the Attorney-General to that body. All these were victories for Blathwayt. So was the important order that all 'freeholders', rather than 'freemen' admitted to corporate privileges, should have the right to vote, a crucial point in the demolition of the colony's corporate constitution under the old charter.[54]

The agents' response was prompt. An undated petition, presented between 25 June and 17 July, pleaded against these alterations in the Attorney-General's draft[55] and some of the concessions gained as a result were of real importance, especially the fixing of a date for the meeting of the assembly, irrespective of the will of the governor.[56] But the Committee resolutely refused to allow the General Court to appoint judges, J.P.s, sheriffs or important officials or the assistants to elect the deputy-governor or the freeholders to elect the assistants, suggestions by which Mather sought to reduce the royal and executive powers desired by Blathwayt.[57] Yet the council was to be elected by the lower house, an important departure from the practice in most of the American colonies.

Finally the agents fought to preserve two privileges: one was control of the judiciary by the General Court, the other that the governor should have no right of veto in the election of Councillors (assistants).[58]

The first real decision about the new charter had been taken at the end of April 1691 when the King ordered that the appointment of the governor should rest with the Crown. William also took a last substantial decision in August when he refused to countenance further objections from the agents and ordered that the final form of the charter should be decided by the Committee.[59] Even so, as late as August and September, Mather still pressed for concessions, mainly for a limitation on the governor's powers in relation to his council and for all civil officers to be appointed in the colony.[60] This rather impudent gesture did achieve results, for the Committee, on 2 September, agreed in substance to several of his proposed amendments.[61] Mather's final shots in the struggle to adapt the provisions of the charter to his interpretation of the colony's best interests were to come on 15 September,[62] when the final wording of the charter had already been prepared. Again some of his points were accepted, although the one which interested him most, because of its importance for Harvard College, was not; no mention was made in the final charter of the General Court's positive right to incorporate schools of learning.[63]

The negotiations over the charter also involved territorial questions since Massachusetts sought jurisdiction over Maine and New Hampshire. Here Mather had mixed success.[64] Despite the objections of Blathwayt and the Gorges family, Maine was confirmed as part of

Massachusetts. More surprisingly, so were Nova Scotia and Plymouth. (The former grant was made after the intervention of William Paterson, one of the founders of the Bank of England, who was interested in the region for possible further Scottish colonization and after lengthy memoranda about the value of Maine and Nova Scotia as sources of naval stores.) The decision to incorporate Plymouth, although the possibility of joining it to New York or Massachusetts had been mentioned as early as October 1690, is less readily comprehensible, since the Committee had not noticed its affairs after that date. Mather knew that Plymouth wished to remain independent; he was also informed that should this seem impossible incorporation with Massachusetts rather than with New York was preferred. He seems to have urged this latter course on the English government, and his critics, with what fairness it is hard to say, claimed that he worked less for Plymouth's independence than for Massachusetts' gain.[65]

Mather's final actions were aimed at consolidating his position in Massachusetts because during the course of 1691 a predictable difference of opinion had arisen between Mather and Ashurst on the one side and Cooke and Oakes on the other.[66] Neither of the latter finally favoured accepting the charter of 1691 on the grounds that it had annulled too many of the colony's former privileges. What alternatives they suggested beyond withdrawing from the negotiations is not known. But both men had informed their allies in Massachusetts of their stand and both knew they would be able to count on the support of the old charter group. In a letter of 4 November 1691 Cooke had already hinted at the deficiencies of the charter and at the conduct of Mather and Ashurst, points which he would develop more fully on his return to Boston.[67] For his part, Mather not only published his own account of the negotiations in London but included in it a highly favourable letter signed by several eminent English nonconformists and arranged for other friends to write in his support to Massachusetts.[68] Perhaps more to the point, on 18 September 1691, Mather and Ashurst had alone put their signatures to a single sheet of paper containing twenty-nine names, those of the future governor and council of the new and enlarged Province of Massachusetts:[69] Sir William Phips as governor and William Stoughton as deputy-governor headed the list. The names of Elisha Cooke and Thomas Oakes were absent from it, nor had they had any hand in its preparation.

Omitted also were five other members of the existing government, elected assistants by the freemen in the spring of 1691. These were Thomas Danforth, deputy-governor of the colony in 1686 and for several years before, who had taken up his place again in 1689; he was a stalwart defender of the old orthodoxy. So was William Johnson, first elected an assistant in 1684 as an opponent of the charter's surrender. John Smith and Peter Tilton were probably also strict charter men. Isaac Addington's exclusion probably had no political overtones, since he was appointed the Province's Secretary. But he was later to oppose Phips and the royal government. The new men brought in by Mather included John Foster, Bartholomew Gedney, Adam Winthrop and Peter Sergeant, known moderates, and John Richards, Mather's political and personal friend, rejected by the electorate in 1690 and 1691. It is not clear when Mather had been first told that he might name the new government, but his choices were carefully considered. The council members selected included a fair share of the colony's old leaders, but these were men likely to accede in the result of Mather's English negotiations; the support of the named political moderates was certain. As far as this was possible, Mather had secured his own power base for his homecoming. Phips, the governor, was in many ways a protégé of the Mathers, as well as a military man satisfactory to the Crown.

Mather's acceptance of the charter of 1691 symbolizes the shift in both power and political thinking in Massachusetts. The old charter group had opposed any constitutional settlement other than a return to the first charter. Their belief that the old charter was a kind of fundamental law or irrevocable constitution sanctified by its links to the foundation of the colony and to the necessary civil defence of the rights of the churches had in the 1660s and 1670s produced vigorous and defiant polemics against the dangers of English interference. But in the period after 1689 not one tract, pamphlet or other writing (so far as we know) roundly asserted a Puritan ideology comprehending this summation of Massachusetts politics. The group in fact showed all the symptoms of decreasing self-confidence and vitality. In 1689, it could effect a temporary return to the old charter; by 1692, it was unable to rally even a determined protest against its abandonment. Now Mather and other influential men seemed to see the first charter as merely a desirable political instrument for the guarantee of a representative assembly, of a satisfactory measure of self-government and of equitable justice. While both the old charter group and the moderates might describe the first charter as a *Magna Carta* and a bulwark of Massachusetts liberties, the latter were willing first to admit that its restoration should depend on English assent and then with Increase Mather's encouragement to decide that the second charter largely protected the political rights that they had enjoyed up to 1686 and could be accepted as a suitable replacement for it. In this way the old stress on the preservation of a godly society had given way to a more secular and Whiggish emphasis on political and constitutional freedoms.

Mather and his supporters could indeed justifiably argue that the charter of 1691 gave Massachusetts considerable liberties. It allowed the General Court rather than the governor and council the power to create courts and grant lands. These were powers not usually found in royal colonial governments. Moreover, the English government had not only given the colony a strong representative assembly but had made a special concession in granting an elective rather than an appointive council, and had permitted one of the colony's agents to nominate the first governor, deputy-governor and councillors. Yet here was the irony of the situation. Confronted by Mather, and the moderates, to whom they had been hostile since 1689, and having failed to preserve the first charter, the old charter men had suffered a considerable loss of status, experiencing the sense of deprivation that often underlay Anglo-American 'country' opposition to the fancied or real increasing powers of the 'court' executive. They were now political 'outs' pushed from the place of power they had held before 1686 into a factional position and they formed the nucleus of an almost certain opposition. And, by the English grant of a new charter with a strong colonial assembly, they were provided with a base of operations that they could fully and familiarly exploit, for many of them were former deputies in the old General Court. This intersection of charter and politics was compounded by the weakness of the colonial executive, provided in typical fashion with formal powers unsupported by the financial independence necessary to support them. And the special provision of an elective rather than an appointive council both lessened the governor's powers of patronage, and, because of his controversial veto powers over these elections, contributed—as did the other factors mentioned—to the potential instability of Massachusetts' politics.[70]

For a time indeed there were even various moves to restore the old charter, or the privileges it had contained. In 1692, for example, the House of Representatives passed a virtual bill of rights and in 1696 resolved that an agent should be sent to England and 'Address made unto his Majesty for Supplies, as also for the restoration of the Ancient Priviledges of the Charter of the Colonie of the Massachusetts, and New Plimouth'. In 1701 the Council resolved—but the House, for obscure reasons, did not—to address the King for a 'restoration of some of our former Priviledges Vizt the Choosing of a Governor, Lieut. Governor and Secretary and Such others as the Court should think fit'.[71] Both Elisha Cooke, Mather's fellow agent, and his son, an even more successful politician, made their career in opposition to royal government and the royal charter.

Yet the more important, less remarked later story of the charter is its transformation in the colony from 'the badge of defeat to a symbol of liberty which, when finally altered by Parliament, led inevitably to war in 1775'.[72] John Wise in his *Churches Quarrel Espoused* (Boston, 1705) praised the New England constitution but Jeremiah Dummer in his *Defence of the New England Charters* (1721) stated that the 'new charter ... is not much more than the shadow of the old one' and that he did not propose to enquire into the 'mismanagement or other cause' that made Massachusetts the only 'loyal corporation ... either in Old or New England, that did not recover its lost liberty under our late glorious King William'. Yet by 1730, in a centenary sermon, Thomas Prince announced that God's special mercy had resulted in the people of Massachusetts ('there never was any People on Earth, so parallel in their general History to the ancient Israelites') having 'greater civil and religious Privileges than almost any others'.[73]

By 1763, the 'inestimable worth' of the charter of 1691 was fully accepted. In the struggle between Great Britain and the colonies, New Englanders rested their first line of defence on their charters. John Adams considered that 'There is so much of a Republican Spirit, among the People, which has been nourished and cherished by their Form of Government . . .',[74] that the charter had allowed them numerous representatives 'too frequently elected to be corrupted' and that 'their consellers were not absolutely at the nod of a minister or governor, but were once a year equally dependent on the governor and the two houses . . .'.[75] Yet even he could reflect that 'the passivity of this colony in receiving the present charter in lieu of the first, is, in the opinion of some, the deepest stain on its character. There is less to be said in excuse for it than the witchcraft, or hanging the Quakers.'[76] None the less Adams also boasted that 'our allegiance to his majesty is not due by virtue of any act of a British parliament, but by our own charter and province laws. It ought to be remembered that there was a revolution here, as well as in England, and that we, as well as the people of England, made an original, express contract with King William.'[77] The charter of 1691 had undergone its full apotheosis.

## NOTES

1. For further discussion and references, see R. C. Simmons, 'The Massachusetts Revolution of 1689; Three Early American Political Broadsides', *Journal of American Studies*, II, no. 1 (April 1968) 1–12.
2. Simmons, *Journal of American Studies*, pp. 3–4.
3. Public Record Office (P.R.O.), C.O. 5/855, p. 59.
4. P.R.O., C.O. 5/855, p. 157.
5. P.R.O., C.O. 5/855, pp. 153–154.
6. R. N. Toppan, ed., *Edward Randolph including his Letters and Official Papers* . . ., Vols. IV, V (Prince Society, Boston, 1899) *passim*.
7. Massachusetts Archives (M.A.) (State House, Boston), *Court Records*, VI, 29 January (1690) 107–108.
8. M.A., Court Records VI 28 May (1690) 133.
9. P.R.O., C.O. 5/855, pp. 255–259, 293–295.
10. P.R.O., C.O. 5/856, p. 142.
11. M.A., XXXVI, 231.
12. Mather's own record of his day-to-day contacts appears in two of his unpublished diaries. His diary for 1688–89 is in the collections of the American Antiquarian Society and that for 1691 is in the collections of the Massachusetts Historical Society.
13. Mather published a written account of his agency in London, in 1691, *A Brief Account Concerning Several of the Agents of New-England.* It has been reprinted in W. H. Whitmore, ed., *The Andros Tracts*, Vol. II (Prince Society Publications, Boston, 1868–74) 271–298. Also useful is his autobiography. The most recent and best edition is by M. G. Hall,

published by the American Antiquarian Society in 1962. K. B. Murdock, *Increase Mather* (Cambridge, Mass., 1925) is a valuable biography but the account of the agency is mainly based on printed sources.

14. Dr William's Library, London, Roger Morrice, 'Entreing Book', II, 480–481.

15. P.R.O., C.O. 391/6, pp. 201–204.

16. Hall, *Autobiography*, p. 332.

17. P.R.O., C.O. 391/6, pp. 203–204.

18. P.R.O., C.O. 5/905, p. 81.

19. See *Andros Tracts*, III, 151, n2.

20. Morrice, 'Entreing Book', II, 543.

21. See R. S. Dunn, 'The Imperial Pressure on Massachusetts and Jamaica 1675–1700', in A. G. Olson and R. M. Brown, eds., *Anglo-American Political Relations 1675–1775* (New Brunswick, 1970).

22. C. M. Andrews, *The Colonial Period of American History*, Vol. IV (reprinted, New Haven, 1964) pp. 368–390.

23. *Commons Journals*, X, 17.

24. For Boscawen, and for other relevant information, see D. R. Lacey, *Dissent and Parliamentary Politics in England 1661–1689* (New Brunswick, 1969) *passim*. For a list of the members of the committee see *Commons Journal*, X, 15.

25. Mather wrote of seeing 'Mr Hampden', 'Diary 1688–89', s.v., 11 January 1689. Both Hampdens were members of the Committee.

26. 'Diary 1688–89', s.v., 3, 14–15, 22, 25 February; 15, 16, 18 March 1689.

27. *Commons Journal*, X, 19, 25, 35, 41–42.

28. See p. 74 and n. 34.

29. *Commons Journal*, X, 51.

30. *Commons Journal*, X, 112, 119, 233.

31. Hall, *Autobiography*, p. 339.

32. *Commons Journal*, X, 277, 294, 311–312, 323.

33. *Commons Journal*, X, 329–330; *Lords Journal*, XIV, 410.

34. Most of these have been reprinted. See *Andros Tracts*, II, 113–123, 137–147, 151–170, III, 3–9, 13–16. Murdock, *Mather* reproduces a facsimile of an additional tract, *A Further Vindication of New England*, probably written by Mather. See also the memorandum 'of the bill [for restoring corporations]', P.R.O., C.O. 5/856, pp. 485–486.

35. H. C. Foxcroft, *Life and Letters of . . . Halifax . . .*, Vol. II (London, 1898), p. 244.

36. H.M.C., *12th Report. Appendix Part VI* (London, 1894) pp. 422–429.

37. Hall, *Autobiography*, p. 342.

38. H.M.C., *12th Report . . .*, p. 432.

39. Thomas Brinley to Francis Brinley, 28 May 1690. Rhode Island Historical Society, Miscellaneous Manuscripts.
40. Hall, *Autobiography*, pp. 340, 342–343.
41. Hall, *Autobiography*, pp. 342–343.
42. 'Brief Account', in *Andros Tracts*, II, 276.
43. I have not been able to find this petition or any certain copy. But in the Massachusetts Archives is a paper 'the Humble Petition of the Agents of the Colonies of the Massachusetts in New England' (together with a preliminary and very rough draft of the same expressed in stronger language) asking directly for a charter containing the same privileges as their former one. M.A., XXXVII, 175a and 175.
44. P.R.O., C.O. 5/856, pp. 506–508; C.O. 5/855, p. 355.
45. P.R.O., C.O. 5/905, p. 258.
46. P.R.O., C.O. 5/856, pp. 535–572.
47. P.R.O., C.O. 5/905, pp. 270–271.
48. For Mather's own version of these events see 'Brief Account', *Andros Tracts*, II, 280–282.
49. There is no evidence, however, that Mather had read or been influenced by radical political writings as had, for example, William Penn, by the same date.
50. P.R.O., C.O. 391/7, p. 21.
51. P.R.O., C.O. 5/856, pp. 418–501.
52. For an example see P.R.O., C.O. 5/856, pp. 580–587.
53. P.R.O., C.O. 5/856, pp. 570–576.
54. P.R.O., C.O. 391/7, pp. 30–35.
55. P.R.O., C.O. 5/856, pp. 578–579.
56. P.R.O., C.O. 391/7, pp. 34–35.
57. P.R.O., C.O. 5/856, pp. 596–597 lists the points at issue between the agents and the Committee at the end of July 1691.
58. P.R.O., C.O. 391/7, pp. 47–49.
59. P.R.O., C.O. 391/7, pp. 40–41. See Earl of Nottingham to King 31 July 1691 and Viscount Sydney to Nottingham 10 August 1691, H.M.C., *71*, *Finch*, III, (London, 1957) 187–8, 199.
60. P.R.O., C.O. 5/856, p. 612.
61. P.R.O., C.O. 391/7, pp. 42–43.
62. P.R.O., C.O. 5/856, pp. 664–665.
63. P.R.O., C.O. 391/7, p. 50.
64. The documents referring to Maine and New Hampshire are to be found in P.R.O., C.O. 5/856, 5/924 and 391/7.
65. Ichabod Wiswall to Thomas Hinckley 6 July and 5 November 1691,

*Collections of the Massachusetts Historical Society*, 4th series, Vol. V (Boston, 1861) pp. 285–286, 299–301.

66. This division was reported by Charles Lidgett in a letter to F. Foxcroft, 5 November 1690, *New England Historical and Genealogical Register*, XXXIII, 406–408. Thomas Hutchinson, *The History of . . . Massachusetts Bay . . .* (London, 1760) p. 404 and note states that Cooke did not sign the petition for the new charter. Increase Mather states that three agents signed it but does not say which three. Cooke, however, writes of 'our petition'. See Cooke to Simon Bradstreet, 9 May 1691, Prince MSS., I, 61, Massachusetts Historical Society.

67. Elisha Cooke to Simon Bradstreet, 10 September and 4 November 1691, Prince MSS., I, 63, Massachusetts Historical Society.

68. See note 13 above; also Sir Henry Ashurst to [Massachusetts General Court?], 28 December 1691, Curwin Papers, III, 41, American Antiquarian Society.

69. P.R.O., C.O. 5/856, pp. 666–667.

70. For the general significance of gubernatorial weakness in the colonies see the discussion in B. Bailyn, *The Origins of American Politics* (New York, 1970).

71. Professor John Murrin of Princeton University kindly provided me with the references in this paragraph: *Acts and Resolves of Massachusetts*, Vol. I (Boston 1869) Cap. 11 and M.A., 'Legislative Records of the Council' [Court Records], VII, 216, 220.

72. The phrase is Professor Murrin's.

73. Thomas Prince, *A Sermon Delivered at Cambridge . . .* (Boston, 1730) pp. 21, 32.

74. John Adams, *Diary and Autobiography*, Vol. II (Cambridge, Mass., 1962) p. 93.

75. John Adams, *Novanglus* in *Works*, Vol. IV (Boston, 1851) p. 91.

76. John Adams, *Works*, IV, 128.

77. John Adams, *Works*, IV, 114.

# 4

# English Dissenters and the American Revolution

## C. C. BONWICK

It is well known that English Dissenters enjoyed a profound sympathy for the American colonists and were strongly affected by the experience of the Revolution. Memories of a shared intellectual ancestry in seventeenth-century Puritanism sustained a rich bond of affection and were fortified by close ties of friendship and a warm sense of community which far outlasted the formal severance of the imperial connection. The association was wide-ranging and complex in nature and its interests were constantly modified by the needs and pressures of circumstance. During the second half of the eighteenth century public affairs pressed harder on both Dissenters and colonists and the fabric of the transatlantic community adapted itself to accommodate new concerns; although theological and other cultural interests continued to provide its central components, its political dimension became increasingly important as time passed. As official relations between Britain and her colonies deteriorated into war, revolutionaries in America looked to their English friends for assistance; they found many of their staunchest overseas supporters in the ranks of Nonconformity. For American patriots the ultimate prize was independence and republican government. There was also a reciprocal effect in England.

Dissenters were, of course, primarily anxious for the fate of their American friends, but they were also convinced that the Revolution offered much of general relevance to their own needs and circumstances. They saw the United States as an 'asylum' both for men oppressed by tyranny elsewhere and as a haven for the sacred principle of liberty. In doing so they measured the suitability of the American political experiment as a model for emulation in England; in particular they were firmly persuaded that the new relationship between church and state which was emerging across the Atlantic had much of pertinence to their own situation as victims of religious discrimination at home. Less happily the Revolution had other consequences for their position in English society. Their American sympathies had a highly unfortunate effect on their public reputation. It became all too easy for the orthodox to accuse them of disloyalty and republicanism since the evidence seemed close at hand and the demonstration apparently irrefutable. Their standing in the country worsened considerably and their Anglican fellow-subjects were even less willing to grant them concessions than they had been fifty years earlier. Sir Lewis Namier once described the Revolution as the greatest disaster to strike English Dissent since the days of the Great Rebellion, and Anthony Lincoln, the most perceptive historian of Dissenting political ideas, has remarked that it played a crucial part in alienating Nonconformists from the prevailing political order.[1] But such assessments, necessarily made in general terms, require closer inspection since in several crucial respects wide discrepancies separated popular opinions from the realities they purported to explain.

## I

Any examination of the implications of the American Revolution for English Nonconformists is especially concerned with the responses of a small group of intellectuals drawn from the three congregations of Presbyterians, Congregationalists and Baptists. It is not concerned with the views of Methodists and Quakers since they were not usually regarded as Dissenters in the eighteenth century. Nor is it necessary to explore the activities of the Protestant Dissenting Deputies (in effect the executive arm of Nonconformity) since although they occasionally spoke and acted on behalf of the laity they normally confined themselves to dealing with specific issues affecting the lives of their constituency. They were willing to assist the New Englanders in their resistance to the Church's plan to appoint a bishop in the colonies but refused to speak out on the more general issues involved in Anglo-American relations. While a roll call of the names of Thomas Hollis, Thomas Brand Hollis, Capel Lofft and Benjamin Vaughan is sufficient to dismiss any suggestion that laymen were unwilling to participate in political affairs in one way or another, they took second place to their clergy and schoolmasters in enunciating the position of Dissent in public discourse. Men such as James Burgh and the ministers Caleb Evans, Richard Price and Joseph Priestley not only debated the central issues of theology but were regarded by Anglicans and Nonconformists alike as implicitly speaking for Dissent on broader matters of national policy. They argued the case for religious freedom and repeal of discriminatory legislation and, as ideologues in the commonwealth tradition, assumed responsibility for speaking on behalf of the American colonists. In addition many other ministers such as Newcome Cappe of York, Rees David of Norwich, Samuel Stennett of London and Joshua Toulmin of Taunton gave support during the war by using fast day and 5 November sermons to castigate government actions and set the Revolution in the framework of their overarching ethical system. But though most ministers who publicly expressed their views belonged to the liberal wing of Dissent, one of the most advanced, Theophilus Lindsey, was more cautious. Having recently left the Church to found the first explicitly (and unlicensed) Unitarian chapel in England, he reluctantly yet prudently abstained from political controversy rather than risk inciting further hostility.[2]

Not that all Dissenters sympathized with the Americans. Students at the Warrington Academy might light their windows to celebrate American victories but a good many others joined the majority of their fellow-subjects in condemning rebellion in the colonies. Evans declared that many Baptist laymen, including several members of his own congregation in Bristol and some ministers whom he knew personally, supported the government. Josiah Wedgwood, the potter, reported that Dr John Roebuck, a government publicist, had enjoyed considerable success among Dissenters during a tour of Yorkshire and in 1776 a former agent for Massachusetts, Israel Mauduit, published an anonymous attack on the colonists. Nor did all ministers approve of American actions; several, including John Martin who also printed a hostile pamphlet, approved government policy, while in Parliament Sir Henry Hoghton, one of the most prominent Dissenting laymen who made several attempts to secure relief for Nonconformists, remained loyal to Lord North's administration to the end.[3] Here was direct proof that there was no solid cohort of

Dissent even if the orthodox often declined to distinguish between those who supported the Americans and those who did not.

Among those intellectuals who were especially the target of conservative criticism, one factor gave great strength to their interest in American affairs. As a group they shared a more powerful sense of community with their counterparts in the colonies and had closer associations with America than any other Englishmen save the Quakers. Many enjoyed close personal friendships with individual colonists, several of whom became prominent Revolutionaries, and used the opportunities thus created to discuss a wide range of political subjects including the worsening tensions between Britain and America. They had also read widely in colonial history and American pamphlet literature, to which they made frequent reference in their own tracts.

From sources such as these their knowledge of America and its inhabitants directed them to a far more favourable understanding than was customary in England. Joseph Priestley went directly to the heart of the matter when he roundly declared that the Americans, particularly in New England, were 'chiefly Dissenters and Whigs'.[4] Being well-read in the hagiography of early Puritanism they accepted that the first settlers had fled to the new world as victims of old-world oppression. Thomas Hollis, in general a warm admirer of colonial society, remarked caustically that the New England fathers 'were persecutors with the stigma of persecution fresh bleeding upon themselves' but most Dissenters were more forgiving of earlier behaviour.[5] Nor was this most surprising since their understanding was drawn in good measure from their friendships with Jonathan Mayhew, Charles Chauncy and other prominent liberal ministers, and the work of an earlier Dissenting minister, Daniel Neal, whose *History of New England* was heavily dependent on Cotton Mather's *Magnalia Christi Americana*. They had less knowledge of other areas except perhaps Pennsylvania; to a considerable degree their conception of American society was New England writ large. In political matters they were fully aware that the colonists shared their own ideological principles, a unity of belief which was not entirely coincidental since over the years they had sedulously fostered the growth of commonwealth Whiggism in America and now the fruits of their labours were ripening. Thus the colonists were believed to adhere to the two most desirable elements in the English tradition. Similarly Dissenters were impressed by the essentially agrarian character of colonial society and its relative lack of class distinction when compared with England, and in cultural terms no one who knew Benjamin Franklin as well as Price and Priestley did could doubt that the colonies had already achieved a high level of maturity. They were, of course, embarrassed by the historical record of persecution—as they were by the continuance of slavery—but in other respects America stood for Dissenters as a paradigm for the operation of those social and political principles to which they were determinedly attached. As Price remarked in 1776, here were 'a number of rising states in the vigour of youth inspired by the noblest of all passions, the passion of being free; and animated by piety'.[6]

## II

The Revolution, when it came, was a complex movement and Dissenters responded to it on several planes. In many respects their views were shared by radical Anglicans such as Catherine Macaulay and Granville Sharp, but in others their reactions were distinctive and unique. At one level they were united with other Englishmen in their alarm over the imperial crisis (though they differed in the construction they placed upon it), and at another they observed its character as an experiment in political organization. A third aspect was of particular interest to Nonconformists and is deserving of independent and special consideration. This last dimension was the advance of religious liberty which, though incomplete in their own generation, stimulated great excitement among them. When evaluating the importance of the Revolution they assessed it in relation to three principal criteria. They gave primacy to an ethical system which was explicitly theological in its premises, then looked at it in the light of the political principles of the commonwealth tradition and the vital need for the evidence of experience to vindicate its theories. Lastly, they considered it in relation to the requirements of their own distinctive position in English society.

Moral judgements were vitally important. A powerful strain of millenarianism ran through the Dissenting mind and controlled its attitudes towards political issues. To Nonconformist ministers the systems of human politics ought to be directly regulated by the ethical imperatives of a theological cosmology. Though largely emancipated from the harshness of Calvinistic predestination and persuaded that God's intentions towards the human race were benevolent, they remained convinced that Divine Providence exercised an active superintendence over the affairs of mankind. He was more than a divine workman who had constructed a world and set it loose in the universe to seek its own salvation; rather, He permitted a wide freedom of action but was capable of imposing severe retribution on those men and nations who transgressed sacred law. Thus the optimism inherent in 'rational' Christianity was tempered by fear that any moral decay would provoke Divine punishment. A belief in the possibility of human improvement was the secular counterpart of theological optimism. Here, too, the prospect of progress lacked absolute certainty and was dependent on rigorous adherence to the rules of virtuous conduct.

The political implications were intensely alarming. Dissenters were sharply aware of the corruption of contemporary English society and came to regard the disasters suffered during the Revolutionary war in moral as well as political terms. Until recently England had been a haven of liberty and had been rewarded accordingly; Dissenters were as proud of the triumphs of William Pitt's *annus mirabilis* as any other Englishmen. Since that happy period, the country had gone into decline. Price remarked in 1774 that it had sunk far into distress and that luxury had undermined the foundations of public liberty; five years later he lamented 'Never, perhaps, was there a time when men shewed so little regard to decency in their vices, or were so shameless in their venality and debaucheries'.[7] Toulmin drove home the message that 'by public calamities nations are disciplined' and his sentiments were echoed by ministers all over the country.[8] Inescapably they were driven to believe that their country deserved punishment and that the disasters of the American war were truly a manifestation of the workings of Divine Providence in the affairs of mankind.[9]

Comparison with America was humiliating yet ultimately comforting. Colonial society could be tried by the same moral and political standards as those by which they judged their own country, and instead of appearing corrupt and decadent it emerged as a model of the virtuous polity. The contrast became still sharper after the imperial dispute degenerated into war; as Price lamented, 'In this hour of tremendous danger, it becomes us to turn our thoughts to Heaven. This is what our brethren in the Colonies are doing. From one end of North America to the other, they are fasting and praying. But what are we doing? Shocking thought! We are ridiculing them as Fanatics and scoffing at religion. We are running wild after pleasure, and forgetting everything serious and decent at Masquerades. We are gambling in gaming houses; trafficking for Boroughs; perjuring ourselves at Elections; and selling ourselves for places.'[10] Such moral rectitude was opportune for under such circumstances America could assume the role of asylum of liberty which England seemed to be wilfully abandoning; whereas before 1775 it had shared this responsibility with Britain, after that year it was on its own.

Accordingly the American cause acquired fresh importance—all the more so to the rational Dissenters who had effectively redirected their emotional demands away from a passionless theology towards the world of politics. With the collapse of liberal administrations on the continent of Europe and the apparently rapid approach of a similar disaster at home, America would have to carry the burden of their millenarian hopes for human improvement. And since they did not believe that progress could be sought along broad and certain avenues, but had to be achieved by passing along the razor's edge, they had added reason to watch the progress of the war with deep concern and exercise an anxious supervision over the United States during the difficult years immediately following its conclusion.

As an asylum of liberty, America had two principal duties to perform. The first, though also the lesser, was to provide a haven for those who believed themselves to be potential victims of oppression at home. Here was a responsibility long sanctified among Dissenters and after the Revolution there was a steady trickle of Nonconformist emigrants. For a time in the 1790s the trickle became a flood as men fled from the fear of prosecution. Priestley and Thomas Cooper were the most famous but there were many more, and yet others who considered the possibility and rejected it; among these latter was the unfortunate Thomas Fysshe Palmer who was later transported to Botany Bay.[11] Yet this function proffered only a limited contribution to the international advancement of liberty since although its benefit to particular individuals was often incalculable, it had if anything a negative effect on the promotion of reform at home by enticing away many of those who might otherwise have continued the fight in England. The second, and far more important, form of asylum was incorporated in the concept of an experiment in the government of an orderly but free society. Since, as Robert Robinson remarked, modern Nonconformity naturally led to the study of government, Dissenting ideologues were greatly interested in the new models.[12]

Dissenters were firmly persuaded that there were many interactions between the Revolution abroad and the need for parliamentary reform at home. The stresses of the imperial crisis revived among them the latent commonwealth ideology which had lain dormant for several decades. As they observed the steady worsening English relations with the colonies they came to believe that there was system and purpose behind the unfolding of government policy. At first they were inclined to regard the Stamp Act affair as worrying but aberrant; with the imposition of the Townshend duties, the Boston Massacre, the Tea Party and Coercive Acts they took a graver view of the situation. The government's simultaneous refusal to accept the election of John Wilkes as member for Middlesex encouraged them to believe there was a single crisis of liberty affecting both branches of the empire and that the outcome of the conflict on one side of the Atlantic would impinge upon the resolution of the dispute on the other—a judgement assiduously cultivated by American propagandists in London. Worse still, as a minority group whose position was dependent on the goodwill of the dominant majority, Nonconformists feared that they would be among the victims should the forces of tyranny triumph.[13] They began looking to the colonies as a haven of liberty before the outbreak of war. Their dependence on America as a model of liberality and moderation increased greatly once fighting began, and when it became evident that the United States was certain to become independent they were exultant at the prospect for the future.[14] They were also active in the reform movements which sprang up during the war. Since many of them were vigorously engaged in sweeping out what they considered as centuries of accumulated corruptions in Christian doctrines it seemed appropriate that a similar broom should be applied to the house of politics. In this they were not alone however. Many Anglicans joined the associated counties movement, the metropolitan reform agitation and the Society for Constitutional Information, nor were they indifferent to the American example. For this reason further discussion of Dissenters' part in reform politics can be left for another occasion. But after the war ended Dissenters maintained a closer awareness of the American experiment than their Anglican colleagues. Just as they had enjoyed a warm friendship with Franklin before the war, so Price, John Jebb (until his death in 1786), Brand Hollis and others established a close association with John Adams during his term as United States minister to the Court of St James's. Political discussions were a prominent feature of the friendship and in particular the Dissenters were much impressed by the argumentation of Adams's *Defence of the Constitutions of Government of the United States* which he composed while in London.[15]

### III

In another respect the American Revolution had a special and unique relevance for Dissenters. One of its consequences in the United States was a substantial extension of religious freedom which, though incomplete by the end of the eighteenth century, represented a position far in advance of that obtaining in England. Although the Dissenters' campaigns began long before Anglo-American relations became a critical issue in English politics, the Revolutionary model played an important part in formulating their attitudes, demands and argumentation. Before the war Nonconformists had admired the Massachusetts system of conjoining establishment of one church with public support to Dissenting sects, and accepted it as a legitimate compromise between the extremes of English establishment and Pennsylvanian liberality. After independence they were exhilarated by the example of Thomas Jefferson's Virginia Statute for Religious Freedom. In it they found explicit and pragmatic proof of the validity of propositions they had been arguing on abstract grounds for generations. They cited it frequently during their unsuccessful attempts to secure relief from discriminatory legislation in the following years.

Religion and the ecclesiastical polity of eighteenth-century England were dominated by the ubiquitous presence of the national Church. The object of the religious settlement was the political one of promoting the authority and stability of the secular order; Church and state stood together as twin pillars of the constitution. Statutory arrangements for an established Church modified by limited toleration for protestant Nonconformists (and minimal toleration for Catholics) were immensely satisfying to Anglicans but far from agreeable to others. The Test and Corporation Acts were a special grievance since they required officeholders to take Communion in the Church as a condition of appointment. In contrast, Dissenters believed that religious liberty—that is, freedom from secular discrimination on confessional grounds as well as liberty of private conscience—ought to march hand-in-hand with civil and political liberty. They struggled hard and long, if intermittently, to modify the system in their favour; apart from obtaining a modest relief for ministers and schoolmasters in 1779 they met with negligible success until the nineteenth century.

The debate was extended and complex on both sides of the question but can be reduced to two issues, one substantive and the other procedural. The first centred on the conflict between individual rights and the interest of the state; the second was the requirement that Dissenters would have to persuade an overwhelmingly Anglican parliament both of the moral propriety of their demands and the safety and wisdom of conceding them. On the first matter Dissenters insisted on the right of the citizen to enjoy full freedom of conscience and, concurrently, full civil rights; they grounded their argument on the theory of natural rights and its concomitant, the Lockean postulate of a social contract. The conservative counter-argument comprised an assertion that in the interest of the community at large the state possessed authority to intervene in matters of religion if they could be demonstrated to be of communal concern. At the beginning of the eighteenth century this had been a not unreasonable claim, but by the middle of the century it could well be argued that the establishment of one favoured sect and the limited toleration of those which were un-favoured was redundant. Certainly the protestant Nonconformists had acquired a well-justified reputation for loyalty to the house of Hanover. Yet suggestions that discriminatory legislation should be repealed (there were few demands for disestablishment) were met with intense horror and atavistic fears that the outrages of the previous century were about to return. And where the argument of natural rights formed the understructure for Dissenting rhetoric, the argument of the interest of the state was the axe which cut away the vital prop. It was a weapon which had to be blunted if Dissenters were to have any hope of relief; and thus they were required to demonstrate that the needs of the community could be congruent with the rights of the individual to enjoy liberty of conscience without secular penalty.

Broadly speaking there were two possible and reciprocal lines of argument, both based on empirical evidence rather than abstract logic, which could be deployed for this purpose. One was to demonstrate that an increase in the number of protestant sects and sectarians had taken place to such a degree that public safety would be better secured by an extension of rights rather than the continuance of special privileges for a single group, however large. The other alternative was to prove that the number of sectarians had diminished to such an extent as to render them politically innocuous. In both cases the argument could be advanced only by reference to experience—and in practice the latter circumstance had in reality prevailed in the eighteenth century though the former was to mature in the nineteenth. There was, however, a possible deficiency inherent in the argument from empirical evidence. Dissenters could argue from the experience of recent English history that they no longer posed any conceivable threat to the body politic (persuasively in the eyes of an external observer) and that they could be trusted with the same rights and privileges as those enjoyed by members of the established Church. What they could not do was to demonstrate from the experience of their own country what the consequences of emancipation would be in actuality. Thus they would still remain vulnerable to the argument of safety and the desirability of avoiding risks. But the force of this argument could be weakened if the grounds of experience could be extended to incorporate other, similar, societies. If reference could be made to other nations which had safely emancipated their Dissenters it could be argued by analogy that the two pillars of Church and state were not irrevocably doomed to collapse if England followed the same course.

It was at this point that the American Revolution acquired a distinctive relevance to the English situation. Admittedly the analogy between English circumstances and American experience was imperfect but there was considerable consonance between them and the parallel had much merit. In America the process of liberalization and secularization took substantial and significant steps forward; subsequent experience suggested that the confessional state was no longer an essential requisite of social and political stability and confirmed that Dissenters could be safely let off the leash. Should such a programme be considered too hazardous for emulation in England, the case of New England also suggested a means by which the maintenance of an established Church could be rendered less obnoxious and devices by which Nonconformist sects could participate to some degree in the benefits of state protection. As yet the United States had a long way to go along the path to a total separation of Church from state, but by the 1780s it had already amassed a corpus of empirical evidence which became available for use in English battles. As it did so Dissenters became increasingly aware of its utility to their own cause.

Before the war Dissenters were more concerned for the defence of their co-religionists in the colonies than with drawing implications for their circumstances at home. Several gave aid to the New Englanders in their resistance to the foundation of a bishopric in America. The Protestant Dissenting Deputies operated as a pressure group in influential places and Thomas Hollis acted as an agent for colonial propaganda by reprinting and distributing tracts by Jonathan Mayhew and others.[16] The lines of the English argument were already clear. The objection to an American bishop lay not in the exercise of his powers as 'a religious officer, to ordain, confirm and perform the other spiritual duties belonging to that character' but in the potentiality of secular power.[17] Since the Church and state marched together in England they feared that the whole apparatus of ecclesiastical discipline, tithes and authority, and the introduction of religious tests for secular office would follow the arrival of a bishop in America. But apart from the opportune publication of Franklin's newspaper article entitled 'Toleration in Old and New England', little direct reference was made to an American model during the debates of the early 1770s.[18] The pleas of liberal Anglican clergy such as Lindsey and Jebb to be relieved from the obligation to subscribe to the Articles of Religion, and the request for similar relief for Nonconformist ministers and schoolmasters were made in terms of abstract rights, theoretical principles and the operation of logic; at this stage there was felt to be little need for any reference to experience.[19]

The vital change came in 1786. In that year the commonwealth of Virginia finally implemented Thomas Jefferson's Statute for Establishing Religious Freedom. Copies arrived in England the same summer and made an instantaneous, profound and lasting impression on Dissenters. Among them Brand Hollis had it printed in his local paper the *Chelmsford Chronicle*, Lindsey's brother-in-law John Disney (who had recently followed him into Dissent) printed it in his memoirs of Jebb, and Price had a modified version published as a broadsheet.[20] It was reprinted on other occasions besides. Jefferson's masterpiece was in many ways an appropriate model for English Nonconformists. It went to the limit of their demand for intellectual freedom and formalized the final disestablishment of an Anglican church. It also enunciated the lack of utility in an establishment and the safety possible in denominational equality; its reasoning was drawn in good measure from the same intellectual system to which Dissenters adhered and the pamphlets that they themselves had composed during pre-war debates.[21]

Writing to Arthur Lee in February 1787, Price declared that the widespread circulation of the Virginia Statute had not been without effect.[22] He may well have been right, for within a few months of its publication in England the Dissenters began their second great campaign of the century to secure the repeal of the Test and Corporation Acts. Three attempts were made, in 1787, 1789 and 1790, and the whole question of the secular position of Nonconformity was debated once more. The lay Dissenting Deputies, who directed the campaign since it was concerned with the rights of laymen rather than ministers, abjured the extreme arguments of Price, Priestley and Robinson, in favour of the more cautious arguments of those such as Philip Furneaux; they also concentrated on stressing the disabilities suffered by Dissenters in preference to the more aggressive radical criticisms of establishment.[23] Important tactical consequences flowed from this decision. As it was necessary to demonstrate the safety to the constitution at large of the course they were advocating, it was desirable to assign greater importance to the evidence of experience: and here the American example was apposite. As Lofft remarked in transmitting the Repeal Committee's resolutions to the *Gentleman's Magazine*, the Dissenters were appealing to the same principles as those inherent in the Virginia Statute which it had recently printed (probably on Price's initiative).[24] During the next three years frequent reference was made to the American example in various forms. Article XI of the official

*Case,* prepared by a subcommittee including Adams's friend Andrew Kippis, made explicit reference to the American evidence 'that a Dissenter from the established religion of a country may be a true friend to its general interests and prosperity'; Samuel Heywood's semi-official tract *The Right of Protestant Dissenters to A Compleat Toleration Asserted* (part of which was probably revised by Adams) incorporated references to the Virginia Statute as 'a masterpiece, deserving record in letters of gold' and quoted Franklin's letter of 1772 at great length; and the American Quakers' Address to President Washington of 3 October 1789 and his reply were reprinted in a Birmingham collection.[25] After the final failure of the century, Dissenters continued to draw encouragement from the American success.[26]

Dissenters' perception of the extent of religious liberty in the United States, which they so enthusiastically judged to be a notable triumph, may not have always accorded precisely with reality, but this was not the point. They did not observe the American scene in a spirit of academic detachment, nor were they solely concerned with the welfare of the American people, though they certainly wished them well. Instead they constantly asked, implicitly or explicitly, whether the American experience had any relevance for England in general and themselves in particular. If they decided that it did, they carefully selected those elements which seemed apposite to their own needs; thus they largely ignored the disestablishmentarian logic of the Virginia Statute in order to use it for their own more limited purposes. Faced as they were with a powerful and apparently intractable opponent in the Church of England they urgently needed encouragement from the successes of others and, more important, they required empirical confirmation of the operability of their theoretical principles of religious liberty and, yet farther advanced, the viability of a separation of Church and state. Such evidence could be invaluable both for their own self-justification and their vain attempts to persuade their opponents either (at the occasion of the applications for relief) of the needlessness of their fears of the consequences, or (after the event) of the folly of their resistance. All this evidence in favour provided powerful support to the argument from principle. Moreover, whereas the advocates of political reform could refer their opponents to the paradigm of the ancient constitution, there was no comparable example to justify religious liberty. Here the ambiguity of the American position was especially fortunate. For although the American model was unique and distinct to the circumstances of an independent nation, it could be regarded at the same time as functioning within the broad context of the English tradition. As an experiment in political behaviour, the Revolution gave considerable stimulus to the advancement of one of Dissent's most cherished causes.

## IV

In its character as a rebellion, the consequences of the Revolution were notably less happy. Between 1760 and 1790 the position of Nonconformists in English society deteriorated considerably. Anglicans who had condescendingly applauded their loyalty during the Jacobite rebellion of 1745 accused them of disaffection and subversive behaviour thirty years later. No longer, their critics declared, could the House of Hanover look to them for certain support; instead they were accused of hostility to the very fabric of society, Church and state. At a petty level this hostility manifested itself in the refusal of Birmingham clergy to share their carriages with Dissenting ministers during a funeral procession, but there were more serious implications. Old charges of king-killing were revived from the embers of past controversy and Dissenters were accused once more of republicanism. Conservative animosities were further strengthened by accusations that they had fomented resistance in the colonies, encouraged and assisted rebellion and applauded the new United States. An anonymous pamphleteer, directing his venom against Price in particular, summarized popular hostility by describing him as 'this modern Calculator, American, Patriot, Republican'.[27] Nor were the attacks made only by the obscure and unimportant or confined to the intellectuals; they were also made by men in authority and levelled against the whole body of Dissenters. Samuel Horsley, Bishop of St David's, substantially advanced his reputation in ecclesiastical circles by pointing to an alleged incompatibility between their purported affection for democratic government, as demonstrated by their admiration for the American Revolution, and their claims of continued loyalty to the crown.[28] Although the Archbishop of Canterbury, John Moore, grudgingly admitted that Dissenters were friendly to a Protestant government in the sense that they would rather be tolerated by an

Anglican administration than persecuted by a Catholic one, this was the limit of what he was prepared to concede; he went on to insist, 'I know not what farther Pretensions they have to the name of good Subjects. Their almost avowed Republican Principles, their constant & active Endeavours to depress the Power of the Crown; Their Conduct in fomenting the Revolt in America—would leave them very little Title to the Favour & Confidence of the State, even if the Church was wholly out of the question.'[29]

These were serious charges. If true, they would certainly justify parliament's refusal to consider repeal of the Test and Corporation Acts. They would also demonstrate that there had indeed been a major change in the public attitudes of Dissent and prove that Nonconformists were alienated from the central postulates of English society. But were such accusations justified by anything more substantial than ill-judged rhetoric such as Price's laudatory reference to the United States as 'a rising Empire, without Bishops, without Nobles, and without Kings'?[30] Of the virulence of Anglican antipathy there can be no doubt. Yet the fears of the orthodox were based on a complex series of misconceptions. Dissenters were neither republicans nor democrats (in the extreme definition of that term): nor were they promoters of rebellion in America, or in any other part of the country. Far from the American Revolution encouraging them in political apostasy, paradoxically it confirmed them in the temperance of their political objectives. Further-more, with few exceptions this was as true for the liberal intelligentsia as it was for those Nonconformists who approved the government's unsuccessful attempt to suppress the colonial rebellion.

The actual record of liberal Dissent was one of determined loyalty throughout the Revolution. Before the outbreak of fighting the intellectuals agreed with Priestley that the continued welfare of the empire depended 'on Union and on Liberty' and consistently directed their energies towards this goal.[31] In establishing this dual objective they were, unfortunately, setting themselves a task more difficult of fulfilment than that of either the government or the Americans. For members of the administration the preservation of union was the prime consideration; if necessary the Americans' liberty could be subordinated to it for such time as it took to re-establish British authority. On the other side, the preservation of liberty was the over-riding ideological goal; should it prove necessary the revolutionaries were entirely willing to jettison the union in the interest of a higher imperative. Neither of these alternatives were open to Dissenters and other radicals. Although in the course of time they were driven to recognize the ultimate supremacy of their concern for liberty, they pursued their dual goal until the last possible moment. It is safe to say that at no point did Dissenters encourage American separatism. When Thomas Hollis promoted the circulation of colonial pamphlets in England, he did so in the hope (vain as it turned out) that his actions would stimulate a better understanding of the American position. None of the tracts he distributed advocated independence, nor did he intend to encourage it, nor did he view the prospect with pleasure.[32] In the first substantial tract on the American question by a Dissenter Priestley lamented in 1768 that the iron hand of oppression was being extended to the colonies and, seeing the Wilkes affair as part of the same crisis, argued that the two countries shared a common interest. Similarly Micaiah Towgood, an Exeter minister, hoped that the conflict would be resolved within the empire, while Wedgwood feared that government policy was likely to provoke independence a century earlier than the normal course of events would have dictated.[33] As their alarm deepened with the Coercive Acts of 1774, Dissenters came to realize that the Americans might be forced to fight in defence of their liberty, but though they offered their sympathy they regarded the resort to arms as a last resort born of endless provocation and the prospects of worsening tyranny. Seeing the forms of government established in Canada by the Quebec Act and being attempted in New England as prototypes of the forms of government proposed for Great Britain, they feared for their position in England but had no thought of inciting rebellion on either side of the Atlantic. If some colonists hoped for a complementary rising in Britain, they were doomed to disappointment.[34]

After Lexington the Dissenters continued to support the colonies within the context of hope that the conflict would be resolved within the empire. The central thrust of Richard Price's pamphlet *Civil Liberty*, published in February 1776 and the object of vituperative condemnation, was the construction of a system whereby the legitimate interests of both Britain and America could be contained within a modified imperial structure. His tract was widely admired among Dissenters and may be taken as representative of their views, but if either the Americans or the government at home construed it as an incitement to separation, they were wrong. Significantly the Dissenters almost completely missed the significance of both Thomas Paine's *Common Sense* and, a little later, the Declaration of Independence. Whereas John Dickinson's essentially moderate *Letters from a Farmer in Pennsylvania* remained an important text long after its original publication in 1768, Paine's pamphlet had little influence (except on Caleb Fleming who was reported as applauding the sections which treated the King 'as the dog deserved') though it was widely read.[35] Nor did the Declaration of Independence have much effect among Dissenters. Initially Price believed it marked an end to hopes of reconciliation, but in his *Additional Observations on the Nature of Civil Liberty*, published early in 1777, he offered a forlorn plea for reconciliation. Franklin's friend Benjamin Vaughan probably felt likewise a year later, while Jebb still hoped for reunion in 1779, and still later Lofft apparently hoped that parliamentary reform might lead to a federal union.[36] Of the leading figures, only Priestley seems to have anticipated separation before Congress declared independence, although news of the surrender at Saratoga and the Franco–American alliance moved them one-by-one to an acceptance of the inevitable.[37] When they did so, it was with exultant expectations for the future of the United States and hopes that harmonious relations could be speedily restored.

Their critics were, of course, correct in asserting that most articulate Dissenters were sympathetic towards the American cause. It was the construction they placed on this sympathy which was defective and the conclusions they drew which were myopic and unjust. Dissenters (including the ideologues) were not little Englanders, nor did they find the exercise of military strength *ipso facto* repugnant; they were as concerned to promote Britain's commercial prosperity and global power as the most patriotic jingoist. Quite apart from any question of liberty, one of their constant criticisms of government policies towards America, especially during the war, was that they would weaken rather than strengthen the nation's strategic position. Successive attempts to coerce the colonies were not only improper, they were also imprudent and likely to be counterproductive since they failed to take account of the pragmatic need to secure the assent of the colonists to the continuance of British authority in North America.

Thus prudential considerations ran in tandem with ethical imperatives and reinforced Nonconformist claims to have a sharper perception than conservatives of the necessities of the situation if, as they all ardently wished, the empire was to be preserved.

The second charge was that Dissenters were republicans, whose latent enmity towards the established order was resuscitated by the American example. In part, evaluation of the accuracy of such an accusation depends on the essentially semantic question of the meaning of the term 'republican'. If, as seems reasonable in an English environment, the concept is required to contain rejection of monarchy as an essential ingredient, it can be affirmed that, with rare exceptions, the Dissenters were not republicans. Certainly Nonconformists constantly repudiated the charge. In the looser sense that it implied a more general disloyalty it can be argued that far from stimulating alienation from the existing political system, the American Revolution did much to encourage and fortify Dissenters' continued acceptance of the fundamental principles of the English constitution. Although they were deeply moved by their observation of the process of creating a new nation and acknowledged it as an experiment in political behaviour whose example was already proving influential in England, they persistently reiterated that they were loyal citizens and denied that they had any intention of importing the machinery of American republicanism into England.[38]

In reality the stimulus of the American model lay elsewhere. At one level, the Revolution vindicated Dissenters' faith in the possibility of secular progress. If Britain was in decline and being punished for moral corruption by Divine Providence, the Americans were encouraging resistance to tyranny, providing a refuge for the victims of oppression and disseminating the rights of mankind. By their actions they were creating a new era in human affairs, and although Price was indulging in hyperbole when he suggested that the American Revolution might prove the most important stage in human improvement since the introduction of Christianity, he was giving expression to an enthusiasm widely felt among Dissenters.[39] At another level, when they came to relate the American model to British circumstances, their response was both diametrically opposite to that claimed by their critics and in a sense paradoxical. In America the dispute with Britain and the colonists' growing suspicions that they were the intended victims of a systematic conspiracy led to a positive and vigorous affirmation of republicanism (including the rejection of monarchy) as the only legitimate form of good government. But in England exactly the same crisis led Dissenters to a notably different conclusion. And in spite of the disasters and pessimism of these years it confirmed them in their belief that the grave political defects of the period were only temporary aberrations, and not systemic defects in the fabric of the constitution.

Effectively, the experience of the American Revolution modernized Dissenters' political attitudes. It did much to stimulate a revival of outspoken radicalism among them, but the forms of that radicalism were more remarkable for their moderation than their subversiveness. Advanced ideology had long existed in the Dissenting mind but had been dormant for some years; now it was awakened once more by the conjunction first of the imperial dispute and the Wilkite affair and then by the outbreak of war. Such a major crisis demanded a far-reaching reformation in the operation of parliamentary representation—and Nonconformists were not alone in believing (erroneously) that the war was a consequence of a corrupt legislature and that reform might lead to reunion. The need to relate general principles of liberty to actual circumstances required them to consider matters of method and structure. At this point the Dissenters' observation of American experimentation, far from leading them away to republican speculation and demands for an overthrow of the existing order, led them back to a reinforced confidence in the legitimacy and relevance of long-respected propositions. In their opinion it completely validated the principles enunciated in the Glorious Revolution—including monarchy —and updated the model of the ancient constitution. After the war John Adams helped his English friends to this understanding by encouraging them to remain within the limits of traditional reform. Like them he insisted on the sovereignty of the people over kings and governments, but his *Defence of the Constitutions*, which was much admired by his Dissenting friends and was probably composed after discussions with them, provided a potent antidote to extremism and a persuasive vindication of balanced and tripartite government as exemplified in the English constitution.[40] Unfortunately Adams's influence was felt only in private. As had happened in the past an injudicious choice of language in public utterances such as Price's notorious 1789 address *The Love of Our Country* misled the critics of Dissent by disguising the essential moderation of Nonconformist politics and the true nature of the response to the Revolution.

Nor did the example of American society lead Dissenters back to the levelling theories of the previous century. They greatly admired the relative absence of social distinctions when compared to their own society but also appreciated that their American friends were members of broadly the same social rank as themselves. Aristocratic the Lee brothers may have been in Virginia; in London they were indelibly middle-class. Similarly Dissenters were also much impressed by the preponderantly agrarian character of American society.[41] In this respect it exercised a conservative and retrograde influence on their understanding and analysis of the problems of contemporary English society. Already they were failing to adjust to the accelerating processes of industrialization and urbanization which were generating social problems of an altogether new order. The evident success of the American model confirmed them in their attachment to the virtues of an agrarian order as a remedy for social ills.

The key to understanding the Dissenters' interpretation of the Revolution lies in their belief that Americans and Englishmen were members of a single transatlantic community and shared a common ideological heritage. Before the war this concept was inherent in the imperial connection but even after the United States had abandoned the formal association Dissenters considered that the Americans were continuing to operate within the same overarching ideology as themselves. Accordingly they placed the American experiment firmly in the context of their own political traditions and argued that it confirmed the propriety of the fundamental propositions of their own constitutionalism; the more successful it proved to be, the more it confirmed the validity of their own political principles. Its attraction was especially enhanced by the Americans' evident ability to redefine the relationship between sectarian affiliation and the secular state in terms more readily acceptable to Nonconformists. By their achievement in advancing the cause of religious liberty they had demonstrated the efficacy of propositions which had previously existed only in abstract theory—and Dissenters attached great importance to the value of experience.[42] It also gave substance to their millenarian hopes for the moral and secular improvement of the human race; if Divine

Providence was presently punishing Britain for her moral decadence, its treatment of the United States suggested that progress remained possible for mankind in general.

In relation to the domestic growth of Dissenting politics the Revolution was a triumph, not a disaster. Unhappily it also inflicted severe damage on the standing of Nonconformists in the nation. As a triumph it provided them with a model which could be adapted to the requirements of English circumstances; still more important it directed them firmly along the path of gradualist reform rather than incited them to root-and-branch revolution. The orthodox failed to appreciate this. Aided by the implications of some ill-considered rhetoric, Anglicans could only believe that Dissenters had encouraged rebellion in the colonies and, inspired by the rebels' example, had reverted to their earlier republicanism. In this respect the Revolution undoubtedly had an unfortunate effect on Nonconformists. It was their misfortune that conservatives misconstrued their enthusiasm, rejected their protestations of loyalty and branded them as enemies to the constitution of Church and state. Dissenters were certainly distressed by the treatment they received, but if they became alienated it was a consequence of orthodox rejection rather than wilful withdrawal.

## NOTES

1. Sir Lewis Namier, *England in the Age of the American Revolution*, 2nd ed. (London, 1961) p. 39; Anthony Lincoln, *Some Political and Social Ideas of English Dissent: 1763–1800* (Cambridge, 1938) pp. 24–27.

2. Thomas Belsham, *Memoirs of the Late Reverend Theophilus Lindsey* (London, 1812) pp. 147–148.

3. H. McLachlan, *English Education under the Test Acts* (Manchester, 1931) p. 224; Caleb Evans, *A Reply to the Rev. Mr Fletcher's Vindication of Mr Wesley's Calm Address to Our American Colonies* (Bristol, 1776) p. 85; Josiah Wedgwood to Thomas Bentley, 6 February 1775, Wedgwood Letters, Josiah Wedgwood and Sons Ltd; Richard Price to William Adams, 14 February 1776, Gloucestershire Record Office; Lincoln, *English Dissent*, pp. 21–22; Sir Lewis Namier and John Brooke, *The House of Commons: 1754–1790*, 3 Vols (London, 1964) II, pp. 628–629.

4. Joseph Priestley, 'An Address to Protestant Dissenters' [1774], *The*

*Theological and Miscellaneous Works of Joseph Priestley*, ed. John Towill Rutt, 25 Vols (London, 1817–31), XXII, p. 486.

5. Thomas Hollis to Jonathan Mayhew, 24 June 1765, Bernhard Knollenburg, ed., 'Thomas Hollis and Jonathan Mayhew: Their Correspondence, 1759–1766', *Mass. Hist. Soc. Proc.*, LXIX (1956) p. 170.

6. Price, *Observations on the Nature of Civil Liberty*, 3rd ed. (London, 1776) p. 98. Where possible, contemporary tracts are cited by short titles.

7. Price, 'A Sketch of Proposals for Discharging the Public Debts, Securing Liberty, and Preserving the State' [*c.* 1774], Shelburne Papers, CXVII, 43, William L. Clements Library, University of Michigan; and *A Sermon Delivered to a Congregation of Protestant Dissenters* (London, 1779), pp. 27–28.

8. Joshua Toulmin, *The American War Lamented* (London, 1776), p. 12. Cf. Rees David, *The Hypocritical Fast* (Norwich, 1781); Newcome Cappe, *A Sermon Preached on the Thirteenth of December* (York, 1776); and Ebenezer Radcliffe, *A Sermon Preached at Walthamstow* (London, 1776).

9. Price, *The Importance of the American Revolution* (London, 1784) p. 3; George Walker, *The Doctrine of Providence Illustrated and Applied* (London, 1784) pp. 26–28; Samuel Stennett to James Manning, 14 May 1783, Manning Papers, Brown University.

10. Price, *Civil Liberty*, p. 98.

11. Thomas Fysshe Palmer to James Smiton, 20 July [1793], Thomas Jones Howell, ed., *A Complete Collection of State Trials*, Vol. XXII (London, 1817) p. 325.

12. Robert Robinson, 'Plan of Lectures on Nonconformity', *Miscellaneous Works of Robert Robinson*, 4 Vols (London, 1807) II, p. 248.

13. Thomas Brand Hollis to [Simeon Howard], 4 January 1775, Boston Public Library; Price to Lord Chatham, 9 February 1775, Chatham Papers, LIII, p. 209, Public Record Office, and *Civil Liberty*, p. 102; Stephen Sayre to Samuel Adams, 5 June 1770, Samuel Adams Papers, New York Public Library; [Arthur Lee], *The Political Detection* (London, 1770) pp. 65–67; and *An Appeal to the Justice and Interests of the People of Great Britain*, 4th ed. (London, 1776) p. 23; Priestley, 'Address to Dissenters' [1774], *Works*, XXII, pp. 483–486.

14. Price to Henry Marchant, 2 November 1773, Marchant Papers, Rhode Island Historical Society; John Jebb to William Chambers, 16 July 1775, *The Works . . . of John Jebb*, 3 Vols (London, 1787) I, p. 148; Price, *The General Introduction and Supplement to the Two Tracts on Civil Liberty* (London, 1778) pp. xiv–xvi; and to Benjamin Franklin,

18 November 1782, Franklin Papers, Bache Collection, American Philosophical Society; [Andrew Kippis], *Considerations on the Provisional Treaty with America* (London, 1783) pp. 7–24, 30–31; Price, *American Revolution*, p. 5.

15. John Adams to Price, 20 May 1789, John Adams Letters, Pennsylvania Historical Society; to Jebb, 21 August 1785, Adams Family Papers, Microfilm Edition, reel 107, Massachusetts Historical Society; Abigail Adams to John Quincy Adams, 21 July 1786, Adams Papers, reel 368.

16. Carl Bridenbaugh, *Mitre and Sceptre* (New York, 1962), part II; 'Hollis–Mayhew Correspondence', *passim*; Hollis, Diary, Houghton Library, Harvard University, *passim*.

17. Kippis, *A Vindication of the Protestant Dissenting Ministers*, 2nd ed. (London, 1773) p. 101; Price to Ezra Stiles, 2 November 1773, Gratz Collection, Pennsylvania Historical Society; and *Introduction to Two Tracts*, pp. xii–xiii.

18. *London Packet*, 3 June 1772.

19. E.g. Israel Mauduit, *The Case of the Dissenting Ministers* (London, 1772) and Philip Furneaux, *An Essay on Toleration* (London, 1773).

20. *Chelmsford Chronicle*, 14 July 1786; Jebb, *Works*, I, p. 100n.; Price, ed., *An Act for Establishing Religious Freedom* (London, 1786).

21. *The Papers of Thomas Jefferson*, ed. Julian P. Boyd, 19 vols to date (Princeton, N.J., 1950–) I, pp. 544–550; James Madison to William Bradford, 9 May and 28 July 1775, *The Papers of James Madison*, ed. William T. Hutchinson and William M. E. Rachel, 8 vols to date (Chicago, 1962–) I, pp. 145, 160, 162n.

22. Price to [Lee], 4 February 1787, Autograph Collection, Houghton Library.

23. Ursula Henriques, *Religious Toleration in England: 1787–1833* (London, 1961) pp. 58–59.

24. *Gentleman's Magazine*, LVII (1787) pp. 237–240.

25. *The Case of the Protestant Dissenters* (London, 1787); [Samuel Heywood], *The Right of Protestant Dissenters to a Compleat Toleration Asserted* (London, 1787) pp. 108–109, 222–227; *Extracts from Books and Other Small Pieces*, 2 Vols (Birmingham, 1789–90) II, pp. 28–31.

26. *A Letter to the Public Meeting of Friends of Repeal of the Test and Corporation Acts* (London, 1790), appendix, p. 15; David Bogue and James Bennett, *History of Dissenters*, 4 Vols (London, 1809) IV, p. 148.

27. *A Scourge for the Dissenters* (London, 1790) p. 38.

28. [Samuel Horsley], *A Review of the Case of the Protestant Dissenters* (London, 1790) p. 31.

29. 'Answer to the Case of the Dissenters in 1787', fols. 14–15, MS. in Arch P/A Moore, Lambeth Palace Library.

30. Price, *Introduction to Two Tracts*, p. xvi.

31. Priestley, 'Address' [1774] *Works*, XXII, p. 498.

32. [Francis Blackburne], *Memoirs of Thomas Hollis*, 2 vols (London, 1780) I, pp. v, 125; 'Biographical Account of Thomas Hollis', fol. 128, Boston University.

33. Priestley, 'The Present State of Liberty in Great Britain and her Colonies', *Works*, XXII, pp. 381, 393, 398; James Manning, *A Sketch of the Life and Writings of the Rev. Micaiah Towgood* (Exeter, 1792) p. 68; Wedgwood to Bentley, 27 May 1767, Wedgwood Letters.

34. Price to Charles Chauncy, 25 February 1775, 'The Letters of Richard Price', *Mass. Hist. Soc. Proc.*, XVII (1903) p. 279.

35. *The Diary of Sylas Neville*, ed. Basil Cozens-Hardy (London, 1950) p. 245.

36. Price to William Adams, 14 August 1776, Glos. R.O.; and *Additional Observations on the Nature of Civil Liberty*, 2nd ed. (London, 1777) p. 89; Benjamin Vaughan to Lord Shelburne, 14 April 1778, Benjamin Vaughan Papers, Am. Phil. Soc.; Jebb, *An Address to the Freeholders of Middlesex* (London, 1779) p. 17n; Capel Lofft, *Observations on Mr Wesley's Second Calm Address* (London, 1777) pp. 108–115, and *An Argument on the Nature of Party and Faction* (London, 1780) p. 57.

37. Priestley to Franklin, 13 February 1776, Franklin Papers, IV, 79, Am. Phil. Soc.

38. Price to [William Smith, M.P.], 1 March 1790, National Library of Wales; Hollis to Andrew Eliot, 'summer 1767', 'Biographical Account'; James Burgh, *Political Disquisitions*, 3 vols (London, 1774–75) II, p. 29; Priestley, 'View of the Principles and Conduct of the Protestant Dissenters', *Works*, XXII, p. 354. Brand Hollis described himself as a republican (to Adams, 5 October 1787, Adams Family Papers, reel 370).

39. Price, *American Revolution*, pp. 2–5.

40. Adams to Brand Hollis, 18 October 1787; Brand Hollis to Adams, 15 February 1787; Lindsey to Adams, 23 February 1787; Price to Adams, 5 March 1789, Adams Family Papers, reels 370, 369, 372; Price to William Bingham, n.d., *Massachusetts Centinel*, 30 June 1787; Priestley, *Familiar Letters Addressed to the Inhabitants of Birmingham* (Birmingham [1790]), p. 12.

41. Price, *American Revolution*, pp. 69, 77–78.

42. Priestley, 'First Principles of Government', *Works*, XXII, p. 55.

# 5

## *The Loyalists*

### ESMOND WRIGHT

It has for long been fashionable to say that the Loyalists constituted the least known, and least researched, topic in American Revolutionary history. Apart from Lorenzo Sabine's remarkable two-volume collection of family-by-family references first published in 1847 and reprinted in 1864; C. Van Tyne's study of 1902 (devoid of bibliography); and two penetrating, and some interesting but less penetrating, articles, until two decades ago hardly any serious scholarly work had been done on the Loyalists.[1] The notable exception was indeed not an academic historian but a novelist, Kenneth Roberts, whose work, especially *Oliver Wiswell* (1940), saluted them honourably. Nor is the neglect surprising. It is possible to attribute it to shame on the American side and embarrassment on the British, to the natural preference of full-blooded Americans for a history that tells of success rather than failure, to distaste for Toryism in a persistently Whig climate of opinion in both countries, and to British sensitiveness in exploring a delicate area in the Anglo-American experience.[2] Certainly until the Loyalists are studied it becomes impossible to be precise about the causes of the Revolution, and to determine whether the Patriots were driven by passionate radical fervour against the Tories, or were themselves 'conservative' of their own just rights and of their claims to property. Clearly the Loyalists are crucial to the understanding of what the Revolution signified.

The real reason for the neglect, however, has little to do with these mutual sensitivities, or with historical psychology. It has a much simpler origin. No serious research in Loyalism is possible until the Loyalist material in the Public Record Office has been probed, or at least until a finding list to it has been prepared. Until that is done, guesswork and mythology can safely reign; and ignorance with them. There are 1450 volumes in the Colonial Office 5 series, which cover mainly the years from 1748 to 1776. Nor can other volumes in the C.O. collection be neglected—they run to at least 390 in number. Treasury 1 (the incoming letters from 1557 to 1920 for which a typescript two-volume index exists) has some 12,625 volumes, boxes and bundles. The War Office is even more daunting and has, inevitably, only been dipped into by scholars. The Artillery alone (W.O. 10) (1708–1878) has 2876 volumes. The extremely useful muster-rolls and pay lists (W.O. 12) (1732–1878) extend to 13,000 volumes. Perhaps only a computer could adequately explore, index and reduce to meaning material on this scale.

But even the resources of the Round Room in the Record Office can mislead. Every Loyalist researcher begins with the Audit Office Papers, and notably with A.O. Series 12 and 13, for which a useful index exists. In each of these series are some one hundred and forty volumes—one hundred and forty-six volumes of Claims by Loyalists in Series 12, and the matching supporting evidence, one hundred and forty-one, in Series 13. All in all, 5072 Loyalist claims were put before the British Commissioners in the years from 1782 to 1789; nine hundred and fifty-four were withdrawn or not followed through; 4118 were examined, of which 1401 were from claimants who were by that time in Canada. The total amount of money claimed by the American Sufferers, as they called themselves, was £8,026,045. The amounts allowed came to £3,292,452. Eighty years ago, the American bibliographer and collector, Benjamin Franklin Stevens—for whom the A.O. Index was compiled—had transcripts made of many of these papers, and copies of them exist in the New York Public Library and in the Library of Congress. There, however, they are known as the Loyalist Transcripts, and references to them do not follow the same serial numbers as in the original P.R.O. material. So, quite apart from the mass of ill-digested material, there has to be noted a special extra dimension of confusion for British researchers.

In the last two decades, however, some major studies have appeared. In his *Prelude to Independence, the Newspaper War on Britain*, published in 1957, Arthur Schlesinger, Senior, paid as much attention to Loyalist editors as to Patriot. In 1961 there appeared a scholarly edition of Peter Oliver's *Origin and Progress*, and William Nelson's essay *The American Tory*, which gives, however, little guidance on sources and draws almost exclusively on printed diaries. Since then we have had

L. S. F. Upton's admirable edition of Chief Justice William Smith's *Diary* (1963–65) and his biography of Smith, *The Loyal Whig* (1969); Callahan's sketchy two volumes *Tories of the Revolution* (1963) and *Flight from the Republic* (1967); Wallace Brown's excellent two studies, *The King's Friends* (1964) and *The Good Americans* (1969); William Benton's interesting intellectual history, *Whig-Loyalism* (1969); Mary Beth Norton's *The British Americans* (1972); Robert M. Calhoon's massive if knotty and somewhat uncoordinated *The Loyalists in Revolutionary America 1760–81* (1973); and Andrew Oliver's new and thoroughly revised edition of Samuel Curwen's *Journal* (1973). Now Loyalist research is beginning to be sustained, thorough and scholarly in quality. We have moved from the impressive but amateur work of Sabine and Siebert into a new professionalism.

If this is so, it owes much to an interesting and indeed unique venture in international scholarship, and to the enterprise of two men, Professor Robert East of the Graduate Center at the City University in New York and his son-in-law, Dr James E. Mooney, then Editor of Publications at the American Antiquarian Society at Worcester, Mass., and now Director of the Historical Society of Pennsylvania. Professor East, author of *Business Enterprise in the American Revolutionary Era* (1938) and *Connecticut's Loyalists* (1974), had long been interested in the Loyalists, and thought that one way of saluting the Bicentenary of the Revolution would be by tackling in depth, and as an international exercise, the study of them. Abetted by a small exploratory grant from the American Council of Learned Societies and by a larger one from the National Endowment for the Humanities, an international group came together, and the Loyalist Papers Project was launched under the auspices of the City University of New York, the American Antiquarian Society, the University of New Brunswick at Fredericton and the Institute of United States Studies of the University of London. Professor East serves as Executive Editor of the Project in New York, with national editors in each country. The Canada Council in Canada and the Leverhulme Trust in Britain have also generously assisted the Project. The first target is the collection and publication of an authoritative finding list of Loyalist sources. The Canadian list running to some 2500 items of unpublished material has already been printed in *The Proceedings of the American Antiquarian Society* (Vol. 82 Part I, April 1972) and the British and American will follow. Working conferences have been held at intervals (in Lehigh, Pennsylvania 1969, at the invitation of the late L. H. Gipson, in New York, 1970, in Fredericton, 1972, at Tarrytown on Hudson, 1973 and London, 1974) and letterpress volumes of journals and diaries are likely to follow on particular Loyalist themes as scholars begin their detailed examination. Andrew Oliver's edition of the *Journal of Samuel Curwen, Loyalist* (Harvard University Press in co-operation with the Essex Institute), though begun before the Project was launched, can be seen as the first printed volume; and some Canadian studies are now in the pipeline. Dr Catherine Crary, who was a research associate of Professor East's, and whose death early in 1974 was a sad blow to Loyalist studies, collected some one hundred and eighty extracts from lesser known figures (*The Price of Loyalty*, New York, 1973). Her collection is a dramatic indication of the variety of experiences and of the tragedies suffered by Loyalists from all walks of life. It captures vividly the human element in the story. But there is no intention of launching—nor in today's economic climate would it be possible to contemplate—a series of volumes on the lavish (and over-ambitious) scale of the Presidential papers. What is planned is simply the making available for scholars on both sides of the Atlantic of guides to Loyalist material thus far unlocated or unexplored. An international index is the first goal, and microfilming and xeroxing of records the second. If there could be, as a fairly speedy follow-up, the publication of a modern-day Sabine, cast—let's say—in Namier-like form, all of us would think the Project well worth while.

By happy coincidence the P.R.O. itself decided to aid Bicentennial studies by bringing forward for publication its own programme of printed Calendars of State Papers bearing on American material. In 1973 the Irish University Press published the first volume of a *Calendar* of documents from the Colonial Office records, with two companion volumes of transcripts of selected documents, under the editorship of K. G. Davies.[3] The series begins in 1770, with the advent of Lord North to power. The *Calendar* is a piece of impeccable scholarship; it notes every surviving document concerning the North American colonies and is to be followed by many more. The editor has handled five hundred volumes and bundles of manuscripts containing an estimated 120,000 folios for these thirteen years; the first volume calendars no less than 1761 items. The two volumes of transcripts give select documents in full, with the aim of recreating 'the situation as regards information in which the Secretary for the American Department found himself'. News from Boston dominates it, but it is as well to be reminded that the concerns of London included Indian affairs, the problems of Quebec and East Florida, of Barbados and Jamaica and the future of the Mississippi; the standpoint is that of the Whitehall administrator running an empire. Within a few years it will be possible to follow very smoothly the American problem as seen by Whitehall in the decade of the Revolution. It remains, of course, true that, important though these reports are, they were often ignored, and that the views of British officials were shaped by their own assumptions, convictions and prejudices as well as by the facts, themselves sometimes partially presented, that reached them.

It is clearly premature to offer conclusions at this stage, for this is very much 'work in progress'. What has become clear is that there is a rich cache of material in Colonial Office 5, in the Treasury 1 series and still more in the War Office Papers; and there is considerable material as yet unexplored in County Record Offices in Britain, known to exist from the lists in the possession of the National Register of Archives, and from the earlier investigations of L. H. Gipson, B. R. Crick and Miriam Alman.[4] There are at least a dozen British cities which have material on the Loyalists. There is matching war material in the Clinton, Germain, Mackenzie and Gage papers in the Clements Library in Ann Arbor, in the Ward Chipman Papers in the Huntington Library, San Marino, and in the Haldimand Papers in Ottawa (on which Professor Stewart McNutt is researching). And in each of the original thirteen colonies scholars are now combing archives and records for Loyalist material.

One of the most difficult issues is of course the word Loyalist itself. It has a distinct and honoured connotation in Canada, whose national origins are bound up with the story of the United Empire Loyalists. In the early years of exile in London, they called themselves, all too accurately, not 'Loyalists' but 'Sufferers'. Only in 1779 with the setting up of the Board of Associated Loyalists, did the word Loyalist become acceptable.

What did Loyalism mean, and how was it proven? This last became the key question if a claim for 'suffering' was submitted. Presumably up to 4 July 1776, all American colonists were automatically Loyalists

—or at least loyal? Presumably too there was always a premium on evasion, on fence-sitting and fence-mending, and—when things got violent—a preference for quiet anonymity. Loyalism in one state was often much easier to admit than in another. As early as January 1775 Henry Pelham in Boston wrote to John Singleton Copley in London asking him not to make political observations in his letters lest they fall into the wrong hands. He hoped to be left 'to scrabble through this turbulent and Dangerous Contest' as well as possible (C.O. 5/39/331). In fact he soon sailed for Britain. With the British in Boston (up to March 1776) and in New York City from July 1776 to 1783, Loyalism there called for no courage, and both cities became for these periods Loyalist sanctuaries. So it was when General Howe and his men wintered in Philadelphia in 1777–78. But Howe was left with no illusions. He refused to divide his force for a Southern expedition in January 1778. Writing from the snugness of Philadelphia to Germain, he said 'Experience has proved that the most the British troops could expect from the loyalists is an equivocal neutrality' (C.O. 5/95/64). In the Valley of Virginia and the pine barrens of the Carolinas it was usually easier to evade declarations of loyalty altogether—although a savage war came to King's Mountain and to Moore's Creek Bridge. Paradoxically many highlanders who had fought for Bonnie Prince Charlie and against George II in 1745–46, were found, 4000 miles away and thirty years later, fighting for George II's ungrateful grandson. Among them was the same Flora Macdonald who after Culloden helped to save her (equally ungrateful) prince.[5] But history is richer in paradox than in gratitude. It was difficult after July 1776 to know which way the wind would blow in many areas, especially in that No Man's Land north of the Bronx, the country ravaged by those known as Cowboys and Skinners. And, if it was rarely easy for any Loyalist or Patriot to choose, the nature of the choice facing the office holder, the merchant and the man of business was different from and usually more difficult than, that posed to artisans, indentured servants and tenants. Even our statistical and demographic knowledge has been shifting and uncertain until recently.[6]

It is possible now to be reasonably precise about the numbers of those who actually exiled themselves. Esther Clark Wright calculates that over 6000 exiles settled in New Brunswick.[7] But the province was also a major point of debarkation for disbanded regiments, so these figures are deceptive. We know that some 10,000 reached the St John's district of the Bay of Fundy in 1783. Among them were thirteen separate corps of soldiers, the De Lancey's and the Second Battalion of the King's American Dragoons, the New Jersey Volunteers, the Maryland Loyalists, the 42nd regiment (a fragment of the Black Watch), the Prince of Wales American Regiment, the Royal Pioneers, the Pennsylvania Loyalists and Arnold's American Legion. Allowing for some obvious duplication, Sabine also tabulates some 6200 names; Wallace Brown and Mary Beth Norton in their studies conclude that there were some 7000 to 8000 exiles in Britain.[8] As we have seen, 5000 submitted claims for losses, but at least 1350 of these were examined in Nova Scotia.

The statistical analysis of the claimants by Wallace Brown has become a subject of some controversy. Eugene Fingerhut has argued that the claimants did not necessarily constitute a representative sample of all the Loyalists.

Several important qualifications must be considered if the Loyalist claims are to be studied quantitatively. The petitioners with several occupations may have had as many economic interests. Many of those who took the British side did not emigrate, and most of the emigrants were not claimants. The petitioners' homes were not distributed throughout the colonies in the same manner as were all loyalist residences. Inflated currencies, collusion among petitioners, and fraud raised many claims above their true values. On the other hand, missing legal proofs of ownership, the commission's regulations on property possessed, and requests merely for lost salaries probably caused some understatements. In addition, the graphic representations of the claims indicate that their values were grouped in an unexpected pattern. Further complications could result, moreover, when two distortions occurred in the same claim. For example, the conversion of currency to sterling probably inflated values, but omission of property from the claim reduced the number of items presented to the commission. Therefore, since the emigrants are not a statistically valid sample of the loyalists, since the claimants are not representative of the emigrants, and since the transcripts do not present accurate quantitative data about the claimants' possessions, one may seriously question a statistical use of this source to describe anything beyond what compensation or pensions the petitioners sought.[9]

E

Accepting the validity of this comment, and accepting the obvious fact that the great majority of the Loyalists would, of course, be passive and not seek, after 1783, to reveal their loyalism, the facts remain that the 5000 claims are thoroughly documented. Any comment on the Loyalists must surely be based primarily on this substantial evidence in the Audit Office Papers, supported by the Colonial Office 5 series.

Can there be, then, any accurate and agreed estimate made of Loyalist numbers? John Adams thought that perhaps one-third of the colonists had been opposed to the Revolution. But it has been argued that his phrase 'full one third were averse to the Revolution' was a reference, ironically, not to the American Revolution but to the French.[10] On the other hand, in 1814 Thomas McKean the Patriot leader of Pennsylvania came up with a similar estimate of one in three. The contemporary Loyalist, Phineas Bond, later a British consul in Philadelphia, put the total number of exiles at 80,000–100,000 (out of a total population of 2,500,000). This would represent the loss of approximately one in thirty of all white families. Professor R. R. Palmer has suggested that the American Revolution produced twenty-four émigrés per 1000 of the population compared with only five per 1000 in the French Revolution, and that the confiscation of property was similar in both Revolutions.[11]

The most detailed analysis in fact is that of Paul Smith working in the War Office papers and provincial muster rolls.[12] His conclusion is that about 19,000 Loyalists formally took up arms in the service of the Crown against the Patriots. Since eight hundred and ninety-five of the 6000 Loyalists tabulated by Sabine were in the Provincial Service, or 15 per cent, Paul Smith assumes that the 19,000 enrolled constitute approximately 15 per cent of all adult male Loyalists. There were therefore, he claims, 128,000 adult male Loyalists; and, assuming a ratio of one adult male to four members of family, the total numbers of Loyalists in the colonies as a whole was approximately 500,000 or 19 per cent. The number of Loyalists is thus on this analysis one-fifth, not one-third. Paul Smith's work is tentative and cautious, and he is careful to say that 'efforts to classify persons in a revolution run afoul of insuperable problems of definition'. But his research and his conclusions are impressively buttressed by statistics and will now be hard to refute.

However, numbers alone do not take us far towards the answer to the question: Who were the Loyalists? Tom Paine's answer was crisp and clear: 'Interested men who are not to be trusted; weak men who cannot see; prejudiced men who will not see; and a certain set of moderate men who think better of the European world than it deserves.' This question however can only be answered on a state-by-state basis. In 1776 there were after all thirteen states, not one, in rebellion; the Founding Fathers were in a measure diplomats from individual colonies seeking and manufacturing alliances.[13] The pattern state by state is bewildering, and, thus far, only a series of broad generalizations can be offered. Loyalist sympathy was strongest of all in New York. One in four of all authentic claimants for compensation from Britain (1107 out of 4118) were New Yorkers. These constituted 0.5 per cent of the population of the state, which was then estimated to be 203,000; and the claims from New York City equally constituted approximately 0.5 per cent of its population (estimated at 25,000). Bearing in mind that only a tiny minority would be claimants, these figures again go some way to confirm the contemporary references made by both John Adams and by Alexander Graydon who both said, and independently, that in 1776 'half the population of New York was Tory'. Alexander Flick in his study of New York Loyalists published in 1901 came to a similar conclusion; the Loyalists, he says, numbered 90,000 out of 203,000, and of these 35,000 emigrated. Moreover, New York was loyal in the real sense of the word; it put its men into action. Two out of three of the New York claimants claimed to have served in the Armed Forces, which in the eyes of the investigating commission was, of course, the arch test of loyalty. Although New York ranked, in size of population, seventh out of the thirteen states, it provided 23,000 men for the British Armed Forces out of a likely total American contribution to them of some 50,000 in all. This was clearly twice the size of the largest force Washington ever had under his command, so that in numbers they could have been significant.

Loyalist sentiment was strong also in New Jersey and—for very different reasons—in the distant colonial frontier outpost, Georgia, skilfully controlled by its Governor, Sir James Wright. It was strong in other regions where and when the British Army was prominent or successful, as, exotically, in the Carolinas or in Pennsylvania. John Adams summed it up years later when he said that New York and

Pennsylvania were so nearly divided—if indeed their propensity was not against independence—that, if New England on the one side and Virginia on the other had not 'kept them in awe', they would have joined the British.[14] Timothy Pickering called Pennsylvania 'the enemy's country', and Curwen thought that Dutchmen and Quakers were too concerned for their property and for their comfort to put either at risk. In Maryland, Governor Robert Eden was popular, and only the zealous campaigning of Samuel Chase and Charles Carroll converted it to the Patriot cause. Loyalism was weakest in Massachusetts, Connecticut and Virginia.

Virginia was in economic character a land of great estates, run by seigneurs, whose Georgian homes—Westover and Shirley, Stratford and Nomini Hall—still stand intact and gracious on the banks of the James, the York and the Potomac. From the tidal rivers and from the Chesapeake, the tobacco fleets carried their staple crop direct—or as direct as French privateers and smugglers allowed—to Bristol, Glasgow and London. Thomas Jefferson calculated that by 1776 the Virginian planters were two million pounds in debt to their London agents. Those who were most British in character and in style of living—like Washington—were apt to feel permanently at the mercy of Scotch factors, London agents and—always—the British government. At the top it was a gracious society, and it was an open one. Property was widely held, and with property went the suffrage. But whatever the democratic form and however easy the progress up the rungs of the ladder, voting was oral, and a few men were lords of vast acres. Society was deferential and kinship-linked. Virginia was run by a cousinhood and was breeding leaders. They looked West now as well as East and to the future.[15]

As a result Virginia, despite its English style of gracious living and its economic dependence on the Mother Country, was not Loyalist country. Sabine mentions only one hundred and fifteen Virginian Loyalists. Of the claims lodged for loss of property, only one hundred and forty were from Virginia. Some potential Virginian Loyalists left early; they included Washington's friend and patron, George William Fairfax and his wife Sally, whom some say is the only woman Washington ever loved. (He had been tempted but not tempted enough by Mary Phillipse, whose father became a Loyalist and died at Chester, England in 1785; Mary married Roger Morris, who too became a Loyalist; she died at the age of ninety-six and is buried at York.) The Fairfaxes had gone in 1773, and one of Washington's melancholy tasks after his return from the First Continental Congress in 1774 was, on their behalf, to sell their belongings at Belvoir, the estate next to his own at Mount Vernon. Sir John Randolph, the King's Attorney-General in Virginia left with his daughters in 1775— but his brother Peyton and his son Edmund became Patriots; indeed Edmund was later a Governor of Virginia and the first Attorney-General of the United States; Peyton presided over the First Continental Congress. This was a Civil War, with brother separated from brother, father from son.

But Virginian Loyalists are even more interesting for who they were not. It has long been said of the Loyalists that they were drawn heavily from the colonial Establishments. Thus, Thomas H. Johnson, in consultation with Harvey Wish, *The Oxford Companion to American History* (New York, 1966): 'Loyalists were to be found in all the colonies and in every walk of life, but they were proportionately more numerous among the well-to-do, the Anglicans, officeholders and other conservatives.'[16] This is the basic formula, drawn mainly from C. H. Van Tyne. He listed the categories somewhat baldly and with much generalized truth.[17]

They were, he said, office-holders, whose income was at stake. Those gregarious persons whose friends were among the official class . . . Anglican clergymen, many of whom had motives similar to those of the Crown officials . . . Conservative people of all classes, who glided easily in the old channels . . . 'Dynastic' Tories who believed in kings . . . 'Legality' Tories, who thought Parliament had a right to tax . . . 'Religious' Tories whose dogma was 'Fear God and honor the King' . . . 'Factional' Tories whose actions were determined by family, friends and feuds and old political animosities.

It is clear that such categorization needs and can now be given much sharper definition. Indeed if there is one new generalization that can be risked it is that the Loyalists came from no particular class and from no one region; they were a cross-section of the population, as they must have been if they numbered 20 per cent. When in June 1776 a number of people were arrested in New York on suspicion of plotting to kill George Washington, they included the Mayor of New York, and some officials, but also farmers, tavern-keepers, two gunsmiths, two doctors, two tanners, one silversmith, one saddler, one shoe-maker, 'a pensioner with one arm', and an unfortunate man described only 'as a damned rascal'. When an Act of Banishment was passed against three hundred Loyalists in Massachusetts in 1778, one-third of them were described as merchants or professional men and gentle-men, but another one-third were farmers, and the rest artisans, labourers and small shopkeepers. In June 1778 Delaware listed forty-six Tories to whom it refused to give a general pardon. They included two captains, three physicians, one lawyer, and seven described as assembly men, office-holders and wealthy citizens. But the list also included nine husbandmen, two yeomen, two innkeepers, three pilots, three shallop men, two mariners, two labourers, three coopers and one weaver, one coppersmith, one tailor, one saddler, one bricklayer, one hatter and one cordwainer. When his transport ship *The Union*, Consett Wilson, Master, sailed from Huntington, Long Island on 11 April 1783, with a group of Loyalists mainly from Connecticut, bound first for New York then for the St John River, over half were 'farmers', quite a few 'shoe-makers', and a number were 'carpenters'. Most of those who settled in Canada were poor and signed their names with a cross.

There is certainly some truth in the charge that only those could or would claim compensation who had some measure of literacy, some awareness of legal process, and much self-confidence, and that they were thus unrepresentative. Fingerhut has a point in implying that many Loyalists' names would simply not be among the claimants at all. This may well explain why relatively few Virginians did claim. The one hundred and forty Virginian claims came from ninety-three individuals. Of these, thirteen were officials, eight ministers of religion, eight planters, four doctors and three teachers; no less than fifty were merchants. Again only thirteen of the ninety-three describe them-selves as natives of Virginia; sixty-four describe themselves as natives of the British Isles, 'temporarily resident in Virginia', and of these all but fifteen arrived after 1760. What this indicates is that much of the carrying trade in Virginian tobacco was in the hands of Scottish factors at the ports; few of them identified with Virginia, or stayed long. Norfolk was one of the few Loyalist centres in Virginia; its inhabitants lived by trade, and needed peace and harmony. When Dunmore felt his grip going, it was in Norfolk that he and his one hundred and twenty-five soldiers took refuge. The Glassfords and Jamiesons of

Virginia Street in Glasgow—the more distinguished among the red-robed 'Tobacco Lords' of the Glasgow Saltmarket—were still pressing their claims for debts on a still reluctant British government over fifty years later, in the reign of George IV. The Scotch—to give them their contemporary spelling, since this noun has not yet in the United States nor in Canada become synonymous with the liquid—were very unpopular.[18] Alongside the Scottish merchants were the Scots–Irish of the frontier. John Connolly and 'several hundred inhabitants of transmountain Augusta' assured Dunmore of their loyalty in July 1775. Among them were John Campbell, Alexander McKee, Simon Girty, Alexander Ross and Edward Ward. But the Scots had survival value. Neil Jameson was an active trader in New York throughout the Revolution. One hundred and twelve Scots merchants from Virginia opened shops in Philadelphia when General Howe occupied it. There is some evidence that, in other colonies also, the Loyalists included many such recent immigrants not yet thoroughly Americanized, 'conscious minorities', as W. H. Nelson calls them, notably Germans, as well as Scots.[19]

It is always assumed that the Church of England ministers were Loyalists; but even this generalization needs careful examination. Only five of the twenty Episcopalian ministers in South Carolina were Loyalists. Of the hundred Episcopalian ministers in Virginia in 1776, no less than eleven were members of local committees of safety; a further thirty-four were Patriot; and of thirty-nine there is no evidence either way.[20] This leaves only sixteen who were Loyalists, and as we have seen eight were active claimants. Of these Episcopalian ministers Jonathan Boucher is often thought to be typical. But what of Peter Muhlenburg from Dunmore County? He found it possible, like the fighting Bishop Leonidas Polk in the Civil War a century later, to reconcile service to God with service to state and to be a patriot Major-General, and to lead his troops in battle. As Harrell put it in 1926, though 'sprinkling' is probably not the correct word to use:[21] 'No social or religious differences divided the Loyalists and patriots in Virginia. From all classes and all sects there came a sprinkling of Loyalists.' He is certainly and sadly correct when he added 'But at no time were they sufficiently numerous or active to menace greatly the patriot success.'

It is impossible to convey in a few sentences the diversity of the

Loyalist experience. The published journals and diaries of the more prominent Loyalists like Jonathan Sewell and Samuel Curwen, Thomas Hutchison and Jonathan Boucher are familiar.[22] What the Loyalist Papers Project is revealing is the experience of more ordinary people. It is almost universally of course a story of suffering and tragedy. Thus, when Mrs Elizabeth Ivey of Rhode Island reached the Scilly Isles on her journey home, even the ship on which she was a passenger was shipwrecked; she staggered ashore, herself heavily pregnant, after watching her husband and two sons drown; all she had in the world were the soaking clothes she was wearing. Or consider the case of Mrs Christian Amiel. She was sixty-seven and she claimed that none of her six sons could help her because they were all grown up and were not with her. In fact their names are a roll-call of Loyalism: John was a Major of Brigade with the 60th Regiment; Peter a Lieutenant of Marines; Robert a Lieutenant in the 17th Regiment 'Trying to live off his pay'; Henry an Ensign in the 22nd Regiment of Foot; Otto, formerly in the 17th Foot, had sold out and was making his fortune in the West Indies; and Philip, lately a Midshipman, was master of a vessel bound for the West Indies and struggling to earn a living. We have in other words a picture of a break-up of a family, once affluent, and no doubt as officers seeking to keep up appearances, but all totally dispersed by the war.

Or consider the account of his difficulties given by the Reverend Ebenezer Dibblee, a graduate of Yale and the Anglican Rector of St John's Church, Stamford, for fifty-one years. When the war came he thought it his duty 'faithfully to discharge the duties of our office and yet carefully to avoid taking any part in the political disputes as I trust my brethren in this colony have done as much as possible'. But in 1785, in writing to the Reverend Samuel Peters, he revealed the personal danger and the cost of his attempt 'to ride out the storm or perish in the Ruins of the Church and Country'.

The Banishment of my Son Frederick in Nvr 1776 till Spring, then lately graduated at Kings College, New York, to Lebanon (with about 20 of my Parishioners, chiefly heads of families) supported at my cost. Myself Obliged to flee in March 1777 to my Dauter at Sharon to be inoculated for smal Pox. The town then a Hospital Town, and the smal Pox brought in by ye return of Soldiers, prisoners at Fort

Washington. The flight of Frederick (left to take care of the family in my Absence) to save his life (Occasioned by ye alarm of his Excellencies Genl Tryons Excursion to Danbury) to his brother on Long Island. My Sons looking to me for Assistance, not daring to enter into Service wh they might have done to advantage, in regard to my safety; cost me better than 150 sterling in Bills Drawn and privately conveyed; wanted for my own Support. Add to this the diminution of my Parish by the flight of numbers, reputable families and (best) support of the Chh. The Dangers attending my person. One bold attempt on my life being Shot at as I was going to attend a funeral, Waylaid, and not presuming to return the same way but seldom, when I went to attend the private Duties of my Cure. The billeting and Quartering of Soldiers upon me, sometimes a Company of a Troop of Horse, or a Militia Company, Officers and Men. Terrors by night and Day for fear of the Violence of Lawless Mobs & ungoverned Soldiery. The Ruin of one of my Daughters by frights, for a long time wholly insane; and to this Day not wholly recovered her former composure and tranquility. Ad to this the Burden of Publick Duty since our Churches were opened (wh mine was Christmas 1779) wh I never neglected within or without our Lines, when permission could be obtained to pass and repass; and for one or two years before the peace I met with less Interruption.

I have given you some general hints, my Dear Sir, before of those past occurrences; and my preservation, I can ascribe to nothing but the providential care of Almighty God.[23]

The Loyalist Papers are rich in these human stories. But they are rich also in their revelation of the personalities of many contemporary figures, and much that they tell is not only revealing but bizarre. It is clear, for instance, how damaging were the activities of Governor Dunmore in Virginia. His calling on the Blacks to rise in revolt pushed many Conservatives into the Patriot ranks. Solid Tories like Edward Pendleton and Robert Nicholas denounced him. Landon Carter, who was devoted to Britain, found words inadequate to express his contempt for that 'Damned Dunmore'; after ten of his own slaves had taken silver from his house, food from his stores, and in a new boat from his wharf had gone off to 'join the devil', Carter was 'Compeled to independency'.[24]

When the Reverend Henry Caner, Rector of Kings Chapel, Boston, sailed away from the city in 1776 for Halifax under the protection of the British fleet, he was seventy-six years old. He had long been campaigning for the establishment of a resident bishop in America and was, as a result, very unpopular with Congregationalists and Presbyterians. He had had a long ministry in America, twenty years in Fairfield, Connecticut, and twenty-eight in Boston. Neither his age nor his spiritual concerns led him however to neglect the removal of all the vestments, plate and records of his church when he went on board the rescuing ship. He refused to return these in 1784 and turned them over to the Society for the Propagation of the Gospel. His letter book is a very valuable source of Loyalist material.[25]

Or consider the splendid 34,000 acres owned by Philip Skene along both sides of Wood Creek east of Lake Champlain. Skene had fought for Bonnie Prince Charlie in 1745, and in the French and Indian War in America. In 1775 he was appointed Lieutenant Governor of Fort Ticonderoga and Crown Point. As an avowed Loyalist his person and his estates were an obvious target for the Green Mountain Boys. But when in May 1775 John Barnes's Company seized his estate and took off his sister and daughters to Connecticut, they discovered that Skene himself was still *en route* from England back to Philadelphia— he was in fact seized on shipboard as he landed in June 1775. What they found in his home came as a surprise: 'They found the corpse of his wife in a small apartment partitioned off in the cellar. It was laid in a very nice wooden coffin, superior to anything which the carpenters of the country could make. And this was enclosed in a lead coffin, which was sealed and soldered up so as to render it quite air tight. His wife had a legacy left her of a certain sum per day whilst she was above ground and Skene had placed her here to receive this legacy.'

Major Skene was a larger than life figure. In person he was big and heavily set. Under arrest in 1775 in Philadelphia, he was lodged perhaps unwisely in the city tavern. Alexander Graydon takes up the story:

The officer to whose charge he was especially committed was Mr. Francis Wade the brewer, an Irishman of distinguished zeal in the cause and who was supposed to possess talents peculiarly fitting him for the task of curbing the spirit of a haughty Briton, which Skene undoubtedly was.

I well recollect the day that the guard was paraded to escort him out of the city on his way to some other station. An immense crowd of spectators stood before the door of his quarters and lined the streets through which he was to pass. The weather being warm, the window sashes of his apartment were raised and Skene, with a bottle of wine upon the table, having just finished his dinner, roared out in the voice of a Stentor, 'God save great George our King!' Had the spirit of '75 in any degree resembled the spirit of Jacobinism, to which it has been unjustly compared, this bravado would have unquestionably brought the major to the lamppost, and set his head upon a pike; but as fortunately for him it did not, he was suffered to proceed with his song and the auditory seemed more generally amused than offended.[26]

Thus far it might seem that recent research is serving to blunt lines rather than to sharpen them. It is certainly making clear how very narrow a line in fact separated some Loyalists from some Patriots. It is hard to see why some Randolphs and Fairfaxes, for instance, went one way and others another. De Lanceys in New York became Loyalists, because the Livingstons were Whigs. The Dunker and Germantown publisher Christopher Sower was a Loyalist because of the religious persecution that his father had suffered at Patriot hands. One reason for the vendetta of the Otises against Governors Bernard and Hutchinson, a vendetta that in the end reached the height of madness was due to frustration over the judgeship. It is possible to see why Benjamin Franklin, despite his liking for comfort in London, threw in his lot with the Revolution: his humiliation in the Cockpit went deep. We are only now beginning to have research done on William Franklin, and further research on him is eagerly awaited.[27]

A civil war can be used by a number of individuals as a cover to wipe out old scores. But why did Galloway go one way, and Dickinson another? They were of about the same age: Dickinson had been born in 1732, Galloway in 1731. Each worked professionally in Philadelphia and each came from a propertied family in Maryland. Each had married money, and was a successful lawyer. Each of them feared the effect of Yankee levelling, and was seen as, in essence, Tory. But Galloway, Franklin's earlier ally against the Penns in Pennsylvania and wise thinker in 1774, ended up as a Loyalist in London, miserably criticizing Howe for losing the war, and claiming damages on a considerable scale. Dickinson, a lawyer also, and a man of means, author of *Farmer's Letters* and one of the first of Britain's critics, refused to sign the

Declaration of Independence, but he did volunteer to serve in the Continental Line, he helped to draft the Articles of Confederation, and he became a vigorous champion of the rights of small states. Why were Van Cortlandt and Schuyler, the patroons of the Hudson Valley patriots, and Frederick Philipse, a neighbour with matching wealth and similar origins, and his son-in-law Beverly Robinson, Loyalists?

We enter here the most intriguing but almost impenetrable area of taste and preference, courage and cowardice, self-interest and opportunism, judgement and calculation, conscience—and chance. A penetrating light has been thrown on this problem by a recent study, William Benton's *Whig-Loyalism*. Noting that a number of prominent men supported the pre-Revolutionary movement but in 1776 and afterwards changed their minds, Mr Benton has charted the course of their intellectual journeys. The men he studied were William Smith and Peter Van Schaack of New York, William Samuel Johnston of Connecticut, Daniel Leonard and Benjamin Church of Massachusetts, Andrew Allen of Pennsylvania, Robert Alexander and Daniel Dulany of Maryland, and William Byrd III of Virginia. In the case of one of these, Peter Van Schaack, what seems to have swayed him was the timing of a series of family tragedies which he suffered in 1775: the death of two sons in July, the ill health of his wife, the loss of an eye and the threat of blindness. After the impact of these calamities, his country's troubles seemed unimportant and remote in comparison with his own grief. In any event he was a man who put loyalty to his conscience above loyalty to the state. William Byrd anguished even more, and committed suicide in 1776.

The list could be continued indefinitely, as Galloway's and Dickinson's careers make plain. Landon Carter of Virginia faced the same dilemma. He had welcomed the revolution originally but he came to feel by 1775 that a republic was just as dangerous as a monarchy. In an independent state 'We might fall into a worse situation from internal oppression and commotions than might have been obtained by a serious as well as a cautious reconciliation'. He feared Patrick Henry far more than he feared the King. So that 13 July 1776 seemed to him a happy day. As his diary records it brought the news—accurate as it proved—of the departure of the royal governor Lord Dunmore; it also brought the news—as it proved totally inaccurate—'That Patrick Henry the late elected Governor died last Tuesday evening.

So that being the day of our batteries beginning to play on Dunmore's gang and they being routed, we ought to look on those two joined as two glorious events particularly favourable by the hand of Providence.' Unhappily for Landon Carter, Patrick Henry was all too much alive. But Carter died before he had to make his agonizing choice. Richard Saltonstall refused to fight on either side and went into voluntary exile. Benedict Arnold, for whatever reasons of mercenary calculation or thwarted ambition, made his agonized decision four years later, and whatever his vices, at least physical cowardice and military folly were not among them, for he was probably the ablest soldier of the war.

The Reverend Jacob Duché, the minister of Christ Church, Philadelphia, swayed to and fro. He was chaplain to both the First and Second Continental Congress. In July 1775 he preached a sermon 'The Duty of Standing Fast in our Spiritual and Temporal Liberties'; he was loyal to his king, but pro-American, for he saw no distinction then between the two sentiments. Intellectually he was consistent, but events compelled a decision, and he found that hard to make. He threw in his hand—and his Christian conscience—and came down on the Loyalist side; perhaps he did so only because he was fortified by Howe's presence in his city in 1777–78? Was he consistent? No. Was he a coward? Perhaps. The line was hard to draw, and some who became Loyalists—William Smith, Joseph Galloway, Daniel Leonard, W. S. Johnston—might well have become distinguished Patriot leaders, had their Whig sentiments of 1765 held through the trials of the decade from 1765 to 1774, or had the dice fallen the other way.

A study of the Whig Loyalists is useful corrective reading today when the scholarship of the Revolution is in fact dominated by the research into contemporary records of men like Bernard Bailyn of Harvard and Edmund Morgan of Yale.[28] Thoroughly steeped in the pamphlet literature of the period and apt to see the events of 1776 in terms of the stereotypes of those pamphleteers and sermon-writers, these scholars see 1776 as an American replica of 1649, with George III sometimes appearing to some contemporaries indeed as a latter-day Charles I. They see clear parallels to 1649 and to 1688 also. Although it is now established that George III was in fact no tyrant, and that his limitation was executive weakness, vacillation and inconsistency rather than the reverse, nevertheless the neo-Whig position of these scholars is apt on occasion to be not only neo-Whig but neo-Bancroftian. It constitutes, however, today's orthodoxy. They minimize the part played by the revolutionary mobs, and the degree of organization—of caucuses, committees of correspondence and minutemen—brought to bear by Samuel Adams and other Patriots, and all but totally missing on the Loyalist side. Perhaps too the essential Puritanism of Sam Adams is hidden by today's emphasis on him as the ringleader of a secular conspiracy. There was much of the *saint manqué* in him, as in his distant cousin, John.

For what emerges from even a cursory survey of the Loyalist papers is that there was an alternative intellectual stance to that taken by the Whigs. The intellectual conflict of 1776 was in fact not between Whig and Tory but between Whig and Whig, or, to use Burke's language—between Old Whig and New. A few might speak the language of Sir Robert Filmer, of Throne and Altar. But both sides took Locke and Coke, Trenchard and Gordon, as their texts, and rested their case on the achievements of the Glorious Revolution: a balanced constitution, a harmonious order of ranks and classes, a religion that emphasized obedience and virtue, an acceptance of property as the basis of suffrage and office-holding. Before March 1776 all but a few Americans saw this British Constitution as their model of government. The narrow difference was that to men like Boucher, Cadwallader Colden and Joseph Galloway, to Hutchinson, De Lancey and Carter this meant primarily loyalty to Crown and Governor; to Richard Bland and John Dickinson it meant primarily loyalty to colony and assembly. In the last analysis it was not a matter of ideology but of emphasis, temperament and circumstance. This was well expressed by G. H. Guttridge:

Whiggism and toryism can be explained but not defined, and the appropriateness of the terms is often a matter of opinion. They arose in the twilight of a political order based on religious sanction, and they flourished before the concept of organised change had emerged. Thus they represent an intermediate stage between religious creeds and political programmes. The creeds were vague, but the programmes not yet positive ... The division between Whig and Tory was rather in temperament and interpretation of society.[29]

Or in the words of the *Town and City Magazine* for 1778, one must

recognize the difference between 'the opposite pillars of the constitution: the one vigilant lest government start into despotism; the other,
lest it sink into anarchy'. This antithesis is a matter of temperament and
a permanent feature of all history. It is not a matter merely of semantics.
Many Tories—i.e. Old Whigs—were as emphatic about the right of
resistance to tyranny as the New or Radical Whigs; even Hutchinson
and Galloway agreed on this. William Smith, calling himself one of the
last of King William's Whigs, was for 'Liberty and the Constitution'.
What this meant was that American Whigs were for the same rights of
property and trade, the same respect for charters, the same control of
taxation which had been the backbone of Whiggism in seventeenth-
century England. Later they wanted a bicameral system, for uni-
cameralism means democracy and as such was dangerous, and an
independent senate. Even Thomas Jefferson later wanted members of
state senates to be 'perfectly independent of their electors'. George
Mason would have required Virginian senators to be substantial
landowners of at least £2000. John Adams, who was appalled at the
thought of an unchecked democracy based on universal suffrage,
exerted his influence to ensure that the Massachusetts Constitution
recognized distinction of property, and similar devices were adopted
in most of the other states. This was to be a Whig Revolution indeed.

There was no sharp polarization of opinion; nor was Loyalism
determined by class or status. All but a few men accepted and followed
the principles of Locke. Even General Burgoyne, who was also a
writer and man of ideas, said: 'Gentlemen, I am no stranger to the
Doctrines of Mr. Locke and other of the best advocates for the rights
of mankind, upon the compact always implied between the governing
and the governed, and the right of resistance in the latter, when the
compact shall be so violated as to leave no other means of redress. I
look with reverence almost amounting to idolatry upon those immortal
whigs who adopted and applied such doctrine during part of the reign
of Charles I and in that of James II.' But it was Locke with a difference.
Cecelia Kenyon brought out the point in a paper delivered in 1960
to a Seminar at Colonial Williamsburg:

The philosophy associated with republicanism and with the Revolution
was also radical. It was the philosophy drawn from Locke's *Second
Treatise*, but it was Lockeianism with an American Gloss. A survey of

Revolutionary literature both before and after 1776 reveals a number of modifications in and deviations from the original treatise which the Americans made as they used the great philosopher for their polemical purposes. The most familiar was the substitution in the Declaration of Independence of the *pursuit of happiness* for *property*. Another somewhat less familiar and certainly less clearly defined change was the American refusal to make a sharp distinction between the state of nature and civil society. These and other differences were apparent before the final break with England. The establishment of republican governments induced still other differences, of which the most important were an emphasis on equality, an intensification of individualism, and the identification of Locke with republicanism. The result was a subtle but substantial simplification and radicalization of the doctrine of the *Second Treatise* . . . Furthermore, the ideas were rooted in the colonial past and were therefore not unfamiliar. Yet the total complex was radical in implication and operation, especially when linked with the belief in, as well as the practice of, republicanism.[30]

Moreover, Locke was emphatic on the importance and the centralized character of Parliament. Locke believed in a supreme power in the State and in the necessary existence of *one* legislator. To him, irrespective of the size of the Atlantic, the authority of Parliament was co-extensive with the Empire; there could be no 'colonial' Parliament, and no division of sovereignty. This point was made repeatedly by secular-minded men like Daniel Leonard, Martin Howard and Peter Van Schaack, and by ministers of religion like Samuel Seabury and Dr Myles Cooper. It was also made—uncompromisingly—by William Blackstone whose first volume of his *Commentaries on the Laws of England* came out in the same year as the Stamp Act. 'There is and must be in every state a supreme irresistible absolute and uncontrolled authority in which the *jura summa imperii* or rights of sovereignty reside, and this supreme power is by the constitution of Great Britain vested in the King Lords and Commons.' Or as Boucher put it, 'All Government is in its nature absolute and irresistible'.

In other words the Tories cited Locke for one reason, to emphasize the supremacy of the Crown in Parliament and the right of Parliament against the Crown. The Whigs cited Locke for another—with their local colonial assemblies in mind, and it was for these that they demanded liberty. But this was a distortion, because the authority

Locke supported was that of the British Parliament. Thus Myles Cooper in his *Patriots of North America* could notice this perversion in verse.

> Behold a vain, deluded Race,
> Thy venerable Name, disgrace;
> As Casuists false, as Savages rude,
> With Glosses weak, with Comments crude,
> Pervert they fair, instructive Page,
> To Sanctify licentious Rage.

When the issue was squarely raised by the Whigs, the Tories stated flatly their position—two independent legislatures cannot exist in the same state. Or as Isaac Hunt put the proposition: 'Two *distinct independent powers* in *one civil state* are as inconsistent as *two hearts* in the same natural body. . . . A due subordination of the less parts to the greater is therefore necessary to the *existence of* BOTH. . . .'

The empire was thus viewed by the Tories as a single state, geographically but not politically divided, with its government established by the Constitution; to deny the established authority of any part of that government was to destroy the whole. Daniel Leonard clearly saw, as he wrote in 1774, that to deny the authority of Parliament was to destroy the framework of the Constitution and with it the 'priceless claim' to all the rights guaranteed by that Constitution. On the same reasoning, Samuel Seabury labelled the Whig contention that the colonists owed allegiance not to Parliament but to the King a self-contradictory heresy:

It is a distinction made by the American republicans to serve their own rebellious purposes—a gilding with which they have enclosed the pill of sedition . . . The King of Great Britain was placed on the throne by virtue of an act of parliament . . . And if we disclaim that authority of parliament which made him our king, we, in fact, reject him from being our king—for we disclaim that authority by which he is king at all.

Yet if the line was one drawn with difficulty in an agreed corpus of Whig theory, and if all proudly shared the legacy of 1688 and 1689, there is in Loyalism one other dimension. That dimension is missing from subsequent American Conservatism, despite the elaborate efforts of writers like Russell Kirk and the late Clinton Rossiter to find eighteenth-century roots for Conservative thought in the United States.[31] If we admit the logic of Louis Hartz that the United States inherited liberalism without having to fight for it, we must also admit that since it was never feudal it also never acquired a religious establishment. It could never produce those ingredients of true Conservatism—aristocratic leadership, instinctive respect for authority in Church and State, and a doctrine of Christian pessimism.

There ran through the sermons of the Revolution two distinctive theories. From Congregational pulpits the note was of criticism of the present, a call, often lurid and evangelical, to a Golden Age of innocence and virtue; the state as well as the soul would be made over. On the other there was the voice of Jonathan Boucher:

Liberty is not the setting at nought and despising established laws—much less the making our own wills the rule of our own actions, or the actions of others—and not bearing (whilst yet we dictate to others) the being dictated to, even by the laws of the land; but it is the being governed by law, and by law only. The Greeks described Eleutheria, or Liberty, as the daughter of Jupiter the supreme fountain of power and law. And the Romans, in like manner, always drew her with the pretor's wand (the emblem of legal power and authority) as well as with the cap. Their idea, no doubt, was that liberty was the fair fruit of just authority and that it consisted in men's being subjected to law. The more carefully well-devised restraints of law are enacted, and the more rigorously they are executed in any country, the greater degree of civil liberty does that country enjoy. To pursue liberty, then, in a manner not warranted by law, whatever the pretence may be, is clearly to be hostile to liberty: and those persons who thus *promise you liberty* are themselves the servants of *corruption* . . . So far from our having a right to do everything that we please, under a notion of liberty, liberty itself is limited and confined—limited and confined only by laws which are at the same time both it's foundation and it's support. . . .

Boucher himself paid tribute to the Loyalists in his *View of the Causes and Consequences* by adapting the lines of *Paradise Lost*:

Among the faithless, faithful chiefly they—
Among innumerable false, unmov'd,

Unshaken, unseduc'd, unterrified,
Their *loyalty* they kept, their love, their zeal:
Nor number, nor example, with them wrought,
To swerve from truth, or change their constant mind

The Anglican clergy were in a special position. They had a special connection with British Authority; many of them were born in the British Isles; all of them had been ordained there; those who were missionaries of the Society for the Propagation of the Gospel received all or part of their incomes from England; and all of them, like the officials of government, were bound by special oaths of allegiance and obedience to their king. It is not to be wondered at that a large proportion of them remained either actively or passively loyal to the mother country in the struggle. To quote the Rev. Ebenezer Dibblee of Stamford, Connecticut (28 October 1765) they sought, 'both in public and private, to inculcate the great duty of obedience and subjection to the government in being, and steadfast adherence to that well tempered frame of polity upon which this Protestant Church of ours is built, a constitution happily balanced between tyranny and anarchy'.

Many Anglican clerics recognized that there was a 'deep-rooted republicanism, democratic levelling principles, ever unfriendly to monarchy' at work. They believed that Church and State mutually supported each other and that this republicanism was a threat both to secular and to religious authority. 'A republican spirit can never rest', explained Henry Caner; 'the same levelling principles which induced them to withdraw from the wholesome establishment of the Church operate with equal force in throwing off the restraints of civil government.' The Reverend Charles Inglis argued that 'One of the principal springs of the rebels' conduct was their desire to destroy the Anglican Church in America'. The Reverend Samuel Seabury of Westchester wrote 'The independent mode of religion is from its very nature incompatible with monarchical government'. And Henry Caner had from the beginning few illusions. Writing to Governor Wentworth, 8 November 1773, he said:

My friends at Boston were exercised with the disagreeable entertainment of tumultuous riots, mobs and Town Meetings which continued almost the whole time of my absence and have not yet ceas'd. The pretended ground of this disorder is the India House Tea; but every Species of rude and indecent language at the Governor and others whom they are pleased to look upon in an unfriendly light, attended with threatnings [*sic*] of violence extended to life itself were openly avowed in their Town M . . . such are the Effects of popular Government, Sedition, Anarchy and Violence and all this flame kindled and kept alive by about half a dozen men of bad principles and morals.[32]

The Reverend Dr George Micklejohn of North Carolina, in the Regulator troubles, declared firmly that the powers that be are ordained of God, and that 'subjection to lawful authority is one plain and principal doctrine of Christianity'. The line might be between one form of Whiggism and another. It was also, and more sharply, between Anglican and Dissenter. The parallel is not only with 1688 or with 1649, but with the Act of Supremacy of 1532, or with 1604—'No Bishop, no King.' These were the sentiments of Samuel Seabury of Westchester, Myles Cooper and Charles Inglis of New York, and Thomas Bradbury Chandler of Elizabethtown, N.J.

To some Dissenters, these men were not High Anglicans but simply Papists. The Reverend William Gordon in Roxbury and Jonathan Mayhew in Boston used their pulpits as revolutionary platforms against the 'popery' of these Anglican Tories. The Quebec Act in all its liberalism was seen as devil's work. And to some like Hessian Captain Heinrich the Quakers were worse than any Presbyterian.

Call this war, dearest friend, by whatsoever name you may, only call it not an American Rebellion, it is nothing more or less than an Irish-Scotch Presbyterian Rebellion. Those true Americans who take the greatest part therein, are the famous Quakers. The most celebrated, the first ones in entire Pennsylvania and Philadelphia and Boston are, properly speaking, the heads of the Rebellion. I am not allowed to write you explicitly, just how the matter developed but you can guess at what I have omitted, and you will hit it pretty fairly . . . For the first you must assume two Rebellions proper. The former was fomenting fifty years ago. It was the result of a state projected upon false principles, whose citizens consisted of seemingly hypocritical pious imposters, and downright cheats. These hypocrites are the Quakers. I cannot tell you all of the infamy I hold these people capable of; for I can think of nothing more abominable, than to practise, under the guise of Religion—malice, envy, yea even ambition, (thirst of power). In Pennsylvania they are the first, the most respected. They know the origin of the Colonies, and knew how to centralize the power in themselves by degrees.[33]

Yet despite the fact that the Revolution was led in part by dissenting ministers, there was no strain in the American Revolutionary situation of that virulent campaign against a decadent Church that marked Voltaire's thought. Tories like Daniel Leonard saw the dissenters as driving a dangerous 'political engine', and John Adams was driven to remind Leonard that in all ages and countries the church is likely to be on the Tory side. But—Thomas Jefferson apart—American liberals did not need to transform their revolution into a religious crusade, precisely because their religion was itself already revolutionary.

But it is worth adding that there is much more in Boucher than just authoritarianism. He criticizes the social compact theory vigorously: 'The supposition that a large concourse of people, in a rude and imperfect state of society, or even a majority of them should thus rationally and unanimously concur to subject themselves to various restrictions, many of them irksome and unpleasant, and all of them contrary to all their former habits, is to suppose them possessed of more wisdom and virtue than multitudes in any instance in real life have ever shown.' There was in Toryism a healthy scepticism for all causes and creeds. Perhaps its most vigorous expression came in the page of *The Gentleman's Magazine*, when the content of the Declaration of Independence was still a shock.

## THOUGHTS ON THE LATE DECLARATION OF THE AMERICAN CONGRESS.

The declaration is without doubt of the most extraordinary nature both with regard to sentiment and language, and considering that the motive of it is to assign some justifiable reasons of their separating themselves from Great Britain, unless it had been fraught with more truth and sense, might well have been spared, as it reflects no honour upon either their erudition or honesty.

We hold, they say, these truths to be self-evident: That all men are created equal. In what are they created equal? Is it in size, strength, understanding, figure, moral or civil accomplishments, or situation of life? Every plough-man knows that they are not created equal in any of these. All men, it is true, are equally created, but what is this to the purpose? It certainly is no reason why the Americans should turn rebels because the people of Great Britain are their fellow creatures, i.e. are created as well as themselves. It may be a reason why they should not rebel, but most indisputably is none why they should. They therefore have introduced their self-evident truths, either through ignorance, or by design, with a self-evident falsehood: since I will defy any American rebel, or any of their patriotic retainers here in England, to point out to me any two men, throughout the whole World, of whom it may with truth be said that they are created equal.

The next of their self-evident truths is, that all men are endowed by their Creator with certain unalienable rights (the meaning of which words they appear not at all to understand); among which are life, liberty, and the pursuit of happiness. Let us put some of these words together. All men are endowed by their Creator with the unalienable right of life. How far they may be endowed with this unalienable right I do not yet say, but, sure I am, these gentry assume to themselves an unalienable right of talking nonsense. Was it ever heard since the introduction of blunders into the world that life was a man's right? Life or animation is of the essence of human nature, and is that without which one is not a man, and therefore to call life a right, is to betray a total ignorance of the meaning of words. A living man, i.e. a man with life, hath a right to a great many things; but to say that a man with life hath a right to be a man with life is so purely American, that I believe the texture of no other brain upon the face of the earth will admit the idea. Whatever it may be, I have tried to make an idea out of it, but own I am unable. . . .

The next assigned cause and ground of their rebellion is, that every man hath an unalienable right to liberty; and here the words, as it happens, are not nonsense, but then they are not true: slaves there are in America, and where there are slaves, there liberty is alienated.

If the Creator hath endowed man with an unalienable right to liberty, no reason in the world will justify the abridgement of that liberty, and a man hath a right to do every thing that he thinks proper without controul or restraint: and upon the same principle there can be no such things as servants, subjects, or government of any kind whatsoever. In a word, every law that hath been in the world since the formation of Adam, gives the lye to this self-evident truth, (as they are pleased to term it,) because every law, divine or human, that is or hath been in the world, is an abridgment of man's liberty. . . .

An Englishman[34]

As a cause and creed, then, Loyalism was conservative, the creed of the friends of government. They saw all change as disruptive. If it was not necessary to change it was necessary not to change. That change was being asked for was not in itself new, for there was little new in recorded history. 'Those who are governed are always ready to set themselves against those who govern,' said Boucher. 'In every society there always have been, and too probably there always will be, men of restless and ambitious minds who are never long satisfied with any system of government or with any administration.' There were 'Artful, wicked and desperate men around', and Loyalist literature is rich in synonyms for them: 'Ambitious and needy adventurers', 'pretended patriots', 'mostly bankrupt and mean people'. There was a firm assumption—shared by both sides—that the people were the victims of a Great Conspiracy. On this Bernard Bailyn has written with authority. New England had always been prone to conspiracy and factions. Now they had bound themselves in alliance with similar voices in England in what George Chalmers described as 'A Cabalinarian Combination'. The Loyalist position was High Tory, rooted in pessimism over the human situation and its future; it was more clearly religious in origin than was the Patriot case. Noting the considerable number of colonial historians who became Loyalists— Thomas Hutchinson for Massachusetts, William Smith for New York, Robert Proud for Pennsylvania, George Chalmers from Maryland and Alexander Hewat for South Carolina and Georgia—Professor East has concluded that there may have been 'a bond of sympathy between the thinking of men who habitually took "the long view" and the thinking of the Loyalists of 1776'.[35]

This is essentially a report on work in progress. I have said nothing on the part played by the Loyalists in the war, which is still a largely unworked area, although tribute should be paid to the Honourable Piers Mackesy for his study *The War for America 1775–1783* (1964) and to Paul Smith for his *Loyalists and Redcoats* (1964). What needs a new telling is the part played by spies on both sides of the line. Lewis Einstein told this story vividly in his *Divided Loyalties* published in 1933, as did Carl Van Doren in his *Secret History of the American Revolution* (1941). There is now, however, considerable wealth of material here and some vivid stories to be told, notably, for instance, of the roles played by Christopher Sower in Pennsylvania,

Beverley Robinson in New York, and James (Jemmie) Rivington, the Loyalist newspaper editor, in New York City. His *New-York Gazetteer*, which began publication in 1773, rapidly made itself unpopular because of its objective approach, which in the eyes of Patriots was unwelcome. Rivington's plant was attacked and destroyed on the 27 November 1775, by a New York mob led by Isaac Sears. Rivington sailed away to Britain in January 1776, but returned to start publication in October 1777 of a strictly Loyalist paper entitled *Rivington's New-York Loyal Gazette*, which in December became *The Royal Gazette*. It is now clear however from Dr Crary's research that he was sending secret information to the Patriots in 1781.[36]

When the Americans reoccupied New York Rivington removed the Royal Arms from his paper, changed its name to *Rivington's New York Gazette and Universal Advertiser* and continued publication. But his paper was silenced for ever on the 31 December 1783 after he had been called upon, once again, by Isaac Sears and Alexander MacDougal. Rivington tried unsuccessfully to stay in business as a bookseller and stationer, aged now fifty-nine, but he failed, and died a pauper in 1802. He composed his own reflections on the strange events in his career in verse.

> The more I reflect, the more plain it appears,
> If I stay, I must stay at the risque of my ears,
> I have so-be-peppered the foes of our throne,
> Be-rebeled, be-deviled, and told them their own,
> That if we give up to these rebels at last
> Tis a chance if my ears will atone for the past.
>      [If there is an evacuation.]
> Yet still I surmise for aught I can see
> No Congress or Senates would meddle with me.
> For what have I done, when we come to consider,
> But sold my commodities to the best bidder?
> If I offered to lie for the sake of a post
> Was I to be blamed if the kind offered most?
>      [Ridicules Honor and Fame when compared with emolument]
>      [True the Tories might defend New York, but he doubts it]
>      ... As a very last shift
> We'll go to New Scotland and take the king's gift.

Good folks do your will—but I vow and I swear
I'll be boiled into soap before I'll live there.

.    .    .

Of all the vile countries that ever were known
In the frigid or torrid or temperate zone,
(From accounts I have had) there is not such another;
It neither belongs to this world or the other.
A favor they think it to send us there gratis
To sing like the Jews at the river Euphrates.
And after surmounting the rage of the billows
Hang ourselves up at last with our harps on the willows.
Ere I sail for that shore may I take my last nap:
Why it gives me the palsy to look on its map.
And he that goes there (Tho' I mean to be civil)
May fairly be said to have gone to the devil.
Shall I push for old England and whine at the throne?
Alas they have jemmies enough of their own!
Besides such a name I have got for my trade,
They would think I was lying whatever I said.

.    .    .

In short, if they let me remain in this realm,
What is it to Jemmy who stands at the helm?

Nor have I said anything here of the experiences of the Loyalists in exile in London, nor of those who settled in Canada.

Perhaps in conclusion two points should be made. If the story of the Loyalists is seen first and last as the record of a failure, the failure was only in the North American colonies south of what is now the State of Maine. If they failed in the United States they succeeded overseas: 35,000 of them settled in Canada, and they are essentially its founding fathers. They were important in Nova Scotia, New Brunswick and Prince Edward Island and they created Ontario. Without them Canada would hardly have been strong enough to survive ultimate American annexation. And under their leadership it did not, or at least did not until recently, become the melting pot that happened south of the 49th Parallel. The promise of the Quebec Act was made real by the fact of Loyalist influx, and Canadian nationalism was built on Loyalist foundations. Similarly in the Bahamas: all the names on Bay Street are of Loyalist descendants. And Loyalists are, of course, the founders of Sierra Leone; its élite of doctors and lawyers for long were called the Nova Scotians because they came via Nova Scotia

The second point that needs emphasis is of their loyalty to Britain itself and its consequences. The 7000 to 8000 people who exiled themselves between 1776 and 1782 made a real contribution to British and European history. Some of them, indeed, became notorious in different ways: Dr Jefferies was one of the first trans-Channel balloonists Colonel Armstrong served with Miranda; Benjamin Thompson became a Count of the Holy Roman Empire; William Cunningham was executed as a criminal; Lloyd Dulany was killed in a duel in Hyde Park; at least one became a prostitute, and at least one had a spell in Newgate Jail for debts. But their major legacy was to the British Services. Of those who came to Britain, or their sons, at least three held senior rank in the Royal Navy, one of them being a son of Mary Phillipse; eight held the rank of Colonel; at least two were army surgeons; and no less than four were full Generals. Sir David Ochterlony became a Major-General in the Army of the East India Company and died at Meerut in 1825. Sir John Stuart, a Major-General in the British Army, was the son of the John Stuart who served as Superintendent of Indian Affairs to the Southern Department, after coming to Georgia with Oglethorpe. And three of Beverley Robinson' sons had careers of distinction: Morris a Lieutenant-Colonel; Sir Frederick a Lieutenant-General; and Sir William as head of the British Army's Commissariat. It was not a mean legacy.

## NOTES

1. Lorenzo Sabine, *Biographical Sketches of Loyalists of the American Revolution*, with a historical essay (Two Vols; Boston, 1864); C. H Van Tyne, *The Loyalists in the American Revolution 1776–1783* (New York, 1902); Moses C. Tyler 'The Party of the Loyalists', *American Historical Review*, I, No. 1 (October 1895); L. W. Labaree, 'The Nature of American Loyalism', in *Proceedings of the American Antiquarian Society*, LIV (1944) 15; Wilbur Siebert, 'American Loyalists in Eastern Quebec', *Royal Society of Canada Transactions*, VII (1913); 'The Legacy of the American Revolution to the British West Indies', *Ohio State University Bulletin*, XVII (1913); 'Loyalist Settlements on Gaspé' *Royal Society of Canada Transactions*, VIII (1914); 'The Exodus of Loyalists from Penobscot', *Ohio State University Bulletin*, XVII

(1914); 'The Dispersion of American Tories', *Mississippi Valley Historical Review*, I (1914); 'Loyalists in the Niagara Peninsula', *Royal Society of Canada Transactions*, IX (1915); 'Loyalist Refugees of New Hampshire', *Ohio State University Bulletin*, XXI (1916); 'Refugee Royalists in Connecticut', *Royal Society of Canada Transactions*, X (1916); 'Loyalists in West Florida', *Mississippi Valley Historical Review*, II (1916); 'Loyalists in Pennsylvania', *Ohio State University Bulletin*, XXIV (1920); 'Kentucky's Struggle', *Mississippi Valley Historical Review*, VII (1920); and 'Loyalist Troops of New England', *The New England Quarterly*, IV (1931).

2. H. E. Egerton, ed., *The Royal Commission on the Losses and Services of the American Loyalists 1783–1785* (Oxford, 1915); G. O. Trevelyan, *The American Revolution* (Six vols, 1899–1914) republished in a one-volume condensation, ed. R. B. Morris (1965). Trevelyan wrote history that, as his son put it, 'did not take account of nuances'.

3. K. G. Davies, ed., *Documents of the American Revolution 1770–1783* (Colonial Office Series) Vol I: Calendar 1770–1771, Vol II: Transcripts 1770, Vol III: Transcripts 1771 (Shannon, 1973).

4. L. H. Gipson, *The British Empire Before the American Revolution* (New York, 15 vols, 1936–1970); B. R. Crick and Miriam Alman, *A Guide to Manuscripts relating to America in Great Britain and Ireland* (London, 1961).

5. Flora Macdonald was 24 when she rescued Bonnie Prince Charlie after Culloden. She lived in Skye until 1774 when, impoverished, she emigrated with her family to North Carolina. When the Highlanders in the back country of North Carolina rallied to the King in 1776 and prepared to march to Cape Fear, Flora Macdonald, mounted on a snow white horse, addressed the men at Cross Creek in Gaelic, and then rode up and down the lines of troops reviewing them. At Moore's Creek Bridge, half the force of 1700 men were casualties; 850 were taken prisoner, among them Flora Macdonald's husband Major Alan Macdonald. In November 1777, his property was confiscated and her two daughters were ill-treated. In 1779, at her husband's insistence, she returned to Skye, selling their silverware to raise money for the journey for herself and four children. Even then her troubles were not over. The ship was overhauled by a French privateer and she suffered a broken arm in the engagement. She died in 1790; her son John reached the rank of Colonel in the British army.

6. J. Potter, 'The Growth of Population in America 1700–1860', in D. V. Glass and D. E. C. Eversley, ed., *Population in History* (Chicago, 1965) pp. 631–688, and U.S. Bureau of the Census, *Historical Statistics*

*of the United States, Colonial Times to 1957* (Washington, 1960) pp. 743–774.

7. Esther Clark Wright, *The Loyalists of New Brunswick* (Fredericton, N.B., 1955).

8. Wallace Brown, *The King's Friends: The Composition and Motives of the American Loyalist Claimants* (Providence, 1965); Mary Beth Norton, *The British Americans* (Boston, 1972).

9. Eugene Fingerhut, 'Uses and Abuses of the American Loyalists' Claims: a Critique of Quantitative Analyses', *William and Mary Quarterly*, XXV (1968) 244.

10. The context implies that the Revolution referred to was the French, not the American. In any event John Adams's figures on Loyalism were always erratic. When in Holland in 1780, he said that no more than 1 in 20 of his countrymen were loyalists. *The Works of John Adams*, Vol. X (Boston, 1856) pp. 87, 193.

11. Phineas Bond, *Letters* (American Historical Association, *Annual Report 1896*, 2 vols., Washington, 1897); R. R. Palmer, *The Age of the Democratic Revolution* (Princeton, 1959) p. 188.

12. Paul Smith, 'The American Loyalists: Notes on their Organization and Numerical Strength', *William and Mary Quarterly*, XXV (1968) 259–277. But cf. C.O. 5/7/557, August 1778, which gives numbers in the provincial service as 7749.

13. Note: Professor East's comment on Connecticut as almost an 'independent republic' made up of 72 more-or-less independent towns. East, *Connecticut's Loyalists*, p. 6.

14. *Works of John Adams*, Vol. X, p. 63.

15. C. S. Sydnor, *Gentlemen Freeholders: Political Practices in Washington's Virginia* (Chapel Hill, 1952); Robert E. and B. Katherine Brown, *Virginia 1705–1786: Democracy or Aristocracy?* (East Lansing, 1964).

16. *Oxford Companion to American History*, p. 489.

17. C. H. Van Tyne, *The Loyalists in the American Revolution 1776–1783*, pp. 25–26.

18. Cf. Philip Vickers Fithian, *Journal and Letters* (Williamsburg, 1945); or, as Governor Morton wrote to Gage, 26 May 1775, 'While the loyalty of many of the country people cannot be depended upon, the Scotch will remain firm' (C.O. 5/92/217).

19. William Nelson, *The American Tory* (1961).

20. I. Harrell, *Loyalism in Virginia* (New York, 1926) pp. 63–65.

21. Harrell, p. 65.

22. For the Loyalists in London, where, in Susanna Copley's phrase, 'they mustered very thick' (C.O. 5/38/192), see Mary Beth Norton's *The*

*British Americans*, and Esmond Wright 'The Loyalists in Britain' in Wright, ed., *A Tug of Loyalties* (London, 1975); cf. Bernard Bailyn, *The Ordeal of Thomas Hutchinson* (Cambridge, Mass., 1974).

23. Crary, *The Price of Loyalty* (New York, 1973), p. 108.

24. *Diary* of Landon Carter, ed. J. P. Greene, 2 vols (Chapel Hill, 1965) *passim.*

25. Henry Caner, *Letter Book*, ed. K. C. Cameron, Transcendental Books (Hartford, 1972).

26. Crary, pp. 36–38; Alexander Graydon, *Memoirs of His Own Times* (New York, 1846) pp. 126–128.

27. Catherine Fennelly, 'Governor William Franklin of New Jersey', *William and Mary Quarterly*, VI (1949) 361.

28. Bernard Bailyn, *The Ideological Origins of the American Revolution* (Cambridge, Mass., 1967); Bailyn, ed., *The Pamphlets of the American Revolution 1750–1766*, Vol. I (Cambridge, Mass., 1965–); Bernard Bailyn, 'Political Experience and Enlightenment Ideas in Eighteenth-Century America', *American Historical Review*, LXVII (1962), 339–351. Bernard Bailyn, 'The Central Themes of the American Revolution', Kurtz and Hutson, eds., *Essays on the American Revolution* (New York, 1973); Edmund S. Morgan, *The Birth of the Republic* (Chicago, 1956); 'Colonial Ideas of Parliamentary Power 1746–1766', *William and Mary Quarterly*, V (1948) 311; 'The American Revolution considered as an Intellectual Movement', in Arthur M. Schlesinger, Jr, and Morton White, eds., *Paths of American Thought* (Boston, 1963); 'The Puritan Ethic and the American Revolution', *William and Mary Quarterly*, XXIV (1967) 3. Cf. Caroline H. Robbins, *The Eighteenth-Century Commonwealthman* (New York, 1959); Merrill Jensen, 'Democracy and the American Revolution', *Huntington Library Quarterly*, XX (1957) 321–341; Clarence L. Ver Steeg, 'The American Revolution Considered as an Economic Movement', *Huntington Library Quarterly*, XX (1957) 361–372; Thad W. Tate, 'The Coming of the Revolution in Virginia: Britain's Challenge to Virginia's Ruling Class, 1736–1776', *William and Mary Quarterly*, XIX (1962) 323–343; Thad W. Tate, 'Social Contract in America, 1774–1787; revolutionary theory as a conservative instrument', *William and Mary Quarterly*, XXII (1965) 375–391; R. Buel, Jr, 'Democracy and the American revolution: a frame of reference', *William and Mary Quarterly*, XXI (1964) 165–190; R. M. Calhoon, 'William Smith, Jr's alternative to the American revolution', *William and Mary Quarterly*, XXII (1965) 105–118.

29. G. H. Guttridge, *English Whiggism and the American Revolution* (Berkeley, 1942).

30. Cecelia Kenyon, 'Republicanism and Radicalism in the American Revolution', *William and Mary Quarterly*, XIX (1962) 153.

31. Russell Kirk, *John Randolph of Roanoke* (New York, rev. ed., 1964); Clinton Rossiter, *Seed-Time of the Republic* (New York, 1953); Arthur Schlesinger, Jr, pointed out—in his own pre-Camelot days—that Locke was the name of a South African golf player and Burke the winner of the United States Open in 1937.

32. Caner, *Letter Book*, p. 153.

33. 'Letter-Book of Captain Johann Heinrich', *Pennsylvania Magazine of History and Biography*, XXXII (1898) 137–139.

34. *The Gentleman's Magazine*, XLVI, 403.

35. Robert A. East, *Connecticut's Loyalists*, p. 10.

36. Catherine S. Crary, 'The Tory and the Spy: the double life of James Rivington', *William and Mary Quarterly*, XVI (1959) 61–72.

*6*

# The American Revolution and the Anglo-American Relationship in Historical Perspective

## H. C. ALLEN

By the rude bridge that arched the flood,
Their flag to April's breeze unfurled,
Here once the embattled farmers stood,
And fired the shot heard round the world.

. . .

On this green bank, by this soft stream
We set to-day a votive stone;
That memory may their deed redeem,
When, like our sires, our sons are gone.
(R. W. Emerson, 19 April 1836)[1]

Was the shot heard round the world? Was it even *to be* heard round the world? Above all, did mankind's 'memory their deed redeem'? Or was Emerson, with patriot's license, just giving vent (in a somewhat if not wholly uncharacteristic fashion) to Fourth-of-July-oration, 'Yankee-doodle'[2] chauvinism?

Certainly American participants in the American Revolution wanted it to be heard around the world, not only by their friends in Britain and, more practically, by Britain's chief traditional enemy, France, but also by a much wider public. 'When in the course of human events, it becomes necessary for one People to dissolve the political bands which have connected them with another, . . . a decent respect to the Opinions of mankind requires that they should declare the causes which impel them to the separation'.[3] In the words of the historian of the United States and Europe, 'The American War of Independence, or (as the insurgents called it) the American Revolution, was rooted in an appeal to the conscience of Europe'.[4]

And Europe, which was, despite more than two centuries of empire-building and its recent cult of Nature, a social structure in many respects corrupt, was still very much the dynamo which galvanized that great commercial, industrial and demographic revolution which was rapidly transforming the face of the globe, and which historians can still accurately describe as the Expansion of Europe. The ancient cultures of China and India (for example) notwithstanding, European 'civilization' constituted in some sense 'the world' around which the sounds of the War of American Independence did echo.

That it seemed an echo, of course, was part of the appeal, for many Europeans—and especially discontented ones—saw Americans as having improved, but, more than that, as being an improved version of themselves. The improvement was not merely depicted as a fact but held out as a continuing aspiration not only for Americans but also for Europeans. As the Frenchman Guillard de Beaurieu declared: 'Americans, with you there are no large towns, no luxury, no crimes and no diseases. You are as Nature commands us all to be.'[5] The successful establishment of a new independent state by 'the People of the United States',[6] on the other side of the Atlantic still seemed to many in Europe to fulfil Bishop Berkeley's prophecy ('Westward the course of Empire takes its way . . . Time's noblest offspring is the last.')[7], although not quite in the form he expected. What is without doubt, however, is that, in Silberschmidt's words, 'The new development had a profound effect on Europe. It delighted all European devotees of liberty and provoked a surge of love and affection for America [For these devotees the emotional words are not too strong]. Interest in America was over-shadowed for a time by the outbreak of the French Revolution', which 'though not directly set in motion by the American example, was clearly inspired by it.'[8]

It would, of course, be wholly wrong to depict the universal European reaction as one of warm approval for the revolutionaries of the United States. One of the foremost agents of that Revolution, Jefferson himself, declared in 1786 of Britain: 'That nation hates us, their ministers hate us, and their king more than all other men.'[9] And he had much justification. But even if many in Europe, and particularly in Britain, heard the firing of American Revolutionary arms with mistrust, hatred and sometimes fear, they did hear it. When the Revolution was over, feeling subsided, and was in any case, as

Silberschmidt points out, heavily overlaid by the much more potent emotions of those same people, both Europeans and British, about the much more alarming French Revolution, which was so much closer to home.

It was in fact alarming enough to prompt a not unimportant parallel wave of feelings in the breasts of American Federalists who, distant though they were, went, in some instances, nearly as far as Edmund Burke in their detestation of Jacobinism. As Senator George Cabot declared in 1797: 'If England will persevere, she will save Europe and save us; but if she yields, all will be lost.' 'She is now the only barrier between us and the deathly embraces of our dear Allies—between universal irreligion, immorality and plunder, and what order, probity, virtue and religion is left.'[10]

From Europe's point of vision, however, the United States virtually disappeared from view during the Revolutionary wars except as an increasingly (and ultimately exceedingly) irritating commercial power insistent on what it regarded as its proper neutral's rights in the long war. When the struggle became more severe and bitter in the Napoleonic era the ultimate result was the War of 1812 between Britain and America. This certainly set back Anglo-American relations for many years and did not encourage most Britons to take too kindly to American assertions of the fundamental importance of their Revolution to the future of mankind. Indeed for a period, there was a perceptible sense in Europe that the United States had overplayed its hand. The noble theories which underlay the Declaration of Independence and even the Constitution did not seem to be making much sustained headway in the Europe of Metternich.

Europeans began to act as if the shot had not been heard round the world and was not likely to be. In fact, the political doctrines of democracy and freedom espoused by America were to depend a good deal on American power, and though this was increasing very fast in the first half of the nineteenth century, most Europeans were not aware of the fact or shut their eyes to it. Some of them were infuriated by what they regarded as unjustified American pretensions. The Monroe Doctrine, for example, asserted in 1823 something which would amount to an American hegemony in the Western Hemisphere, an overlordship that the United States government had not the military means at its disposal to enforce, especially at sea. It was not really to

F

have such means until the end of the century. When combined with the aura of moral superiority self-consciously exuded by most Americans when expounding that democratic missionary role in the world which they had first adumbrated in 1776, Europeans found their attitude abrasive, and often maddening.

Sydney Smith gave characteristic expression to this sentiment in a famous passage: 'Other nations boast of what they are or have been, but the true citizen of the United States exalts his head to the skies in the contemplation of what the grandeur of his country is going to be. Others appeal to history; an American appeals to prophecy and with Malthus in one hand and a map of the back country in the other he boldly defies us to a comparison with America as she is to be and chuckles in delight over the splendours the geometrical ratio is to shed over her story . . . The American propensity to look forward with confidence to the future greatness of their country may be natural and laudable. But when they go further and refer to the wished-for period as one in which the glory of England will be extinguished forever, their hopes become absurdities.' Alas, in 1976 not wholly absurd by any means, even though Smith in the end turned out to have had a historical point in what he went on to say, in a passage packed with ironies for our day.

'Let us suppose the time arrived when American fleets shall cover every sea and ride in every harbour for purposes of commerce, of chastisement, or protection, when the land shall be the seat of freedom, learning, taste, morals, all that is most admirable in the eyes of man, and when England, sinking under the weight of years and the manifold casualties by which the pride of empires is levelled in the dust shall have fallen from her high estate. In that day of her extremity . . . might an Englishman . . . not truly say: "America has reason to be proud; but let her not forget whence came the original stock of glory she had laid out to such good account".'[11]

Now that we in the mid-twentieth century have observed (and the past tense may be appropriate) the plenitude of American power, and the alarming, if not the absolute, decline of British strength and will, we may be able to see the whole course of the Anglo-American relationship to date in better proportion. Writing in 1952 my own judgement was that 'Two main themes dominate the history of Anglo-American relations. The first arises . . . from the peculiar relationship which has always existed between the two countries, both physically and psychologically . . . Looking back over the whole course of Anglo-American relations from 1783 to the present day, we can see persistent, even steady, progress from mistrust to cordiality . . . The second . . . theme is concerned, not with the increasing amiability of the relationship, but . . . with the shifting balance of power within it . . . the fact that there is a remarkable reversal in the relative position of the two states between 1783 and 1952.'[12]

My judgement then, in the manner we historians find it so difficult to avoid, was undoubtedly unduly affected by the special circumstances and climate of opinion of the day. My view of the ripening of Anglo-American friendship was somewhat sanguine, not to say sentimental; my view of the temporary nature of the decline of British power perhaps even more so when I wrote: 'But it is to be hoped that the exhaustion of Britain after 1945 was only a temporary condition. She may be an ancient among the nations, but it does not necessarily follow that she is doomed inevitably to the weakness, and ultimately the decrepitude, of senility.'[13] It still does not necessarily follow, but there is room for a good deal more doubt, not to say scepticism, after the passage of nearly a quarter of a century. What is perhaps clear is that those years after the Second World War saw the apex of America's relative international power and that in them its overwhelming nature was exaggerated by the fact that she, alone among the 'Great Powers', was not damaged but was indeed strengthened by the war.

American power to proselytize has depended in very considerable degree on her cruder strengths—economic, political and military. Her situation in 1976 will be very different from that around 1960, let alone 1950. She still has about 6 per cent of the world's population and occupies nearly 7 per cent of its total land area, but whereas in 1951 she produced, according to some estimates, one-third of all the world's goods, and one-half of its manufactured goods (according to Woytinsky the U.S. share of world income increased from 26 per cent in 1938 to 40.7 per cent in 1948),[14] the picture in the seventies is very different. Even since 1963 the American share of world trade has sunk from some 15 to some 13 per cent, and her share of the world's consumption of electrical energy has diminished from 36 per cent in 1961 to something nearer 30 per cent in 1970. In 1962 57 per cent of all the motor vehicles in existence were in the United States: in 1970 the figure was approximately 40 per cent. America's share of gross world product has probably sunk from about a half in mid-century to not much more than a quarter today.

This economic strength has found expression in military power. Even after the unexpectedly short period from 1946 to 1949 during which the United States enjoyed an exclusive monopoly of nuclear weapons, her military (and especially naval) supremacy was clear for many years, except on the actual continent of Europe. In 1954–55, for example, according to *Jane's Fighting Ships*, the United States Navy was 'equal to all the major navies of the world combined'. By 1974, although there was still an effective balance of nuclear terror, it was probable that Russia had more, if not more effective, nuclear missiles than America, while the U.S.S.R. had, crudely estimated, 3400 naval vessels to 2400 American, being weaker in aircraft carriers but much stronger in submarines. Even more notably in military than in economic strength America's lead had declined decisively though she remained, overall, much the world's strongest political unit.

Thus the unique ascendancy of the United States which had been foreshadowed after the First World War but which the American people had refused to recognize until it was finally thrust upon them in 1941 did not endure for more than about twenty years. It owed most to the structural strengths of the American polity—a huge, wealthy and economically well-balanced territorial base; an energetic, enterprising, efficient and well (but not too highly) organized people; and a remarkably stable and effective system of government—but much also to the destructive effect of the two world wars on the other great powers. In some sense the moment of supreme power, real though it was, had an element of the fortuitous, even the artificial in it.

Not that, in the fifteen years since the peak of 1960, America's actual power has declined, but her relative strength has certainly done so. Other powers and groups of powers have gained ground, but they have a long way to go if they are to catch up. The United States remains a remarkably effective power—'the greatest': she can at the touch of a button destroy us all. But she has, short of the ultimate holocaust, come up against the practical limits of her international strength, and the American people have recognized as much. We are, as a result, now able to see the rise of her strength over the last two centuries in better perspective.

The graph of America's relative power, after a surge forward at the time of the Revolution, and some hesitation during the French wars and the War of 1812, rose with remarkable speed thereafter, though confined in its influence during the nineteenth century largely to the North American continent and almost wholly to the Western Hemisphere. Rising more sharply as a result of the process of industrialization, which accelerated rapidly in the second half of the century, her impact after 1898 began to be increasingly felt by the outside world, first in Asia and then in Europe. Her intervention in the First World War gave her the leadership of mankind. It was no coincidence that the 'Great War' has gradually come to be called, in the era of American ascendancy, by the American name 'World War I': the United States was, with the possible exception of Britain, the first truly world power, a role to which her central geographic position as well as her unique strength fully entitled her.

It was at this point that the real power of the United States came for the first time into line with the pretensions to political influence which her messianic ideology (incipient though it then was) had led her to make in 1776. She had had much general influence—in, for example, the realm of ideas—before 1917 but it was now enormously enhanced. Henry A. Wallace once called the twentieth century the century of the 'common man':[15] it has also been called 'the American century', and the two concepts have in some degree been entwined together since the Revolution. The Declaration of Independence contained, as Alistair Cooke has pointed out, 'two sentences' which 'would shake the ordered world' of the eighteenth century. The first was that '. . . all Men are created equal, that they are endowed by their Creator with certain unalienable rights, that among these are Life, Liberty and the Pursuit of Happiness'. 'The second sentence was the stick of dynamite'; '. . . that to secure these rights, Governments are instituted among Men, *deriving their just powers from the consent of the governed.'*[16] Here, at the very beginning of the independent history of the United States, was the banner with the strange device, 'Democracy'.

Of course, in another sense this idea that the Declaration was democratic is wholly untrue. Among what Rufus Choate called (with the Yankee scepticism of a New England Whig) 'the glittering and sounding generalities of natural right which make up the Declaration of Independence',[17] there was no mention of democracy.

Even less did the Constitution, conservative, even counter-revolutionary document that it was, give America a democratic government, but it did make the evolution of democracy possible—one is tempted to say predestined—and when the ferment of those generalities of 1776 was well advanced (first fermentation under Jefferson, second fermentation under Jackson) it was not necessary to put the new wine in new bottles: the Constitution of 1789 was new enough and sufficiently flexible.

It was in these years around the second quarter of the nineteenth century that the brew of the Anglo-American economic, cultural, and even in a sense political connection really began to develop renewed and increased strength. As Frank Thistlethwaite has written of it: 'The Anglo-American connection transcended the facts of economic geography. Along the North Atlantic trade route there moved, not only goods, but people, the carriers of technical, philanthropic, religious and political ideas. The Atlantic economy supported a structure of social relations which bound together important elements in Britain and the United States.'[18] The importance of the economic connection was to weaken steadily after the Civil War, the cultural connection was to persist right up to the present day, and in due course the political connection was in some respects to get stronger, at least until immediately after the Second World War.

A friendly political connection was not yet, by early nineteenth century, firmly established in the sphere of formal international relations. Here the legacy of the American War of Independence was still much too strong. George Canning, that 'malevolent meteor',[19] who was still in the firmament till 1827, was described by John Quincy Adams, as an 'implacable and rancorous enemy'[20] of America. Adams himself had risen from the Secretaryship of State to the Presidency in 1825, and Canning's cousin, Sir Stratford Canning, British Minister in Washington, described his hatred of the British as 'ravenous'.[21] But Canning, certain liberal proclivities notwithstanding (at least compared with those of Castlereagh), was a Tory, an anti-Jacobin, and a figure of the establishment, albeit always in some degree an outsider because of his youthful poverty. He 'made it' inside the establishment, and so approved of the British system.

There were many who did not, and who saw the United States of America in a wholly different light. They were sympathizers with the sentiments of a poem in *The Political Magazine* of June 1832, quoted by G. D. Lillibridge:

> The People, the People, remember them, too
> When America vanquished the Red and the Blue;
> And rose with her stars full of freedom and light,
> A firmament blazing thro' slavery's night. . . .

As Lillibridge himself writes,

'To these people American democracy had set off a chain reaction destined to reach far across the Atlantic into all of Europe and destroy the chains of European bondage. Again and again radical spokesmen were to note that the impact of American ideas was "almost beyond calculation". The course of American development had proved beyond a shadow of doubt that democracy was no longer to linger in the minds of men as a utopian ideal—its principles "have been submitted to a long experience . . . and the question is settled". And from a center of radicalism, the London Working Men's Association, came a thundering flash of light: "The Republic of America . . . is a beacon of freedom" for all mankind.'[22]

These antiphonal strains continued well beyond the middle of the century. They could be heard in the characteristic words of two men as different as Viscount Palmerston and John Bright; the former gave expression to the lack of diplomatic harmony between the two countries, the latter to the deep accord of working-class opinion among the two peoples. As Palmerston put it in 1857: 'These Yankees are most disagreeable Fellows to have to do with about any American Question; They are on the Spot, strong, deeply interested in the matter, totally unscrupulous and dishonest and determined somehow or other to carry their Point.'[23]

Bright in effect rebuked him when he declared of the Union in the Civil War: 'Privilege thinks it has a great interest in this contest, and every morning, with blatant voice, it comes into your streets and curses the American Republic.'[24] By contrast, the Republic (he asserted on another occasion) has 'the most free government and the noblest constitution the world has ever seen'.[25] 'The existence of that free country and that free government', he continued at a later date, 'has had a prodigious influence upon freedom in Europe and in England

... by the ... great example of ... its political institutions' which are 'free ... beyond all other countries'.[26]

By the turn of the century the two strains, foreign and domestic, had begun to converge, for not only had the Reform Bills of 1867 and 1885 taken Britain a long way down the path to democracy which Bright had sought to follow, but the voice of Palmerston had been succeeded—the timbre was not dissimilar—by that of Joseph Chamberlain, expressing the desire in 1898 that 'the Stars and Stripes and the Union Jack should wave together over an Anglo-Saxon alliance'.[27] We are entering now upon that rise of Anglo-American friendship which its historian declares must 'take first rank' among 'the decisive events of modern history'.[28] The yeast of the ideas of the American Revolution was still to work in Britain for some years to come, and the long-term effects of its democratic tendencies were thus sustained and became in some respects permanent.

Nor, as Bright had noted, was its continental European legacy unimportant, especially when continued, at second hand so to speak, through the French Revolution of 1789 and its successors in France and elsewhere in the nineteenth century, in the manner suggested by Bernard Faÿ in his classic study of *The Revolutionary Spirit in France and America*. Alexis de Tocqueville wrote in *Democracy in America* in 1835: 'I confess that in America, I saw more than America; I sought the image of democracy itself ... in order to learn what we have to fear or hope from its progress.' The inspiration of the book, which is itself a monument to the influence of the revolutionary spirit of America upon Europe (was not Tocqueville also author of *L'Ancien Régime et la Révolution?*), was 'not so much curiosity about America as concern for France especially, and for the Old World in general. America was, it seemed, merely the laboratory; the findings were designed for application abroad'.[29]

Even as late as the Russian Revolution of February 1917 some Americans at least could believe that the leaven of 1776 was still at work. As President Wilson said two months later in his message to Congress asking for a declaration of war on Germany, 'Does not every American feel that assurance has been added to our hope for the future peace of the world by the wonderful and heartening things that have been happening within the last few weeks in Russia? ... The autocracy that crowned the summit of her political structure ...

has been shaken off and the great, generous Russian people have been added in all their naive majesty and might to the forces that are fighting for freedom in the world, for justice, and for peace.'[30] The triumph of Lenin and the Bolsheviks in November abruptly changed all that. Before long the United States, along with France and Britain, was intervening in Russia against the Soviets, and Attorney General Palmer was setting, in the Red Scare of the early twenties, a pattern of near hysterical anti-Communism, which was to be repeated in an even more pronounced and frenetic manner thirty years later.

Here, in its most dramatic form, appeared a deep, and deepening, political and socio-economic chasm between the 'old' radical forces, which the Americans had in considerable degree represented in 1776 and since, and the new radical forces of Communism which, until the emergence of Mao Tse-Tung's China, became ever more closely identified with the Soviet Russian leadership. (Only in technology did a common interest seem to maintain a bridge between Russia and America, which as nations had always been conscious of a certain geo-political affinity.) The origins of this fissure, the end result of which was the super-power confrontation of the 1950s, lay deep in the rise of modern industrialism and in the impact of the writings of Marx and Engels. They had early become apparent in a small way in the relations between *America and the British Left*, to use the phrase which is the title of its historian's work.[31]

If we may use this French Revolution based, *sinister-dexter*, terminology, the English 'left' in the heyday of Gladstonian liberalism and Cobdenite radicalism looked to America for inspiration, as we have seen in the case of Bright, who with Cobden indeed came to be known in the House of Commons as 'the honourable members for the United States'. But with the extremely swift rise in the late nineteenth century, on the one hand, of *laissez faire* industrial capitalism in the United States, soon to become incomparably the world's greatest industrial power and, on the other hand, the parallel growth of the working-class, socialist, Marxist-influenced, Fabian, Labour critique of capitalism, America rapidly tended to become to many no longer a 'beacon of freedom' but the very citadel of the hated international capitalist (and later imperialist) system. British workers saw across the Atlantic 'an exacerbation of the class conflict and a deterioration of the condition of the workers, which they were determined to avert in

Britain. The power of the trusts, the brutality of the struggle between capital and labour, the damaging effects of the "speed-up"—these impressions formed the main features of the picture of American labour conditions that they had in their minds.'[32]

By this time, however, it can plausibly be argued that the ferment of the American Revolution had worked itself out, at least in the sense that it could no longer be regarded as leading the thought of the left, but this may be the point at which the left-hand, right-hand metaphor breaks down altogether. Thus 'British Liberals and Labour leaders alike expressed unbounded enthusiasm for Wilson's war aims'[33] and for the League of Nations during and after the First World War. After November 1917, in fact, the British working-class movement was schizophrenically divided between its feeling for democracy on one side and its desire for full-blooded socialism on the other: this dichotomy could now be seen as one between capitalist democratic America and autocratic Soviet Russia. In a very real sense, however, the United States, as the long-maintained consistency of her constitutional processes (themselves in part conservative at birth) suggests, still did represent adequately some aspects of her own Revolutionary traditions. It is time to examine a little more closely what those traditions were, before we assess their impact within the Anglo-American relationship.

We have observed the theoretic universalist implications inherent in the Declaration of Independence. These notions, naturally, had deep roots: they did not spring full blown from the goddess-head at the sound of the firing at Lexington in 1775. The structure of American political ideas was underpinned by English seventeenth-century history and by the works of such men as John Locke, and it was encouraged by American study of the political theories of the ancient world as well as of the contemporary Enlightenment in Europe. It is doubtful how many even of literate Americans had read Jean Jacques Rousseau's clarion call, 'L'homme est né libre, et partout il est dans les fers',[34] but it is clear that he and his European contemporaries were much moved by the American, New World, experience and especially (in his case at all events) by the concept of the supposedly Noble Savage. It is also clear that the American Revolution owed something to the intellectual stirrings in Continental Europe. It is even clearer that it in its turn had a profound influence on the events that led up to the French Revolution which broke out in the year that the American Constitution was inaugurated.

But there was the American War of Independence before there developed the fact, and the name, of the American Revolution, and it was primarily a national movement. Those—and they include some historians—who have been primarily drawn to their interest in the United States by its role as the peculiar prophet (and fulfiller, in part at least, of its own prophecies) of democracy, have often been inclined to ignore or underrate the nationalist, even chauvinist, climate of American opinion. In the theoretical liberal democratic structure of 'civilized' human society, that society is global but it is in the full sense of the term international. Government by consent may be by the consent of individuals—by counting heads instead of breaking them, by the ballot and not the bullet (to use the American apothegm)— but it also very much assumes, with true American pragmatism, that it is the consent of people in groups (God-given groups almost) and above all 'popular' national groups.

Thus, as we have noted, the actual opening words of the Declaration of Independence are, 'When in the Course of human Events, it becomes necessary for one People to dissolve the Political Bands which have connected them with another, and to assume among the Powers of the Earth, the separate and equal Station to which the Laws of Nature and of Nature's God entitle them. . . .' If, in the course of the War of Independence, radical views emphasized more and more the revolutionary universalist implications of the Americans' actions, the conservative reaction which led to the formulation and ratification of the Constitution was profoundly national in character and inspiration. If Tom Paine in *Common Sense* (1776) declared that 'Society in every state is a blessing, but government, even in its best state, is but a necessary evil; in its worst state an intolerable one', and in the *Rights of Man* (1791) was to declare 'My country is the world, and my religion is to do good',[35] the framers of the Constitution were for the most part more orthodox, even godly, men, and there was nothing universalist in the opening words of their down-to-earth national document. 'We the People of the United States, in order to form a more perfect Union, establish justice, insure domestic tranquillity, provide for the common defence, promote the general welfare, and secure the blessings of liberty to ourselves and our posterity, do ordain and establish this Constitution for the United States of America.'[36]

If there was sober idealism here, it was neither thorough-going, nor radical, nor fully democratic, nor Messianic. It was certainly rather nationalist than universalist; and indeed there has even been argument, notably at the time of the Civil War, as to whether it was truly national, whether the real allegiance of the revolutionary generation was not still to their separate States. The clear balance of historical judgement is that Lincoln had the best of the argument when he pointed out in his First Inaugural that, 'The Union is much older than the Constitution', which was framed in part for the declared object of forming 'a more perfect Union'. 'I hold', he asserted, 'that, in contemplation of universal law and of the Constitution, the Union of these States is perpetual. Perpetuity is implied, if not expressed, in the fundamental law of all national governments.'[37] The Civil War proved once and for all that the Union, the United States of America, was in every sense of the term a nation.

The liberal democratic American ethic has only been able to operate effectively, or at all, in international affairs through nation states. The titles of the great American international artifacts, the League of Nations, the Organization of American States and the United Nations, are highly significant. Our modern, in some ways anarchic, world of some 130 far from united nations is in considerable measure the result of Woodrow Wilson's concept of nationalism, and it is as well to remind ourselves that our international society, which America has done so much to bring into being, is just that, a global collection of sovereign, autonomous, nation states.

The American Revolution, however, did not merely signalize potential universal democracy and national separatism, for 1787 and 1789 put not merely a national but a conservative and propertied stamp on the upheaval precipitated by the War of Independence. The Revolution was, in Denis Brogan's striking phrase, the only revolution in history which stopped where its authors intended it to stop, and the final embodiment of this capitalist conservatism, as well as nationalism, was the Constitution. It owed as much to fear of inflation and Shays's Rebellion as to a liberal belief in self-government, and there were those in the Philadelphia Convention, like Alexander Hamilton, who deeply distrusted demos; as he himself said, 'The people are turbulent, and changing; they seldom judge or determine right'.[38] This was the strand in American development which was to do so much to make the United States an unprecedentedly effective democratic, capitalist, agrarian, commercial and ultimately industrial nation. She was indeed to follow and rapidly to surpass Britain as the world's first commercial and industrial power. This arose in considerable measure from the special economic relationship of the two peoples: as Frank Thistlethwaite has written: 'Political economists as different in outlook as John Stuart Mill, Edward Gibbon Wakefield, and Karl Marx considered the United States, along with the British colonies, to have a special connection with the United Kingdom outside the normal definition of international trade: a matter, rather, of inter-regional-relations within a single economy embracing the entire Atlantic basin.'[39]

There have been some historians who have used a stronger word than 'connection' to describe the Anglo-American relationship; Bruce M. Russett, for example, called his study of it *Community and Contention: Britain and America in the Twentieth Century*.[40] Others would regard that name as too strong for all save such an exceptional period as that of the Second World War, but, although the term has for some years now (despite its revival by President Nixon) fallen into disrepute, there has certainly been something which can be called at a number of periods since 1783—such as the second quarter of the nineteenth century and the first years of the twentieth—a special relationship.

This derived in some degree from, and was certainly illustrated by, the essentially civil-war character of some aspects of the American Revolution itself. There was always a large number of Britons favourable to the American cause, and Esmond Wright, in another essay in this volume, has validated Paul Smith's estimate that something like one-fifth of Americans sympathized with Britain. As the Elder Pitt put it to the House of Commons, in his dramatic fashion, as early as 1766, long before actual hostilities were thought of: '..., Sir, ... I have been charged with giving birth to sedition in America. ... The gentleman tells us America is obstinate; America is almost in open rebellion. I rejoice that America has resisted. Three millions of people, so dead to all feelings of liberty as voluntarily to submit to be slaves, would have been fit instruments to make slaves of the rest.'[41] The United Empire Loyalists who emigrated to Canada were a living embodiment of the internecine nature of the conflict.

The dialogue between the two sides of the Atlantic very largely broke down in the War of Independence, but it was resumed quite soon, during the decade of what Bradford Perkins has called the 'first rapprochement'. He quotes the words of Talleyrand, visiting America privately in 1795: 'America is . . . completely English, that is England still has the advantage over France in drawing from the United States all benefit that one nation can draw from the existence of another.'[42] It was not to be wholly disrupted again, even during the War of 1812: indeed, the actual diplomatic negotiations, that part of the dialogue which is often the first to be dropped, did not cease during that conflict. Waxing and waning, it has continued ever since, at all levels, diplomatic, political, economic and social.

It flourished during the second quarter of the nineteenth century, at the beginning of the twentieth century, after America's entry into the First World War, and during and for many years after the Second World War. It increasingly transcended party boundaries, so that whereas Conservatives could talk readily to Republicans, and Liberals shared many convictions with Democrats in the years before the First World War, by the Second World War the Democratic Roosevelt could be reported as saying of Winston Churchill that 'no one could have been a better ally than that old Tory'. This dialogue was possible because of fundamental agreement between the two societies on certain elemental principles to which we have referred already— national independence, the right to hold certain views of the international goals which men should pursue, self-government with its associated freedoms of thought and speech, and ultimately full democracy with a universal franchise. Even today when any form of really special diplomatic relationship is at an end, there is perhaps a wider Anglo-American exchange of ideas through all the media than at any previous time. This is even more apparent, to cite just one example, at the level of the counter-culture than at that of the establishment: the points of contact are extraordinarily numerous and variegated.

The importance of the common language in the maintenance and expansion and proliferation of the dialogue, hackneyed cliché though it is, cannot quite go without saying. It is far wider than the Anglo-American community, and it is indeed an interesting reflection that that offspring of Anglo-Saxon imperialism, the English-Speaking Union, has in fact undergone a sufficient metamorphosis to outlive the British Empire, both fact and word; it has done so simply because it has become exactly what its name implies—an association of those who speak and write the English language. Much of the hybrid vigour of the tongue has resulted from the Anglo-American interplay, and it would be hard, politically or historically, to underestimate the importance of English/American, which is the nearest thing we have to a modern lingua franca. Its role, for example, in India, where it has survived as the only near-common tongue, is far more impressive than the historic mediaeval role of Latin. In the Western world it has made possible the direct impact of the American Revolution and its political tradition on Britain.

We are possibly only just beginning to realize the full significance of languages in human history. The intermingling, the mutual influence, the stimulating effects of, among others, the English and American branches of the language have been of immense importance to each other and to mankind. C. D. Darlington has noted the parallel, if it is no more, between the breeding of human groups and their linguistic development; languages 'split into dialects as peoples split into breeding communities . . . The development of language was bound to interact with every other evolutionary development'.[43] The extreme vigour of the hybrid Anglo-American language may direct our attention to, if it is not symptomatic of (or even in part caused by), the arguably most successful nature of the gene pool constituted by the Anglo-American community. We may possibly apply to it the comment of Darlington on a much earlier era. 'Great expansions of human population were therefore likely to be expansions of people who had new abilities and new ideas . . .; in other words, to use a practical definition of a modern term, more "intelligent" people.'[44]

Darlington argues, if I understand him correctly, that there are two sides to anthropology, which is fundamentally biologically based. On the one hand, in Flinders Petrie's words, 'The rise of . . . new civilization is conditioned by an immigration of a different people . . . it arises from a mixture of two different stocks', in other words from the vigour of hybridization; on the other hand, there is the 'stagnation and frequent loss of culture' of immobile, stratified societies, with a balanced but essentially unchanging gene pool. There are opposite evolutionary risks, typified by the extremes of 'Hindu society with its well-preserved professional castes' and the Western European societies 'with their flexible classes and increasing though always limited mobility'.[45] The best hope for advance seems to lie between these 'opposite poles of inbreeding and outbreeding. With inbreeding heredity is all-powerful; determination is absolute; the group, the population, the caste or the race are invariable; they can be destroyed or removed but if they remain nothing can change them. With outbreeding heredity disintegrates; recombination produces unpredictable variability, endless innovation. Uncertainty, organized uncertainty, dominates not the organism but the population; determination in controlling the evolution is transferred to the selective power of the environment. Between these two extremes, it now appears, every species . . . is adapted to preserve some kind of balance.'[46] In a different age and in different language Frederick Jackson Turner was saying something similar when he noted that 'our early history is the study of European germs developing in an American environment', but went on to say that 'too much attention has been paid to the Germanic origins, too little to the American factors'.[47]

It may be argued that the evolution of the people of the United States, in which the American Revolution probably played a crucial, even quintessentially typical, part marked a decisive step in human development. The original British stock provided a sufficient, a just sufficient, element of stability, of inbreeding, while the virtually uncontrolled mass immigration which followed upon independence introduced a quite unprecedented degree and speed of outbreeding, and hence genetic change. The Anglo-American–European–African–Indian–Asian gene pool constituted by the socially exceedingly flexible population of the United States can plausibly be regarded as a phenomenon unprecedented in human history, as indeed the changes wrought in the world in the era of American ascendancy have been unprecedented. As *The Economist* rightly claimed on 4 January 1975, under American leadership 'the third quarter of the twentieth century . . . has been by far the most successful in history. During it real gross world product has more than trebled, so that we have added more than twice as much to annual productive power in these brief 25 years as in all previous aeons of our planet.'

Perhaps the most persistently remarked of all American characteristics has been that of energy, of hustle. As Thackeray put it long ago: 'There is some electric influence in the air and sun here which we don't experience on our side of the globe; people can't sit still . . . they must keep moving.'[48] (G. K. Chesterton put it somewhat more tartly:

> The Yankee is a dab at electricity and crime,
> He tells you how he hustles and it takes him quite a time.[49])

It does seem plausible that, at the biological level, this should in considerable part be the result of the hybrid vigour of an unprecedentedly outbreeding society. Perhaps it is not wholly fanciful to see some of America's recent troubles in East and South East Asia as the result of expecting all societies to react and behave as America has come to do, to think of the Americans as ignoring Kipling's 'epitaph drear, "A Fool lies here who tried to hustle the East" '.[50]

The act of liberation which came to be called the American Revolution reinforced this process, released further energies. The reestablishment of British authority must in some degree have had the opposite effect. Whether by one of the possible compromises mooted at the time (had there been the will and wisdom to effect it), such as Burke's foreshadowing of the later concept of the British Commonwealth or Chatham's groping towards an Anglo-American federal system, it might have proved possible to get the best of both worlds is just one of the fascinating might-have-beens of history. One suspects that the full realization of the American social, political and economic miracle needed total independence. (It is possibly no accident that Australia has really 'taken off' only in the last quarter of a century, since she began to accept immigration, especially perhaps non-British immigration, on a scale unsurpassed in relative terms even by the United States itself.)

At the very time of the Revolution Adam Smith, whose proposed solution to the problem was the interesting one of American representation in an imperial parliament at Westminster, saw clearly what had been the secret of the prosperity of the American mainland colonies. On the economic side, 'Plenty of good land, and liberty to manage their own affairs their own way, seem to be the two great causes of the prosperity of all new colonies', and on the political side 'above all, equal and impartial administration of justice which renders the rights of the meanest British subject respectable to the greatest, and which, by securing to every man the fruits of his own industry, gives the greatest and most effectual encouragement to every sort of industry'.[51] These conditions were provided in even fuller measure by the American system evolved after the Revolution. It can be contended that the organizational and human key to America's prosperity has lain in this magnificently healthy economic balance between the liberation of the individual and group energies of the people on the one hand and the preservation of just enough law, order and discipline to preserve stability on the other. It is a balance reminiscent of, perhaps related to, that between inbreeding and outbreeding in their gene pool.

But the Revolution had a more obvious and direct (if not immediate) effect on Britain than these relatively long-term cross-fertilizing effects of national self-government, democracy, immigration and capitalist commercial and industrial development. This was its effect on the development of the British Empire.

The disastrous loss of what came, significantly, to be called the First British Empire evoked two British attitudes (somewhat akin to the two American attitudes, Federalist and Republican, which were in this context to reach their tensest confrontation at the time of the Hartford Convention of 1814). The first, strongest in the opponents of the late war and influenced by the new liberal economic ideas of Adam Smith, wished for the dismantling of that protectionist mercantilist system associated with the Navigation Acts, which had been the main and longest standing aspect of the Empire, and its replacement by a basically free-trade system, in necessarily close association with the United States. The second, typified in a man like the Earl of Sheffield, hated the Americans and believed in the reassertion, in a dangerous world, of the old concepts of Empire, necessarily excluding the United States.

In the climate of mutual hostility which prevailed even during the 'first rapprochement', and which was soon to be reinvigorated by the French wars and then the War of 1812, the narrow traditional view prevailed both economically and politically and ideas of some form of

Anglo-American commercial union came to nothing. But deep beneath the surface the leaven was at work. After the catharsis of the Battle of the Quarterlies in the years following the Treaty of Ghent, the most extreme manifestations of anti-Americanism and even anglophobia began to fade, and, perhaps most important, the growth of free-trade ideas in Britain in the second quarter of the century led to a profound British rethinking of the lessons of the American Revolution and of the nature of the Second British Empire. This was the period when most Britons began to accept with equanimity the idea that colonies would inevitably fall off the imperial tree like ripe plums. Even Disraeli, in many respects the prophet of the revived imperialism of the late nineteenth century, was a Little Englander in these years.

The crucial (or at least, in the view of some younger scholars, the symbolic) turning point in this change of heart was the Durham Report of 1838, which pointed forward to the self-government of Canada in domestic affairs which was to begin in the late 1840s. (Canada always tends to be a touchstone of, as well as a mutual hostage in, the Anglo-American relationship.) The principle was soon applied to Australia and New Zealand, and became the foundation of the ultimate development a century later of the free association of independent nations which is now called The Commonwealth. Much water, it is true, was to flow under the bridge before, in the years after the Second World War, the principle was systematically and energetically applied to British colonies of every race and clime; there was, for example, a vigorous revival of imperialism in the last years of the nineteenth century. No doubt happily for Anglo-American relations as such, this coincided with a partial and temporary though very effective American bout of popular, old-fashioned, European-style, imperialist fervour, symbolized in many respects in the career of Theodore Roosevelt. But fundamentally the ultimate dissolution of the British Empire can be seen in considerable degree as the long-term result of the American Revolution. Admiral Alfred Thayer Mahan was right to say: 'Since she lost what is now the United States, Great Britain has become benevolent and beneficent to her colonies.'[52]

This is not, however, simply a case of a remote, if root, cause working its way out through history. With the exception of the era of American (mostly Republican) Imperialism, America was always there, a living embodiment of the anti-imperialist spirit. The United

States, born in revolution against the British Empire, remained the embodiment of what came to be called, in mid-twentieth century, anti-colonialism. In the invention of the Mandate system of the Versailles settlement, in the framing of the Atlantic Charter in 1941, and in the rapid, some would say helter-skelter, dissolution of the British Empire after the Second World War, many Americans behaved as an exceedingly effective anti-imperialist pressure group. The second Roosevelt was, according to his son Elliott at least, a striking example of this spirit: 'I've tried to make it clear to Winston—and the others—that, while we're allies and in it to victory by their side, they must never get the idea that we're in it just to help them to hang on to the archaic, medieval Empire ideas . . . Great Britain signed the Atlantic Charter. I hope they realize the United States Government means to make them live up to it.'[53] This feeling was in large measure bipartisan; Wendell Willkie got from British colonial administrators in the Middle East, on his 'one-world' tour, 'Rudyard Kipling, untainted even with the liberalism of Cecil Rhodes'.[54]

During the war Churchill, old-line Tory imperialist supporter of the Indian Raj, fought off what he regarded as this threat. As he said in the House of Commons, in words now plainly seen to be directed at America: 'Let me, however, make this clear, in case there should be any mistake about it in any quarter. We mean to hold our own. I have not become the King's First Minister in order to preside over the liquidation of the British Empire.'[55] He did not quite have to do so during his second administration but by the time of his successor but one, Harold Macmillan, the wind of change was quickly and boisterously blowing the world's last great strictly colonial empire almost out of existence. The process happened—and certainly happened with, relatively speaking, so little violence and bloodshed—not only because of sensible British calculations of their capacity to hold on to their colonies by force, but also, it seems fair to say, because of a now deep-seated conviction that it was right to let their peoples go.

That they believed this, was, originally, the result of reflection on the American Revolution, and on its successful application in the 'Old Commonwealth' in the nineteenth century and more recently, after dire birth pangs, on the Indian subcontinent. It was also the result of the living influence, indirect and direct, of the United States, a veritable incarnation of anti-colonialism. That the pressures exercised by America in the direction of instant self-government were not excessive, or at least not excessively effective, is perhaps demonstrated by the fact that, despite terrible disasters like Nigeria's civil war, in long historical perspective the strategic manoeuvre of withdrawal from dominion, especially in its timing, was not conducted without skill.

The tactics of withdrawal, and in some respects United Kingdom life in general, were also influenced by the model—if one may use the phrase—of conservatively revolutionary American behaviour based fundamentally on the American Revolution (and on the English seventeenth-century civil war—submerged in subsequent British experience—before it). The American political tradition has always been willing to contemplate radical new starts; not all, or indeed most, Americans have gone as far as Thomas Jefferson when he advocated remaking, root and branch, American political institutions in every generation, but, at the state level, not only were all the states except the original ones created from scratch, under only the very general auspices of the Federal government, but their constitutions are, broadly speaking, in a continuous state of renovation and, on occasions, of total overhaul and even re-creation *de novo*.

This is perhaps not surprising in a nation every member of which is an immigrant or the descendant of an immigrant, and emigration, for all the mental and material baggage an emigrant may take with him, is the quintessence of starting anew. The references in both the Declaration of Independence and the Constitution to naturalization, a wholly new concept at the time, and one flat contrary to the English belief in indefeasible allegiance, is symptomatic, and the steady and literally vital American pursuit of the doctrine's international recognition in subsequent history clearly shows its importance. This is not unconnected with the American attachment to the doctrine of social contract and to the idea of a static written constitution, compared with the British (English one might almost say) addiction to the idea of organic growth and development and to the concept of an unwritten constitution. The roots of this divergence were apparent at the time of the Revolution, and it was, indeed, very significant in its causation. It has been lessened somewhat in recent years with the development in the United States of the notion of continuing legal adaptation and development, but it has been a notable feature of the long-term influence of the Revolution in Anglo-American history.

It cannot, however, compare in importance with the issue of imperialism and anti-colonialism. One curiously related issue which has been a very substantial one is that of racial equality. For many years, centring on the second quarter of the twentieth century, Americans who attacked British colonialism were likely to receive a beam-in-thine-own-eye reply which pointed sharply to the American treatment of its own racial minorities, especially the Negro; India was set in the balance against the South. This was not wholly hypocritical in the British, for only small and mostly transient racial minorities existed in Britain and many of these were well-to-do or very wealthy, and in a curious way the English class system, if it did not easily recognize overtly the racial equality of an Indian Prince or even an African Chief, did accept them and regard them collectively as a group separated from the rest of the population by the circumstances of birth.

Historians have not perhaps sufficiently remarked that the American post-Reconstruction era, with its re-establishment of White supremacy in the Southern states around the turn of the century, coincided with the onset of European and American Imperialism in foreign affairs. Once that phase was over—betrayal, as it seemed to be, of the great principle of national independence and international equality of rights raised by the American Revolution—the people of the United States again began to see that they also appeared to be violating the even greater principle that 'all men are created equal'.

As Americans had influenced Britain over the disbandment of the Empire, so in the late 1950s and the 1960s American movements pressing for racial equality at home had a perceptible effect on the British attitude to their large-scale immigration of coloured peoples. There plainly were deep domestic factors and principles in the United Kingdom which raised the same issues, but in a number of spheres the American influence is clear, particularly those of legislation and of administrative machinery for community relations and in coloured organizations for the assertion of their civil rights. And it is not absurd to see this as a long-term effect of the American Revolution.

Abraham Lincoln has frequently, and very frequently in recent times, been accused at mildest of racial conservatism and *à outrance* of sheer racism. He said on 21 August 1858, 'I have no purpose to introduce political and social equality between the white and the black races. There is a physical difference between the two, which, in my judgment, will probably forever forbid their living together upon the footing of perfect equality; and inasmuch as it becomes a necessity that there must be a difference, I, as well as Judge Douglas, am in favor of the race to which I belong having the superior position.' But, he—even he—then went on, 'notwithstanding all this, there is no reason in the world why the negro is not entitled to all the natural rights enumerated in the Declaration of Independence—the right to life, liberty, and the pursuit of happiness.' The Declaration was indeed a heady mixture: as Lincoln, deeply conservative though he was on this issue, concluded of the Negro, 'in the right to eat the bread, without the leave of anybody else, which his own hand earns, he is my equal and the equal of Judge Douglas, and the equal of every living man'.[56] In mid-twentieth century this aspect of 'the spirit of '76' still has potent force in Anglo-American affairs.

The legacy of the American Revolution as a whole, indeed, can be held, without stretching the truth, to have been in considerable degree responsible for that community, if by no means always unity, of interest which has made the 'great rapprochement' and the subsequent alliance of the mid-twentieth century possible. As British, 'Whig', historians such as George Otto Trevelyan early saw, the lesson of the Revolution for Britain in imperial affairs, was that she should, in the last resort, never again follow the same course of refusing independence, and on the whole, in the end, she never has.

But with the rise of democracy in Britain in the second half of the nineteenth century the accord was able to go a great deal further. Some Britons, such as John Bright, warmed at the time to the now familiar though not yet corny (in truth still moving) words of Lincoln at Gettysburg in 1863: 'Fourscore and seven years ago our fathers brought forth on this continent a new nation, conceived in liberty, and dedicated to the proposition that all men are created equal. Now we are engaged in a great civil war, testing whether that nation, or any nation so conceived and so dedicated, can long endure.'[57] Far more Britons could assent to, nay enthusiastically support, the lofty idealism of Woodrow Wilson half a century later in calling upon Congress in 1917 to declare war on Germany: 'We shall fight for the things which we have always carried nearest to our hearts, for democracy, for the right of those who submit to authority to have a voice in their own

Governments, for the rights and liberties of small nations, for a universal dominion of right by such a concert of free peoples as shall bring peace and safety to all nations and make the world itself at last free.'[58]

He went on clearly to identify the source of his and so many of his countrymen's ideas when he said, 'the day has come when America is privileged to spend her blood and her might for the principles that gave her birth and happiness. . .'.[59] Lincoln made the point even more directly in Independence Hall, Philadelphia, on 22 February 1861, when he said, 'all the political sentiments I entertain have been drawn, so far as I have been able to draw them, from the sentiments which originated in and were given to the world from this hall. I have never had a feeling, politically, that did not spring from the sentiments embodied in the Declaration of Independence.'[60]

The Western world, the 'free world' to use its own phrase, of the mid-twentieth century, of which (at least for a couple of decades) the Anglo-American community was uniquely at the heart, owed its political inspiration in large degree to the American Revolution. The United States was then and is now persistently accused of imperialism by the economic determinists and hard-line socialists, deeply imbued with dialectical materialism and Marxist–Leninist belief in the dictatorship of the proletariat and the supremacy of the Communist state. Looking for its inspiration to the class struggle—in the words of the *Communist Manifesto*, 'The history of all hitherto existing society is the history of class struggles'—and to the disappearance of the nation—'In proportion as the antagonism between classes within the nation vanishes, the hostility of one nation to another will come to an end'[61]—international Communism in all its often mutually and bitterly hostile manifestations is deeply dedicated to the equal material welfare of the working class in theory, whatever its wholly different policies in practice.

The inspiration of the English-speaking world was indeed a world away from this: political liberty, the autonomy and co-operation of nations, private enterprise and property (albeit increasingly tempered by state regulation) and equality of opportunity though not of accomplishment. The testing time of the two systems is not yet over with the fading of the Cold War: many Communists indeed believe that the final crisis of capitalism is now at hand, and in 1975 it is not easy to remain convinced that this belief is necessarily wholly wrong. The malfunctioning of national and international capitalism, the widespread surge of violence, the apparent risk of losing the capacity for effective and necessary group action in the emphasis on individual desires, the difficulty in maintaining the distinction between license and liberty—these things and more put a question-mark over the future of the Anglo-American community and the Western world as a whole.

At such a time of doubt we may with benefit remind ourselves of earlier periods of doubt and of the fundamental principles of our society which have so many of their roots in 1776. As Lincoln said, on the eve of America's greatest trial as well as his own, that day in Independence Hall:

I have often pondered over the dangers which were incurred by the men who assembled here and framed and adopted that Declaration. I have pondered over the toils that were endured by the officers and soldiers of the army who achieved that independence. I have often inquired of myself what great principle or idea it was that kept this Confederacy so long together. It was not the mere matter of separation of the colonies from the motherland, but that sentiment in the Declaration of Independence which gave liberty not alone to the people of this country, but hope to all the world, for all future time. It was that which gave promise that in due time the weights would be lifted from the shoulders of all men, and that all should have an equal chance. This is the sentiment embodied in the Declaration of Independence.[62]

## NOTES

1. 'Hymn Sung at the Completion of the Battle Monument, Concord', *Complete Works of R. W. Emerson*, Vol. I (London, 1873) p. 494.
2. William Gordon, *Independence of United States*, Vol. I (published by author, 1788) Letter xii, p. 482.
3. Declaration of Independence, 1776.
4. Max Silberschmidt, *The United States and Europe, Rivals and Partners* (London, 1972) p. 14.
5. Quoted Silberschmidt, p. 15.
6. Constitution of the United States.

7. George Berkeley, Bishop of Cloyne, *On the Prospect of Planting Arts and Learning in America* (1752), Stanza 6.

8. Silberschmidt, p. 15.

9. J. P. Boyd, ed., *The Papers of Thomas Jefferson*, Vol. IX (Princeton, 1954) p. 445.

10. Quoted S. E. Morison and H. S. Commager, *The Growth of the American Republic*, Vol. I (New York, 1942) pp. 371–372.

11. Article in *The New Monthly Magazine and Literary Journal*, February 1821, quoted in J. B. McMaster, *A History of the People of the United States, from the Revolution to the Civil War*, Vol. V (New York, 1903) pp. 332–333.

12. H. C. Allen, *Great Britain and the United States: A History of Anglo-American Relations, 1783–1952* (London, 1954) pp. 26–28.

13. Allen, p. 28.

14. W. S. and E. S. Woytinsky, *World Population and Production, Trends and Outlook* (New York, 1953) pp. 392–394.

15. Quoted John Bartlett, *Familiar Quotations* (London, 1957) p. 948b.

16. *Alistair Cooke's America* (London, 1973) p. 122.

17. Letter to the Maine Whig Committee, 1856, quoted Bartlett, p. 490b.

18. *The Anglo-American Connection in the Early Nineteenth Century* (Philadelphia, 1959) p. 39.

19. Metternich's description quoted in H. Temperley, *The Foreign Policy of Canning* (London, 1925) p. 456.

20. Quoted S. F. Bemis, *John Quincy Adams and the Foundations of American Foreign Policy* (New York, 1949) p. 445.

21. Quoted F. Merk, *Albert Gallatin and the Oregon Problem: A Study in Anglo-American Diplomacy* (Cambridge, Mass., 1950) p. 21.

22. *Beacon of Freedom* (Philadelphia, 1955) pp. 1, 5.

23. Quoted R. W. Van Alstyne, 'Anglo-American Relations, 1853–7', *American Historical Review*, XLII, no. 3 (1937) p. 500.

24. Quoted G. M. Trevelyan, *The Life of John Bright* (London, 1925) pp. 307–308.

25. Quoted Harold Hyman, ed., *Heard Round The World* (New York, 1969) p. 41.

26. Quoted Hyman, p. 96.

27. Quoted R. B. Mowat, *The Diplomatic Relations of Great Britain and the United States* (London, 1925) p. 558.

28. L. M. Gelber, *The Rise of Anglo-American Friendship* (Oxford, 1938) p. 27.

29. H. S. Commager, ed. (London, 1953) p. xii.

30. Quoted George F. Kennan, *Russia and the West under Lenin and Stalin* (Boston, 1962) p. 24.
31. Henry Pelling (London, 1956).
32. Pelling, p. 107.
33. Pelling, p. 127.
34. The opening words of *Du Contrat Social* (1762).
35. Quoted Bartlett pp. 370(a), 371(a).
36. H. S. Commager, ed., *Documents of American History*, Vol. I (New York, 1958) p. 139.
37. John G. Nicolay and John Hay, *Abraham Lincoln, Complete Works*, Vol. II (New York, 1894)-p. 3.
38. Quoted H. C. Allen, *The United States of America* (London, 1964) p. 63.
39. Thistlethwaite, pp. 4-5.
40. (Cambridge, Mass., 1963.)
41. Max Beloff, ed., *The Debate on the American Revolution 1761–1783* (London, 1960) p. 100.
42. Bradford Perkins, *The First Rapprochement: England and the United States 1795–1805* (Philadelphia, 1955) p. 1.
43. *The Evolution of Man and Society* (London, 1969) pp. 36–37.
44. Darlington, p. 37.
45. Darlington, pp. 672, 677.
46. Darlington, pp. 674–675.
47. F. J. Turner, *The Frontier in American History* (New York, 1947) p. 3.
48. W. M. Thackeray, *The Virginians* (London, 1899) p. xvii.
49. *A Song of Self-Esteem*, quoted Bartlett, p. 867 (b).
50. *The Naulahka*, quoted Bartlett, p. 814 (b).
51. *The Wealth of Nations*, Vol. II (London, 1920) pp. 69, 107.
52. A. T. Mahan, *Lessons of War with Spain, and Other Articles* (London, 1900) p. 243.
53. Quoted Chester Wilmot, *The Struggle for Europe* (London, 1952) p. 634.
54. *One World* (London, 1943) p. 14.
55. Quoted R. E. Sherwood, ed., *The White House Papers of Harry L. Hopkins* (London, 1948) p. 653.
56. Nicolay and Hay, I, p. 289.
57. Nicolay and Hay, II, p. 439.
58. H. S. Commager, *Documents of American History*, Vol. II (New York, 1958) p. 312.
59. Commager, II, p. 312.
60. Nicolay and Hay, I, pp. 690–691.
61. Quoted Bartlett, p. 593 (a), 593 (b).
62. Nicolay and Hay, I, p. 691.

## 7

# Immigrants, Steamships and Governments: The Steerage Problem in Transatlantic Diplomacy, 1868-74

## MALDWYN A. JONES

The latter half of the nineteenth century was in many respects a period of growing international collaboration. Improvements in communication and transportation bound nations together more closely but at the same time created or exacerbated problems which transcended national lines. In a wide variety of fields—commerce, travel, education, public health—there was an increasing sense of interdependence and a feeling that the common interest demanded reciprocal international arrangements and uniformity of standards.[1] Some of the products of this impulse are well known: the International Red Cross, the Universal Postal Union, the International Copyright Convention, the Permanent Court of Arbitration at the Hague, the International Office of Public Health. In addition there were international conferences on a large number of other problems which all states faced but none could solve alone: the rule of the road at sea, the prime meridian, calendar reform, the white slave traffic, the control of infectious diseases, currency exchange, patent law. So numerous, indeed were the examples of intergovernmental co-operation on matters of common concern that on the eve of the First World War men were tempted to believe that the world was moving towards that ideal of peaceful unity held up in Tennyson's *Locksley Hall.*

This illusion was of course shattered by the events of 1914–18. The national antagonisms which exploded the First World War were seen to be infinitely stronger than any vague yearnings for international brotherhood. This had in fact been equally true of the preceding decades. International commerce in the nineteenth century, far from being characterized by co-operation, bore all the marks of an economic struggle between competing nation-states. So, too, did the efforts of the industrialized powers to extend their influence to the less developed parts of the world. Thus, because of the intense hostility felt by the Great Powers for one another, international co-operation tended to be confined to those spheres in which there were not only tangible mutual advantages to be gained but in which agreement could be reached without any surrender of national sovereignty.

Just how narrow were the limits within which international co-operation was possible was demonstrated by an episode which historians have almost totally ignored. This was the abortive attempt by the United States and the European maritime powers to agree on an Emigrant Ship Convention whose object was the protection of emigrant steerage passengers on the voyage across the Atlantic. The need for such protection was universally acknowledged. To be sure the 'horrors of the steerage' were sometimes exaggerated: serious outbreaks of disease were in fact rare and deaths during the crossing much fewer than might be inferred from sensational newspaper articles. Yet, even after 1870, when steamships had virtually ousted sailing vessels from the emigrant traffic the Atlantic crossing remained an ordeal. Steerage conditions were always crude and uncomfortable and they could sometimes be squalid, even scandalous. Even in the best ships the accommodation provided for emigrants was cramped, dark and ill-ventilated, the food coarse and ill-prepared and there were frequent complaints that members of the crew assaulted and abused passengers, especially females.

From 1803, when Britain adopted its first Passenger Act, most of the maritime countries of Europe passed laws designed to prevent overcrowding and to ensure that vessels carried sufficient quantities of food and water.[2] Similar measures were adopted by the United States, the first of them in 1819. But although by the 1860s successive amendments had produced more stringent and elaborate codes on both sides of the Atlantic, most of the provisions of the respective Passenger Acts were a dead letter because of the absence of adequate enforcement machinery.[3] The fact was that steerage conditions could not be effectively regulated by purely national legislation, no matter how well devised.

Enforcement had been difficult enough in the days of sail, when a large proportion of the vessels engaged in the transatlantic emigrant trade had been American. Emigrant ships flying the Stars and Stripes were immune to European law the moment they began the westward voyage, and although they were subject to American law in respect of offences committed on the high seas, a lack of summary jurisdiction, coupled with the reluctance of emigrants to remain in ports of arrival in order to give evidence, meant that offenders usually escaped punishment. But the problem became infinitely greater once the emigrant traffic was monopolized by European steamships, as happened in the 1860s. Jurisdiction over offences allegedly committed on the high seas on board, say, British vessels belonged exclusively to British courts, but that jurisdiction could not be exercised because the witnesses were in America. Yet in America there was no authority competent to enquire into complaints. The resulting dilemma was neatly summed up in 1868 as follows by T. W. C. Murdoch the chairman of the Colonial Land and Emigration Commissioners: 'where there is evidence there is no jurisdiction, and where there is jurisdiction there is no evidence, so that under present circumstances there is practically no redress for emigrants who may be ill-treated or defrauded on the voyage'.[4] International co-operation was thus a necessity if the emigrant was to be protected. For, as Murdoch went on to remark, 'nothing that can be done in the country from which the vessel sails will be effectual unless there are the means of enquiry and redress in the country in which the vessel arrives'.[5]

International regulation of the emigrant traffic had first been mooted during the heavy mid-century emigration. The unsuccessful attempt in 1850 of the British philanthropist, Vere Foster, to institute a prosecution against the ship's officers of the American sailing ship *Washington*, whom he had seen grossly ill-treating the passengers, exposed the ineffectiveness of British passenger legislation against foreign ships the moment they were clear of the land.[6] The Colonial Land and Emigration Commissioners were unable to suggest any effectual remedy for this state of affairs but, at the suggestion of its chairman, T. W. C. Murdoch, the Select Committee on the Passengers' Act recommended in 1851 that an attempt be made to secure the enactment by the American Congress of a law similar to the British Passenger Act and the appointment of officers at ports of arrival in the United States specially empowered to enforce it.[7] The Colonial Secretary in Derby's first Cabinet, Sir John Pakington, had several interviews on the subject with the American Minister to London, Abbott Lawrence, but nothing came of them.[8]

The heavy mortality from cholera on board emigrant ships in the autumn of 1853 again focused attention on the subject and in January 1854 Palmerston characteristically suggested that pressure be brought to bear upon the United States to compel its co-operation in enforcing the British Passenger Act on American ships. Since Palmerston was then at the Home Office, this was none of his business and Newcastle, the Colonial Secretary, bluntly told him to stop intermeddling. In any case the Emigration Commissioners believed that to follow Palmerston's suggestion would be dictatorial and would only result in lessening facilities for emigration.[9] All that the British Government did at this point was to ask for and obtain the co-operation of the United States in ascertaining the state of health of immigrants arriving from Europe.[10] But the Emigration Commissioners were now convinced that the only real remedy for the abuses that occurred on emigrant ships was the assimilation of the British and American Passenger Acts. The Commissioners recognized, however, that the United States would find this course difficult because the United Kingdom was by no means its only source of immigrants. The Passenger Acts of the different European countries from which emigrants sailed, they declared in April 1855, differed so widely that it would be impossible for the United States to frame an Act so general as to embrace the provisions of the several European laws. With this statement the problem of assimilation was dropped for more than a decade.[11]

Its revival in 1868 marked the opening of a diplomatic episode that was to last with hardly an interruption for six years and which was to involve Germany as well as Great Britain and the United States. What brought the subject to the fore once more was the filthy and diseased state in which two German emigrant ships from Hamburg had arrived in New York during the previous winter. They were among the few sailing ships now left in the emigrant traffic and both had suffered heavily *en route* from ship fever. The *Lord Brougham* which arrived on 6 December 1867, had lost 75 passengers out of 383 during the crossing and the *Leibnitz*, which reached New York on 15 January 1868, had lost 105 out of 544. The New York Emigration Commissioners concluded after a detailed investigation that 'the shocking mortality on board the *Leibnitz* arose from want of good ventilation, cleanliness, suitable medical care, sufficient water and wholesome food'. They therefore petitioned Congress for amendment of the existing American Passenger Act.[12]

The Treasury Department, which had responsibility for these matters, did in fact prepare a new Passenger Bill, though it was destined not to reach the statute book.[13] Meanwhile it attempted to enforce more stringently the existing Passenger Act of 1855. The result was that several British steamships were seized at New York for alleged infringements of the American law and ordered to give bonds for considerable sums—amounting in some cases to more than $100,000. These British vessels had been fitted up in accordance with the provisions of the British Passenger Act and on previous voyages to New York had not attracted the attention of the American authorities. Now, however, they were prosecuted for failing to comply with the somewhat different requirements of the American law, particularly the requirement that berths should be 24 inches wide, as opposed to the 18 inches prescribed by British regulations.[14] Sir Samuel Cunard and the representatives of the other British steamship lines protested bitterly, if somewhat disingenuously, to the British Consul at New York at 'the injustice of being subjected to the prevailing American law after having been obliged in England to fit up vessels in accordance with British law'.[15] Accordingly in March 1868 the British Minister in Washington, Edward Thornton, proposed to Seward that the British and American passenger laws should be assimilated and suggested that each country should appoint 'some practical man' to confer on the matter.[16] But Seward discouraged the idea by saying 'that the attention of Congress was so entirely engrossed by the President's [impeachment] trial that it would take no new measure into consideration' and that in the present mood of retrenchment 'anything like the appointment of a Commission involving even a small expenditure would probably be rejected'.[17]

At about the same time, however, Baron Gerolt, the Minister of the North German Confederation at Washington, suggested to Thornton that the British Government might want to consult with the Prussian Government for the purpose of combining together in some attempt at assimilating their passenger laws with that of the United States.[18] This proposal was one of a number of indications that the Germans had been shocked by the cases of the *Lord Brougham* and the *Leibnitz*.

The New York Emigration Commissioners' report on the *Leibnitz*, a copy of which had been sent to Gerolt, had complained of negligence on the part of the Hamburg authorities. Accordingly in February 1868 Bismarck appointed a commission to visit both Hamburg and Bremen to enquire into the arrangements for regulating emigration. Then, when the commission reported a month later that the regulations at both the Hanseatic towns were defective and the manner of their enforcement lax, Bismarck decided to place emigration under federal supervision. At the same time he authorized the opening of negotiations with the United States on the question of international regulations for the protection of emigrant passengers.[19]

The consequence was that a proposal which the United States had found unacceptable when made by Great Britain alone was acceded to when backed also by the Germans. In August 1868 the Secretary of the Treasury, Hugh McCulloch, instructed the head of the Steamship Inspection Bureau, Captain William M. Mew, to go to Britain and Germany to discuss with the relevant authorities the assimilation of the passenger laws of the three countries. Captain Mew found that the British and the Germans were both ready to co-operate but that the former felt that something more was needed than the mere framing of a common code of regulations. The crucial question, Murdoch insisted to him in London, was that of jurisdiction for even if the respective laws were identical legislation would to some extent be futile so long as there was no agreed enforcement procedure. Finding Murdoch's arguments convincing, Mew concluded that the best way of solving the problem would be by means of a treaty which embraced the question of jurisdiction as well as that of an assimilated code of regulations. Moving on to Berlin, Mew was gratified to learn that the Government of the North German Confederation was of the same mind. Before leaving for home Mew had reached an informal understanding with German officials about the terms of an Emigrant Ship Convention between the North German Confederation and the United States.[20]

But when a Draft Convention drawn up by the Germans on the basis of the Berlin discussion was submitted to the Treasury Department, many of its provisions were strongly opposed. McCulloch was particularly critical of Article XIX, which proposed to establish at the leading American ports Boards of Joint Commissioners which would

G

have judicial powers and which would have both American and German representatives. In notifying Gerolt of McCulloch's objections, Seward expressed his belief that the Senate would never approve a treaty which allowed foreigners to be members of a court which exercised jurisdiction in the United States.[21]

Seward's successor as Secretary of State, Hamilton Fish, was no stranger to the problem of protecting emigrants during the crossing. In 1853 he had presided over a Senate Committee which produced a lengthy report on sickness and mortality on emigrant ships.[22] Now, on examining the Draft Convention with Germany, he found that he shared McCulloch's constitutional objections and decided to refer the matter to the legal advisers of the Government. In any case he was convinced that 'no scheme could be successful which did not contemplate the co-operation of all the maritime powers'.[23] Hence, on 1 October 1869 Fish addressed a circular to the United States Ministers to Great Britain, France, Italy, the North German Confederation, Belgium, Denmark, Sweden and Holland instructing them to propose negotiations to produce uniform regulations for emigrant vessels and to establish at the principal ports of arrival in the United States what were vaguely referred to as 'international tribunals'.[24]

All the countries addressed were in due course to accept the proposal in principle, but before any of them had had time to reply Fish instructed American diplomatic representatives to submit to them as a basis for negotiation a Draft Convention acceptable to the United States. The German Draft to which McCulloch had objected earlier had sought only to assimilate the passenger laws of the North German Confederation and the United States. The document Fish circulated, however, represented an attempt 'to harmonize the various and conflicting provisions of the Passenger Acts of the United States and of the several European Powers which [had been] invited to join in the negotiations'.[25] That had involved making changes, sometimes substantial ones, in the regulations proposed by the Germans governing such matters as the passenger space allowance, the size of berths, sanitary and ventilation arrangements and the dietary scale.

But the most striking innovation contained in the American Draft lay in Article XXIII, which dealt with the composition and functions of the tribunals to be established in American ports and to be known as Emigrant Courts. The legal officers of the Government had now given it as their opinion that no court could be established in the United States with the power to impose fines and enforce them whose judges had not been appointed in the prescribed constitutional manner —that is, nominated by the President and appointed by and with the consent of the Senate—and who did not fulfil the constitutional requirement that all judicial officers shall be bound by oath or affirmation to support the Constitution. This advice confirmed Fish's belief that mixed tribunals would be unconstitutional. Hence he caused Article XXIII to be so worded as to restrict to American citizens the exercise of the judicial functions of the Emigrant Courts. The Article did, however, provide that Foreign Consuls, as the representatives of the other contracting party to the Convention, could participate along with American representatives in what Fish termed the executive or administrative functions of the Emigrant Courts, that is, in the preliminary investigation of alleged offences.

The composition and function of the proposed Emigrant Courts now became the key issue in the parallel, but separate, negotiations which the United States embarked upon with Germany and Great Britain. As might have been expected the North German Government reacted very unfavourably to the American Draft, and especially to Article XXIII. In a despatch to Gerolt the president of the chancery of the North German Confederation, Delbrück, complained that the United States had 'utterly abandoned the principle adopted as the basis of all previous negotiations', namely, that infractions of the proposed Convention committed on the high seas were to be tried by 'international tribunals'—a phrase which, as Delbrück pointed out, Fish had used in his circular of 1 October 1869. Delbrück had understood that phrase to mean mixed bodies made up of both Americans and Germans. Yet Article XXIII in the American Draft proposed to confer jurisdiction upon Emigrant Courts from which, at least in their exercise of judicial functions, 'every non-American element would be rigidly excluded'. This was not, he asserted, an arrangement which he was prepared to accept.[26]

Delbrück's views were reported to Fish at the end of January 1870 along with the more pungently expressed objections of Dr Johannes Rösing, the Consul-General of the North German Confederation at New York. Article XXIII, declared Rösing, 'took full account of American interests but none at all of ours'. The Confederation, he felt, could only contemplate such an 'unprecedented concession of juris-diction' over its vessels on the high seas if the idea of a mixed inter-national tribunal were accepted. To deprive German interests of all share in jurisdiction would only mean that 'our passenger vessels would become to a higher degree tributary than they are at present to the various customs and quarantine authorities in this port'.[27]

Fish in reply protested that the Constitution of the United States made it impossible to concede what the Germans requested. At the same time he denied that only Americans would be concerned in the work of the Emigrant Courts and sought to reassure Gerolt that since the foreign consul would be a party to any investigation of an alleged offence, he would in fact be able to influence the outcome.[28] But Gerolt was not impressed. His answer was to send Fish a lengthy extract from a report of the Bremen Chamber of Commerce.[29] The Bremeners produced a long list of objections to the regulations proposed by the Americans, especially to the dietary scale which they described as unsuited to the German palate. But their heaviest fire was reserved for Article XXIII. The proposal that the convention should be enforced by an American rather than an international Court must, they asserted, 'on no account be conceded'. The inclusion of the Consul in the preliminary enquiry would be of very little practical value.

While Fish and Gerolt were deadlocked in Washington, George Bancroft, the American Minister in Berlin, was making great efforts to overcome German misgivings. Bancroft's intimacy with Bismarck and other German leaders meant that the discussions in Berlin were conducted in a more friendly spirit than those between Fish and Gerolt. Indeed, they seemed for a time to have a better chance of success. Like Fish, Bancroft was adamant that 'the judge in an American court, on American soil, must be an American'.[30] But by March 1870, after lengthy conferences with Bismarck and Delbrück an acceptable compromise formula seemed to have been found. This provided that the powers of criminal jurisdiction to be granted to the proposed Emigrant Courts should be so distributed that, when charges were brought against foreign ships, a mixed jury or Commission should decide on the facts, while a purely American court should determine the appropriate punishment.[31]

This formula was not so very different from that which Fish had been vainly pressing on Gerolt. Hence the Secretary of State had little hesitation in accepting it. Of the two alternatives discussed at Berlin Fish preferred a mixed Commission to a mixed jury, but he was content to leave the choice to Bancroft's discretion. However, he felt that it was desirable that whatever was agreed on by Bancroft and Bismarck should also be acceptable to such other powers as were disposed to join a Convention. As a preliminary to a general negotiation in Washington, Bancroft was instructed, as soon as he had reached a firm agreement with Bismarck, to seek its endorsement by the Berlin representatives of all the European maritime powers.[32]

But agreement with the North German Confederation was further away than Fish and Bismarck had believed. Bismarck was secluded on his Pomeranian estate for much of the spring of 1870 and it was Delbrück with whom Bancroft had now to deal. He proved to be less co-operative than the Chancellor had been. Though professing himself anxious to reach agreement with the United States Delbrück prevaricated and stressed the difficulties whenever Bancroft urged him to make explicit proposals about the working of the proposed mixed commissions. When at the end of May he finally did so it was with the reservation that the revised Article XXIII he submitted should be looked upon as a basis for discussion and not as something binding him or his government. On examining the revised Article, moreover, Bancroft discovered that there was still a sizeable gulf between the American and German positions. Delbrück insisted that the proposed Emigrant Courts must render their decisions in accordance with the reports of the mixed commissions and not, as Bancroft had proposed, in accordance with the testimony. In practice that meant, as Bancroft pointed out, that 'the commissioners should be judges alike of the law and of the evidence, and that they, and not the Emigrant Court, should decide on the guilt or otherwise of the party complained of'. What was more Delbrück was firm that a division of opinion between the commissioners should have the same effect as an equal division of a jury.[33]

Delbrück's attitude showed that agreement was still as far away as ever. And before the matter could be discussed further the outbreak of the Franco–Prussian War in July 1870 brought negotiations for the moment to an end. Bismarck, Delbrück and, indeed, Bancroft now had more pressing matters to attend to and the subject of an Emigrant

Ship Convention was not to be taken up by them again for well over a year.

Meanwhile the parallel Anglo-American discussions were following a remarkably similar course. After a deadlock lasting several months there came a moment when agreement seemed within reach. Then the difficulties reappeared and, although the diplomats continued to worry at the problem, the prospects of success gradually withered. And once again it was the problem of jurisdiction that proved insoluble.

The crucial importance of that problem had been appreciated by British officials from the outset. While the Emigration Commissioners and the Board of Trade were at one in favouring the assimilation of the British and American Passenger Acts, both they and the Foreign Office anticipated that there would be great difficulty in agreeing with the Americans about the proposed tribunals.[34] These attitudes coloured the instructions given to Thornton on receipt of the American invitation of 1 October 1869 to discuss an Emigrant Ship Convention. Clarendon authorized the British Minister to enter into negotiations with the United States but since it was not clear from the invitation what precisely was being proposed he was to say that the United Kingdom Government reserved its position both as to the regulations and as to the constitution of the tribunals.[35] Doubts about American intentions were, however, to some extent removed when in December Thornton forwarded to the Foreign Office a copy of the Draft Convention under discussion between the United States and Germany. 'You will see', wrote Thornton, 'that the United States has no intention that the tribunals shall be mixed, but composed of natives.' This was a principle he would be opposed to in an Anglo-American Convention[36] and, moreover, he was certain that Parliament would never agree to Americans having exclusive jurisdiction over British ships on the high seas.[37]

In British official circles the American proposal provoked a variety of responses.[38] The Board of Trade, for example, was prepared to waive jurisdiction providing that there were safeguards against unfair proceedings, as well as against 'undue stringency' in the regulations themselves. The Law Officers of the Crown, on the other hand, were not prepared to sanction the idea of 'international tribunals', but thought that the object in view might be attained by a Convention, accompanied by British and American Acts which made reciprocal grants of jurisdiction over the ships of each country to the ordinary tribunals of the other.

Clarendon was inclined to the Law Officers' view but, before committing himself, asked Thornton in February 1870 to clarify the position regarding the constitution of the tribunals.[39] On receiving confirmation from Fish that they were to be wholly American, Thornton referred to the precedent of the mixed Slave Trade Commissions which Britain had set up with the United States, and indeed with other countries. Fish commented that he had always believed such commissions to be unconstitutional because of their composition and that their sentences, had any been passed, would not have been valid in the United States. Fish added reassuringly that the proposed Emigrant Courts would be federal tribunals and would thus be of a higher standard than state courts and free from local influences. He also stressed that the waiver of jurisdiction would be reciprocal. But, as Thornton pointed out, that was illusory because there was no emigration from the United States to Europe.[40]

Having received this clarification Clarendon instructed Thornton to state that the British Government could not consent to 'a stipulation by which the important British interests concerned to carry out emigrants to the United States would be subjected to the jurisdiction of a court, the composition of which would be foreign in its nature'. Thornton was also to point out that the French, German and Dutch governments, with all of whom the British government had been in communication, fully shared his objection.[41]

All the same Clarendon was reluctant to see the negotiations fail. Despite his sore feelings at the Senate's rejection of the Johnson–Clarendon Convention the previous year, he believed that an agreement protecting emigrants on the high seas was of such importance that a further effort ought to be made to reach it. The Foreign Secretary felt that what the situation required was that a British official conversant with emigration should go to America to confer about the intricacies of the problem. On asking the Colonial Office whether they could spare anyone he learned that Sir Clinton Murdoch, as he had now become, who had been chairman of the Colonial Land and Emigration Commissioners since 1847, was then in Canada to investigate the system of free land grants to settlers. Murdoch was therefore instructed to go to Washington to discuss the proposed Convention.[42]

Murdoch arrived in Washington on 20 May 1870 and together with Thornton had several interviews with Fish and the Assistant Secretary of State, J. C. Bancroft Davis. The discussions were almost wholly about the proposed tribunals. Murdoch suggested that three objects should be kept in view in establishing such bodies: first, they should be set in motion only by some public official; that would put a stop to the extortion 'heretofore practised by common informers'; secondly, there should be a fair representation on each tribunal of the country to which the inculpated ship belonged; and finally, the proceedings of the tribunals should be summary so as to avoid the inconvenience and expense both to shipowners and emigrants of protracted litigation. Fish and Bancroft Davis at once assented to these principles and discussion then centred upon how they might be implemented. After some further exchanges Fish proposed an arrangement very similar to that recently under discussion in Berlin between Bancroft and Delbrück. In cases of alleged violations of the Convention there should first be a preliminary enquiry as to the facts by two referees, one to be appointed by the appropriate consul, the other by the Emigrant Court. The two referees should report their conclusions to the Court, which should then 'pronounce judgment in accordance with that conclusion'.[43]

This plan was accepted in principle by Murdoch. It would, he believed, attain the three objects he had had in view and it would have advantages both for the shipowner and the emigrant. Murdoch thus left Washington confident that a satisfactory arrangement would soon be arrived at. But by the time he had reached London he had had second thoughts. The formula he had agreed with Fish, he now realized, was defective in certain respects. In particular it did not deal with the possibility that the two referees might not agree. In that case, Murdoch felt—as Delbrück had done—that the charges should be regarded as unproven.[44]

Murdoch returned, moreover, to find the powerful British steamship lobby up in arms at the prospect of an Emigrant Ship Convention with the United States. Their objections had been set forth at great length in a document submitted to the Board of Trade in February 1870 by Gray Hill, Secretary of the Liverpool-based North Atlantic Steam Traffic Conference.[45] While the Conference did not dispute that abuses had taken place on sailing vessels it claimed that they had had no parallel on steamships. The British Passenger Acts, it was asserted, had worked well, as was proved by the low death rate among emigrant passengers travelling to America by Conference steamers: in 1869 there had been only 154 deaths out of a total of 221,403 emigrants. Moreover, the proposed changes would mean converting existing steamers, at great cost to their owners, and would entail an increase in emigrant fares. Hence the proposed changes in the regulations were as undesirable as they were unnecessary. As for the proposed Emigrant Courts, these 'might exercise their powers in an arbitrary and un-satisfactory manner'.

The statement submitted by the Conference did not, however, fully reflect the strength of feeling among the Liverpool shipowners. In a private letter to the Foreign Office Gray Hill revealed that in addition to the objections set forth in the statement the Conference had other motives which they preferred not to mention in a document which might be seen by American officials. To have done so might have jeopardized the interests of British shipowners in the United States. The British steamship lines, Gray Hill claimed, had learned from experience that they were the objects of American jealousy and ill-will and suspected that the Convention had been suggested out of a desire to injure them. They had also learned from experience that justice was not impartially administered in the courts of New York. They believed indeed that 'owing to the want of principle which exists among the Government officials at New York, any authority given to them will be subject to great abuse and be used principally as an instrument of extortion'. Hence the Convention should be rejected or, if adopted, it should be shorn of all its objectionable provisions.[46]

These complaints, accompanied by a wealth of illustrative detail, were reiterated in the summer of 1870 in a series of private letters to the Foreign Office from one of the leading Liverpool steamship owners, William Inman, founder of the Inman Line. As well as impugn-ing American motives in proposing the Convention Inman contrasted Sir Edward Thornton's 'supineness' in protecting British interests from American attack with the stout defence of German interests by Baron Gerolt—a contrast which, according to Inman, could be explained by the fact that Gerolt was a shareholder in the North German Lloyd Steamship Company.[47] Faced with this barrage of criticism Lord Granville, Clarendon's successor as Foreign Secretary, replied that he had no reason to doubt American motives. But he felt it essential that their objections should be seriously weighed.[48]

Yet despite its dislike of the proposed Convention the North Atlantic Steam Traffic Conference soon modified its attitude. This was the result of the pressure exerted upon it by the Board of Trade. At a meeting in London on 11 November 1870 the Conference's representatives were told that, in the Board's view, the proposed Convention could, if suitably amended, work to the advantage of the British shipowner. By assimilating the British and American Passenger Acts, by providing for summary jurisdiction and by ensuring that the British Consul would be a member of the tribunal which was to enquire into alleged offences, the Convention would protect the British shipowner against the oppressive prosecutions of the past. Furthermore, the Board argued, it was probable that, unless such a Convention could be agreed upon, the United States would act unilaterally, adopting a Passenger Act which might press harder upon shipowners than any provisions the Convention might contain. The Board added the veiled threat that if, in response to the Conference's request, the Government decided to oppose the Convention, it would not subsequently feel itself bound to interfere to protect British shipowners against any new regulations the United States might decide to introduce. However, if the Conference accepted the Board's advice and agreed to a Convention, everything would be done to ensure that it contained no provisions harmful to the British shipowner.[49]

Confronted with such an ultimatum the Conference felt it had little option but to comply. But it proposed a long list of amendments to the regulations to be incorporated in the Convention and insisted on safeguards against frivolous and blackmailing prosecutions.[50] In January 1871 a conference was held between representatives of the shipowners, the Board of Trade and the Emigration Commission at which these matters were thrashed out. The outcome was a revised Draft Convention which, in the opinion of T. H. Farrer, the Permanent Secretary of the Board of Trade, met the views of the Emigration Commission on behalf of the public, 'without unduly favouring the shipowners'.[51] The most important changes related to the question of jurisdiction. The Board believed it was unnecessary to create the Special Courts envisaged in the Fish–Murdoch Draft Convention, but wondered whether the regular American Courts sat often enough to prevent unreasonable delay. To meet this difficulty the revised Draft proposed that jurisdiction should be entrusted to 'competent courts'. Furthermore, to prevent 'offensive and vexatious litigation', the consent of the Consul of the country to which the vessel belonged would be required before any prosecution could be instituted.

When Foreign Office officials examined the revised draft, however, they found much to object to. In the first place they insisted that a convention could not be entered into until the Merchant Shipping Code Bill, due to be considered shortly by Parliament, became law. The proposed Convention was intended to embody the emigrant ship regulations to be incorporated in the Bill; but the Convention, if agreed upon in advance of the Bill, would need alteration if the latter were amended, as it almost certainly would be, during its passage through Parliament. Secondly, there was a more fundamental objection: that it was, in the opinion of the Foreign Office, inappropriate, improper even, to bind two governments by a formal treaty to such a mass of petty detail as some of the clauses of the revised draft contained—those in Article VI, for example, which prescribed regulations about privies, water closets and cooking utensils. To include such minutiae in a formal instrument would mean that a new treaty would be required whenever it was decided to make the slightest change in the regulation. Such matters, it was argued, belonged rather in an Appendix or schedule attached to the treaty.[52]

Lord Tenterden, the Assistant Under Secretary for Foreign Affairs, felt in view of these considerations that the whole question ought to be carefully considered *ab initio* and that for the time being the draft treaty 'should be allowed to sleep'.[53] This was also the view taken by Granville. The most that could be done at the moment, thought the Foreign Secretary, would be to communicate unofficially to the United States those provisions of the Merchant Shipping Code Bill which constituted the first twenty-two articles of the Draft Convention and to ask whether those clauses would meet with American approval if subsequently incorporated in an international convention.[54]

The carping attitude of the Foreign Office and its leisurely approach to negotiation exasperated Board of Trade officials. Having with great difficulty overcome the objections of the Liverpool shipowners to the proposed Convention, they saw their hopes of an early agreement dashed by what they saw as an eleventh-hour volte-face by the Foreign Office. Farrer's irritation at the turn of events, expressed in a number of sharply worded notes to Tenterden, was not difficult to understand.[55] The Foreign Office had never before objected to the form of the proposed Convention, though it had known for more than two years that most of its clauses embodied the kind of detailed regulations now complained of. Nor could it have been easy for Farrer to understand why the Foreign Office, having first laid it down as a principle that legislation must precede negotiation, should then have insisted that Parliament could not act upon the Merchant Shipping Code Bill until the British Government had ascertained what the United States would agree to.

It is by no means clear why Granville and Tenterden suddenly cooled towards the notion of an Emigrant Ship Convention with the United States. But their change of heart coincided with the revival by the Americans of their claim for 'indirect damages' in respect of the activities of the *Alabama*, a claim which produced an angry outcry in Britain and placed Anglo-American relations under great strain for several months. With the fate of the *Alabama* arbitration in the balance the Foreign Office may well have thought it prudent to defer formal negotiations on other sensitive issues. At all events on 13 January Thornton was instructed simply to communicate informally to Fish the relevant portions of the proposed Merchant Shipping Code Bill.[56] Nothing was to be said for the time being about revising Article XXIII of the Draft Convention agreed to by Fish and Murdoch in 1870. In fact almost another year was to elapse before the British again broached what had all along been the main stumbling block in the negotiations —the character and functions of the tribunal which was to decide upon alleged breaches of the regulations.

Fish's belated reply to Thornton's overture revealed, perhaps for the first time, the full extent of the difficulty of assimilating the British and American Passenger Acts. In theory it should have been a straightforward exercise; in practice each country tended to interpret assimilation to mean the adoption of its own regulations by the other. Thus, after examining the British draft regulations, Grant's Secretary of the Treasury, George S. Boutwell, suggested that several were defective and might be improved by bringing them into line with American requirements. Among other things he wanted the width of berths and the amount of deck space per passenger increased to standards laid down in the American Passenger Act of 1855.[57]

These proposals were perhaps unexceptionable in themselves—although British shipowners were to object strongly to them. But it was strange that Boutwell did not see fit to mention that a wholesale revision of the 1855 Act was in train. Yet only a week after Fish had transmitted to Thornton the Treasury Department's suggested amendments to the proposed British regulations the President sent a special message to Congress recommending fresh legislation to protect the emigrant both during the crossing and on his arrival in the United States. Accompanying the message was a report on emigrant transportation by J. Fred Myers, a Treasury Department official, who had been sent to Europe to investigate emigration problems in the summer of 1871. After inspecting a number of steamships at the main emigrant ports Myers had reported that although he was 'inclined to exculpate all the great steamship companies from intentional brutality or neglect', he was nevertheless 'decidedly of the opinion that the present steerage system should be greatly modified or abolished'. He complained of the squalor, impropriety and discomfort resulting from the fact that groups of between twelve and twenty passengers of all ages and both sexes were accommodated in small and undivided compartments. There was an urgent need, he declared, for more space and greater privacy. In endorsing this recommendation Grant made a brief reference to the desirability of an international agreement if emigrants were to be given complete protection during the crossing. But the main emphasis of the presidential message was upon the need for fresh legislation by Congress.[58]

With the Congressional session about to end Grant's plea fell on deaf ears. But an outcry in the New York press in the autumn of 1872 against the alleged ill-treatment of emigrants on the voyage from Europe gave renewed impetus to the demand for steerage reform.[59] Thornton believed that he could see the hand of the Administration in the agitation. 'I strongly suspect', he wrote, 'that the criticism has been encouraged, if not instigated, by Fish and other members of the Administration, and its principal object was, as in almost every step that is taken here, to influence the votes of a portion of the people with reference to the Presidential election'.[60] What he meant, as he later explained, was that Grant and his advisers were trying to win

German–American and other immigrant votes for the Republican party.[61] There is no evidence that this was indeed the Administration's motive, although there is no doubt that the President's supporters were worried during the 1872 presidential campaign lest German–American hostility to Grant should be aroused by the Congressional enquiry, sponsored by Schurz and Sumner, into the sale of War Department arms to France during the Franco–Prussian War.[62] Thornton believed that the outcry in the American press was undeserved so far as British steamers were concerned. But fearing that it might result in more stringent Congressional regulation of the emigrant traffic he urged a speedy conclusion of the Emigrant Ship Convention. He was apprehensive, he told Tenterden in October 1872, that the next session of Congress would see the introduction of a new Passenger Bill, which 'may contain, either from malice against our flag or [from] ignorance, provisions which might become extremely vexatious to our shipping interests'. Would it not be better, he argued, to forestall such a measure by acceding to the American wish for a Convention? That course would give the British an opportunity 'to lead the United States into the right road' with regard to steerage regulations. And, even if the Convention were not fully accepted by Parliament, the fact that it was under negotiation would 'tend to prevent Congress from taking vexatious proceedings on the question'.[63]

Not surprisingly the British steamship lines reacted indignantly to the criticism levelled against them in the New York press. In November 1872 they issued a long and detailed statement asserting that the charges of overcrowding, ill-treatment and immorality were 'in all material points false and unfounded' and proceeded from people who had no real knowledge of the facts.[64] Murdoch shared these views. He believed, for example, that the statements of the 'Amateur Emigrant' in the *New York Tribune* were 'grossly exaggerated and in many respects untrue'. But he admitted that there was room for improvement in the carriage of emigrants and reiterated his long-held belief that the only effective protection for emigrants during the voyage was an arrangement with the United States that would allow summary prosecution before a tribunal in the port of arrival.[65]

Early in 1873 the problem became in Murdoch's view more urgent with the news that a bill regulating emigrant ships had been introduced into the House of Representatives by Congressman Owen D. Conger of Michigan.[66] Most of the provisions of the Conger Bill differed little from those of the British Passenger Act but two of its clauses were in Murdoch's opinion 'utterly inadmissible'—one which required American consuls to inspect emigrant ships in foreign ports before they sailed for the United States, another which gave United States District Courts summary jurisdiction over all offences committed at sea on emigrant ships. Murdoch believed, correctly as it turned out, that there was little chance that the Conger Bill would pass, but until agreement about steerage regulations was reached with the United States the question would 'constantly be brought up in the House of Representatives and be made a text for exaggerated and sensational declamation'. He felt it desirable, therefore, that negotiations for a Convention, the broad outlines of which had been agreed during his visit to Washington in May 1870, should be pressed to a climax.[67]

The Foreign Office had already reached the same conclusion. It felt that, with Congress evidently threatening to act unilaterally, the Emigrant Ship Convention had become an urgent necessity—not, it should be noted, in order to protect the emigrants whose welfare had first prompted the proposal but in order to safeguard the influential British shipping interest. Parliament had still made no progress with the Merchant Shipping Code Bill, whose passage the Foreign Office had earlier deemed an essential preliminary to further negotiation. Nevertheless, Granville was now prepared to make a fresh effort to reach agreement.

The revised Draft Convention approved by the Foreign Office in December 1872 for submission to the United States was a much shorter document than the draft of the year before: it contained only six Articles compared with twenty-three.[68] This was because the detailed code of regulations for emigrant ships contained in the earlier draft had now, in order to meet the views of Granville and Tenterden, been placed in a separate Annexe, consisting of twenty-seven clauses. These regulations were the product of protracted discussions between the Board of Trade and the Liverpool shipowners. The North Atlantic Steam Traffic Conference, having considered Boutwell's suggested amendments to the regulations, found nearly all of them objectionable. Some of the American proposals, such as those increasing the width of berths or providing emigrants with more space, it deemed to be unnecessary. Others, like the proposed requirement that rafts be carried on deck were held to be impracticable. Moreover, the effect of the proposed alterations, so the shipowners claimed, would be to reduce the numbers steamships could carry and thus raise fares.[69]

The Board of Trade was not as uniformly hostile as were the shipowners to Boutwell's proposed amendments. Some of them were in fact incorporated in the revised Draft of December 1872. But most of the American suggestions were rejected, as the North Atlantic Steam Traffic Conference had recommended. The Board's determination to protect British shipping interests was most clearly apparent in the Article concerning the composition and functions of the tribunal that was to decide in America upon alleged breaches of the regulations. As before, it provided that the tribunal should be a federal and not a state court and that the consent of the British Consul should be required before proceedings were instituted against British ships. The Foreign Office was equally anxious to insist upon these points. But before finally deciding to adopt the Board of Trade's suggestions— which it ultimately did—it was asked by Thornton to consider a new German proposal which Fish thought might solve the problem of jurisdiction.[70]

German–American discussions of the proposed Emigrant Ship Convention, suspended at the outbreak of the Franco–Prussian War, were not resumed until October 1871 and made little further headway for several months after that. During the interval Delbrück's position on the crucial question of jurisdiction, always somewhat unyielding, had hardened still further. As newly-appointed President of the Imperial German Chancery, he was even less disposed to cede judicial powers to the United States than he had been as President of the Chancery of the North German Confederation. His attitude now was that the deck of a German vessel on the high seas was in fact as in law German territory. Hence the revised Draft Convention which he instructed the German Minister in Washington, Kurd von Schlözer, to submit to the State Department in May 1872 contained no mention of the mixed tribunals that Gerolt and Fish had discussed earlier. Instead Delbrück proposed that persons charged with having committed offences on board emigrant ships should be surrendered to the country of which they were citizens, to be tried and punished there by its own tribunals under its own laws. Given that the emigrant traffic from Germany was monopolized by German ships, manned largely by German crews, that would mean in practice that German courts would have exclusive jurisdiction.[71]

This proposal Fish promptly rejected as unworkable and as affording no protection to emigrants. Among other objections the Secretary of State pointed out that unless the wronged emigrant or some other witness were sent back to Germany along with the alleged offender, the latter would have to be released for want of evidence.[72] Schlözer, perhaps recognizing that that was an unanswerable argument, then suggested an alternative method of proceeding. It closely resembled the plan which Bancroft and Delbrück had discussed two years before. What Schlözer proposed was a Court of preliminary enquiry to deal with cases arising under the Emigrant Ship Convention. It would consist of two Commissioners, one to be appointed by the United States, the other by the government of the country to which the ship in question belonged and who might be the Consul of that country. Any emigrant who wanted to make a complaint should do so to his Consul, who would then refer it to the Commissioners before whom both the plaintiff and the defendant would have the right to appear. After hearing evidence obtained by means of subpoenas issued by a judicial body, the Commissioners would draw up a report which would then be submitted to a United States District Court by which judgement would be passed.[73]

Fish believed Schlözer's suggestion offered a possible way out of the deadlock over jurisdiction, providing he could be satisfied as to the constitutionality of the proposed Joint Commission. Meanwhile he passed on the German plan to Thornton in order to obtain the British reaction.[74] This turned out to be unfavourable. The British Consul General at New York, E. M. Archibald, whom Thornton consulted in the matter, thought that since the two Commissioners would represent opposing interests they would be unlikely to agree. He felt, moreover, that the suggested procedure would be at variance with the usual mode of administering justice and would in practice be a good deal less summary.[75] The Board of Trade, whose opinion was also sought, raised the same objections as Archibald and in addition expressed doubts as to whether the United States would in the end find the Schlözer proposal constitutionally acceptable. In the Board's view a plan which gave an American court power only to enforce a judgement previously arrived at by a mixed commission was 'an erosion of the spirit of the Constitution'. The Board reiterated its preference for Federal Courts rather than Special Courts, but stipulated once again that if a grant of jurisdiction were made no proceedings against British vessels could be instituted without the consent of the British Consul.[76]

Accordingly it was the scheme of jurisdiction proposed by the Board of Trade that formed the basis of the revised Draft Convention which, along with the annexed Code of Regulations, Thornton was instructed on 31 December 1872 to present to the State Department.[77] On receipt of the British proposals, Fish referred them to the Treasury Department and at the end of February 1873 received a report from Boutwell which, while grudgingly leaving the door open to further negotations about the Regulations, amounted to a total rejection of the British scheme of jurisdiction. Boutwell acknowledged that some of the defects he had complained of in the original British draft of regulations had been remedied or had been 'so explained as to show that they were not of so grave a character' as he had supposed. But other defects remained and believing that such details could only be settled 'by experts commissioned to devise a system satisfactory to both governments', he believed that a prolonged correspondence would be unavailing.[78]

Boutwell went on to criticize the stipulation, contained in Article III of the proposed Convention, that no proceeding should be taken under it in any American court without the prior consent of a British Consular officer. He believed that in practice no British Consular officer would be predisposed to discover breaches of the regulations by British vessels, 'especially when by giving his consent to a prosecution he would be liable to incur the enmity of any powerful corporation engaged in the transportation of emigrants'. In Boutwell's view, therefore, the stipulation contained in Article III virtually annulled any effective penalty by which the regulations could be enforced. Finally, Boutwell expressed disinclination to comment further upon the British proposals because of a conviction 'that if any convention of the kind be entered into, it should be accepted by all the powers whose vessels transport emigrants to this country'. He suggested therefore that whatever measures might be contemplated in this direction, they should be so shaped as to secure a general concurrence and not simply that of the United Kingdom.[79]

Fish, when pressed by Thornton for a reply, chose not to divulge the whole of Boutwell's letter. Perhaps he felt that to do so would reveal the depth of the Treasury Department's lack of interest in, indeed hostility to, bilateral agreements and thus bring the negotiations with Britain to an abrupt end. Hence the Secretary of State disclosed to Thornton only that part of Boutwell's letter which referred to the appointment of experts.[80] Granville's response to this was to instruct Thornton on 21 April to invite the United States to send experts to England to assist in drawing up an agreed code of regulations.[81] It took Thornton several months, however, to get a reply to this invitation, despite repeated reminders to Fish. And when in September he finally succeeded, he found it difficult to conceal his irritation with the Secretary of State's equivocation. Fish's response to the British invitation was to say that no appropriation was available for defraying the expense of sending experts to England and, with Congress not in session, there was no early prospect of obtaining one. To avoid delay he proposed that the British send their experts instead to the United States.[82]

Fish can hardly have expected the British to be convinced by so hollow an excuse for inaction or to take seriously a counter-proposal so patently disingenuous. And in fact the British did neither. Rather did they conclude from Fish's reply that the United States was no longer prepared to negotiate seriously for an Emigrant Ship Convention. 'I regard it as absolutely hopeless', wrote Tenterden to Farrer of the Board of Trade on 6 November, 'attempting to make the United States Government send people here about Emigration and a renewal of the proposals as a waste of time; but your Department and the Shipowners can judge for themselves whether they will break off on this head'.[83]

In the event neither the Board of Trade nor the North Atlantic Steam Traffic Conference wanted the Government to break off negotiations. Both feared that if it were to do so Congress might be encouraged to pass one of a number of Passenger Bills then under consideration, all of which contained new and more stringent provisions. But both the Board of Trade and the North Atlantic Steam Traffic Conference were strongly opposed to the code of regulations being settled in America. The framing of such regulations, wrote Gray Hill, was a complicated matter which American officials at Washington did not understand. If an error were to be made even on an apparently insignificant point, it might have disastrous consequences for those engaged in the emigrant trade.[84] Farrer agreed and insisted that the only way to settle the details of the regulations was for American experts to come to England.[85]

This was the view expressed by Thornton to Fish in a rather frosty note sent on 2 December 1873. The British Government, he remarked, would have had as much justification as that of the United States in pleading lack of funds as a reason for declining to send experts across the Atlantic. But that would have been no obstacle had it been really desirable to discuss the framing of regulations in the United States. The fact was, he insisted, that such a mass of detail concerning the build, fitting and conduct of ships could only be settled in the country where they were built and owned and in concert with the owners. Furthermore, Thornton concluded, the really difficult question which still remained to be settled was that of jurisdiction and, in the opinion of the British Government, that could be better settled through ordinary diplomatic channels than by special experts.[86]

Thornton's oblique invitation to reopen the question of jurisdiction brought no response from Fish. In fact this appears to have been the last occasion on which the matter was mentioned in Anglo-American exchanges. The Germans, despairing of reaching a solution, had long since lost interest in the subject. Now Great Britain and the United States, after discussing the matter intermittently for six years, tacitly agreed that there was no likelihood of agreement. The Emigrant Court, about whose character and function there had been so much detailed discussion, was henceforth to be no more than a historical curiosity.

Nor did the proposal to assimilate the American and British Passenger Acts meet a better fate. Here again there was no formal winding up of negotiations; they spluttered on until the autumn of 1874 and then petered out. Thornton's renewed invitation to send experts to England was referred by Fish to Boutwell's successor as Secretary of the Treasury, William A. Richardson. He in turn passed it on without any recommendation to the House Committee on Appropriations which ignored it.[87] On 18 May Thornton reported that there was no prospect of Congress making an appropriation for sending experts to England, a project 'which I have so pertinaciously pressed upon Mr Fish's attention'.[88] This news did not, however, worry the Board of Trade as it might have done earlier for it was becoming increasingly clear that for reasons of domestic politics there was little immediate prospect of Congress adopting a revised Passenger Act.[89]

There the matter ended, except for a languid exchange of views in the autumn of 1874 about the Woodworth Report, a Treasury Department enquiry into steerage conditions. This Report, undertaken in compliance with a Senate resolution of 11 March 1873, demonstrated the Treasury Department's preference for national rather than international regulation of the emigrant traffic. Only one of the Department's investigators even mentioned international regulation of the emigrant traffic and he did so only to dismiss it. 'Matters of the kind in question . . .', wrote Thomas B. Sanders, referring to steerage conditions, 'instead of being adjusted by the cumbrous working of an international convention, ought to be governed more simply by regulations of the legislature, which can be altered in part, as occasion may require, without endangering the whole or making it necessary to obtain the consent of another government'.[90]

Those words may serve as an epitaph for the Emigrant Ship Convention. Looking back at the six years during which it was under discussion it is difficult to feel that there was ever a time when agreement was possible. National sentiment would always have militated strongly against any surrender of sovereignty to a powerful rival, especially in so historically sensitive an area as maritime rights. This was all the more true at a time when relations between two of the parties to the negotiations were exceptionally strained because of the *Alabama* claims and the Fenian raids. In such circumstances agreement could only have been reached had it offered the promise of mutual advantage. Yet given the fact that emigration flowed in only one direction and that all the ships involved in the emigrant traffic were owned in Europe the vital element of reciprocity was lacking. This being so, failure was inevitable. While there was genuine concern on both sides of the Atlantic for the welfare of emigrants there was an even stronger concern for national interests. Against such an obstacle the tide of benevolence was bound to beat in vain.

## NOTES

1. The growth of such a feeling in the United States in the late nineteenth century is the theme of Oscar Handlin, *One World: The Origins of an American Concept* (Oxford, 1974).

2. The Passenger Acts and other laws affecting emigration passed by the different European countries are discussed in Gustave Chandèze, *De l'intervention des Pouvoirs publics dans l'Emigration et l'Immigration au XIXᵉ siècle* (Paris, 1898).

3. For the ineffectiveness of early British legislation see Oliver MacDonagh, *A Pattern of Government Growth: The Passenger Acts and their Enforcement, 1800–1860* (London, 1961).

4. Murdoch to Elliot, 24 April 1868 (enclosure in Elliot to Hammond, 11 May 1868), F.O. 5/1453 (Public Record Office).

5. Murdoch to Elliot, 24 April 1868, F.O. 5/1453.

6. MacDonagh, *A Pattern of Government Growth*, pp. 222–224.

7. *Report of the Select Committee on the Passengers' Act, 1851*, P.P. 1851, XIX (632), p. xxxii.

8. *Fourteenth General Report of the Colonial Land and Emigration Commissioners, 1854*, P.P. 1854, XXVIII [1833] pp. 31–32.

9. H. U. Addington to Colonial Land and Emigration Commissioners, 21 January 1854; Commissioners to Addington, 28 January 1854, C.O. 384/92 (P.R.O.).

10. *Copies of two communications from Her Britannic majesty's minister to the Secretary of state, relative to the health on shipboard, of immigrants from foreign countries to the United States*, 33rd Cong., 1st sess., Senate ex. doc. no. 73.

11. *Fifteenth General Report of the Colonial Land and Emigration Commissioners, 1855*, P.P. 1854–55, XVII [1953] p. 27.

12. *Annual Report of the Commissioners of Emigration of the State of New York for the year ending December 31, 1867*, State of New York Assembly Documents, 1868, Vol IX, no. 111, pp. 5–7, 125–132.

13. *Letter from the Secretary of the Treasury, communicating . . . information in relation to existing laws regulating the carriage of passengers in steamships and other vessels*, 40th Cong., 2nd sess., Senate ex. doc. no. 47.

14. E. M. Archibald to Edward Thornton, 7 March 1868 (enclosure in Thornton to Stanley, 30 March 1868), F.O. 5/1453.

15. F. W. J. Hurst to Archibald, 3 March 1868; Cunard to Archibald, 6 March 1868 (enclosures in Thornton to Stanley, 30 March 1868), F.O. 5/1453.

16. Thornton to Stanley, 30 March 1868, F.O. 5/1453.

17. Thornton to Stanley, 30 March 1868, F.O. 5/1453.

18. Thornton to Stanley, 30 March 1868, F.O. 5/1453.

19. Heinrich von Poschinger, *Fürst Bismarck und der Bundesrat*, 5 Bde. (Stuttgart u. Leipzig, 1897) Bd. I, pp. 150–153.

20. *Report on Conferences held with the authorities of Great Britain and Germany on the subject of Emigration by Captain William M. Mew of the Treasury Department* (Washington, 1869).

21. Seward to Gerolt, 13 February 1869, Department of State, General Records, RG 59, *Notes to Foreign Legations: German States and Germany* (National Archives, Washington, D.C.).

22. *Report of the Select Committee of the Senate of the United States on the Sickness and Mortality on board Emigrant Ships*, 33rd Cong., 1st sess., Senate Rep. no. 386.

23. Fish to Gerolt, 24 January 1870, RG 59, *Notes to Foreign Legations: German States and Germany*.

24. Fish to Gerolt, 26 November 1869, RG 59, *Notes to Foreign Legations: German States and Germany*; Fish to Thornton, 27 November 1869, RG 59, *Notes to Foreign Legations: Great Britain*.

25. Fish to Bancroft, 26 November 1869, RG 59, *Diplomatic Instructions of the Department of State: Germany*.

26. Delbrück to Gerolt, 30 December 1869 (enclosure in Gerolt to Fish, 20 January 1870), RG 59, *Notes from the Legations of the German States and Germany*.

27. Gerolt to Fish, 25 January 1870, RG 59, *Notes from the Legations of the German States and Germany*.

28. Fish to Gerolt, 24 January 1870 and 9 February 1870, RG 59, *Notes to Foreign Legations: German States and Germany*.

29. *Extract from a Report of the Chamber of Commerce to the Bremen Senate on the proposed Draft Convention with the United States for the protection of emigrants, dated 16 February 1870* (enclosure in Gerolt to Fish, 26 March 1870), RG 59, *Notes from the Legislations of the German States and Germany*. For the importance of the emigrant traffic to the Bremen economy see Rolf Engelsing, *Bremen als Auswandererhafen, 1683–1880* (Bremen, 1961), especially ch. III.

30. Bancroft to Fish, no. 75, 7 March 1870, RG 59, *Despatches from United States Ministers to German States and Germany*.

31. Bancroft to Fish, no. 75, 7 March 1870, RG 59, *Despatches from United States Ministers to German States and Germany: Prussia*. Bismarck's involvement in the discussions is evident from Bismarck to Lord Augustus Loftus, 18 March 1870 (enclosure in Loftus to Clarendon, 19 March 1870), F.O. 5/1454.

32. Fish to Bancroft, 4 April 1870, RG 59, *Diplomatic Instructions . . .: Germany*.

33. Bancroft to Fish, no. 92, 27 May 1870; no. 95, 30 May 1870; no. 97, 3 June 1870, RG 59, *Despatches from United States Ministers . . .*

34. Murdoch (C.L.E.C.) to Rogers, 26 October 1869; T. H. Farrer (Board of Trade) to Under Secretary, Foreign Office, 25 August 1868; Memorandum by C. Spring Rice (Foreign Office), 3 November 1869, F.O. 5/1453. The author of the last named document was Charles Spring Rice, Under Secretary of State for Foreign Affairs, the father of Cecil A. Spring Rice, later British Ambassador to the United States.

35. Clarendon to Thornton, no. 41, Commercial, 24 December 1869, F.O. 5/1453.

36. Thornton to C. Spring Rice, 13 December 1869, F.O. 5/1453.

37. Thornton to C. Spring Rice, 3 January 1870, F.O. 5/1454.

38. Memorandum by C. Spring Rice, 3 January 1870, F.O. 5/1454.

39. Clarendon to Thornton, no. 8, Commercial, 1 February 1870, F.O. 5/1454.

40. Thornton to Clarendon, no. 9, Commercial, 19 February 1870, F.O. 5/1454. No slave ship in fact ever came before an Anglo-American Commission. See Leslie Bethell, 'The Mixed Commissions for the Suppression of the Transatlantic Slave Trade in the Nineteenth Century', *Journal of African History*, VII, no. 1 (1966) 92.

41. Clarendon to Thornton, no. 18, Commercial, 19 March 1870, F.O. 5/1454.

42. Foreign Office to Colonial Office (Draft), 18 March 1870; Murdoch to Rogers, 15 June 1870, F.O. 5/1454.

43. Thornton to Clarendon, no. 38, Commercial, 23 May 1870; Murdoch to Rogers, 15 June 1870, F.O. 5/1454.

44. Murdoch to Rogers, 15 July 1870, F.O. 5/1454.

45. *Statement of Members of the North Atlantic Steam Traffic Conference with reference to the draft of a proposed Convention between the United Kingdom and the United States* (enclosure in Gray Hill to Spring Rice, 4 March 1870), F.O. 5/1454.

46. Gray Hill to Spring Rice, Private, 4 March 1870, F.O. 5/1454. Despite their strictures on the administration of justice at New York, what the shipowners had in mind was the venality not of the courts but of the Customs officers whose duty it was to report violations of the Passenger Act to the United States District Attorney. The New York Custom House was the largest single federal office in the country and the greatest source of patronage. Congressional enquiries in 1867 and 1872 revealed that it afforded the spoilsmen unrivalled opportunities of plunder and

extortion. See Ari Hoogenboom, *Outlawing the Spoils: A History of Civil Service Reform 1865–1883* (Urbana, Ill., 1961) pp. 17–18, 101–105 and, more particularly, William J. Hartman, 'Politics and Patronage: The New York Custom House, 1852–1902', unpublished Ph.D. Dissertation, Columbia University, 1952.

47. Inman to W. H. Wylde, 23 August 1870; Inman to W. Stobart, 10 September 1870, F.O. 5/1454. Inman's feelings were summed up in the following passage: 'You say Mr Wylde thinks I am unreasonable in saying that the Yankees are trying to pay us off for the *Alabama* . . . I *repeat*, it will be the most *suicidal* act for our Government to consent to the Convention. I can . . . only feel very sorry that our Government can be so "taken in" by the Americans and here I must protect myself by saying that I am considered to be more of an American than almost any Englishman (except it be John Bright) . . .'; Inman to Stobart, 10 September 1870.

48. Foreign Office to Board of Trade (Draft), 8 November 1870, F.O. 5/1454.

49. T. H. Farrer to Secretary, N.A.S.T.C., 25 November 1870, M.9964/70; Gray Hill to Secretary, Marine Dept, Board of Trade, 4 February 1871, M.T.9/95, File M.1127/71 (P.R.O.).

50. Gray Hill to Secretary, Marine Dept, Board of Trade, 4 February 1871, M.T.9/95, File M.1127/71.

51. Farrer to Under Secretary, Foreign Office, 20 November 1871, F.O. 5/1454.

52. Memorandum by Lord Tenterden, 21 November 1871; Memorandum by J. B. Bergue, 28 November 1871, F.O. 5/1454.

53. Memorandum by Tenterden, 29 November 1871, F.O. 5/1454.

54. Granville to Board of Trade (Draft), 8 January 1872, F.O. 5/1455.

55. Farrer to Tenterden, 2, 3, 9 January 1872, F.O. 5/1455.

56. Granville to Fish, no. 1, Commercial, 13 January 1872, F.O. 5/1455.

57. Boutwell to Fish, 13 March 1872 (enclosure in Fish to Thornton, 7 May 1872), F.O. 5/1455.

58. *Message of the President of the United States recommending Legislation in relation to the transportation of immigrants to and within the United States*, 42nd Cong., 2nd sess., Senate ex. doc. no. 73.

59. Murdoch to Herbert, 2 November 1872, M.T.9/67, File M.11994/72.

60. Thornton to Tenterden, Private, 15 October 1872, F.O. 5/1455.

61. Thornton to Granville, no. 58, Commercial, 16 December 1872, F.O. 5/1455.

62. Allan Nevins, *Hamilton Fish: The Inner History of the Grant Administration* (New York, 1937) pp. 603–604.

63. Thornton to Tenterden, Private, 15 October 1872, F.O. 5/1455.
64. *Statement by the Steam-Ship Lines Engaged in the Emigration Trade to North America in reference to Recent Published Comments upon the Conduct of that Trade* (Liverpool, 1872).
65. Murdoch to Herbert, 2 November 1872, M.T.9/67, File M.11994/72.
66. Minute by Murdoch, 4 February 1873, F.O. 5/1455.
67. Minute by Murdoch, 4 February 1873, F.O. 5/1455.
68. *Draft of a Convention between Her Britannic Majesty and the United States of America for the better protection of Steerage Passengers between the British Islands and the United States, December 1872* (enclosure in Foreign Office to Thornton, no. 31, 31 December 1872), F.O. 5/1455.
69. Gray Hill to Assistant Secretary, Board of Trade, 13 August 1872, M.T.9/95, File M.8681/72.
70. Thornton to Granville, no. 57, Commercial, 8 December 1872; Farrer to Under Secretary, Foreign Office, 1 January 1873, F.O. 5/1455.
71. Schlözer to Fish, 11 May 1872, RG 59, *Notes from the Legations of the German States* . . .
72. Fish to Schlözer, 17 July 1872, RG 59, *Notes to Foreign Legations: Germany.*
73. Schlözer's proposal was described in Thornton to Granville, no. 57, Commercial, 8 December 1872, F.O. 5/1455.
74. Thornton to Granville, no. 57, Commercial, 8 December 1872, F.O. 5/1455.
75. Archibald to Granville, 17 December 1872, F.O. 5/1455.
76. Farrer to Under Secretary, Foreign Office, 1 January 1873, M.T.9/95, File M.1446/72.
77. Granville to Thornton, no. 31, Commercial, 31 December 1872, F.O. 5/1455.
78. Boutwell to Fish, 28 February 1873, *Letter from the Secretary of the Treasury . . . in relation to sending experts to England to aid in framing the necessary regulations, &c, as to emigrant-ships,* 43rd Cong., 1st sess., House misc. doc. no. 123, pp. 2–4.
79. Boutwell to Fish, 28 February 1873, *Letter from the Secretary . . . in relation to sending experts to England . . .,* pp. 2–4.
80. Fish to Thornton, 7 March 1873, F.O. 5/1455.
81. Granville to Thornton, no. 21, Commercial, 17 April 1873, F.O. 5/1455.
82. Fish to Thornton, 9 September 1873 (enclosure in Thornton to Granville, no. 39, Commercial, 15 September 1873), F.O. 5/1455.
83. Tenterden to Farrer, Private, 6 November 1873, M.T.9/95.
84. Gray Hill to Farrer, 4 November 1873, M.T.9/95, File M.16606/73.
85. Minute by Farrer, October 1873, M.T.9/95, File M.14903/73.

86. Thornton to Fish, 2 December 1873, M.T.9/95, File M.3620/73.
87. Fish to Richardson, 5 December 1873, *Letter from the Secretary . . . in relation to sending experts to England . . .*, p. 5.
88. Thornton to Derby, no. 21, Commercial, 18 May 1874, M.T.9/95, File M.6802/74.
89. Virtually all the bills introduced into Congress during Grant's administration with the object of reforming steerage conditions were the work of mid-Western Congressmen. Most contained provisions that forbade the individual states from levying head taxes on immigrants. For this reason such measures were invariably blocked by Congressmen from New York, which derived large sums from head taxes. British officials were fully aware of these sectional implications. See, for example, Murdoch's minute of 4 February 1873, F.O. 5/1455.
90. *Letter from the Secretary of the Treasury, communicating . . . information in relation to the space allotted to each steerage-passenger on board ship*, 43rd Cong., 1st sess., Senate ex. doc. no. 23, p. 86.

# 8

# Edward J. Phelps and Anglo-American Relations

## CHARLES S. CAMPBELL

Edward John Phelps was sixty-three years old when President Grover Cleveland named him United States Minister to Great Britain in 1885. He had already had a distinguished career. He graduated from Middlebury College in 1840 and then entered the Yale Law School. He began the practice of law in Middlebury, Vermont, but soon moved to Burlington, where he made his permanent home. Originally a Whig, Phelps became a Democrat following the break-up of the former party. After serving as Comptroller of the United States Treasury under President Fillmore, he became a highly successful lawyer in Vermont. He also played an important part in state politics, and in 1880 ran unsuccessfully as Democratic candidate for governor. But his career was not mainly in politics. He was appointed professor of law at Yale College in 1881 and he held that position until his death in 1900, except for his four years as Minister in London.

At the time of Phelps's appointment to London in 1885, Anglo-American relations were better than they had been for many years. Cleveland and more particularly his Secretary of State, Thomas F. Bayard, were temperamentally sympathetic to Britain and anxious to see the ties of friendship strengthened. Phelps seemed to be an excellent choice for the important post of Minister. A man of broader culture than many American diplomats of the day, with charm and social graces, and a good public speaker, the new Minister had qualities that made him welcome in Britain.[1] Although lacking diplomatic experience, he had outstanding legal qualifications; apparently Cleveland selected him for this reason. Questions seemed likely to arise between Britain and America involving interpretations of treaties and other matters of law, and the advice of an expert in the London Legation would be useful.

Despite the auspicious outlook, however, serious controversies were to arise between the two countries during the next four years, so serious that in 1888 the United States dismissed the British Minister at Washington, Lord Sackville, and early the next year Phelps left London for good, before his term had expired. New Ministers were not appointed until the Republican administration of Benjamin Harrison took office in 1889. Three major controversies caused the sharp deterioration in relations. They centred upon the North Atlantic fisheries, the Bering Sea fur seals and Lord Sackville himself. In each instance Minister Phelps reported inaccurately and gave bad advice. He thus showed himself unable to fulfil a prime duty of a diplomat: to keep his government well informed. To Phelps, consequently, must be assigned an appreciable share of the responsibility for the lamentable state of Anglo-American relations at the end of Cleveland's first administration.

The old Anglo-American dispute over the North Atlantic fisheries revived shortly after Phelps took up his new post in London. By the Treaty of Washington of 1871 American fishermen had received the right to fish in Canadian and Newfoundland waters from which they had previously been excluded, and in partial exchange Canada and Newfoundland were permitted to export their catches to the lucrative American market free of duty. But by the early 1880s American fishery interests had become convinced that they were injured more by the tariff concession than they gained from the fishing privilege. They succeeded in persuading the Government to notify London in 1883 that the fishery articles would terminate in 1885, the earliest date permissible under the 1871 treaty.[2]

After 1885 fishing rights reverted to the position set out in an older treaty, the treaty of 1818. It barred Americans from many of the inshore waters to which they had grown accustomed in recent years and barred them, too, from Canadian and Newfoundland ports except for the purposes of obtaining wood, water, shelter and repairs. The Canadians were determined to enforce these restrictions. Deprived of tariff concessions themselves, they most certainly would not allow the United States to enjoy the free use of their waters and ports.

Consequently, when the fishing season of 1886 arrived, Americans discovered that they were no longer permitted to enter Canadian ports for the valuable and long-familiar purposes of buying bait and ice, trans-shipping catches, and hiring crews, and that if caught when fishing in banned waters their vessels were liable to confiscation. The first experience with the Dominion's harsher policy came in April and May 1886, when the Canadians seized three American fishing ships. One of them, the *David J. Adams*, was held three years, until 1889, when she was condemned and sold by court order. Throughout the remainder of the season of 1886 there were numerous other incidents, though no more seizures. By the end of the year 116 American fishing vessels had been warned or detained.[3]

Minister Phelps in London viewed these developments with rising ire. A native of Vermont, he presumably had first-hand acquaintance with Canada, although he is not known to have spent much time there. Unlike Secretary Bayard, however, he had no comprehension that the Dominion had outgrown its colonial status and mentality, and that Washington and London no longer could ride roughshod over it. He did not think highly of the Canadian Government. He soon became convinced that petty colonial officials in Ottawa were aggravating the Anglo-American misunderstanding in a most irresponsible manner, and that if only London would pay them no heed a settlement could easily be reached. At a very early date he began to urge retaliation against the Dominion. The United States, he advised Bayard on 29 May 1886, might have to take 'strong and decided ground'; two weeks later he was urging that it 'take very decided and sharp ground' and 'be ready and willing to back it up'.[4] This latter recommendation came when the controversy had just started, a controversy that the United States herself had precipitated by denouncing the fishery articles. In these circumstances there was no excuse for the Minister's truculence.

In this fishery dispute—as well as in the subsequent fur-seals dispute—Phelps's despatches were frequently so belligerent as to make one suspect that he was basically anti-British. This he was not. He liked the British and enjoyed his stay in London. He was in no sense an Anglophobe. To a significant extent his disapproval of Canada was due to his belief that she stood in the way of better Anglo-American relations. His belligerent attitude stemmed from misunderstanding rather than antipathy. In both the fishery and the fur-seals controversies he laboured under a galaxy of misapprehensions: that Canada's case was without merit, that Canada herself was inconsequential, that Great Britain would welcome the United States Government jolting the Dominion into reasonableness, that the British Government was so overweening that it would not negotiate on equal terms unless first given a few sharp kicks. In addition, the Minister by temperament was not suited to be a diplomat. Petulant and sometimes impatient, he could not conform to the calm, deliberate procedures essential to good diplomacy.

In view of these defects of understanding and temperament, it is not surprising that Phelps steadily urged upon Secretary Bayard a strong stand on the fisheries. 'We must . . . give the British Government distinctly to understand that . . . reprisals will be immediately made unless peaceable redress is given'; no favourable response from London would be forthcoming unless a 'vigorous system of retaliation is commenced'; 'Whatever the President says to Congress . . . must be based on the assurance that we can obtain from Great Britain no satisfaction whatever by means of negotiation or agreement. We must enforce it, or go without it'; 'We have now really exhausted arguments.'[5]

Congress too had its advocates of retaliation, for the old feelings against Great Britain died slowly. Committees of the Senate and the House of Representatives, after investigating the fishery controversy, recommended reprisals. As a result a Retaliation Act of 3 March 1887 directed the President, at his discretion and whenever he should be satisfied that American fishermen were being unjustly treated, to deny entry into United States waters to Canadian and Newfoundland ships, and also to ban fish 'or any other product of said dominions'.[6]

Phelps probably favoured mandatory rather than discretionary retaliation, but he thought that the legislation was 'moving in the right direction' and that 'retaliatory measures that would bring Canada to reasonable terms, would not be disagreeable to the British Government'.[7] But Cleveland and Bayard heeded neither Congress nor Phelps's frequent admonitions from London. Although they did protest the interference with American shipping, they did not invoke the Retaliation Act, but instead continued to negotiate. They invited Canada's Minister of Finance, Sir Charles Tupper, to Washington for unofficial talks. Phelps became uneasy. He thought it a mistake to show friendship to the Dominion. What Great Britain wanted, he reported, was 'pressure enough put upon Canada to bring them to reasonable terms'.[8] His advice was not taken. After further discussion, Washington, London and Ottawa agreed to convene a joint British–American commission to make a comprehensive settlement of the dispute.

Phelps, who 'preferred an *ad interim* arrangement', made his customary prediction that England would 'never give a hair's breadth . . . unless compelled'.[9] Once again events proved him wrong. The joint commission, meeting in Washington in late 1887 and early 1888, drew up a treaty regulating the fisheries, which it signed in February 1888. The British members in an accompanying protocol announced the terms of a *modus vivendi* that they were prepared to put into effect for two years pending the treaty's ratification. By the terms of the *modus* American fishing vessels would be permitted, upon the purchase of annual licences, generally unrestricted use of Canadian Atlantic coast waters and Newfoundland waters; the licences would be free if the United States abolished her duties on Canadian and Newfoundland fish. Although the Senate rejected the treaty, the *modus*, which of course was not subject to legislative approval, came into force. It worked out so successfully that Great Britain kept renewing it until 1912, when London and Washington negotiated a final settlement.

In this fishery controversy one cannot say that Phelps's advice had any disastrous effect. But this was only because Cleveland and Bayard disregarded it. They adopted a policy diametrically opposed to their Minister's recommendation. Phelps urged retaliation, not negotiation. Although Congress did provide for retaliation and although this must have affected British thinking, it is clear that the settlement of 1888 resulted far more from the negotiations sponsored by Cleveland and Bayard than from the Retaliation Act. The President never invoked the act, and Great Britain manifestly did not capitulate as a result of it. She continued to support her Dominion so staunchly that the only treaty acceptable to London was quite unacceptable to the Senate. Patient diplomacy, not reprisals, led to the *modus vivendi* of 1888.

In the other two major controversies in which Minister Phelps was involved his advice, unfortunately, was not disregarded. One of these concerned the fur seals of the Bering Sea. As part of the Alaska purchase of 1867 the United States had acquired the Pribylov Islands in that sea. During the summer months these islands were the breeding ground of the enormous North Pacific herd of fur seals. In 1870 the Treasury Department had awarded a private American company a twenty-year lease granting killing rights on the islands, under carefully prescribed conditions. All went well until the 1880s, when serious competition arose from sealers, many of them Canadians, who killed the seals in non-territorial waters of the Bering Sea. After President Cleveland took office in 1885, demands became insistent that the government stop this kind of sealing (pelagic sealing, it was called): demands from the American sealing company whose profits seemed endangered, from the Treasury Department which feared declining revenue paid by its lessee, and from naturalists who envisaged the destruction of the great herd. Almost coincidentally with the Canadian seizures of American fishing vessels in Canadian territorial waters of the North Atlantic, the United States began in 1886 to arrest Canadian sealing ships in the open waters—well outside the territorial waters— of the Bering Sea. Further arrests occurred in 1887. Great Britain denounced them as contrary to international law, which indeed they were. The United States defended them as necessary to save the herd from extinction, which they may have been. Soon the American Minister at the Court of St James found himself busy with another explosive Anglo-American controversy.

Common sense pointed to an obvious solution. If only the nations concerned would agree to limit the slaughter of seals at sea, as well as on land, sufficiently to ensure the herd's preservation, they could continue sealing in both areas—in the Bering Sea and on the Pribylov Islands. Acting under instructions from Secretary Bayard, Phelps in late 1887 suggested to Prime Minister Salisbury that regulations be drawn up. The Prime Minister, he reported to Bayard, 'promptly acquiesced' and asked for specific proposals. Then on 22 February 1888, having received new instructions from Washington, Phelps at a meeting with Lord Salisbury made a formal offer of regulations that would ban pelagic sealing in the Bering Sea between 15 April and 1 November and between 160 degrees longitude west and 170 degrees longitude east. After the meeting he wrote Bayard optimistically on 25 February that Salisbury 'assents to your proposition'.[10]

A significantly different account of the interview, however, was given by the Prime Minister. He wrote Minister Sackville in Washington

H

that 'I expressed to Mr. Phelps the entire readiness of Her Majesty's Government to join in an Agreement with . . . the United States to establish a close time for seal-fishing north of *some latitude to be fixed*.'[11] If the area to which the agreement was to apply was as yet unknown, it was manifestly incorrect to depict Lord Salisbury as having accepted the American proposal.

As between the two versions of the interview, one must accept the Prime Minister's as closer to the truth. The fact that he wrote to Sackville on the very day of Phelps's visit, whereas Phelps's account was dated and presumably written three days later, favours Salisbury's version. Salisbury later observed that it was not surprising that Phelps, reporting three days afterward an interview at which no notes were taken, 'slightly misconceived' what had occurred.[12] Moreover, it is impossible to believe that the Prime Minister, whose career was marked by caution and deliberation, would have committed himself to the American offer before consulting his colleagues in London and also officials in the Dominion of Canada. Throughout his life Salisbury was a scrupulously accurate reporter; the same cannot be said of Minister Phelps.

Phelps left London in early April 1888, and was away until 22 June. On returning he discovered that no progress towards an agreement on the fur seals had been made. The British Government was waiting to hear from Ottawa. Disappointed, the Minister wrote Salisbury urging 'immediate action', and on 13 August he had a long discussion with him at the Foreign Office. But by that time Canada had come out in firm opposition to a treaty limiting sealing at sea but not on land, and Salisbury warned his visitor not to expect an early settlement.[13]

Phelps perceived, as was obvious enough, that Canada was behind the Prime Minister's hesitation; and, with this additional reason for thinking ill of her, he exploded with two highly injudicious communications to the State Department in Washington. Great Britain, he wrote Bayard, would not make a treaty without Canada's consent, and such consent was unlikely. The United States, consequently, had two possible courses: do nothing, and contemplate the inevitable extinction of the seal herd; or prevent that melancholy outcome by capturing the ships of the pelagic sealers. Phelps had no doubt as to which course was preferable. 'I earnestly recommend, therefore [he wrote], that the vessels that have been already seized while engaged in this business be firmly held, and that measures be taken to capture and hold every one hereafter found concerned in it. If further legislation is necessary, it can doubtless be readily obtained. There need be no fear that a resolute stand on this subject will at once put an end to the mischief complained of. It is not to be reasonably expected that Great Britain will either encourage or sustain her colonies in conduct which she herself concedes to be wrong and which is detrimental to her own interests as well as to ours.'[14] He followed this despatch with a private letter to the Secretary: 'You may be sure that England will not back up Canada in this business. . . . I have no doubt it would be satisfactory to the British Government to have us put a stop to it. . . . We *must* show Canada that she cannot outrage us with impunity. And the moment we take a firm stand, all the trouble will cease. That is the surest way to avoid difficulty. *And you may be sure it will be satisfactory to the present British Government. . . .*'[15]

The chances are strong that Cleveland, had he stayed in office, would not have acted on Phelps's recommendation; after all, he had not followed the Minister's advice in the fishery dispute; and it is noteworthy, too, that in 1888 he and Bayard refused to sanction arrests of Canadian sealing vessels—and consequently no arrests occurred that year. But only a few months remained before his term expired, and after March 1889 it fell to his successor, President Benjamin Harrison, and the latter's first Secretary of State, James G. Blaine, to decide on policy in regard to sealing in the Bering Sea. The decision of Harrison and Blaine was to revert to the seizure policy of 1886 and 1887. To the fury of Ottawa, United States revenue cutters arrested four Canadian sealing vessels outside territorial waters in 1889. Documentary evidence is lacking, but one may be confident that Minister Phelps was partly responsible for the new seizures. Although he had terminated his mission and left Great Britain at the beginning of February 1889, his despatches to the State Department were the most recent available, and it would be remarkable if Secretary Blaine had not consulted them. Particularly is this so in view of Blaine's—and President Harrison's—respect for Phelps, whom they were soon to recall to public service in connection with the fur-seals dispute. Presumably Blaine was reassured by Phelps's categorical assurance that London would not oppose a 'firm stand'; and the policy adopted by the new administration was precisely the one urged by the former Minister.

But if the new President and his Secretary of State expected their action to be welcome to Great Britain, they were speedily undeceived. Instead of acquiescing as envisaged by Phelps, the British Government supported Canada, even to the extent of preparing to use force. Not only did Britain vigorously protest the seizures of 1889, but she ordered four warships to enter the Bering Sea should the United States arrest British sealers the following year. An alarming crisis developed. It ended only when the United States, bowing to the British threat, rescinded an order to make arrests in 1890.[16]

Phelps's inaccurate reporting over the fur seals had another unhappy consequence. Looking through material in the State Department archives, Blaine in 1890 happened to find the despatch of 25 February 1888 in which Phelps erroneously depicted Lord Salisbury as having accepted America's proposed limitation of pelagic sealing. Blaine apparently thought he had discovered some valuable evidence. Calling Phelps—the exaggerated rhetoric was characteristic of the Secretary— a man well known to be 'accurate in the use of words, and discriminating in the statement of facts', the Secretary on two occasions and in blunt terms formally accused Prime Minister Salisbury of having backed down on what Blaine described to Harrison as the 'explicit agreement of Feby 25'.[17] Salisbury rejected Blaine's aspersions in his customarily dignified language, but he would have been more than human if the charge of bad faith, advanced on the strength of Phelps's report, did not harden his attitude.[18] Despite the strained atmosphere, however, the two countries concluded a *modus vivendi* in 1891 that limited the killing of seals on land and at sea. A British–American arbitration tribunal in Paris in 1893 (Phelps was one of the American counsel at the arbitration) imposed more comprehensive regulations, but not until 1911 was a convention concluded which gave the seals sufficient protection for survival.

The dismissal, on 30 October 1888, by the United States Government of the British Minister at Washington, Lord Sackville, gave rise to the last of the three major controversies with Great Britain during Phelps's service in London. On the eve of the presidential election of that year Sackville, in response to a letter from a person claiming to be a former Englishman but now a naturalized American, asking advice on how to vote, most unwisely suggested that his correspondent support Cleveland. The Minister's foolish letter was handed to the press. On its publication an outcry arose across the United States. The apparent evidence that Great Britain favoured Cleveland was quite enough to cause the important Irish–American vote to swing over to Harrison; and horrified Democratic politicians hastened to put pressure on the President to try to repair the damage by dismissing the blundering diplomat quickly, before the election was irretrievably lost.

In this delicate situation Phelps gave Washington most unfortunate advice. His assessment of the probable reaction of the British Government and press in the event of Sackville's dismissal proved completely wrong. He spent the night of Saturday, 27 October 1888, at Hatfield House as a guest of Lord Salisbury. He had just received two telegrams from Secretary Bayard, the first instructing him to notify Salisbury that the United States 'confidently relies upon disapproval action of British Minister', the second stating that Sackville's 'usefulness here has ended' and that 'no time should be lost in letting Lord Salisbury understand the necessity of immediate action'.[19] During a long talk in the evening, Phelps, interpreting these telegrams freely, told the Prime Minister that the United States was requesting Great Britain to recall Sackville. The Prime Minister refused to comply, without more information about the offences charged to the British envoy.[20] Phelps thereupon telegraphed Bayard on 28 October, that 'He [Salisbury] intimated that you can send him [Sackville] away for which there are precedents. Says a recall by British Government would terminate Minister's career. Not necessarily so if dismissed by the Government of the United States. Am satisfied that long delay will occur and no decisive action at last if recourse to British Government is relied on. If you deem the case to require effectual action, I advise that you act upon the hint of Secretary of State for Foreign Affairs [Salisbury was also the Foreign Secretary] and terminate matters at once.'[21]

Did Phelps correctly portray Lord Salisbury's state of mind? It seems certain that he did not. The day after his discussion with Phelps, the Prime Minister telegraphed Queen Victoria that 'I deferred any answer to his request [for Sackville's recall] until we had seen the language imputed to the Minister'.[22] Nothing in this confidential communication indicates that Salisbury had 'intimated' or given a 'hint' that he would not oppose Sackville's dismissal. Later, after the dismissal had occurred, he rebuffed the American Government in fairly strong language: 'It is sufficient under existing circumstances', he wrote Minister Phelps, 'to say that there was nothing in Lord Sackville's conduct to justify so striking a departure from the circumspect and deliberate procedure by which in such cases it is the usage of friendly States to mark their consideration for each other.'[23] But perhaps the best evidence of Phelps's inaccuracy is that he himself came to entertain doubts about his own telegram. After some reflection he confessed to Secretary Bayard that 'I inferred . . . that the British Government would prefer that action should be taken, if at all, by the Government of the United States. It is proper, however, to add that this inference was based only upon the remark above quoted [a remark attributed by Phelps to Salisbury "that a recall by his own Government would be ruinous to Lord Sackville, whereas such a result would not necessarily follow if he was dismissed"], and though I believe it to be correct, was not justified by any more direct expression of Lord Salisbury.'[24] With only this inference to support his characterization of Salisbury's wishes, the Minister had acted imprudently indeed.

In the same incautious telegram of 28 October Phelps made another blunder. He declared to Bayard, 'The tone of English Press sustains you in so doing', that is, in dismissing Sackville. And back at his desk the next day, after the weekend at Hatfield, he repeated the statement: 'All the London papers this morning agree that British Minister must leave. You need not hesitate to act.'[25] The London press that day did agree that Sackville had been indiscreet and that he could not continue in Washington. It did not agree that the United States should dismiss him. The *Times* and the *Daily News* thought that he should be recalled, and the *Standard* that he should resign.[26]

Phelps also erred, oddly enough, about a point of law. He had been appointed because of his legal knowledge, and Secretary Bayard must have waited anxiously for his opinion on a moot point. Was Great Britain obligated to recall her Minister on mere request by the United States? If so, Washington was entitled to dismiss him after Salisbury refused to act without further evidence. Phelps's opinion was reassuring: 'Whatever the reason, and even without giving reasons a Government may ask the withdrawal of an unacceptable minister. He should be therefore at once recalled. . . . I think Lord Salisbury made a mistake in hesitating, and thus gave you a valid ground on which to take action yourself [to dismiss Sackville, that is]. Nor do I think this will ever be controverted. . . . You will doubtless agree with me, that the only way to get rid of Sackville reasonably, was promptly and directly to ask his recall, giving the general reasons and leaving the details to follow. And if compliance was delayed, to dismiss him.'[27] Unfortunately the Minister's opinion has not been supported by authorities on international law. Those who have studied Sackville's dismissal agree that no obligation to recall on request existed in 1888 or any other time. The Minister's prediction that the legality of Washington's action would never 'be controverted' has proven singularly mistaken.[28] Since Phelps's opinion was not rendered until after the dismissal, however, it did no damage except that it must have encouraged Bayard in attempts he made to convince the British that Washington had acted commendably. Further irritation, not conviction, resulted in London.

Far more harmful were Phelps's reports, made before the event, that the Prime Minister and the London press would support, perhaps welcome, Sackville's dismissal. Political exigencies in the United States in late 1888 called for a decisive step, and it may be that Cleveland would have demanded dismissal whether Phelps's assurances had been available or not. But if the Administration had not been so thoroughly misled, it might have followed a different course. Bayard was a man of high principles; he was an admirer of Great Britain and anxious for good relations. If he had been correctly informed by his Minister, he might well have opposed so drastic a move as dismissal. And Cleveland, however acute his political sense, was a stubborn, courageous person. Even the President might have stood against the clamour of the politicians and prevented an act that has tarnished his reputation and that of the United States.

In 1891 Phelps published an article on the fur-seals dispute.[29] A private comment on it by John Bassett Moore, the eminent authority on international law and Third Assistant Secretary of State under Secretary Bayard, is worth quoting because Moore is enlightening both about Sackville's dismissal and also about Phelps's whole career as a diplomat. It was not surprising, Moore wrote former Secretary Bayard, 'that you rubbed your eyes when you read Mr. Phelps's article on the seal question. I only regret that no one who is competent to deal with this argument seems to be in a position to do so. It is amazing that Mr. Phelps should assert as principles of international law theories which Macaulay's "schoolboy" ought to know to be erroneous. Quite as unfounded is his notion that Great Britain would like us to do what he advises. You have an example of the value of his views as to Great Britain's wishes, in the Sackville case. You doubtless remember that he advised you to act on Lord Salisbury's "suggestion" & send Sackville away. . . . his Lordship . . . seems not to have relished it very greatly. . . .'[30] As Moore implied, Phelps's judgement was occasionally poor indeed. In the Sackville affair that defect contributed to a deplorable outcome.

To catalogue Phelps's blunders in the three Anglo-American controversies that he helped to negotiate may give the impression that he was a hopelessly stupid, cantankerous man. On the contrary, he was an able person who in other public careers would probably have served with distinction. President Cleveland in 1888 considered naming him Chief Justice of the United States. In 1890 and again in 1892 Phelps ran unsuccessfully for the United States Senate. He might have been an outstanding Senator had he won either election, though one wonders if he was not too impetuous to be a good judge. Many of his despatches replete with sound information are in the State Department's archives, laboriously penned in his stiff, backward-sloping writing. Always he was diligent and conscientious. He was popular with the British public. When he returned to the United States in 1889, the London correspondent of the New York *Tribune* wrote that 'the English know him [fortunately they did not know his recommendations to Washington], respect him, and admire him as one of the most American of Americans'.[31]

It remains true that Phelps lacked the essential qualities of a diplomat. He was far too impatient with the slow processes of diplomacy, too prone to express himself unequivocally without evidence. He was unsuited particularly for a post in London because of his scorn for Canada. Partly because of his weaknesses Anglo-American relations became needlessly strained. The career of Edward J. Phelps as Minister to the Court of St James's provides an excellent example of the perennial danger of appointing to high diplomatic office a man of ability but without suitable temperament or adequate experience.

## NOTES

1. *Nation*, XLVI (1888) 333–334. For general information concerning American and British foreign policies while Phelps was Minister see John A. S. Grenville and George B. Young, *Politics, Strategy, and American Diplomacy, Studies in Foreign Policy, 1873–1917* (New Haven, 1966) ch. 2; Kenneth Bourne, *The Foreign Policy of Victorian England, 1830–1902* (Oxford, 1970) ch. 5; Charles S. Campbell, *From Revolution to Rapprochement: The United States and Great Britain, 1783–1900* (New York, 1974) chs. XI and XII.

2. *Congressional Record*, 47th Cong., 2nd sess., pp. 1041–42 (10 January 1883); pp. 3055–56 (21 February 1883); p. 3298 (26 February 1883).

3. *Senate Reports*, 49th Cong., 2nd sess., no. 1683 (Serial 2456) p. xi; Lansdowne to Colonial Office, 11 May 1886, Public Record Office (London), Foreign Office 5/1966; *Senate Executive Documents*, 49th Cong., 2nd sess., no. 55 (Serial 2448); *Senate Miscellaneous Documents*, 49th Cong., 2nd sess., no. 54 (Serial 2451).

4. Phelps to Bayard, 29 May, 15 June 1886, Charles C. Tansill, *The Foreign Policy of Thomas F. Bayard, 1885–1897* (New York, 1940) pp. 221, 230.

5. Phelps to Bayard, 20 July, 13 September 1886, Tansill, *Bayard*, pp. 235, 245; Phelps to Bayard, 20 November, 3 December 1886, Papers of Thomas F. Bayard, Library of Congress (Washington).

6. *Congressional Record*, 49th Cong., 2nd sess., p. 929 (24 January 1887).

7. Phelps to Bayard, 25 January 1887, Tansill, *Bayard*, p. 252; Phelps to Bayard, 5 February 1887, Bayard Papers.

8. Phelps to Bayard, 11 June 1887, Tansill, *Bayard*, p. 267.

9. Bayard to James B. Angell, 29 October 1887, Tansill, *Bayard*, p. 279.

10. Bayard to Phelps, 19 August 1887, *Fur-Seal Arbitration . . .*, II, *Appendix to the Case of the United States* (Washington, 1892), I, 168–169; Phelps to Bayard, 12 November 1887, ibid., p. 171; Bayard to Phelps, 7 February 1888, ibid., p. 173; Phelps to Bayard, 25 February 1888, ibid., p. 175.

11. Salisbury to Sir Lionel Sackville West (as Lord Sackville then was), 22 February 1888, Great Britain, Foreign Office, *Blue Book, United States, No. 2 (1890): Correspondence Respecting the Behring Sea Seal Fisheries, 1886–1890* (London, 1890) p. 182. Italics inserted.

12. Salisbury to Phelps, 22 October 1890, Foreign Office 5/2111.

13. Phelps to Salisbury, 28 July 1888, *Blue Book, United States, No. 2 (1890)* p. 209; Salisbury to Sackville West, 3 September 1888, ibid.,

p. 220; Phelps to Bayard, 12 September 1888, *Papers Relating to the Foreign Relations of the United States, 1891* (Washington, 1892) p. 530.

14. Phelps to Bayard, 12 September 1888, *Foreign Relations, 1891*, p. 531.

15. Phelps to Bayard, 12 September 1888, Tansill, *Bayard*, p. 476.

16. Charles S. Campbell, 'The Anglo-American Crisis in the Bering Sea, 1890–1891', *Mississippi Valley Historical Review*, XLVIII (1961) 393–414.

17. Blaine to Sir Julian Pauncefote (British Minister to the United States), 19 July 1890, *Fur-Seal Arbitration*, II, *Appendix to the Case of the United States*, I, 240; Blaine to Pauncefote, 29 May, 19 July 1890, ibid., pp. 213–217, 240–242; Blaine to Harrison, 19 July 1890, Albert T. Volwiler, ed., *The Correspondence Between Benjamin Harrison and James G. Blaine, 1882–1893* (Philadelphia, 1940) pp. 109–110.

18. Salisbury to Phelps, 22 October 1890, Foreign Office 5/2111.

19. Bayard to Phelps, 25, 26 October 1888, Instructions, Great Britain, Department of State Records, National Archives (Washington).

20. Salisbury to Sackville, 27 October 1888, Foreign Office 5/2031; Phelps to Bayard, 28 October 1888, Bayard Papers.

21. Phelps to Bayard, 28 October 1888, Bayard Papers.

22. Salisbury to the Queen, 28 October 1888, George E. Buckle, ed., *The Letters of Queen Victoria, Third Series* (3 Vols, New York, 1930–32), I, p. 444.

23. Salisbury to Phelps, 24 December 1888, Foreign Office 5/2031.

24. Phelps to Bayard, 2 November 1888, *House Executive Documents*, 50th Cong., 2nd sess., no. 150 (Serial 2652) p. 11.

25. Phelps to Bayard, 29 October 1888, Bayard Papers.

26. The *Times*, *Daily News*, and *Standard* (all of London), 29 October 1888. The *Daily Telegraph* (London), 29 October 1888, did seem to favour Sackville's dismissal by the United States rather than his recall by Britain.

27. Phelps to Bayard, 10 November 1888, Bayard Papers.

28. Charles S. Campbell, 'The Dismissal of Lord Sackville', *Mississippi Valley Historical Review*, XLIV (1958) 644–645.

29. Edward J. Phelps, 'The Behring Sea Controversy', *Harper's New Monthly Magazine*, LXXXII (1891) 766–774.

30. Moore to Bayard, 29 March 1891, Bayard Papers.

31. *Nation*, XLVIII (1889) 107.

## 9

# Trusts and Tycoons: British Myth and American Reality

### VIVIAN VALE

Let us begin with a happy ending.

The scene is Buckingham Palace, very early in a morning of 1901. Upon the great lawn there descends from the sky a remarkable aerial machine and from it emerge a small but richly assorted group: the President and Vice-President of the United States; the German Kaiser and his aide-de-camp; our young hero and pilot, an 18-year-old engineer from Colorado; his fiancée, daughter of the Marquis of Romsey; and his sponsor, a Mid-western millionaire. Having refreshed themselves—for Edward VII, we infer, has no qualms about a 6 a.m. breakfast—the party get down to business. They draft, and the three heads of government then sign, an international proclamation forthwith abolishing all trusts, combines and corners 'upon pain of confiscation', and declaring free trade to be universally established. As earnest of their reforming zeal they announce an immediate gold blockade of Imperial Russia. A good morning's work thus completed, the reformers disperse. Our hero and his betrothed head for a 'private but none the less splendid' ceremony at St George's Chapel, Windsor; and the rest of the world presumably settles back into whatever it was doing before trusts were invented.

So bald an account does scant justice to a novel's grand finale. Merely fanciful (by the Coleridgean distinction) it may be: yet this antitrust polemic, entitled *The Lake of Gold*,[1] has certain features which should earn it a reprieve from total oblivion. First, at a juncture (1903) when American antitrust novels abounded, this one is a rare British specimen. Its author called himself Griffith but his real name was Jones. Secondly, it is, like one or two other portions of the Griffith/Jones *oeuvre*, a period piece of science fiction, as the barest résumé will show.

Six months of unremitting toil at the bottom of a disused Colorado mineshaft suffice the young mechanical genius to fashion his aircraft. Borne upon two hundred anti-gravitational fans of toughened glass, and powered by a critical blend of petroleum and coal-dust, it rises, hovers, and then moves rapidly southward to the coast of Chile, where this volcanic lake of gold is sighted. The same impressive mode of propulsion is later adapted to a submarine or two; and then to an ocean liner, whose maiden voyage is an eastward crossing of the Atlantic in rivalry with the pride of the Hamburg–Amerika line. Our magic vessel gives the s.s. *Deutschland* four days' start from the Ambrose Channel light and then overhauls her handily somewhere off Fastnet.

Thirdly, *The Lake of Gold* is a highly moral tract. The deutero-Jones was not anti-American, but he was anti-Bad American. The forces of good are personified by the Mid-western millionaire who finds the $200,000 needed for the flying machine. He stands for truly popular enterprise, and his political views (as we read them) roughly anticipate the Progressive platform of 1912. He and his protégé would apply their new technology wholly to virtuous ends. The lake of gold is excavated, its contents minted and then freely unloaded upon the American market. They prove more than sufficient to clear the mortgage off every farm in the United States. Trusts totter, while tariffs (explains the author) 'automatically abolished themselves because no-one wanted the gold in which the duties had ultimately to be paid'. Beneficial spin-offs are by no means ignored, and it is pleasant to record that Edward VII gets a donation of $5 million towards his hospital fund. In the opposite scale wickedness, too, is personified by an American millionaire: but how different, for he is the sinister head of the U.S. Steel & Iron Corporation. To defend this vast property he relies, not upon substantive due process, but upon a beauteous and evil daughter. She seduces—within the strict limits of contemporary literary convention—a spy in the pay of Russia, whose government shows up pretty badly, and he in turn corrupts the maintenance crew of the marvellous aircraft. It is stolen. And how the ensuing conflict ranges around the globe we must leave to the curious reader to find out.

But perhaps the most durably important feature of this extravaganza is the view it implies of trustification as something which has by now, the first years of the new century, passed beyond ordinary human resources to control or counteract. A homogenized concept of 'the trust' is being projected on to an almost universal plane. The author does not trifle with us by making any nice distinctions between types of industrial consolidation—between the earliest and simplest pooling system resting on a gentleman's agreement among participants, and the trust proper; or between the latter and the device of the holding company which, being less vulnerable at law, had by 1900 largely superseded it. The evil is seen as a generalized one, the struggle against it as virtually cosmic; and such is the adversary's power that victory can be wrested from him only by calling in quasi-supernatural aid— the magic machine, the inexhaustible mineral.

Whatever had the American trusts been doing to earn so sensationally bad an image in the eyes of Europeans, and specifically of the British? The turn of the century, after all, is not implausibly represented in history books as an era of strong even vociferous Anglo-American goodwill, of initiative in many fields, from cultural to diplomatic, for entente between the so-called two great branches of the Anglo-Saxon race now that both were imperial powers. How deep this *rapprochement* really went remains debatable. But certainly, if we accept that at the opening of the present century the main tide of Anglo-American amity was still running freely, we must also be aware nevertheless of a strong contrary current prevailing over certain reaches and producing very choppy water. For industrially and commercially the early 1900s were the years of the 'American invasion'. And our first experience over here of the *défi Américain* was doubly alarming at the time because impinging on industries both old and new: not only a matter of our being overhauled in production of coal and textiles, bridges and railway locomotives, boots and shoes, but of our being anticipated in new fields—electrical engineering, telephones and typewriters, and in certain other new aspects of transport and communication. Much of this novel competition, in Britain's home as well as her overseas markets, could be convincingly explained as the United States' quest for new markets once her last internal frontier had been reached. But popular journalists like W. T. Stead were concerned less with explanations than with shrill prophecies about the imminent 'Americanization of the World'.[2]

How much of this alarm was needlessly exaggerated could not have been evident at the time. Even today we lack any painstaking industry-by-industry study from which to assess the relative impacts of transatlantic competition at this period—where it was most damaging, where it was most stimulating, and where it merely filled a vacuum— although Professor Saul, for one, has suggested how we might set about it.[3] And as to *why* certain American manufacturers were so successfully vying with us in certain areas, conjectures naturally differed, even among those Britons—and there were many at this juncture—who crossed the Atlantic, singly or in teams, with the express purpose of inspecting American industrial methods at first hand. Suffice it here that the speculative capitalization of the New World, the ingrained American habit of building upon future expectations rather than present assets, had encouraged certain sections of British opinion by the early 1900s to make a bogy of something called 'the trusts'— omnivorous creatures who had hitherto lurked within their natural habitat, that is to say behind tariff walls, but were now emerging to invade the European terrain. British industrialists, if free-traders, complained of being handicapped in the fight against them by excessive governmental regulation: if protectionists, they demanded more government help. Some British trade union leaders feared for their organizations, were the American pattern of industrial concentration to be imitated over here; indeed, one historian of British labour has represented this apprehension as accelerating the movement of our unions at the turn of the century towards a political party of labour.[4]

As for the British public at large, were one pressed to say what particular engagement first brought home to them the nature of the new competition, one would mention at once the tobacco war of 1901–2; for that Anglo-American duel presented to retailers and consumers considerations of both patriotism and profit in a most acute form. The campaign opened in September 1901, when the head of the biggest transatlantic tobacco combination, James Buchanan Duke, president of the American Tobacco Company, crossed to Liverpool and bought up at a stroke substantially the whole of the outstanding stock of Messrs Ogden.[5] For this thriving Merseyside concern, producing nationally popular pipe tobacco and cigarettes, Duke paid very nearly $5\frac{1}{2}$ million, and made clear that he was willing to spend as much again on a price-cutting war with a view to acquiring other British tobacco firms. These latter, however, stood ready to repel the invader, for they already had one grim warning fresh in mind. Earlier in the same year the Diamond Match Company of America had suddenly swooped upon our biggest match producers, Messrs Bryant & May—which had been paying 20 per cent dividends and looked safe as houses—and had carried them off by dint of superior machinery and pre-emption of patents. The tobacconists were not to be caught napping; and a dozen of them, with Wills at their head, immediately formed a British counter-concentration as the Imperial Tobacco Company of Great Britain and Ireland. There ensued nearly a year of bitter warfare between the Imperial and American companies. Bonus was met with bonus, gift coupon with gift coupon; and had the retailers been better organized they might as *tertius gaudens* have wrested more from the combatants than they did. In June 1902 Imperial carried the war into the invaders' territory by acquiring several large factories, storage facilities and building land in Richmond, Va. In the following September, Duke capitulated and a treaty was signed whereby the invaders withdrew, Ogden's was surrendered to Imperial, and respective British and American markets were redetermined. But the contest had been bitterly fought, in a blaze of publicity; and so long as the outcome was uncertain, every Briton was made aware of the threat. Even the non-smoker can hardly have missed the full-page advertisements carried for months by every daily newspaper.

It was while the tobacco war was at its height, and public opinion therefore at its most sensitive, that a seemingly far more serious menace to British prosperity, indeed British security, began to rear its head. By the spring of 1902 it became generally known over here that an American trust (or some such combination) had bought up great quantities of our Atlantic shipping—the Leyland Line, the White Star and Dominion Lines—and was laying siege to Cunard. 'Undeniably the sensation of the new century' was how Britain's chief shipping journal *Fairplay* described the transaction. 'The Press', declared one M.P., 'has made it the question of the hour.' 'Bewilderment, alarm, indignation', wrote another, 'such has been the prevailing mood of the public mind since the news . . . burst upon it a few weeks ago. That something was wrong somewhere—that someone had stolen a march on us—that something ought to be done—such was the comment of the man in the street and in the newspapers.' 'London Hysterical over Morgan coup', proclaimed the New York *Herald*, since 'the Combination practically places the American merchant marine in first position in the tonnage of the world.' 'Atlantic to be an American lake', rejoiced the New York *Journal*. And officials of the federal government—the Secretaries of Commerce and the Treasury, for instance—made speeches in the same spreadeagle vein which were duly reported over here. A reciprocal gloom pervaded the British press. 'The supremacy of the merchant marine', complained one organ, 'had slipped from us while we slept.' The American shipping trust, thought another, 'must mark, unless speedily neutralized, the turning point in our commercial fortunes of three centuries'. To one of America's few big shipbuilders, Charles Cramp, it seemed clear that the prospective steamship merger had roused the British from their lethargy 'into an almost feverish realisation of the actual conditions which confront them'. 'Our broken-hearted cousins', commented a New York *Times* leader, had been 'frightened to a degree which discredits their Anglo-Saxon phlegm.' Certainly the prevailing mood here was one of grim foreboding, with large sections of industry, press and public calling on the government for energetic action to avert (as one writer put it) 'an intolerable national humiliation' which would make Britain 'a mere annexe of the United States'.

What particularly alarmed British observers of the new American shipping trust, it is safe to say, was its presumed connection with railways. The shipping lines, men predicted, would be the tentacles of the railroads. And pretty soon it was known over here that behind the shipping combine stood the figure of J. Pierpont Morgan, consolidator of railroads, and now architect of the world's first billion-dollar corporation, the recently formed U.S. Steel. There was some whistling in the dark. In the Commons one or two jests were ventured about Morganizing the Atlantic, and about a putative buccaneering forebear of J. Pierpont—one Henry Morgan, he of the old, bold mate. In another place their lordships relished a subtler pleasantry about Morganatic alliances. But in the popular mind the faceless trust had now acquired a personification, and a pretty simple one at that. For just as Britons did not usually discriminate between one type of American industrial combination and another, so their press was prone to lump the Morgans—the second generation, as we tend to think, of American capitalist, consolidatory, rationalizing and withal aristocratic —together with their predecessors, the piratical Goulds and Fiskes, under one and the same *persona*.

That *persona* we can today partially re-create by deliberately reimmersing ourselves in the popular literature of the period. Here, pending the appearance of some monograph on the theme of the American tycoon in British fiction, a rather random sampling will have to suffice. Perhaps the earliest fully-sustained representation of an American millionaire—sustained, that is to say, over the sheer brute length of the Victorian novel—comes from the pen of that prolific third-rater, Sir Walter Besant. In Besant's first good if not best seller, *The Golden Butterfly* (1876–77),[6] the type appears under the already typified name of Gilead P. Beck. Having amassed much money but little culture in oil prospecting, Beck now comes to visit, perhaps to settle, in England with English friends first encountered when he was poor and in peril in the Far West. His hosts proceed to fool him, though unmaliciously, to the top of their bent. Does he express an interest in painting? At once they take him to a prominent art dealer where he is invited to make an expertise between a number of large but totally worthless canvases. He would like to meet great contemporary men of letters? His hosts forthwith arrange a literary luncheon for which certain of their friends are made up, costumed and briefed in order to be introduced as Mr Tennyson, Mr Browning, Mr Ruskin and so forth (an opportunity for stylistic parody which, alas, Besant is not the man to seize). True to his oft-expressed principle, 'What you can't spend, give', the millionaire is moved to plan several foundations—the Gilead P. Beck National Theatre, the Gilead P. Beck Lying-in Hospital, etc. Less innocently, he is induced by a shady London financier to invest heavily in the flotation of the Isle of Man Internal Navigation Company. The Beck subplot is tied well into the novel's main action (for Besant is nothing if not professional) and a festival of eavesdropping duly leads to the dénouement —a grand sensation scena wherein the financier goes, for purely private reasons, out of his mind, Beck loses his fortune, and philosophically returns to the United States to compile another.

That the American has served as little more than comic relief in a standard melodrama is the more disappointing when one considers that Besant knew something of the United States from several visits there, on his own behalf or for the Society of Authors. Two decades later he was to promote the Anglo-American Union, one of a number of such societies springing up in the 1890s for the entertainment of transatlantic visitors to London. Such contact, to be sure, was intermittent. But even an Englishman who lived in the United States for more than ten years, married an American, and helped edit the New York *Times* does not do much better in the same literary line. Louis Jennings, whose novel *The Millionaire*[7] was serialized by Blackwood's Magazine in the mid-1880s, had undoubtedly a considerable knowledge of New York city politics. Yet none of it avails to enhance the credibility of his fictional protagonist. Where Gilead P. Beck is genial, Dexter File is a dread figure, crouched perpetually over the panel of knobs and switches that afford him instant access to Albany or Philadelphia or Washington, plus a private submarine cable to the stockmarkets of Europe. At his elbow hovers a smooth personage who would today enjoy some such style as 'legislative liaison assistant'. The political depths, however, remain unsounded. A visit to the English countryside, in search of a long-mislaid wife, has a humanizing effect on Dexter File: but nothing can be done to disentangle him from his stage props. So heavily laden with the fantasy of infinite wealth, he and all such creations sink, and our interest with them, at a relatively early chapter.

To be sure, some subsequent British treatments of the same theme, appearing in the 1900s, do indeed place their American millionaire heroes within a wider variety of social context. In one such example[8] the tycoon buys, sight unseen, a decayed castle in the south-west of Ireland where, caught between the romantic natives and the sophisticated Anglo-Irish, he labours vainly for reunion all round. Another venture in this *genre*[9] has the American of enormous wealth and charm acting as umpire, in an English suburban setting, throughout a genteel but terribly prolonged game of sexual mixed doubles. So far from offering any insight, whether informed or imaginative, into the problems attendant upon being an American, and a financier, and immensely wealthy, such writers seem to assume that their readership of fellow Britons will be well enough served by a purely Anglocentric approach that seeks only to amuse. Generally speaking, the more eminent the writer the deeper our disappointment. Even Kipling, whose literary skill was at the disposal of a first-hand experience of the transatlantic scene, is content to pose a very limited question— Is the tycoon, or is he not, assimilable to the English way of life?— and to answer it one way in *An Error in the Fourth Dimension* but contrariwise in *An Habitation Enforced*.[10] And what shall be said of

the Master himself? 'Before the American business-man,' James con-
fesses, 'I was absolutely and irredeemably helpless, with no fibre of my
intelligence responding to his mystery.' Or again, speaking of his
father: 'Business in a world of business was the thing we most agreed
(differ as we might on minor issues) in knowing nothing about.'[11]
Though his father's father had amassed no small fortune in commerce, it seems to be rather the innocence of the self-made man which
most preoccupied the grandson. When *The American* represents himself to Mrs Tristram as 'successful in copper . . . only so-so in railroads,
and a hopeless fizzle in oil', we may suspect Christopher Newman's
diffidence to be James's own.

With these examples before us, do we still hesitate to admit that
popular British depictions of the American tycoon during the last
quarter of the nineteenth and first decade of the twentieth centuries
were unenlightening because superficial? Then another sort of test may
serve to remove any lingering doubts. What, given two minutes' notice,
can we most readily recall about Morgan himself? It is a safe bet that
for most of us recollections will present themselves rather like a
scatter of snapshots; isolated flashbacks of the kind that might well
served as situational nuclei for successive instalments of just such a
serialized novel as we have been surveying. Morgan aboard his steam-
yacht *Corsair*, chugging up and down the Hudson and refusing to
disembark his captive guest until another thousand miles of distressed
railroad have been signed into his surgical care. Jupiter Morgan,
presiding over a pantheon of lesser bankers at 23 Wall Street through
critical days of Treasury panic in 1895 or 1907. Maecenas Morgan,
padding through the galleries of Europe with the pack of art dealers
at his heels; complaining that the French exhibits must have been
chosen by a chambermaid, yet himself credulous before the alleged
relics of Marie Antoinette. Morgan the Magnificent, clambering into
court dress and a coach for Edward VII's coronation procession, while
wags on the pavement peddle licences inscribed 'Permission to remain
on the face of the earth, signed J. P. Morgan'. Or at St Paul's for the
Cecil Rhodes memorial service, installed immediately behind the Dean
and bathed in the refulgence of £9000 worth of electric light, a gift
to the Chapter from his own pocket. Morgan meditative, in his
renaissance marble library, the endless games of solitaire proceeding
beneath the big black cigar and luminous nose. Morgan *furioso*, on the

telephone to a trust-busting President: 'If I've done anything wrong, send your man round to my man and have them fix it up.' Morgan at bay before the Pujo committee of 1912, courteously uncommunicative as to the precise extent of his company's influence. And then, the following spring, Morgan's last vacation; sailing off to die, Pierpontifex Maximus, appropriately in Rome.

That we find ourselves forced to rely so much on impressionistic vignettes like these is of course one measure of the poverty of would-be studies of the House of Morgan in particular, of which the most recent is indeed the least decent. But in a wider sense it is a measure also of the dearth of native American studies of the financier's role in national economic life. Between business histories, which have illuminated the operations of particular firms, and general economic histories, which have usually ignored business procedures altogether, there has long remained a broad and very thinly populated area which some have designated entrepreneurial history. This is properly the field where historians study the relations of business leaders with their counter-parts in other firms, their relationship with the economy as a whole, and the broad socio-economic effects of their decisions. Despite the exemplary willingness of a number of American firms to open their archives to the historian, the latter has cast less light than might have been expected upon the entrepreneur's economic and social role and upon how he himself saw that role. Hence an excessive reliance upon popular myth, especially in its fictionalized manifestations.

How far and in what respects British myth of the tycoon corre-sponded to American reality in the late nineteenth century, we still have too few reliable means of discovering. But from a recent and very thorough case study[12] of one of the most prominent Anglo-American investment banking houses over a twenty-year period it is possible to draw some trustworthy inferences. The investigator of Morton, Bliss and Co.'s operations between 1869 and 1889, for instance, has shown persuasively that the investment banker's role in promoting railroad development during the early *post bellum* decades was at once more extensive and more covert than has been generally supposed. Not only was he the familiar supplier of capital, the mobilizer of other people's money, and *pro tanto* the guardian and spokesman of a (mostly European) creditor clientele but he was also the agent of deliberate, rapid and profitable expansion. Frequently he and his kind were both capital middlemen *and* profit-seeking investors; major stockholders in, as well as creditors of, the lines for which they were selling bonds. Sometimes, for a prudent sharing of risks, they undertook such promotion in conjunction with other banks. But back in the 1870s and early 1880s, between firms in the investment banking community competition for good bond contracts was especially keen. Morgan, and half-a-dozen other such houses, laid their fortunes by going out to seek expansionary railroad business of this nature. That their influence was exerted covertly indicates a natural desire to avoid publicity in a field so bestrewn with scandals. (That the depression of the 1870s only increased that influence is nevertheless probable, in as much as it increased the proprietor's dependence upon the banker's continuing aid.) On this showing, the commonly-held notion of the investment banker as *deus ex machina*, invoked only after the railroad promoters were in trouble, and intervening only at the late stage when it was necessary to impose order upon railroad chaos in the interest of senior security holders, has no relevance to these earlier decades of expansion. If Morgan and his like did eventually resort to banker-induced railroad amalgamation and retrenchment for conservative ends, they did not do so before the late 1880s and 1890s. Until then, their influence was wholly promotional and expansive.

From all of which we may conclude that the popular British image of the American tycoon as a wielder of occult power is probably not without some verisimilitude in regard to the 1870s and 1880s. The myth's deficiency lies in its persistence well into the 1900s after the American economic climate had changed and the financier's function with it. To illustrate the nature of that change we cannot do better than to return to the theme of Anglo-American competition in the North Atlantic as suddenly dramatized by the episode of 1901–3.

That affair, which came before the Cabinet on at least four occasions and was eventually to embroil no fewer than five departments of state, may be said to have begun when Sir John Ellerman, director and largest shareholder of the Leyland Steamship Company, in 1900 sought to add to his fleets one of the very few American-owned steamship concerns of any size in the North Atlantic. This was the Atlantic Transport Co., a Baltimore-based holding company with two small but expanding steamship companies active in both the passenger and freight trades. When negotiations with the latter's manager, Bernard N.

Baker, were almost consummated, however, the shipping world was startled with news of a *volte-face*. For instead, Leyland's North Atlantic service was itself to be bought up by the Philadelphian owner of another—perhaps one should say, *the* other—large-scale shipping man of the United States east coast. Clement A. Griscom was president of the International Navigation Co., a conglomerate holding company working three component enterprises of American, British and Belgian registry under a common funnel. Griscom had large ambitions for native American shipping in the new century, a buoyant optimism that the prevailing boom in the world oceanic carrying trade would continue, and high hopes of profiting from a shipping subsidy bill— one of a long line of such proposals—currently before the Congress. More importantly, his bankers were the Philadelphian subsidiary of the J. P. Morgan Co. With the latter's backing, Griscom in May 1901, having first merged by trustification his own International Navigation Co. with Baker's Atlantic Transport, went on to secure a controlling interest in Frederick Leyland & Co., Ltd, at a price which seemed to European observers extravagant and to Leyland shareholders irresistible.

The gradations by which the House of Morgan came to be drawn into this bold development are interesting to observe. Hitherto, its Philadelphian subsidiary had arranged with Griscom only for the expansion, by new building, of the latter's own lines. Next, Morgan agreed to be banker to the newly-formed trust, advancing cash for its expanding fleet, easing the syndicate's passage by his professional contacts, and arranging to market its preferred stock. The risk at that stage cannot have appeared to him great. Even if Congress failed to pass the subsidy bill, he would possess adequate security in his lien on the new vessels and in the expectation of good working profits from the new Griscom–Baker merger. When the latter combination was enlarged by the Leyland deal, however, the situation was altered. Ellerman, in personal negotiation with Morgan, had raised his cash price for Leyland stock by nearly one-third above its current market valuation. Consequently the House of Morgan, instead of being merely a bank advancing credit and arranging sale of securities, were henceforth implicated (through their London affiliate, J. S. Morgan & Co.) in one of the largest shipping concerns in the United States foreign trade, to the tune of $11 million.

Hardly had the ripples of the Leyland purchase subsided when a fresh shock-wave struck the bows of the international shipping community. On the last day of April 1902 notice was published that the American shipping trust had entered into a provisional agreement to purchase the parent company of the White Star line. With that line went its building connection with Harland & Wolff through whose chairman, William J. Pirrie, the transaction had largely been negotiated. As in the Leyland deal, the price the Americans were willing to pay—albeit only one-quarter in cash, yet at a figure based on the line's record earnings of the year 1900—left informed opinion aghast. For every £1000 White Star share they proposed to offer £1400. At almost the same juncture, too, the American combination signed an offensive-defensive alliance with the two great German shipping companies of Hamburg–Amerika (Hapag) and Norddeutscher–Lloyd (NGL). Here the prime mover was Hapag's energetic head, Albert Ballin. At one of the meetings in New York which preceded signature of the treaty, Ballin extracted two promises from Morgan: that he would agree to the combine's bid for a 51 per cent controlling interest in the Holland–America line, chief competitor of the Germans; and that he would make overtures to Cunard for a similar agreement with them. The former approach was successful. Over Cunard's fate the British were left for a time in suspense.

They already had plenty to worry about. Leaving out of account its two German allies, the projected American combine would evidently control an Atlantic fleet, whether plying under American or British or Belgian flags, of an aggregate tonnage calculably just under one million gross registered tons. Coupled to the American railroad network, would it not enable the United States swiftly to undercut British oceanic freights? Furtherto, the White Star fleet included eight expresses under contract to our Admiralty for use, as armed cruisers or otherwise, in time of war. If war came, moreover, what might befall our island's food supplies? And how would the transfer of such crack vessels into foreign hands, perhaps to a foreign registry, affect our merchant marine's traditional role as nursery of the Royal Navy Reserve? Overnight, Morgan's European image became in popular eyes a depredatory one. Cartoonists drew him knee-deep in mid-Atlantic, towing away or scooping up armfuls of British shipping. Bernard Partridge limned for *Punch* a classic representation of him in Doge's costume, wedding the sea with a (shipping) ring. Yet another impressionist pictured the American eagle rampant over the entablature of the Royal Exchange. From all sides so great an outcry arose in press and parliament that Morgan felt compelled to devote much of his European visiting of 1902 to gestures of reassurance, dining with their Majesties in London, lunching with the Kaiser at Kiel, and being unwontedly generous of his time for press interviews.

For him too the late spring and early summer were an anxious period. Step by step, each costlier than foreseen, his house had been drawn into accepting financial responsibilities toward what was now manifesting itself as the largest commercial armada the world had yet seen, equal in tonnage almost to the entire merchant marine of France and comprising nearly one-third of all dry-cargo tonnage then deployed in the North Atlantic carrying trade. His bank was financing a substantial proportion of the building programme of those American lines entering the combine. A number of these vessels, moreover, had been ordered from native yards at high American prices in groundless expectation of subsidy. After the boom year of 1900 world carrying trade had declined sharply and (more ominous) was still failing to pick up. Yet Morgan's options to complete purchase of Leyland and White Star were fast running out; and once agreement had been reached with the Germans, formal articulation of the Trust could be no longer delayed. Honouring his promise to Ballin he put in a modest bid, through an intermediary, for Cunard; but probably was relieved when the directors declined it. By May he had evidently decided to go ahead. In October the International Mercantile Marine Company (IMM) was formally incorporated in New Jersey, the necessary share exchanges and payments being completed by early 1903. Voting control of the new Trust was vested in a board consisting of five Americans (one of them Morgan's representative, who had been entrusted with the preliminary negotiations) and two Englishmen (Pirrie and Bruce Ismay, of White Star). Its executive and finance committees were all-American. The J. P. Morgan partners were to receive as managers' fee over $2 million of the new stock. Initial cash demands on the Trust ran up to some $50 million—about twice the original estimate of cost and decidedly more than could readily be raised by sale of preferred stock: hence the need to issue as much again in $4\frac{1}{2}$ per cent collateral trust bonds. The total capital of the new corporation was to consist of $60 million preferred stock, carrying a cumulative dividend at 6 per cent p.a.; and $60 million common stock limited to dividends of 10 per cent p.a.; together with the additional $50 million collateral trust debentures.

On paper these figures looked enormous, greatly surpassing as they did the aggregated capital value of the International Mercantile Marine's component companies. Were they therefore exorbitant? Only time and tide would show. But two things were immediately clear to Morgan. He could not afford to incorporate any further lines, and so no provision was made in the trust deed for that. And he would need to retain every penny of the subsidy available to those White Star vessels reserved for war-time use by the Admiralty. Hence it was imperative upon him to come promptly to an agreement with the British Government. With the latter he therefore began in June 1902 to treat through a former Foreign Office official, Sir Clinton Dawkins, who was to be the IMM's British manager. These negotiations, in which the government were represented by Gerald Balfour for the Board of Trade, Selborne at the Admiralty, and Joseph Chamberlain as Colonial Secretary, bore fruit in a twenty-year agreement that was approved by the Cabinet in August and duly ratified after debate by parliament.[13] Under its terms Morgan was assured of continuance of the Admiralty's subsidy for the remainder of its life-span, and was promised that when future subsidies were under consideration the British companies absorbed into the IMM would be treated by the government on the same footing of general equality as other British steamship companies, so long as the IMM refrained from pursuing any policies 'injurious to the interests of the British Merchant Marine or of British trade'. The government for its part secured reciprocal assurances from Morgan that no British vessel in, or hereafter to be built for, the Combine would be transferred to a foreign registry without the Board of Trade's consent, and would remain officered and proportionately crewed by British subjects. The British lines absorbed, in short, would remain British as would a majority of their directors.

By means of this instrument the government had gone far to allay official and public anxiety about Britain's future security in the event of international hostilities. Her commercial prospects in the North Atlantic nevertheless remained highly unsure in the face of the trans-atlantic titan. A twin pillar of government policy must therefore be to strengthen our competitive position there, and to this end it appeared urgently needful to keep the Cunard Company out of foreign hands and to fortify its trading position against the formidable new American rival. Parallel, therefore, to its discussions with Morgan, the same trio of ministers (referred to as 'a committee of the Cabinet') pursued a much more complicated course of negotiation—into whose intricacies we do not here need to go—which led eventually to an agreement with Cunard, laid on the table of the House of Commons simultaneously with the Morgan Agreement and given legal and financial effect by the Cunard Agreement (Money) Act of 15 August 1904.[14] Under its terms Cunard undertook to build two steamships capable of greater speeds than any other afloat. For this the government would lend the company £2.4 million, at 2½ per cent interest over twenty years, repayable at 5 per cent p.a., together with increased working subsidies as soon as the new flyers came into service. Special provision was made to preclude sale of the company's shares to foreigners.

Neither agreement, with Morgan or with Cunard, escaped criticism, for each in its own way was novel in aspect. That with Morgan marked the first occasion on which Britain, the world power, had deemed it necessary to come to a bilateral accommodation over shipping with a challenger. And by its contract with Cunard the government had, in seeming infringement of *laissez-faire*, virtually bound itself in an unprecedented kind of relationship with one particular private company: thereby large and contentious issues were involved, the determining of which was to be influential, not for the current crisis only but for subsequent state policy also. When the question of building the *Queens* arose in the 1930s copious reference was made back to the precedent of 1902.

But what stimulated critics, and in particular those abnormally blessed with hindsight, was the manifest failure in practice of the International Mercantile Marine Co. itself. The report on its first working year, ended 31 December 1903, showed that the much-vaunted combine of over 130 vessels valued at more than £38 million had been losing money hand over fist. Failure to meet even its fixed charges, although precisely nothing had been allowed for depreciation, obliged Morgan to pledge himself to make good the deficit over the next three years. Despite a managerial shuffle the downward trend in earnings persisted during 1904, indeed was accentuated by a ruinous war in which the IMM for some months strove to undercut Cunard's steerage rates for the emigrant trade at a juncture when world freight was also depressed. Internally, too, the combine failed to realize the economies expected from centralization of control; while Congress still refused to come to its aid with a federal subsidy. As investors the American public responded but poorly. Since all securities issued by the House of Morgan were simultaneously showing price declines, it was obvious that the market for new issues was seriously congested. The strain on IMM's underwriters was therefore early and heavy: by March 1905 their commitments had had to be called upon in full. By 1909, after six years of struggle, the Company had still paid no dividends and its bonds had not risen to par. The two German lines, once their ten-year agreement had run its course, declined to renew their association with the Combine, which was saved from extinction only by the expansion of world demand for shipping in the First World War.

Although it proved unsuccessful in the short term, Morgan's venture in support of the IMM demonstrated beyond doubt the availability of capital on a very large scale for shipping promotion in the United States. Its creation represented a vigorous attempt by American shipowners—uncertain about subsidies, denied by law the right to place foreign-built vessels on the American registry, yet subjected to very high native building costs—to take advantage of the working economy and legal security which trustification seemingly offered. Yet, since the type of combination chosen failed to take into account the nature of the commercial medium in which it was to operate (oceanic and international), the story of the IMM is a chapter of misconceptions and losses. For Baker and Griscom these losses must have been fairly considerable, since both had to put up 100 per cent cash for their underwriting commitments and both had demonstrated their faith in the enterprise by engaging heavily. Losses eventually sustained by the House of Morgan have been credibly estimated at between $1 million and $1½ million.[15]

How could the master of capital have so badly miscalculated? In Morgan's eyes the advantage of the steamship combination had appeared twofold. By linking American-owned ships to native railroads it would attract, through lower charges, more of the Atlantic carrying trade into American hands. And on the ocean itself an amalgamation of lines would reduce 'wasteful' competition by 'rationalizing' sea-borne trade, in much the same way that the J. P. Morgan Co. had earlier amalgamated, pruned and systematized the distressed railroad companies which fell into its hands. Unfortunately for Morgan, the analogy between land and sea transit did not hold. Virtual monopoly might be achievable by the owner of a railroad system: a combination of carriers on the high seas, by contrast, cannot acquire any such monopoly over trade routes on an international ocean free to all comers. A railroad right-of-way is by its nature exclusive and grows in value with the population of the territories it serves. But nothing can prevent a promoter of means from introducing a new line of steamships whose parallel operation will cut into the trade of those already plying there. It was upon capturing a hegemony in the oceanic freight trade, moreover, that Morgan (judged by his few public utterances on the subject) was persuaded to build his highest hopes. Yet for line services across the North Atlantic, freight had long been of secondary impor-tance, for rapid development of tramping in the 1870s and 1880s had left liners there with cargo capacity in excess of demand. The liner's service, after all, was relatively inflexible: but the tramp skipper would move in anywhere to undercut.

Even in the passenger trade, moreover, international business is liable to an irregularity which never comparably afflicts domestic railroads. Cyclical alternations of world prosperity and depression, modulated by sudden regional fluctuations in rates and traffic, are unpredictable and only very partially controllable by *ad hoc* pooling arrangements. Despite all attempts by shipping conferences and rings to impose some stability through self-regulation, charges continue to be set by the haggling of the market, and vary from route to route and from port to port to a degree which the railroad traffic manager could neither conceive of nor cope with. From all these considerations the wise shipping-line's board pursues a cautious policy in fleet aggregation and a niggardly one in profit distribution. The IMM, however, was conceived and born in euphoric mood and in an *annus mirabilis* of maritime prosperity. The year 1900 was a dangerously abnormal one for the promoters to take as typical when capitalizing a line's annual earnings, and still more so to base their offers of purchase upon. Even allowing for the ingrained optimism of speculative American capital-izations of that epoch, the prices paid were over-generous to a fault.

In applying to the shipping industry the same principles of consolidation which had succeeded on land, Morgan and his colleagues
imposed upon their new marine enterprise at the very outset an un-
warrantably heavy burden. It was as though his earlier success with
railroads had fostered in the financier a blind and uncritical faith in the
virtue of consolidation *per se*.

In this light it now becomes possible to see Morgan, not as the wily
and dominating financier of popular fiction, but as the victim of his
own inexperience in an unfamiliar medium; in matters maritime a tyro,
not a tycoon. His House, purely as bankers, had scrutinized the plans
of Griscom—a shipping magnate, and as such credibly supposed to
possess the necessary specialist skills—and had presumably deemed it
a financially worthwhile proposition. He had allowed himself to be
towed in the shipowner's wake. Then, beginning with Ellerman's
unforeseen demand for full payment for Leyland in cash, the Morgan
company's role had by swift stages become transformed until its own
funds and those of its depositors had become inextricably involved in
virtual ownership of an enormous marine monster. The IMM's great
fleet was to prove unable either to stifle competition or to control rates,
and did not perceptibly raise productive efficiency in the trade. Instead
of becoming, as the British feared, a dominating influence, its share of
the transatlantic business never reached 40 per cent and constituted no
more than one element in future shipping conferences in that area. It
did not even become a paying proposition until dowered with the
somewhat artificial prosperity of world war. In the afterglow of its
failure the tycoon appears neither as a hero nor as a robber baron;
neither altruistic nor rapacious, but simply misled by those in whose
specialized knowledge he had trusted. For the first time ill-success had
attended one of Morgan's great schemes. Henceforward he attempted
no more trustifications. Slow though his popular image was in crumb-
ling, the first decade of the twentieth century marks the decadence
of the American tycoon.

## NOTES

1. George Griffith, *The Lake of Gold: a narrative of the Anglo-American
conquest of Europe* (London, 1903). It seems to have escaped the vigilant
eye of Mr I. F. Clarke when he compiled his bibliography, *The Tale
of the Future* (London, 1961).

2. W. T. Stead, *The Americanization of the World* (1901) and *passim* in his monthly *Review of Reviews* at this period.

3. S. B. Saul, 'The American Impact upon British Industry, 1895–1914', *Business History*, III (1960) 19–38.

4. H. M. Pelling, 'The American Economy and the Foundations of the British Labour Party', *Economic History Review*, 2nd series, VII (1955) 1–17.

5. For the background history of the American Tobacco Company, see U.S. Commissioner of Corporations, *Report on the Tobacco Industry* (Washington, D.C., Government Printing Office, 1909).

6. W. Besant and J. Rice: *The Golden Butterfly* (London, 1876).

7. L. Jennings, *The Millionaire*, first serialized in *Blackwood's Magazine* CXXXIII (1883) and later published anonymously in three vols.

8. 'Rita' (Mrs E. M. J. Humphreys), *Half a Truth* (London, 1911).

9. W. E. Norris, *Vittoria Victrix* (London, 1911).

10. Respectively in *The Day's Work* (1908) and *Actions and Reactions* (1909).

11. H. James in his own Preface to Vol. XIII of the New York edition of the complete *Works* (1908–09).

12. Dolores Breitman Greenberg, *Financiers and Railroads, 1869–1889*, unpublished Ph.D. Thesis, Cornell University, 1972.

13. Gerald Balfour's own papers on these transactions are P.R.O., Board of Trade 30/60/48. The Morgan Agreement was laid before parliament as Cd. 1704 (1903).

14. 4 Ed. VII c 22. The Cunard Agreement had been laid simultaneously with the Morgan Agreement as Cd. 1703 (1903). Cunard's records of their negotiations with the government were later collected by their solicitors in a pair of volumes which are among the company's archives at the University of Liverpool.

15. Records of Price, Waterhouse & Co., auditors to the J. P. Morgan Co., cited by T. R. Navin and M. V. Sears in *Business History Review*, XXXVIII, no. 4 (1957) 311–314. *The Economist* weekly also kept a watchful eye on the IMM's annual accounts over these early years.

# The Future At Work: Anglo-American Progressivism 1890-1917

## KENNETH O. MORGAN

'The fact is that our political issues are so different that it is hard for either nation to understand the other.' So wrote Herbert Foxwell, a conservative economist in Cambridge, England, to E. R. Seligman of Columbia University in 1895.[1] Fourteen years later, he congratulated Seligman and himself on the contrasts between the two nations. 'Englishmen more than ever envy you the extraordinarily conservative character of your constitution. Democracy seems to have hardly any hold on American politics.' Britain, on the other hand, was plagued by 'the crudest budget of modern times—worthy of the shallow and rhetorical Henry George, whom our chancellor, his namesake, much resembles'.[2]

Foxwell's insular view has been echoed by almost all historians of the Progressive reform movement that swept through the cities and states of America in the first two decades of the twentieth century. It has invariably been assumed that Progressivism can be understood only in a purely American context, as the product of a period of self-examination and inward-looking analysis after the excitement of imperialism and the war with Spain in 1898. It was a time of self-purgation after what Richard Hofstadter called the 'psychic crisis' of the 1890s.[3] Equally, British historians have viewed the political upheavals of the Liberals in the years up to 1914 as a period of introspection after the divisions and disillusionment of the South African War and the gradual retreat from empire that resulted. The House of Lords, Irish home rule, Welsh disestablishment, women's suffrage, above all, the 'new Liberalism' of social reform are all taken to indicate a preoccupation with the internal social and political structure of Britain itself, a high noon of domestic radical change from which a self-contained, insular nation was abruptly wrenched by the advent of total war in August 1914. In so far as the United States did impinge on the awareness of British radical reformers in the Lloyd George era, it has been taken to have served as a threat and a warning—as the supreme symbol of uncontrolled monopoly capitalism in its most irresponsible guise. The intimate transatlantic radical community of *ante-bellum* days, a world that perished at Appomattox, had disappeared. To the British left, socialist and non-socialist alike, the United States now provided the model (and to some extent the source) of the evils from which British radicals sought to save their society. In short, British and American historians of the reform movements in their respective countries appear to agree that each nation was self-contained, preoccupied with its own internal stresses and conflicts, comparatively unmoved by the contemporary experience of the other.

And yet, the evidence from contemporary sources, particularly the British and American newspaper and periodical press, is overwhelming that the Progressive movement in each country was transatlantic in its emphasis. The New York *Forum* commented in October 1906 on 'the unconscious influence that the trans-Atlantic branch of the great English-speaking race exercises on the cis-Atlantic branch, and vice versa'.[4] Political commentators like Lyman Abbott and Benjamin Flower felt convinced that American Progressivism was part of a world-wide movement closely paralleled on each side of the Atlantic.[5] Time and again, this refrain was taken up by journalists and politicians in the Progressive movement in each country. Indeed, British reformers, anxious to consolidate the Liberal–Labour alliance in the period after the 1906 general election, adopted the name 'Progressive' to identify their creed. C. P. Scott in the *Manchester Guardian*, A. G. Gardiner in the *Daily News*, H. J. Massingham in the *Nation*, wrote freely of the 'progressive alliance'.[6] In London, Manchester and other urban areas up and down the land, radicals on local authorities formed themselves into 'progressive parties'. Political commentators observed how Progressivism in the Theodore Roosevelt/Wilson era and Liberalism in the Asquith/Lloyd George period appeared to share common aspirations—the cutting back of political privilege, the substitution of the 'national interest' for that of 'special interest', the replacement of the ethic of competition with that of collective co-operation, the democratization of the political process, the promotion of social justice and of industrial and labour reforms, in the interests both of national efficiency and of humanity. There were those who claimed that, just as the Jacksonian Democrats had struck a common chord with the radical reformers in Britain in 1830, just as the American Civil War had lent new impetus to the revived parliamentary reform agitation in the 1860s, so once again radical reformers on each side of the Atlantic were comrades in a common cause. Of course, some of this was exaggerated. The closeness of the Anglo-American connection in the years after 1900 can be overdone. Since the intimate association of transatlantic radicals in the early nineteenth century, British and American politics had taken very different paths. Partly as a result of this, partly the consequence of changing patterns of immigration to America, the two nations had drifted apart. Further, America's rise as a world power had led to serious Anglo-American diplomatic conflicts, as recently as 1902–3 over the boundary between Venezuela and British Guiana. Historians who try to discern a 'special relationship' in these years, or later, are all too prone to sentimental nostalgia or wish-fulfilment about the 'English-speaking peoples'. Even so, the reality of the interaction between British and American Progressivism is too pervasive to be brushed aside. A study of its character, and perhaps of its limitations, sheds new light on political change in the two countries. In particular, American Progressivism may be seen, not just as an introspective desire for purification and change at a time of relative national prosperity, but as part of a world-wide quest to control urbanization and industrialization, a quest which knew no national boundaries or else soared above them.

Without doubt, the impact of American Progressivism upon British politics in the Edwardian era was episodic and often indirect. American analogies were freely used in debates on the issues by Edwardian politicians—but all too often by Conservatives rather than by radicals. Those checks and balances embodied in the American constitution were widely cited by opponents of the Parliament Bill in 1909–11 to justify the preservation of the House of Lords as a bastion against unbridled democracy. The American idea of a referendum was quoted for the same purpose. The *laissez-faire* climate

I

in which American business had flourished since the civil war was emphasized by *The Times* and Conservatives generally to curb the pretensions of British trade unions, and to oppose the 'socialistic' attacks on wealth and property conducted by Lloyd George and his allies.[7] Above all, sympathy with the United States on alleged grounds of race inspired Joseph Chamberlain and other Unionists to hope for an alliance with the Americans, or at least for a friendly understanding, as a main adjunct to British foreign policy. The war with Spain in 1898 evoked warm sympathy for the American cause from nationalists and imperialists of all shades in Britain, from Chamberlain to Robert Blatchford of the I.L.P.[8] Strategic decisions which led to the United States patrolling Caribbean waters with its own expanded fleet were held to be a valuable support for British naval supremacy in the north and mid-Atlantic.

On the other hand, ministers in the British Liberal government after 1905 viewed the United States with some detachment. The member most closely involved with the United States, James Bryce, the celebrated author of *The American Commonwealth* (1888) went from the Irish Office to Washington as British ambassador from 1907 to 1913. While this enabled him to make his own unique contribution to Anglo-American cultural understanding, of course it removed him entirely from direct contact with the British political scene.[9] The one remaining member of the government consistently anxious to maintain close relations with the United States, though not in the shape of a formal alliance, was Sir Edward Grey, the Foreign Secretary. He believed strongly in the ties created by language, cultural heritage and religion between the two 'Anglo-Saxon' powers, and the diplomatic implications of this. He devoted much time to anxious fence-mending with the Americans, notably over the Canadian reciprocity treaty in 1911—a policy that, incidentally, led directly towards the downfall of Laurier's Liberal government at Ottawa. When Woodrow Wilson became President of the United States, and sagely dispatched Walter Hines Page to the court of St James's, Grey emphasized how closely attuned he felt to the new Democratic administration, headed by an austere, university-trained patrician like himself. Over the Panama tolls issue and policy towards Mexico in 1913–14, Grey made it plain to Wilson that he took a far less narrow view of British national interest than did his foreign office advisers.[10] Conversely, Grey's highly eclectic attitude towards domestic British issues, in which he often formed an unexpected alliance with Lloyd George on labour, land and other questions, owed nothing to developments in the United States. His transatlantic enthusiasms were for export only.

On the other hand, the radical domestic policies of the British government during the years from 1906 to 1914 did find some transatlantic ammunition. In particular, Lloyd George, far from the inward-looking, parochial figure he is often represented to be, took a keen if not always well-informed interest in events in the United States: American journals often featured interviews with him. Characteristically, the American figure who most captured his imagination was Theodore Roosevelt whom he met during the latter's triumphant visit to Britain in 1912.[11] Roosevelt's version of the 'new nationalism', a strong foreign policy being combined with paternalist social reform, chimed in with Lloyd George's own inclinations. Again, Roosevelt's penchant for commissions of experts to examine questions like the trusts and the tariffs in a scientific and detached way followed closely Lloyd George's own proposals. In his memorandum in 1910, in which he advocated an inter-party coalition which would vault above petty partisan politics, Lloyd George had similarly proposed commissions of experts who would look at 'non-controversial' issues like imperial preference, the Ulster question, the Lords veto, and disendowment of the Welsh church.[12] Above all, Roosevelt appealed to Lloyd George (as did Franklin Roosevelt twenty years afterwards) as a symbol of powerful central leadership and of broad executive power who would transcend the mundane issues with which the party politicians of the day were consumed. In the *Truth about the Peace Treaties* in the 1930s, he cited Theodore Roosevelt, along with Botha of South Africa, as a 'big man' who provided a new concept of leadership.[13] Like T.R., Lloyd George believed in executives rather than in legislatures. His bid for a British version of the 'new nationalism', based on military preparedness and social reform, failed in 1910; the reality of Party was too strong for him. But in 1916, when the political world was revolutionized by the impact of total war, Lloyd George's vision found new significance. Then indeed the New Nationalism—or 'nationalist–socialism' as Lloyd George and his new ally, Lord Milner termed it[14] —came into its own. The machinery of central government was overhauled, quasi-presidential power was vested in the man at the centre, businessmen and non-partisan experts were drafted in to run their departments on practical lines. Indeed, an almost uncritical faith in the judgement of down-to-earth, untheological businessmen—a faith applied by him even in trade negotiations with Krassin and the Soviet government in 1920–21—was one indirect legacy of Lloyd George's flirtation with the New Nationalism. At the time, though, Lloyd George was critical of Theodore Roosevelt for rebelling against the Republican regulars and forming the 'Bull Moose' Progressive Party in the 1912 campaign. 'He ought not to have quarrelled with the machine', Lloyd George observed.[15] It was one aspect of the New Nationalism that Lloyd George himself forgot in 1918, with fatal results for his career. In addition, his admiration for Hitler in the 1930s, much on the lines of his earlier enthusiasm for T.R., was ominous. He could select the wrong messiah.

For radicals and socialists outside the Liberal administration also, the United States provided an attractive impulse during these years. William Jennings Bryan, for all his insularity, received generous acclaim from Liberal and Labour backbenchers when he visited Britain in 1906: he was the symbol of democratic power ranged against the wealth and influence of the 'goldbugs', the apostle of international peace who had fought imperialism in America as courageously as the pro-Boers had done in Britain. Even the Labour Party did not necessarily view the United States solely as the ugly symbol of big business. On the contrary, the growth of a vigorous socialist movement in the Mid-West and other regions of the United States, the rise of the American Federation of Labor under Gompers in the face of judicial and other obstacles, re-awakened some of the old faith of the left in America as 'the last, best hope on earth'. While the Fabians (as in Beatrice Webb's American journey in 1898) thought American politics corrupt and incompetent, the more internationally-minded of the Independent Labour Party found much encouragement in the American scene. Ramsay MacDonald wrote enthusiastically of the success of the American Socialist Party in Milwaukee and other areas of the Mid-West. He kept up a regular correspondence with Oswald Garrison Villard of the New York *Nation*.[16] Keir Hardie visited the United States three times in all (1895, 1908 and 1912), and each time found something to gladden his weary heart.[17] He was alarmed always by the unbridled power of trusts and cartels in America. He noted, too, the wide gulf that prevailed between the American labour unions and the Socialist Party, their failure as yet to forge the kind of flexible labour alliance that he himself had helped form in Britain in 1900. He was far from being overwhelmed by Debs's success in polling almost a million votes in 1912; most industrial workers still ignored the Socialists, and indeed Debs's most substantial vote, proportionally, came from rural Oklahoma. Even so, Hardie did not despair of American labour. He had wide-ranging contacts with many wings of the American working-class movement, and so had his intimate associate, Frank Smith, the ex-Salvationist. Through Sam Gompers, Hardie learnt of the progress of the A.F. of L., and its steady, if reluctant, involvement in politics in pursuit of its Magna Carta. One outcome was the creation of the new Department of Labor by Woodrow Wilson in 1913. Through Debs, and ex-Populists like Henry Demarest Lloyd in Illinois, Hardie learnt of the grass-roots strength of American socialism in such disparate areas as the largely German parts of Wisconsin and Illinois, and the remote silver and copper mines of Montana, Wyoming and Idaho. Above all, Hardie was impressed by the success of the American Progressive movement in spreading the ethic of communal and co-operative activity through-out American society, in counteracting and undermining the ugly, brutal creed of free-enterprise capitalism. Just as Hardie saw the rise of the New Liberalism and the flowering of social reform in Britain as vital forces in helping on sympathy and understanding for democratic socialism and the Labour Party, so in the United States, pressure for a socialized, humanized, more moral capitalism would lend momentum to Debs and his followers—always provided that they retained contact with the industrial masses and did not lapse into the sterile dogma of a Hyndman or de Leon. At all events, Hardie, whose international sense was so closely bound up with his perception of the social and political processes in Britain itself from 1906 onwards, was far from viewing the United States with blank despair. Many on the British left, Liberal and Labour, followed his lead.

The impact of the United States on British reformers, however, was intermittent and partial at best. The influence of British liberalism on American Progressives, by contrast, was coherent and continuous. For decades, American reformers had imbibed much of their political philosophy from Britain. Carlyle, Ruskin and Morris helped them towards a moral critique of *laissez-faire*. A. R. Wallace's evolutionary doctrines spurred on the progress of 'reform Darwinism'. Later, Graham Wallas's new 'sociology' impelled the young Walter Lippman and others towards a more scientific methodology in quantifying and assessing social phenomena. He also taught them to take account of the irrational in politics.[18] In Boston from the 1890s onwards, W. D. P. Bliss, Robert Woods, Frank Parsons and other quasi-socialist reformers found in British Fabian socialism, in its *fin-de-siècle* phase, the inspiration for many of their hopes.[19] Until the turn of the century, however, this kind of influence was largely abstract and philosophical: it does not lend itself to precise measurement by the historian. After all, as Frederick Howe commented, with undue exaggeration, in his eulogistic account of British city government, social reform in Britain had been almost non-existent, because of the control exercised by vested interests, particularly the landed classes, on the British legislature.[20]

In the Edwardian years, however, the inspiration of British reform movements for American Progressives became tangible and all-pervasive. Indeed, in many ways, Britain, like Germany, Denmark, Switzerland and other European countries, became for American Progressives a kind of social laboratory where new techniques of political and social planning were being tested and refined. They served as a model of how radical reform could be practical—and good business as well. From the turn of the century, the Anglo-American 'connexion' assumed a highly specific form. A stream of young university teachers, economists, social workers, journalists and civic reformers made their way to Britain, particularly to British cities, to observe the progress of reform in the Old World and to assess how it could be transplanted or adapted to the New. This marked a more outward-looking phase of American reform, part of the supersession of Populism by Progressivism. Populists, largely drawn from remote rural areas of the south and west, preoccupied with domestic issues like the currency and the railroads, viewed Britain as a detested stereotype, the mercantile stronghold of Jewish finance and of the 'cross of gold' on which the American democracy, with the assistance of the Judases of Wall Street, was being crucified. But the mainly urban Progressives viewed Britain in a more positive light. While the Progressive reformers—Jane Addams, John R. Commons, Richard T.

Ely, Charles Beard, Frederick Howe and many others like them—remained profoundly American in their assumptions, convinced that the ailments besetting their society could best be solved within a native context by the application of direct democracy on the traditional American model, they valued the application of social engineering from Europe, too. It served to give their achievements a more enduring quality, long after the class and sectional cleavages of the Populist era had passed into obscurity.

There was much to interest American liberals in the British political scene after 1906. They viewed with admiration the onslaught waged by the British government on special interest groups—on the brewers (the 1908 Licensing Bill was a great encouragement to American prohibitionists),[21] on the landed classes, above all on the House of Lords. They followed with keen attention the crisis occasioned by Lloyd George's 'people's budget' in 1909. It was noted that the main thrust of the budgetary proposals came from new taxes on land, for which American Progressives such as Tom Johnson, Frederick Howe and Joseph Fels had long called. With new taxes imposed on the unearned increment on urban land, with the reversionary duties and other new imposts, it was believed that the British city and the British parliament would be freed from the remaining shackles of feudalism, that new bonds would be forged between the middle and working classes, and that a constantly renewable source of revenue for social reform would be found. American progressives also approved of the decision to hold a new general election in January 1910 so that radical legislation could be given a direct popular mandate.[22] The progress of British democracy in other respects was also applauded—the payment of Members of Parliament, the Franchise Reform Bill of 1912 and, above all, the growing pressure from the suffragettes. However, it was notable that the more militant tactics of the British suffragettes struck few welcoming chords among American women's leaders. Alice Stone Blackwell, in the *Woman's Journal*, wrote sympathetically of the campaign being waged by Mrs Pankhurst and her daughters. But 'one thing upon which in America we are all agreed is that it is not needed here and would not do here', Mrs Blackwell commented.[23] American women's leaders claimed their objectives were achieved by peaceful methods of persuasion on the state and city level: Inez Haynes Irwin, originally a warm supporter of the Pankhursts, noted how thirty-seven states of the union ratified women's suffrage measures from 1913 after a largely non-militant campaign.[24] Even so, close contact was maintained between the women's movement on each side of the Atlantic. The active involvement of American women in the social justice movement made the more socially radical amongst the British suffragettes— Sylvia Pankhurst and Margaret Bondfield, for instance—highly congenial to American women, most notably Alice Paul.

Two areas, above all, helped to inspire American Progressives in their most active and creative period—social justice and civic reform. In these two fields, the impact of British liberal and humanitarian reform was of most direct inspiration.

In the field of social justice, it was the evolution of the British city that in large measure provided the key to the liberal diagnoses of American reformers. It was in Britain and other European countries that the urban stresses arising from uncontrolled industrial expansion were most acute. Episodes like the London dock strike of 1889 afforded British middle-class social critics a new insight into the evils arising from poverty, slum housing and casual labour in the working-class areas of British cities.[25] Marx's analysis of the social residuum who formed the casualties of industrial change seemed all too forcefully borne out: many dreaded the growing appeal of socialism that might result amongst the urban poor. Fear as well as compassion helped on the cause of social reform. These developments, especially Charles Booth's famous survey of the London poor in 1889, were widely read by urban reformers in the United States. In particular, there was the major influence of the British settlement houses, Toynbee Hall in London's East End above all, created by Christian socialists to provide a communal focus for the immigrant and other poor of London. Toynbee Hall had a dramatic impact on the social awareness of American reformers. Jane Addams's memoirs, *Twenty Years at Hull House*, provide a revealing and sensitive testimony to it.[26] She had originally been stirred by Edward Caird's lecture on Abraham Lincoln, which showed her how the intellectual refinement of Oxford could be fused with human sensibility and compassion. In her visit to Toynbee Hall in 1888, she found the institutional means and the spiritual ideals which provided for her the essential key to social justice in the American cities. Hull House in Chicago, to a considerable degree, mirrored the principles on which Toynbee Hall was founded. Like its London counterpart, it sought to create a small, face-to-face community in which the urban poor could be protected from the size and impersonality of the modern city. Like Toynbee Hall, it was based on the premise that the cultural traditions of the residents should be, if possible, preserved and encouraged; thus immigrants in Hull House were urged to maintain their national customs, dress and culture. And finally, Hull House, perhaps even more than Toynbee Hall, was based on the premise that a wide, perhaps widening, gulf existed between the middle and working classes. Its organizers viewed the working-class world from the outside. In return, they gained the consolation of social service and of the fulfilment of Christian obligation. Settlement Houses were, for Jane Addams, 'a subjective necessity'. In a very real sense, the Anglo-American connection in the social justice movement was a Protestant Christian one: Jane Addams's experiment at Hull House was fired by the special sense of mission, even of personal guilt imbibed by a college-trained, middle-class American girl in the later nineteenth century. Many other women reformers—Edith Starr and Vida Scudder, later on Lilian Wald and Florence Kelley—carried on the ideals of Toynbee Hall into other settlements, into the crusade against urban poverty and environmental deprivation, into the campaign for tenement house reform in New York and elsewhere. Several of them went through their formative years in Britain: for instance Vida Scudder, who studied at Oxford from 1884 to 1887 and was deeply influenced by Ruskin's lectures there. Without the impulse provided by the British connection, the American social justice movement would have taken a different course.

As the movement for social reform broadened in America after the turn of the century, the influence of British and other European reform experiments became more and more intense. Eastern Progressive journals, such as the *Outlook*, *North Atlantic Review*, the *Arena*, the *Forum* and the *World's Work*, transmitted them in minute detail to eager American readers. British commentators on social problems, like Robert Donald (editor of the *Daily Chronicle*), Percy Alden M.P. and J. Allen Baker M.P. of the L.C.C., became widely read in America, although they were usually careful to spell out the differences that divided the British and American reform movements. After 1908, the social reforms of Lloyd George and Churchill were widely emulated in the states and cities of America. Labour exchanges, old-age pensions, progressive direct taxation, housing and land renovation, above all the British National Health Insurance Act of 1911, made a dramatic impact on American reformers.[27] Even in Wisconsin, where La Follette's Mid-Western Progressives felt far removed from the European scene—and in important senses hostile to it—'the Wisconsin Idea' borrowed from the British experience featured in the drafting of their social legislation. The limitation of working hours, minimum wage provisions, tax reform, workers' compensation for accidents, and factory inspection were areas where American Progressives drew heavily on European examples. Certainly, Germany was an even more compelling symbol for American social reformers, with its long legacy of legislation dating from Bismarck's measures of the early 1880s. But the experience of Lloyd George and his colleagues showed that liberal reform was compatible with active democratic control as well as with centralized paternalism. The state need not be so servile after all. If some of the more democratic aspects of the Liberal social reforms seemed unscientific and inefficient to a New Nationalist like Herbert Croly in his *Promise of American Life*, they made British Liberalism all the more appealing to the main stream of American social justice pioneers.

Scores of American social reformers made the pilgrimage to London's East End and to other British cities at this period. Amongst the most notable was the historian, Charles Beard, who worked for two years in Ruskin Hall, the working-man's college in Oxford founded by the American, Walter Vrooman, in 1899.[28] Here Beard refined his awareness of the crippling pressures of urban poverty and of the underlying economic factors that caused it. He began, too, his lifelong association with adult education: he was to found the Workers' Education Association of America in 1921. Beard also became intensely involved with the socialist movement. From Keir Hardie he heard at first hand of the way in which socialists and trade unionists had made common cause in the Labour Representation Committee. Beard almost stayed on in Britain to work for socialism. Some other American reformers did so. Dr Stanton Coit, a pillar of the Ethical Church, became a zealot of the Independent Labour Party and strove to become a parliamentary candidate. Joseph Fels, the naphtha soap millionaire, who had founded land cultivation societies in Philadelphia and other American cities, turned to similar ventures in the Essex marshes and elsewhere as a remedy for rising unemployment in Britain. He was actively involved in sponsoring the social work of George Lansbury in London's East End. He also met Keir Hardie and later helped finance Hardie's tour around the world in 1907–8.[29] The American impact on the British labour scene prior to 1914 is too often discussed solely in terms of the impact of de Leonism and the 'Wobblies' in pushing British miners and railwaymen towards direct industrial action in the period from 1910 to 1914. In fact, documents of industrial revolt, like *The Miners' Next Step* published at Tonypandy in 1912, had an indigenous origin, and owed virtually nothing to American syndicalist doctrines. By contrast, men like Fels brought a direct American experience to the mainstream of the British Labour movement. Fels's influence lingered on, even when his land colonies collapsed, and even when the more confiscatory aspects of Labour's programme alienated him (since he preferred the single tax on land as a panacea). In return, the growth of a democratic Labour party, the 'progressive alliance' which enabled Labour and the New Liberals to unite in fulfilling the old Liberal objectives as well as pushing on to new social goals, acted as a powerful stimulus to urban reformers in the social justice movement in the United States. Writers like Sydney Brooks gloried in English Labour's 'stride towards democracy'.[30]

An even more pervasive impact of Britain on the American reform movement came through the medium of municipal and civic reform. This chimed in with one of the most central features of American Progressivism—its urge to democratize and humanize the city. Here Britain, like Germany, was an obvious inspiration. Municipal socialist experiments had been widespread in Britain since the 1870s— Chamberlain's measures in Birmingham, the L.C.C. in London and the municipal reforms of Glasgow were already widely familiar. Much use had been made of British experiences by urban reformers in Boston in the 1890s. One of the most forceful of them, Frank Parsons, a lecturer in the law school of Boston University, extended the argument to demand not only municipal socialism in American cities but the state ownership of public utilities such as railroads, coal and water supplies throughout the nation. While he rejected the class hatred of the Marxists, he cited the nationalization carried out in New Zealand as harmonious instances of socialistic public enterprise in practice.[31]

As the public revulsion against the 'robber barons' was fostered by Ida Tarbell and other muck-raking journalists from 1902 onwards, these collectivist proposals acquired a new appeal and respectability. Another important theorist of urban reform, also much impressed by the British experience, was Albert Shaw, whose *Municipal Government in Great Britain* (1895) attracted wide attention.[32] Shaw emphasized the disinterested and honest nature of municipal government in British cities, and the wide range of services offered by them. Their life was civic, not merely urban. To him, British cities, like those of Germany and Switzerland, seemed to have an independence of spirit and a public-minded ethos which American cities, plagued by corruption and the machinations of selfish private interests, conspicuously lacked. Again, the impact of the 'muck-rakers', notably Lincoln Steffens's exposures of urban graft in St Louis and other cities after the turn of the century, provided a new political momentum for Shaw's teachings.

In city after city from the turn of the century, reform movements were widespread: Progressive reformers like Tom Johnson in Cleveland, 'Golden Rule' Jones in Toledo and Hazen Pingree in Detroit carved out a new nation-wide reputation. The borrowings from Britain were often indirect, although there is a clear link between the spread of commission government and of city managers, and the influence of a municipal civil service in Britain. The National Civic Federation made explicit its interest in the British urban experience: in 1906 it despatched a twenty-two man commission to investigate British municipal government and to promote its major features in the United States. Most urban reformers in this period remained incurably optimistic about the British city, and the popularity of municipal reform in Great Britain. As in the United States they had boundless faith in the natural enlightenment and liberalism of the British free citizenry, quite detached from considerations of class benefit or economic self-interest.

The most instructive and best-informed of these enthusiasts was Frederick C. Howe, a lifelong reformer from his days with Tom Johnson in Cleveland in the 1890s down to the New Deal period forty years later (when Howe worked with Jerome Frank in the A.A.A. programme).[33] Howe saw in the British city a symbol of faith for the American nation. Britain and Germany showed him that the city could become the hope of democracy, instead of its downfall.

He propounded his beliefs in a series of powerful monographs—
*The City: the Hope of Democracy* (1905), *The British City: the Beginnings of Democracy* (1907) and *European Cities at Work* (1913). In
addition, he was an indefatigable contributor to Progressive journals
in the Eastern and Mid-Western states alike. The message was consistent. In Britain, while Parliament was relatively inert because of
the control of the landed aristocracy, 'the city represented the high
water mark of democracy'.[34] Its local authorities were under close
democratic control yet their spirit was generally non-partisan.
Furthermore, municipal councils enlisted the voluntary services of
prominent local businessmen and tradesmen as their members,
without any thought of monetary reward. As a result, there was a
natural congruence between private and public enterprise. Businessmen
councillors showed the same practical, business-like enthusiasm in the
running of municipal services as they did in running their own private
firms. This was a major consideration for Howe: as Lincoln Steffens,
who accompanied him on some of his European tours wryly observed,
Howe 'believed in businessmen'.[35] The results, Howe argued, were
dramatically revealed in British city life—in experiments in municipal
trading in gas and water services, in the growth of municipal tramways,
in the development of local electricity plant, in the creation of garden
cities through a combination of public and private support, and
above all in the wide range of economic, social and cultural services
that the British city naturally provided. They were marked by
emphatic financial benefits, too. Howe, an economist by training,
delighted to point out how municipal trading in Britain provided a
far better return on capital than did private management. Municipal
gas or tramway services were highly efficient, notably cheap for the
consumer, showed a clear profit, and yet provided a high level of
wages for municipal employees.

But the ultimate benefits of the British city were above all, Howe
claimed, ethical and psychological.[36] The extent of activities operated
by British city government, the range of social classes it brought into
its activities, gave a sense of natural identity and involvement between
ordinary citizens and the city in which they lived. The contrast
between this and the stagnation or apathy which marked American
cities, with the layers of corrupt private interests which intruded
between the people and their civic government, was emphasized by

Howe time and again. As Bryce had observed long ago, Americans were not interested in their cities since they did so little. Whereas Americans disliked or feared the city, British people viewed it with hope, even in a city with such acute housing and environmental problems as Glasgow or Manchester. Howe remained generally optimistic about the British city. When the Progressives were defeated in the London County Council elections in 1907, he insisted that this did not imply a loss of faith in progressive municipal government in London, but resulted simply from a local argument about the rates.[37] Howe's main criticism of British cities, indeed, diminished during these years. He attacked the system under which British cities were made powerless by the inflated land values and by the economic stranglehold exercised by the landowners, often absentee. This led to a serious loss of potential revenue for the city, to inadequate city planning and to widespread urban squalor. Howe vigorously condemned the ugliness and low architectural standards of British town centres, and compared them very unfavourably with German cities in this respect.[38] However, to his delight, Lloyd George's 1909 budget made the first serious attempt to tax the unearned increment arising from land after development, and to release urban land for new social purposes. The financial control of the landowners over British cities, a legacy from the Middle Ages, was now dramatically under challenge from a radical Chancellor. Therefore, while Howe was more enthusiastic about German cities, which he rightly felt enjoyed more civic independence, he retained his optimistic faith in British cities also. After Lloyd George's budget, he felt that they might serve even more emphatically as the model and the inspiration for American urban reformers.

Howe's enthusiasm for the British city, faithfully reproduced in many American journals during these years, was partly based on a series of half understandings. Indeed, Howe himself eventually became a migrant from the city, and returned to the rural society from which he had sprung. He was too inclined to ignore factors other than the control of the landed classes which shackled the independence of the British city. In particular, he failed to see the ways in which Parliament and the central government were encroaching on the powers of cities —and were having to bail them out to keep municipal and county services going. One of the main reasons for the form which Lloyd

George's budget of 1909 took was a crisis in local government finance, and the urgent need to find new forms of revenue from the central government to pay for social and educational services.[39] Again, Howe made the government of British cities and counties more neat and tidy than it really was, and largely ignored the overlapping mass of separate authorities for public health, the poor law and (until 1902) education. Had he read more carefully the minority report on the Poor Law in 1909 his faith in the social services which British cities were capable of providing might have been somewhat dented. Even so, his conclusions were generally sound enough. He saw in the British city an active, organic democratic unit, widely respected, ever extending its sphere of operations. By contrast, American cities were passive, despised and relatively powerless. The British city served as a model for American urban reformers from 'Golden Rule' Jones (himself a native Welshman) in Toledo, Ohio, onwards. It suggested that urban reform was practicable in American terms also. Progressivism, like charity, could begin at home.

From these main themes of British inspiration for the American Progressive—social justice and civic reform—a typology of American Progressivism, a kind of profile of one major facet of American liberalism in the Roosevelt–Wilson era can be constructed. This took the form of the rational planner, the detached, non-partisan expert, professional in his administrative operations, yet with the enthusiasm of the well-meaning amateur, élitist in outlook, yet close to the people in his political philosophy. In many ways, he followed on from the Genteel Reform tradition handed on by the Liberal Republicans in 1872, and the later 'mugwumps' who advocated civil service reform on the British pattern, and who achieved the passage of the Pendleton Act in 1883. Like these patrician reformers—Charles Francis Adams, Richard Watson Gilder, Carl Schurz and E. L. Godkin, the Anglo-Irish editor of the *Nation*—American Progressives also admired the prototype of British government: passionless, élitist, based on ideals of public service and social segregation inculcated by a classical education and the public schools. The kind of public school- and university-trained civil servant who had fired the enthusiasm of Godkin in the 1860s (and who still provided an ideal for the anti-imperialists of 1898) was still a model widely admired. New private schools in the United States formed in the last decades of the nineteenth century gave it a new currency. The introduction of new forms of urban and municipal government in the Progressive era after the turn of the century was in some ways an attempt to Anglicize the United States, by curbing the excesses of its democracy with social and political controls. Just as American Progressives admired the detached, philosophical outlook on government which fired non-partisan civic reformers at home, so they were ready to applaud similar examples overseas. The enthusiasm of American Progressives for their own imperialist movement in Cuba, Latin America and China has long been noted.[40] What has not been sufficiently stressed by historians of American Progressivism who have noted the central role played by the 'mugwump' patrician in the reform movement after 1900 is that this was in many ways a direct transplantation of the British Liberal—indeed, Liberal Imperialist—ideal. Patrician, enlightened administrators of the type of Cromer in Egypt or Milner in South Africa provided the inspiration for many Progressive commentators after 1900. The *Outlook* praised the choice of a man like Lord Minto as Viceroy of India in September 1905: 'it may be remarked that Great Britain never chooses any but able and diplomatic men for this important post'.[41] This kind of imperialist stereotype was particularly appealing for New England and other Eastern Progressives who favoured the New Nationalism of Theodore Roosevelt and Croly. Often the class or racial assumptions that underlay this essentially Anglo-Saxon ideal were bluntly underlined. 'The British Empire has been, and is, a tremendous force for the advancement of civilization throughout the world.'[42] It is no surprise that many (though by no means all) Progressives called for restriction of the flood of 'new immigrants' from the Latin and Slav countries of Europe.

Time and again, emphasis was laid on the fact that British administrators and social reformers were Oxford- and Cambridge-trained, of public school background, and that other British universities were emulating their élitist example. The *Outlook* was lyrical in its praise of the type of man who composed the Liberal government that took office in Britain in December 1905. There were, it noted, eleven men from Oxford, five of these from Balliol, 'These represent the highest and finest traditions of self-culture'. Furthermore, these men included the president of the National Physical Recreation Society, an expert golfer, boxer, cricketer, oarsman, fisherman, footballer and 'pedestrian'.[43] (A bird-watcher might also have been added to this galaxy of talent.) Britain's zeal for the active outdoor life, redolent of the public school antecedents of its governors, was never more widely canvassed. Conversely, the presence in the Cabinet of an outsider like Lloyd George, a product of a poor Welsh cottage and Llanystumdwy National School, entirely self-made and largely self-educated, aroused less attention. Some years later, Walter Hines Page, then the American Ambassador, took up the same theme. He lavished praise on the British ruling class—symbolized by Morley, Grey and Lulu Harcourt in the Liberal government in 1913—'gently bred, high-minded, physically fit, intellectually cultivated'.[44] It was British universities above all, particularly Oxford, which kindled the Progressives' patrician ideals: 'for generations English university life has been a preparation for participation in English public life'. The *Outlook* praised the detached, critical spirit in which its products viewed current shibboleths. Morley's proposals for India in 1906, for instance, were commended for adapting political democracy to Indian conditions—that is, not basing it on universal suffrage. Morley, it claimed, had freed himself of some of the traditional errors of the American Liberal, notably the standard belief that universal suffrage was an automatic, universal right.[45] With the proper leadership, a similar style of reform was feasible in the United States also. In their different ways, Theodore Roosevelt, sprung from a Dutch patroon family in the Hudson valley, trained at Groton and Harvard, and Woodrow Wilson, an austere Presbyterian who had taught at Johns Hopkins before moving on to Princeton, represented similar ideals of élitist leadership in the United States. They each symbolized a contrast with the business and manufacturing classes. They could be expected to put Liberal Imperialism into effect at home. Abroad, America already had her own social imperialist models ready to hand—for instance, General Wood whose improvements of the roads and other civic amenities of Havana provided an antiseptic, Anglo-Saxon Utopia for the advancement of lesser, Latin breeds. British Liberal Imperialism meant for many American Progressives an updated version of the Rome of the Antonines, confident, rational, ordered—and above all clean. The vision of 'spotlesstown', of a clean, organized civilization, in place of the squalor, racial tensions and overcrowding of American cities, was in many ways the ideal of the American Progressives. S. S. McClure wrote of his admiration for the hygienic, crime-free character of British cities by comparison with the urban ghettos of America.[46] Britain, and its Liberal Imperialist élite, provided much of the framework for this ideal. In these ways, then, Britain provided much of the momentum for the American Progressives in the era between the Spanish–American war in 1898 and the United States' entry into the First World War in 1917.

At the same time, it is clear that this British influence had its limits. Urban reform in America owed its impetus to native sources as well. The pressure for direct democracy—for primaries, the direct election of senators, the initiative, referendum and recall—were in explicit contrast to the indirect democracy that flourished in Britain. Indeed, Germany, another model for the Progressives, was in major respects profoundly anti-democratic in its social and political system. Furthermore, the stereotype of the patrician university-trained Anglo-Saxon élitist had its appeal mainly for Progressives in the north-eastern states of America. Even here, there were Progressive critics of it. For instance, Herbert Croly condemned Britain's inefficient methods of economic and commercial management, and its dependence on free trade, which would, he claimed lead to Britain's ultimate decline as a major power. 'The best English social type was a gentleman—but a gentleman absolutely conditioned, tempered, and supplemented by a flunky.'[47] Marcus Aurelius was degenerating into Bertie Wooster.

In the Mid-West, La Follette and other Progressives of the insurgent wing of Republicanism, reacted sharply against the patrician ideal: this was the kind of schism which produced the decisive breach within the Progressive movement between Theodore Roosevelt and La Follette in 1912, and which ultimately led to the latter throwing his support behind Woodrow Wilson. Here in the Mid- and Far-West, as for the Populists who preceded them, Britain seemed to most Progressives less of a social model than a symbol of the class enemy.[48] However forward-looking in its social policies, Britain for the La Follettes and Norrises still represented a hierarchical, monarchical, interest-ridden society, dominated by reactionary landowners as it was in 1776, and further reinforced by the insidious capitalistic concerns of the City of London. When war broke out in Europe in August 1914, La Follette's sympathy for the social reforms of the

British Liberal Government or for his French forbears in no way led him to identify with the *entente* powers. Indeed, he believed that British finance imperialism was in large measure responsible for bringing the war about—with the incidental assistance of the arms manufacturers, later to be christened 'merchants of death'.

Other Progressives were also disillusioned by the more undemocratic aspects of the British scene, long before 1914. These were emphasized for many Progressives by British policy towards Ireland which repelled many Liberals beyond the restricted confines of Irish–American circles. Lincoln Steffens was another prepared to borrow reforming techniques from Britain while rejecting the essence of its social structure. He believed that in Britain there lurked some of the graver evils of the American scene, but in a more subtle form. Corruption, openly displayed in America through political graft, was quietly diffused in Britain through its education system—the career of Cecil Rhodes was an illustration of this.[49] Where America had financial interests, Britain had class privilege, in many ways much more entrenched and more dangerous. There was, Steffens felt, need for a British muck-raking press to expose conditions across the Atlantic. Even Frederick Howe fell somewhat short of a total admiration for the British social and political system. Despite all the reforms introduced by the Asquith government since 1908, he noted that privilege and the power of the landed interest was still pervasive in Britain; a more determined effort was needed to uproot it than the government, even Lloyd George, had so far attempted. Howe was dismayed by the crude imperialism rampant amongst the Liberal social reformers he admired: 'even the Labour Party had a confused veneration for Empire'.[50] Howe did not want an empire that was a greater Birmingham, but rather a Birmingham which was a crown colony writ small with a Chamberlain as its viceroy. When European war broke out in 1914, Howe felt as detached from the *melée* as did La Follette. After all, the two countries whose social experiments he most admired were ranged on opposite sides.

The criticism of Britain voiced by American Progressives took varying forms. To Croly, and in a sense to Steffens, what was wrong with Britain was that, politically, it was too democratic. All manner of social groups and classes were given freedom to operate and organize—for instance, the influence of the religious denominations on the British primary education system was the despair of many American radicals. In Croly's view, this pluralist system meant a suppression of the concentrated forces of the true 'popular energy'.[51] He favoured a powerful, centralized paternalism, with a heavy concentration on the executive: there were those later who accused him (perhaps unfairly) of Fascist implications. Steffens also admired strong government: hence his distaste for the confusions and ultra-democracy of the British Labour Party, and his later enthusiasm for the totalitarian dictatorship in the Soviet Union. The future 'worked' in Moscow as it simply did not in Manchester or Merthyr Tydfil. Steffens (and Ernest Bevin) despised the I.L.P. radical 'whose bleeding 'eart ran away with 'is bloody 'ead'. Conversely other Progressives felt that Britain remained too undemocratic, its social justice movement unduly based on class segregation, its civic reformers too superior and isolated. Howe had praised the British city because only a small number of its officials were popularly elected;[52] but this could easily be inverted into a major criticism. The moral was starkly pointed out by the mysterious and secretive manner in which Britain, directed by Grey, the very exemplar of the Liberal Imperialist patrician admired by American Progressives, went furtively to war in August 1914. Britain was not a social democracy and a political democracy only with serious qualifications.

There was another, wider aspect of British Liberalism in these years which tended to alarm Progressives of most shades—its unduly close links with organized labour. Despite their concern for the working man, American Progressives viewed his plight from the outside, as they also viewed the farmer, the immigrant and the Negro. Progressives felt far removed from Gompers and the world of American labour unionism; they deeply feared the violence and class upheaval symbolized by the 'Wobblies'. Progressives wanted civic and humanitarian reform, but in a conservative, capitalist setting. They did not, in general, openly pose fundamental questions about the distribution of wealth or the control of economic power. They preferred a co-operative commonwealth to a socialist state: Denmark was their 'middle way' as Sweden was for Marquis Childs during the New Deal.[53] Ultimately, perhaps, most Progressives hoped to reform men rather than institutions, to change society through moral enlightenment and civic education rather than through structural reform. Upton

Sinclair found that his novel, *The Jungle*, an account of the horrific labour conditions in the meat-packing factories in Chicago, appealed to the middle-class consumer not to the working-class producer. It produced the Pure Food and Drug Act, not factory legislation. Meanwhile, labour conditions in Chicago remained as uncivilized as before. Workers went on voting Republican and Democratic, rather than Socialist, just the same. Sinclair, as he wrote in disgust, had aimed at the public's heart and hit its stomach instead.[54] By contrast, British Liberalism released new formidable forces beyond the capacity of a patrician élite to control. Asquith could not play 'finality Jack' to the Labour movement. The industrial unrest in Britain in 1910–14, at a time of alarming manifestations in the United States with violent strikes and the upsurge of the 'Wobblies', emphasized for many American Progressives that their reforming zeal had its firm limits. It could remould capitalism, but it should not destroy it. It was planned for the working men but did not arise spontaneously from their needs. Even the tenement house reformers were often careless of the wishes of the proletariat whose wretched conditions they sought to remedy, as Sylvia Pankhurst told them bluntly enough during her American tour in 1911. In the event, most British Liberals felt their links with organized labour in a 'progressive alliance' were becoming closer: in March 1914 there was a real prospect of a Liberal–Labour coalition government. Most American Progressives were still happy to keep their distance from the working man, and to view Debs, distastefully, from afar.

For all its limits, the connection between British and American Progressivism in this period was evidently a close one. Despite the fears of Croly and others, developments in Britain still provided a fund of ideas and inspiration for American reformers down to August 1914. The election of Woodrow Wilson as President in 1912, a man deeply steeped in British political tradition and folklore, a worshipper at the shrine of Gladstonian Liberalism in its most unreconstructed form, seemed to make the links between British and American liberals still more complete. Yet, it was Wilson in fact who dramatically underlined the differences between them. His New Freedom in 1913 had virtually no social content: labour was just another special interest which could claim no privileged treatment from the federal government. His main priorities were the trusts, tariffs and banking: monopoly and the concentration of large-scale industrial and financial power were the main targets. None of these held much significance for British Liberals, the products of a more integrated, less sectional society. Their approach to concentrations of economic power was to place them under public control rather than to dismantle them entirely. In any case, tariff reform had largely been suppressed as a major issue in British politics; it was wider industrial problems, together with the unique hazards of Ireland, that preoccupied British Liberals now. The outbreak of war in August 1914 confirmed the gulf that still existed between Britain and the United States in their political systems and priorities. In any event, the massive immigration into the United States since the 1890s was steadily eroding much of the Anglo-American connection. Despite the temporary enthusiasm of the British left for Woodrow Wilson as a transatlantic Messiah in 1917–18,[55] the old links were never restored. The steady decline of British Liberalism, the rise of Labour, the new polarization between labour and capital as the central fact of British political life after 1918, coincided with a new surge of business ascendancy under Republican rule in the United States. 'Normalcy' largely killed off American Progressivism, and the British associations that had helped to foster it. In the thirties, save for a maverick like Lloyd George, the New Deal failed to kindle the old fire amongst the British left. Franklin Roosevelt's brisk destruction of the World Economic Conference in July 1933 revealed the essential nationalism, even isolationism, of his administration.

Even so, the transatlantic aspects of American Progressivism should not be ignored. They serve to show how American liberalism had emerged from its inward-looking cocoon of the Populist years. They showed, too, how the frankly élitist ideals of the civil service reformers and Genteel Reform patricians had merged with wider democratic currents after 1890. American Progressives did not enlist British and other European ideas because they were the apprehensive victims of a 'status revolution'.[56] In the main they represented (as did their business-men antagonists) social groups which had survived, indeed flourished, throughout the Gilded Age and the Robber Baron era, so-called. To the university teachers, lawyers, journalists and social workers who provided the ethic and the passion for so much of American Progressivism, especially in the cities, the British experience gave them a confident, optimistic, crusading aspect, not a defensive, alarmist one.

Radical reform was again possible, desirable, even profitable, in the United States. It was rooted in basic American ideals dating from the founding fathers and beyond. But, above all, it flourished 'over there', in Britain in the here and now. In the Old World, Frederick Howe and his friends beheld a vision of the future—and it worked.[57]

## NOTES

1. Herbert S. Foxwell to E. R. Seligman, 24 November 1895 (Butler Library, Columbia University, Seligman Papers).
2. Foxwell to Seligman, 23 June 1909 (ibid.).
3. Richard Hofstadter, 'Cuba, The Philippines and Manifest Destiny', *The Paranoid Style in American Politics* (Vintage Books edition, 1967) pp. 148 ff.
4. *Forum*, October 1906, pp. 176–177. These comments were written by A. Maurice Low.
5. Cf. Benjamin O. Flower, *Progressive Men, Women and Movements of the last Twenty-Five Years* (New York, 1914) pp. 134–141.
6. This is discussed at length in P. F. Clarke, *Lancashire and the New Liberalism* (Cambridge, England, 1971). See the same author's 'The Progressive Movement in England', *Trans. Royal Historical Society*, 5th Series (1974) 159–182.
7. Henry Pelling, *America and the British Left* (London, 1956) pp. 70 ff.
8. A. E. Campbell, *Great Britain and the United States, 1895–1903* (London, 1960) pp. 195–200; *American Fabian*, June 1898, p. 4.
9. Cf. Edward Ions, *James Bryce and American Democracy* (London, 1968) pp. 203 ff.
10. Keith Robbins, *Sir Edward Grey* (London, 1971) pp. 274–277.
11. David Lloyd George to Mrs Lloyd George, 16 October 1912 (National Library of Wales, Lloyd George Papers, MSS. 20, 431 C).
12. This memorandum is printed in Kenneth O. Morgan, *The Age of Lloyd George* (London, 1971) pp. 150–155.
13. David Lloyd George, *The Truth about the Peace Treaties*, Vol. I (London, 1938) pp. 226, 231–232.
14. Lord Riddell, *War Diary* (London, 1933) p. 324.
15. Harold Spender, *The Prime Minister* (London, 1920) p. 359.
16. See the Villard–MacDonald correspondence in the Houghton Library, Harvard University, 6.MS.Am.1323.
17. Hardie's views on the United States are discussed in my book, *Keir Hardie: Radical and Socialist* (London, 1975) pp. 85-87, 185-188.

18. Cf. Charles Forcey, *The Crossroads of Liberalism* (Oxford, 1961) pp. 100–101.
19. See Arthur Mann, *Yankee Reformers in the Urban Age* (Cambridge, Mass., 1954) chs. IV–VI and *The American Fabian*.
20. Frederick Howe, *The British City: the beginnings of Democracy* (New York, 1907) pp. 9, 273–309.
21. Samuel J. Burrows, 'The Temperance Tidal Wave', *Outlook*, 4 July (1908) p. 513.
22. *Outlook*, 20 November (1909) pp. 605–607.
23. *Woman's Journal*, 15 June 1912, pp. 188–189. The views of an English anti-militant women's suffragist, A. Maude Royden, were widely cited.
24. 'The Adventure of Feminism', Inez Haynes Irwin Papers (Radcliffe College Library). Only nine western states had by 1912.
25. Cf. Gareth Steadman Jones, *Outcast London* (Oxford, 1971).
26. Jane Addams, *Twenty Years at Hull House* (New York, 1910) pp. 39–40, 81, 89 ff; Allen F. Davis, *American Heroine* (New York, 1973), pp. 48–52.
27. Gertrude Amy Slichter, 'The European Backgrounds of American Reform' (University of Illinois, Ph.D. Thesis, 1960).
28. Richard Hofstadter, 'Charles A. Beard', *The Progressive Historians* (Vintage Books edition, 1970) pp. 172–179.
29. Mary Fels, *Joseph Fels: his Life-work* (London, 1920) pp. 58–59; Ramsay MacDonald to Bruce Glasier, 29 August 1908 (Independent Labour Party archive); *La Follette's Magazine*, 1 January (1910).
30. *Outlook*, 7 April (1906) pp. 797–800.
31. See Parsons's articles in *The Arena*, December (1906); January, February, March, April, October (1907).
32. Slichter, 'European Backgrounds', p. 191.
33. Apart from the works by Howe cited in the text, his *Confessions of a Reformer* (New York, 1925) is also well worth reading.
34. Howe, *The City: the Hope of Democracy* (New York, 1905) p. 136.
35. Lincoln Steffens, *Autobiography*, Vol. I (New York, 1931) p. 648.
36. Howe, *The British City*, p. 123.
37. Howe, ibid., p. 213 n.
38. Howe, ibid., p. 243; idem, *European Cities at Work*, p. 323.
39. See Lloyd George's 1909 Budget speech, printed in *Better Times* (London, 1910) pp. 60 ff.
40. William E. Leuchtenburg, 'Progressivism and Imperialism: the Progressive Movement and American Foreign Policy, 1898–1916', *Mississippi Valley Historical Review* XXXIX (December 1952) 496 ff. There are, of course, many exceptions to this generalization.
41. *Outlook*, 9 September (1905) p. 52.

42. Ibid., 6 January (1912), pp. 4–5.
43. Ibid., 23 December (1905) pp. 957–959.
44. Page to Herbert S. Houston, 24 August 1913 (cited in Burton J. Hendrick, *Life and Letters of Walter Hines Page*, Vol. I (New York, 1924) p. 139).
45. *Outlook*, 25 August (1906) pp. 923–924.
46. S. S. McClure, *Autobiography* (London, 1914) pp. 255–256.
47. Herbert Croly, *The Promise of American Life* (New York, Paperback edition, 1963) p. 238.
48. Cf. *La Follette's Magazine*, 9 January (1909).
49. Steffens, *Autobiography*, pp. 652–653, 704–708.
50. Howe, *Confessions of a Reformer*, pp. 296–298.
51. Croly, *The Promise of American Life*, p. 238.
52. Howe, *The British City*, pp. 234–235.
53. Howe, 'A Commonwealth Ruled by Farmers', *The Outlook*, 26 February (1910). Marquis Childs wrote enthusiastically of 'Sweden: the Middle Way' during the 1930s.
54. Louis Filler, *Crusaders for American Liberalism* (Collier Books, 1961) pp. 165–168.
55. Marvin Swartz, *The Union of Democratic Control in British Politics during the First World War* (Oxford, 1971) pp. 131–135.
56. Richard Hofstadter, *The Age of Reform* (Vintage Books edition, 1955) pp. 131 ff.
57. I am grateful to Professor Carl Degler of Stanford University and The Queen's College, Oxford, for some valuable comments on a draft of this essay.

# Woman Suffrage in Britain and America in the Early Twentieth Century

## DAVID MORGAN

> We who have come down from the last generation
> are reformers, but reformers are poor politicians
> > Carrie Chapman Catt, December 1916

> What a ridiculous tragedy it would be if this
> strong Government and Party . . . was to go down
> on Petticoat Politics
> > Winston Churchill, December 1911

Women first voted in a British parliamentary election in December 1918. By ensuring in America a Republican-led 66th Congress the mid-term elections a month earlier had made it almost certain that women would vote in the presidential election of 1920. Elsewhere women were enfranchized at this period only in revolutionary conditions in Soviet Russia and defeated, newly republican Germany. Victorious France and Italy did not participate in this flood of the feminist tide; both were free of the Marxist necessities of Russia and the German desire to emulate the victors: neither had had strong suffrage movements. Only in Britain and America had there been a long political campaign and large scale organizations, the leaders of which were the acknowledged pace setters of world wide political feminism.

The general outline of the rise of feminism in these two leading countries has been the object of several studies.[1] The final, climactic years when the question was before Congress and Parliament are now more clearly understood.[2] It may, therefore, be possible to attempt a more systematic comparison of elements of the final campaign than has hitherto been possible. It is acknowledged, of course, that such comparison between significantly different societies, economies and policies is fraught with difficulties. The patterns of mass and élite expectation contrasted considerably in the nineteenth century and, indeed, continued to do so after 1900. Yet it was in the early twentieth century that Britain converged more quickly with America in the granting of political rights at the same time as both countries took important steps in the direction of ameliorating gross inequalities in the distribution of political, social and economic resources. In terms of Louis Hartz's analysis[3] Woman Suffrage was granted in both countries precisely at the time when the 'fragment' society returned to 'confront' the parent society and culture. It was granted at a time, moreover, when the political preoccupations of both societies were becoming more similar. Most particularly, it was granted when both countries were deeply involved in a war which forced them, formally at least, to deepen and clarify their attachments to participatory and egalitarian norms. Despite their differences both societies showed similarities in the range and speed of their responses to feminist demands. Suffragists, in both countries, could not fail to notice the similarities in the values lying behind the different political façades. Comparison, then, may be a more valid exercise in this period than in the nineteenth century.

It is already possible to regard the woman suffrage campaigns as the first *feminist* revolution. Revolution in the sense that a significant, if not fundamental, redistribution of power between the sexes took place; first in that we are now in the middle of a second feminist revolutionary impulse which might well be more thoroughgoing in its effects than the first. This second revolution like the first will need, eventually, further legislation and regulation, that is, its outcome will be political actions directly involving the state. Thus, while the Suffrage campaign may be intrinsically interesting to study, it may also be of some interest to examine how such legislation in the past impacted on the political system and how it was moulded by it. In the first revolution the lead was clearly taken by feminists in the United States and Britain and, thus far, the second revolution seems likely to be similarly characterized. In neither country has the political system changed in most critical respects. There may, then, be clues from the Suffrage campaign as to the interaction of Women's Liberation and the political systems in the two countries. More of that later, however.

Feminism came out of eighteenth-century philosophical radicalism, was embodied in nineteenth-century liberalism, and carried to its first major victory by early twentieth-century 'Progressivism'. Britain provided the leading spokeswomen in the first phase, and the most 'militant' activists in the third phase.[4] America had the first real national organization, could show the most widespread and sustained political activity in the second phase, and closely paralleled the British campaign in the third phase.

Feminist ideas spread most widely when feminism and feminists were seen as part of larger causes. Thus, despite the powerful intellectual case made by Mary Wollstonecraft in the 1790s,[5] feminism had to wait a further half century before an organization was created among American women who had come to see feminism as significant, if not vital, to their other causes.[6] Similarly, in England an organization for women's rights came out of the mobilization of radicals and liberals for, *inter alia*, the Reform Act of 1867.[7] In both countries the movements split in the 1870s as the reformist tide ebbed, and reformers, women included, had to establish their priorities. In America, the ostensible cause was the refusal of Radical Republicans to include women in the *post bellum* settlement. The movement there split, and the dabbling of some Eastern feminists in more general revolutionary ideas tailed off. Feminism, thereafter, took on a more Western, homogeneously American, conservative hue.[8] Hence in the 1890s many Populists were sceptical of feminism and refused to endorse it. Not until the movement began to attract women who were 'Progressive' did it advance steadily in the West and then, later, in the East. In general, feminism came to be attractive to the 'clean government' school of thought, the Americanizers of immigrants, the declared enemies of corrupt boss-ridden city politics.[9] Woman Suffrage, like Prohibition, *could* be portrayed as part of a backlash, a last attempt of native Americans to retain their control over American politics and life. But, along with measures allowing voters the Initiative, the Referendum, Primaries, the Recall and the Short Ballot, Woman Suffrage could, by Suffragists and 'Progressives', be set in the context of attempts to refurbish American democracy. For this growing school, only by breaking the grip of party organization could the allegedly flagging faith of voters in their political competence be restored.[10] Thus, while the 1890s gave the feminist cause only two states, Colorado

1893 and Idaho 1896, to add to their former territories Wyoming and Utah, the short period from 1910 to 1912 saw the cause triumph in Washington in 1910, California 1911, Arizona, Kansas and Oregon in 1912. Together, this meant that the women of nine states and a territory (Alaska) voted by the time Woodrow Wilson took office, a significant number in the very section where the party battle was at its keenest precisely because it was becoming the area whose choice was decisive in national elections.

The subsequent campaign may, briefly, be outlined. Wilson's inauguration marked a resurgence of Suffragist interest in pressing for a Constitutional amendment prohibiting state sex discrimination in setting franchise qualifications. This in turn helped split the National American Woman Suffrage Association (N.A.W.S.A.) leading in 1913 to the expulsion of the Pankhurst disciple Alice Paul and her followers and the creation of the Southern States Woman Suffrage Conference which was hostile to the proposed amendment. In 1914, after the Democrats in caucus had declared Woman Suffrage to be a state matter, and only two out of seven state referenda—Montana and Nevada—had succeeded, the N.A.W.S.A. embraced a state-orientated policy symbolized by the proposed Shafroth–Palmer Constitutional amendment. This overcame the problem of securing Suffrage referenda in the states by allowing referenda upon petition of only 8 per cent of the votes cast at the last presidential election. This position was, in effect, endorsed by both parties right up to August 1916 when the Republican presidential candidate, Charles E. Hughes, came out for the original Susan B. Anthony amendment which positively prohibited state discrimination and gave Congress power to enforce the prohibition. One month later the N.A.W.S.A. changed both its officers and its policy and, until 1920, conducted an enormous campaign aimed at securing state victories for the express purpose of enacting the Susan B. Anthony amendment.

Until 1916 Woodrow Wilson had refused to involve himself in the campaign. From his re-election onward, nevertheless, he became steadily entangled. Not, however, until the United States was at war could he be persuaded to press Congress to allow a vote on the amendment, only to find that his own party was principally to blame for the failure to secure the two-thirds vote in the Senate of the Sixty-fifth Congress. In the November 1918 elections the

Republicans became the majority party and hence the amendment passed Congress quickly in the summer of 1919. The ratification campaign was successful in just over a year and Tennessee, the thirty-sixth state, ratified in time to allow both presidential candidates to appeal to the new women voters in time for the November 1920 presidential election. In both the Congressional and ratification campaigns the sectional characteristics of Southern hostility and Western enthusiasm were very clear.[11]

In Britain the nineteenth century saw the franchise extended to men on an instalment basis and, after 1867, to women for local elections if they were qualified, but unmarried or widowed. By 1904 this process of enfranchisement was complete for local government and marriage had long ceased to be a bar. But anomalies and inequities abounded and Liberals, particularly, gave vent to considerable concern. Suffragists, chiefly organized in the National Union of Women's Suffrage Societies (N.U.W.S.S.) had strong reason to hope that the next government would be Liberal and would have to face up to franchise reform quickly. In that process they could hope to persuade or coerce a Liberal government into granting Woman Suffrage. The appearance after 1906 of a *Labour* wing of the Liberal party merely increased these expectations.

The Liberal party at large, however, had other priorities and the clash between the two opposed sets of expectations was the stuff of the violent campaign that followed the Liberals taking office. The party was moving steadily away from the old Gladstonian mould— a half of those elected in the huge majority of 1906 were in Parliament for the first time.[12] Neither the old guard nor the new men put Woman Suffrage anywhere but low on their list of priorities and to this the Liberal–Labour members assented. Campbell-Bannerman, the Prime Minister, though generally sympathetic—as seven-eighths of Liberal M.P.s were—knew that the party was preoccupied with other questions and would not agree easily on a bill. In 1908 on his retirement he was replaced by H. H. Asquith whose strong opposition was intensified by the kind of campaign waged against his government. By 1909 the government had authorized the forcible feeding in prison of Pankhurst 'Suffragettes'—organized in the Women's Social and Political Union (W.S.P.U.).

Only after the Parliament Act of 1911 was on the statute book was there any possibility of Woman Suffrage, and then only a slight one. The government's proposed Franchise Bill—which supposedly could take a Suffrage amendment—added to the growing stress being felt inside the government. The debacle of January 1913 when the Speaker forced the withdrawal of the bill, the subsequent 'Suffragette' fury, the 'Cat and Mouse Act' and a general stalemate on the question were the results. Not until the war broke up this impasse was any advance possible. The question of votes for soldiers brought up general franchise reform and, in turn, Woman Suffrage. The replacement of Asquith by Lloyd George at the head of a broad coalition government created the bipartisan situation in which, *inter alia*, a Suffrage solution was possible. In the event the actual bill went through its stages speedily and women over thirty years of age were enfranchised before the Armistice gave them the chance to vote in their first parliamentary election.[13]

So much for the familiar outlines of the campaigns. What now may be said by way of comparison both of the operations of the political systems, and of the Suffragists? First, it is clear that reactions of political leaders to the issue in both countries were more conditioned by constitutional and party political considerations than they were by considerations of justice, or even the needs of women. More will be said later of Wilson and Asquith personally on this question, but it is idle to see the reactions of either out of the context of, for example, the ramifications of the question of the Lords for Asquith, or the South for Wilson. These and other inhibitions were direct products of the constitutional situations and need elucidating.

In Britain the unitary constitution meant that women must be given the parliamentary vote all over the Kingdom, or not at all. In America, under a federal system, Western states might grant full Suffrage but, at first, this meant little in the East or South. In Britain where, after 1906, the Liberals controlled the Commons and the Unionists the Lords, any government Suffrage Bill stood to be rejected by the Lords, given the political context. In America the actions of the federal government were conditioned, constitutionally, by state control of franchise qualifications and, politically, by the special tie between that and the racial question in the South. The eleven former Confederate States, if they opposed solidly, would need only two allies to prevent the ratification of an amendment to the

Constitution. The task of securing two-thirds majorities in Congress, and thirty-six state ratifications was a huge test of political organization and pressure even without any concerted sectional opposition.

In Britain, the failure to settle the Irish question before 1906 meant that there was something of a British equivalent of the American sectional vote. After 1910 this was of great significance since it fostered the myth among Unionists that the absence of an *English* majority behind the Liberals plus the 1911 curb of the Lords, put the constitution in abeyance and left them free to oppose government measures by virtually—as the Curragh seemed to prove—all means. Again, the American Constitution fixed the timing of elections and this contributed directly to the frustrating of some of Wilson's legislative intentions after 1916. Thus Woman Suffrage may be regarded as a failure for Wilson in the last days of the Sixty-fifth Congress.[14] On the other hand, in Britain, while the constitution gave the government the choice of election dates and issues—within limits— the Parliament Act of 1911 at once narrowed these limits from seven to five years and—via the Lords' two year delaying power—made a legislative log jam inevitable after 1912. The Suffrage position was worsened by this.[15]

Conversely, however, the constitutional and political situations provided compensations. In America, if it was sectional fear that inhibited federal action, it was also sectional pressure in the West that kept the issue before the dominant party and ultimately secured the Nineteenth Amendment. When both parties were bidding for the control of the West, both would have to pay—eventually—part of the West's price of support. In Britain a sectional vote existed—the Irish—and this was largely hostile to Suffrage in the key period from 1911 to 1913, principally to prevent a Cabinet split and preserve the Home Rule Bill. The Cabinet system, however, provided something of a sectional equivalent to the American situation in Congress. While in America the President's cabinet was secondary, in Britain the decisive struggle lay in the Liberal Cabinet where Asquith opposed most of his principal colleagues. By 1912 the fact that Grey, Lloyd George and Haldane were ready to press Asquith very hard on the question meant that Suffrage was 'in the swim', would be before Liberals and the country at the next election, and could not be ignored by Asquith thereafter. The pressure of powerful friends in the Cabinet made up—to an extent—for the fact that, lacking a federal system, British women voted nowhere in parliamentary elections and lacked the leverage of *voters*.[16]

The power of a Prime Minister was great, especially when rivals and not he were hurt by scandal,[17] but it was not overwhelming and Asquith could not have stood indefinitely against a majority of his Cabinet and party. It is interesting to note that, assuming there had been no war, an Irish settlement, and a Liberal victory in 1914 or 1915, Asquith would have had to be 'converted' to Suffrage by 1916, anyway, in order to ensure that—under the Parliament Act—the issue would be ready for an election in 1918 or 1919.

Suffrage could not be made a party issue in either country. A large majority of the Liberals were for it, but until 1911 the Lords would have certainly rejected a Liberal measure. Thereafter, parliamentary time and the sheer weight of legislation told heavily against Suffrage when added to the fears of a Cabinet split held among Irish Nationalists and the Liberals. In America the Democrats controlled the Presidency throughout, and Congress until 1919, but they alone could not provide the two-thirds vote required for an amendment. Both parties had large programmes and resented the forcing of Suffrage on them by a militant direct action policy. Mrs Pankhurst first appeared to Liberals as something of a Labour ginger group and then, later as a Unionist Trojan Horse. Democrats from South and North could rightly regard Suffragists as more a Republican than a Democratic phenomenon. For both parties the issue became a danger when re-election had to be considered. For Liberals this period was around 1912–13 when—because of the Parliament Act—the 1914 or 1915 manifesto had to be envisaged. For Democrats it was during 1916 when Wilson realized that the price of Western support in November entailed some gesture towards Suffrage. The declarations of Roosevelt and Charles Evans Hughes only made the point more explicit. In 1912 Asquith's government could plead the problem of time, while in 1916 Wilson could plead the South. Neither plea had indefinite validity.[18]

For parties and politicians the war was the catalyst forcing conversions to Suffrage, and giving both a way to save face. In Britain, with the Irish question in abeyance, the war issue of 'votes for soldiers' carried Suffrage explosively back into the political swim and, by

K

helping, cost Asquith his position, put an active Suffragist in office as Prime Minister of a coalition government; producing, in short, the conditions most likely to produce a successful conclusion to the campaign.

In America the impact of the war strengthened the President's hand in relation to Congress in general, and his own party in particular. It also weakened the capacity of Anti-Suffragists of all shades and, as in Britain, highlighted the role and status of women war workers. In both countries the extension of political, social and economic democracy became part of the rhetoric of politicians concerned to boost morale and prepare for post-war reconstruction. It is well to note, nevertheless, that in both countries the war would not have been the catalyst it was had there not been the large-scale campaigns of pre-war days. Suffrage was at the edge of the pre-war spectrum of practical politics— the war hastened its move towards the centre. In that process both Irish and Southern objections were disregarded, the Irish having an immediate political price to pay in the destruction of the Nationalists. An irony of the 1918 election in Britain in consequence was that the only woman elected—the Countess Markievicz—could not take her seat, not because she was a woman, but because she was a Sinn Feiner.

On Suffrage the constitutional and party political systems pivoted importantly around the President and Prime Minister, certainly after 1916. The attitudes of both were of great importance. Asquith made no secret of his hostility, while Wilson only very slowly moved to further Suffrage and was never an ardent champion. Asquith was converted too late to be in charge of the Suffrage Bill, but did include the issue in the Speaker's Conference after he had declared for it. Wilson bowed to the South in 1916, but not thereafter and paid the price in his own failure and that of his party in the Sixty-fifth Congress. Subsequently he did his best to repair the damage both in Congress and during the ratification process. In Britain, after the departure of Asquith, Lloyd George had no real difficulty in securing Suffrage via the speedy passage of the Representation of the People Act. Both Asquith and Wilson had fond memories of essentially non-political first wives and lived with second wives who enjoyed their voteless state when it went along with power and influence. Both resented militancy—Asquith with his 'want of imagination' concluding militants to be criminal and unbalanced, while Wilson saw their activities as a direct slur upon his good intentions. Had Asquith swung over in 1912—and insisted on Irish support—it is likely that the Reform Bill could have gone under the Parliament Act and have been ready for implementation in 1914—unless the Lords passed it in an attempt to force an earlier election.[19] Likewise had Wilson been more vigorous in 1916 he might have prevented the solidifying of the Southern position. By being so fearful he allowed racists and 'Wets' to make the running and thus hurt the Democrats in 1918, and even in 1920. Fear and lack of vision in 1916 forced him to work very hard thereafter merely to avoid further damage.

The two cases were not really contemporary. The Americans had before them the example of what could happen should frustration among women boil over into Pankhurst militancy and by 1917 this was beginning to happen. Neither Wilson nor the run of politicians in Congress and the states were ready to accept this—and refused to believe that what had occurred in pre-war Britain simply could not happen in America. In addition to fear, emulation and rivalry had a place. The success of the movement during 1917 was a precedent that Americans might follow. There was a traditional rivalry with monarchical Britain and the fact that the constitutional monarchy stood to look more 'democratic' was an incentive to action in wartime America both among Suffragists and politicians who were unimpressed by Australasian, Scandinavian and even their own Western precedents. This was especially true when, in November 1917, the New York state referendum on Suffrage was carried by the Suffragists —just as the Commons was sending the Representation of the People Bill to the Lords. The New York victory was a turning point for Wilson who swung his influence immediately in favour of a successful House vote. America could hardly lag behind when Britain was preparing to admit that votes for women was necessary for victory and reconstruction. The British victory was, then, of some importance coming when it did. The militancy of the Pankhursts and Alice Paul had shaken American politicians and Suffragists alike— the success of the British movement reassured the politicians and strengthened the Suffrage cause in America.

A noticeable difference between the campaigns was, of course, the overt political machinations of certain business interests in America.

Both the liquor and textile industries opposed Suffrage because each felt directly threatened by a female vote which was presumed to be 'moral' in its outlook. It seems clear, nevertheless, that in Congress when the two industries were counter-attacked in force, they were only successful where their cause coalesced with a more strictly political opposition, namely Southern fears of the Negro. British Suffragists were less joined in the public mind with the image of a specifically moral, crusading temperance vote. Mrs Pankhurst, especially, drove home the notion that Suffragists were, overwhelmingly, people who sought the vote as a right. In America corrupt politics and business saw its enemy in the vengeful native American matron, certainly in 1916 when there was less likelihood of a successful Socialist party. The parties there were more vulnerable to dedicated groups of strategically placed voters. In Britain a Labour party existed and was growing. It, rather than militant women, was cast in the role of nemesis.

Finally, among the political factors, it is worth noting the similarities between the two dominant parties which faced the demand for Suffrage. Both had become more sectionally based and both were at the time facing a backlog of demands for measures of adjustment and compensation for sectional inequalities. They shared a distaste for big business, war and overseas commitments, though both had wings favouring the latter. Within their areas of strength they were 'town and country' parties—outside them they were seeking to be the parties of the lower classes of the growing cities. They were more loosely organized than their opponents and this meant that a question like Suffrage which at first lacked a powerful sectional thrust, or faced a sectional veto, stood little chance of becoming party policy. Both parties had staunch Protestants and Catholics in their ranks—both groups cool or hostile to female emancipation. Both had to face the violent opposition of opponents who had come to see governing as their prerogative and who were not favourably inclined to Suffrage. Both had strong factions who had seized the ground of 'reformism' and resented the fact that their party's treatment of the Suffrage question seemed to make them less 'reformers' than sectional, social, economic 'outs on the make'. It is only fair, then, to add that this was more apparent than real. The two parties were coerced and cajoled into overcoming their sectional prejudices, and it is very doubtful if either opposing party would have acted more quickly or easily in power. Democrats and Liberals alike were much preoccupied with other questions and it is of great importance to realize that Suffrage impinged unfavourably on two very important sources of preoccupation, namely the Irish question for Liberals, and the race question for Southerners.

The Suffragists themselves have been written up more than the politicians they sought to influence. Even so, there are still comparisons and contrasts which can be usefully made in face of the changing political situations the Suffragists dealt with. Again, the connections between the British and American movements after 1905 are worth some clarification.

There are some immediately obvious similarities in the movements. By 1905 both had a history of more than fifty years, both had survived major splits, and both had seen the first generation of leaders give way to younger, more organizationally minded leaders. Both movements were weak in popular support but both entertained high expectations, the British especially. In Britain the rise of the Labour party encouraged some of the older leaders to believe that future gain lay in working for its success, and using its rise to force the other parties to act. Likewise, in America the faith of many Suffragists was put in the Progressive movements of the West and the urban reformers of the Eastern cities.

The time lag in the incidence of militancy is, equally, an obvious contrast. Almost twelve years separated the beginning of American from British militancy—and even then it was initiated by conscious disciples of the Pankhursts. This contrast is somewhat lessened, however, by the fact that militancy *did* occur in America at that moment when, to Suffragists at least, the political context was as promising for them as it had been in England in 1906. Both groups seized their main chance—the Americans twelve years after the British.

The appearance of militant, competing organizations had somewhat comparable effects on both parent movements. In America, after 1913, Alice Paul speeded up the process by which the old movement abandoned its Southern incubus, and proclaimed itself ready to use Western women voters to coerce Northern and Border Democrats and Republicans alike. Likewise, in the same year that Alice Paul appeared on the national scene in America, the older British movement opened negotiations with the Labour party thus signalling its disillusionment with the Liberal party. One movement abandoned a section, the other embraced a party—or so it seemed.

Two features of this change of political alliances may be compared. First, the change for both was largely a matter of legislative tactics and not of ideology. Accepting new allies in the campaign for the vote did not involve any commitment to the political programme of those allies. Thus, when the position in the legislature changed, there was nothing to prevent a return to former allies. Therefore, the American movement by 1919 was ready to gain any Southern support it could get by ignoring Southern women if they were black. Equally, the British movement was quite prepared to ignore the Labour party —as a party—once Lloyd George was Prime Minister and ready to enact its demands in 1917.

Secondly, both leaderships worked very hard to resist the logic inherent in the militant position. The Conciliation Bills of 1910–12 in England and the Shafroth–Palmer amendment of 1914 in the United States were both efforts to obtain Suffrage via a consensus of parties unable, and unwilling, to make the issue a party one. Both moves traded on the influence and power possessed by the older movements within high political circles. In America Mark Hanna's daughter, the Republican Mrs Medill McCormick, and the Tory Lord Lytton in Britain—the respective agents—were both the victims and proponents of the delusion that there must and could only be a bipartisan solution. Formally, at least, they appeared to have been proved correct—both measures were enacted in bipartisan votes. In Britain, however, the old party lines had been transformed into those for and against the Lloyd George government while, in America, the Republicans took care not to provide the necessary votes in the Senate and during Ratification until Democrats had been seen resisting their leader and President in the Sixty-fifth Congress. Woman Suffrage was put through by those in the Executive in Britain and out of it in America. In neither case was its intrinsic factors and qualities of greater importance than the political gain seen in it by its chief sponsors. Women were being recruited by parties rather than accorded 'justice' as such. The component of expediency can be overstressed but, seen from the perspective of party leaderships, it appears to have been the dominant motif.

So much for the movements in general in the final period of their history. Some valid comparisons may also be made of the leaders produced after 1905. First, the two non-militant leaders—Mrs Millicent Fawcett of the N.U.W.S.S. and Mrs Carrie Catt of the N.A.W.S.A.[20] Both were widows and both, by the standards of their societies, were upper-middle class and of independent means. Both had served long apprenticeships in the movement and appeared at its head at about the same time. Both were internationally minded and both retained this outlook through and after the war. As leaders, both were single-minded in the pursuit of the vote and refused to allow other gestures to entangle their campaigns. Hence both resisted their pacifist wings after 1914, and urged war service as a duty which properly used could provide the desired reward. Both, nevertheless, saw the vote as more than a symbol of status, and neither had much of the bitterness towards men apparent among many of their militant co-Suffragists.

Both leaders resisted militancy though conceding that it made political sense at least in the early period from 1906 to 1908 in Britain and early 1917 in America. Both acted decisively when it was clear—by 1912 in Britain and 1915 in America—that persuasion of politicians must give way to party coercion. Both cultivated those who had access to leading politicians—for example Mrs Helen Gardener in America, a friend of Wilson's, and the influential and well connected Ladies Frances and Betty Balfour in Britain—and, while retaining their independence, tried hard to accommodate politicians who were genuinely trying to promote Suffrage.

Mrs Catt and Mrs Fawcett may be justly accused of not giving enough attention to the conversion of male voters who stood behind the male politicians they worked so hard to convert. Yet Mrs Catt in her distance from immigrant males and Mrs Fawcett in hers from working-class men were hardly alone among their social kind. The American middle classes were in this period reacting sharply against the immigrant vote, while their British counterparts could still view Labour M.P.s as a wing of the Liberal party. Formally, at least, so far as the working classes were concerned their chief organizations were in favour of Suffrage. If Suffragists seemed to concentrate too much on the middle-class voters this was surely because they realized that these needed converting and were—because of their education— accessible to the printed and spoken word. To expect that Suffragists should have foreseen the power of organized labour is to ignore the fact that this was not obvious before 1905 when the basic Suffrage strategies were laid down in both countries. Moreover, it is to ignore the fact that, as ardent feminists, both women saw the political advent of voting women as of greater importance than any conceivable Labour faction or political party.

Mrs Catt, unlike Mrs Fawcett, set up in the League of Women Voters, an organization designed specifically to press for feminist objectives using the newly enfranchised voters. That it largely failed, as did both leaders' pleas for women to become active in political parties, may hardly be said to be entirely the fault of the two Suffragist leaders. Both, until their deaths, strove to lead their erstwhile followers in the cause of sex equality and opportunity and also to urge them to participate in the quest for international harmony.

In their dealings with both governments and legislatures both women were sanely realistic. Wilson, Mrs Catt understood, had to overcome the hesitation of the very Southerners he needed for the rest of his programme. Asquith, as Mrs Fawcett saw, had some cause for asserting that after 1911 the Liberal burden was heavy enough until the Home Rule and Welsh Church Bills were safely out of the way. Both women realized that party leaders were busy men who were personally affronted by militant unlady-like behaviour and politically affronted by tactics which smacked of outright blackmail. More importantly they realized that such men had legitimate party concerns. Might there not be a higher Republican than Democrat turnout among women voters? Likewise in England would not Tory women be more likely to vote, and could a Liberal government really believe that a limited property-based extension of the franchise would not favour Tories? In disowning militancy, Mrs Fawcett after 1909 and Mrs Catt after 1917 performed the negative function of pressing their cause and the positive one of offering inducements to politicians who would join it.

The militants by comparison performed a complementary function, namely that, however much detested by politicians, their activities made too spectacular a subject for both hostile and friendly newspapers to ignore and thus kept the movement in daily contact with the public. Non-militants made friends, militants made news—both were needed. Woman Suffrage was an issue which, since they could not adopt, parties would prefer to ignore. It had to have the means of gaining publicity, and that frequently. Soothing ruffled politicians became a routine task which non-militants were well placed to carry out. This task, anyway, was easier for them than the one which would have faced them had there been no militancy, namely that of preventing Suffrage from being ignored through the fears, uncertainties and sheer preoccupations of politicians.

Newsworthiness, however, had its limitations. The militants in both countries found themselves misreported and misrepresented. More, they found themselves tempted constantly to change their tactics in order to keep their publicity. They had, again, the parallel task of controlling the increasingly desperate element recruited by the chance of personal publicity and possible martyrdom. Hence picketing and heckling gave way to attacks on property and this, in turn, to assaults on politicians and threats of worse. In Britain the cycle of militancy—repression—more militancy was fully developed by 1912. The separation of Mr and Mrs Pethick-Lawrence from the Pankhursts meant that there was no check on where Christabel Pankhurst was leading, or not leading, the movement. In America victory came before the pattern included major assaults on property and persons. It is almost certain that there would have been a similar development—Christabel could after all be distracted by the war; Alice Paul was not so distracted in April 1917 and the fury and exasperation engendered in wartime America was as great as anything seen in pre-war Britain.

On balance, however, no accusation that militancy retarded Suffrage will stand. As was noted, the only real chance in Britain of success before 1914 was marred more by Asquith's personal opposition, Lloyd George's political weakness, and the action of the Speaker than by Mrs Pankhurst. Likewise the Negro problem and the Prohibition campaign slowed Suffrage more than did Alice Paul and her activities. Politicians who claimed to be alienated by both would have overlooked much had political considerations allowed or forced them to do so, Southern gentlemen notwithstanding.

The formal leader of the Women's Social and Political Union was Mrs Pankhurst, but the real moving spirit became her daughter Christabel, and it is she who must be compared with Alice Paul.[21] While Christabel was a fluent, forceful platform speaker, the charisma of both was seen more in committee than on the platform. Both acquired an impressive personal following and were quite ready to use this to overawe any opposition in their organizations. Christabel Pankhurst, the more overtly autocratic, felt sure enough of her position virtually to expel both the Pethick-Lawrences and her own sister Sylvia, all the while running the organization from Paris. Both women shared the conviction that the weakness of the Suffrage movement, and the hostility of politicans alike, testified to the need for new tactics. The readiness of the press to report their activities was, they realized, of far greater significance than condemnatory editorials and biased reporting.

Militant tactics in 1906 may have stemmed directly from the personal frustrations of the Pankhursts, but they were continued and later used in America because they were seen as the only way of securing publicity and forcing action on the Suffrage question. Both women realized that militancy had a certain boomerang effect, but they judged this to be less politically important than continuous publicity, and might be allowed for when the reasons for opposition to Suffrage had been exposed and neutralized. The superpatriotism of the Pankhursts during the war, and the absence of militancy during the American Ratification campaign were in part such allowances. Both may be seen as gestures towards politicians then in process of conversion or actively bent on helping Suffrage.

The career of Alice Paul is the most significant example of the inter-action between the British and American movements. Arriving in Britain in 1908 as a student at the Quaker Woodbrooke Settlement School in Birmingham, she departed two years later as a fully-blown Pankhurst militant with imprisonments and forcible feedings to her credit. Arriving as a young American Quaker and social worker convinced of the need for Suffrage as a right and a social necessity, she left having been fully exposed to the charisma of the Pankhursts and their non-Quaker methods of political agitation. Arriving a believer that men as voters and politicians were indifferent, she left having seen how a dedicated group, ready to accept imprisonment and personal indignities, might seize national publicity and convert male amazement and hostility into passive or even active support.

The Pankhurst policy of continuous opposition to the party in power, to Alice Paul, made political sense in England since that party, if converted, could put the issue through the legislature. The policy was modelled on the Irish Nationalist tactics which Mrs Pankhurst believed her husband had been an electoral victim of in the 1886 election. The British system of *party* government encouraged groups and small parties to believe that within a party in power the way to coerce factions—even leaderships—hostile to their aims, was to set against such groups their own party colleagues whose policy proposals—related or not—were actually or potentially in jeopardy because of external or internal opposition or instability. The Irish had used this 'across the board' opposition successfully. The Pankhursts, in short, set out after 1906 to push Liberal ministers into conflict with their backbenchers.

After 1912 Alice Paul was accused of blindly trying to follow this tactic in the different constitutional setting of America where there was a separation of powers, and where no one party had ever secured two-thirds of the seats of both Houses; where in fact a bipartisan policy seemed the *sine qua non* of success. Politically, however, the policy had some justification. So long as both American parties competed for the allegiance of the West, so would they have to be sensitive to the demands of that section. This necessary sensitivity was their Achilles heel to Alice Paul for, after 1912, in the West many women voted. In Britain, opposing the party in power after 1906 meant asking Liberal *husbands* and *brothers* to abstain or vote Conservative. In America, the policy meant asking Western *women* to vote Republican in 1916 and 1918—and this at a time when Wilson was a minority President needing the West for re-election. The possession of the vote by women of the section which decided elections was the crucial element making for success once it was exploited.

As states granted the presidential vote after 1913, Mrs Catt herself was quite ready to use this increasing weight in Washington. She did not, however, go among Western voters and ask them to coerce Democrats. It was left to the Pankhurst-trained Alice Paul to show her that politicians had to be as sensitive to hostility as to co-operation. Western Democratic politicians were grateful to Mrs Catt, but they feared Alice Paul and their fear was as potent a political force as their gratitude.

Much of Alice Paul's success stemmed from the fact that she was well backed from the beginning of her rebellion against the National American Woman Suffrage Association. Prominent among her backers was the imperious Mrs O. H. P. Belmont. She provides an example of an American contribution to British success, since it was she who had helped support Christabel Pankhurst during her exile in Paris in 1912. In Alice Paul she clearly saw an American version of Christabel and backed her forcibly despite her own close connections with the parent organization. Mrs Belmont thus played the American equivalent of the Pethick-Lawrence role in the Pankhurst organization, namely that of the wealthy, well-connected, zealous backer. She was familiar with the Pankhurst organization and not merely via press reports—a familiarity which may be put down as a further British contribution to success in America. For this to be understood it is necessary to turn to the background of the Suffrage victory in New York State in 1917, to the work of Elizabeth Cady Stanton's daughter, Harriet Stanton Blatch.[22]

Mrs Blatch lived in England from 1882 to 1902, met Mrs Pankhurst in the circle of Jacob and Ursula Bright, and participated in the work of the Equal Franchise Committee after it split off from the parent organization in 1889. In addition, she was active in the Women's Liberal Federation, became a Fabian, and was a friend of the Peases and the Webbs. On her return she immediately moved into women's trade union circles in New York, and by February 1907 was appearing at Albany as a labour spokeswoman. In December 1907 she sponsored a visit from the militant daughter of Richard Cobden, Mrs Cobden-Sanderson, and in October 1909, from Mrs Pankhurst herself. Eight months later she organized the first Suffrage parade and, helped by Mrs O. H. P. Belmont and Mrs Mary Beard, she launched the Women's Political Union. Unlike the Pankhursts, seven years earlier, she did not insert 'Social' into the title in order to attract those fearful of its trades union overtones.

Mrs Blatch continued to organize Suffrage parades and, in 1912, took agitation a step further when she set up silent pickets outside the New York State legislature when it debated a Suffrage proposal. In this same year Mrs Blatch introduced Alice Paul to Jane Addams and helped Miss Paul to gain the Chairmanship of the Congressional Committee of the National American Woman Suffrage Association.

From this position Miss Paul went on to an independent and larger status—and a policy of attacking Democrats. This may have been second nature to a Philadelphian, but Mrs Blatch had made Democrats her allies against upstate Republicans and had secured, in 1912, a promise from 'Commissioner' Murphy of Tammany to allow a Woman Suffrage amendment to the state constitution to come to a referendum. National political necessity, as seen by Miss Paul, dictated threatening Democrats. Murphy, happily, resolved the dilemma by ordering the defeat of all amendments including Suffrage in the referendum of 1914. Mrs Blatch merged her organization with that of Alice Paul in January 1916, though she kept up her personal contact with Tammany. By 1917, when New York State again voted on Suffrage, Tammany saw fit to stay neutral and this allowed a New York majority to swing the whole state, crack open the reluctant East and lead directly to the successful January 1918 vote in the House of Representatives.

Mrs Blatch was a minor figure in the national Suffrage picture but, in several respects, she was important. She had pioneered both the Suffrage parade and Suffrage pickets—both used heavily by Alice Paul. In 1912, when she still had influence in the National Association, she helped Alice Paul to become its Congressional Chairman and stimulated Mrs Belmont to take an interest in the new beginning being made in Washington by a disciple of Mrs Pankhurst. Being the daughter of Elizabeth Cady Stanton gave her a certain standing with the press and she capitalized on all of this, when, on 5 October 1916 after Hughes had been 'converted', she revealed Wilson's reasons for refusing to follow as being concerned essentially with the Negro question in the South.

Mrs Blatch can hardly be described as a Pankhurst disciple. Rather, both had shared in the same educational experience at the hands of the Brights, the Fabians and later in the women's trade unions. Mrs Blatch herself, however, remained more as she had begun—the war did not make her bellicose and the peace found her still a socialist. In her role in the Suffrage movement she bore a close resemblance to her old friend and former colleague, Mrs Pankhurst. Both were politically sophisticated widows who, from a sense of frustration in Suffrage organizations, formed separate groups, pioneered new methods of agitation and then saw their movements pass into younger hands. Though Mrs Blatch, unlike Mrs Pankhurst, did not gain a national or international reputation, she yet deserves a mention as a significant figure in the Anglo-American aspects of the Suffrage movement.

The Woman Suffrage campaign lasted seventy-two years in

America and fifty-one years in Britain. On the face of it, this was a long campaign. In fact, the time lapse after the issue had come before Congress and Parliament as a serious question was relatively short—less than ten years in both cases. Partly this was because the Suffrage movement had helped create and sustain an élite and engendered some favourable sentiment in educated, middle-class circles. Much more so this was owed to the fact that the rate of economic and social change had created for this élite a mass of potential followers who might be mobilized not for Woman Suffrage or notions of justice for women but for what might be done with the support of women voters. Inevitably the prior political commitments of such people could give rise to disputes over both the principle and priority of Woman Suffrage. The Irish in England and the Southern Democrats in the United States were very visible in their opposition but there were others, too, who questioned the priority of Woman Suffrage, even among those supposed to be friendly. The delay caused by such factors outweighed any due to the opposition of Asquith, the vacillation of Wilson or the folly of some Suffragists. Woman Suffrage, then, was delayed by potent political issues. In both countries it required the political consequences of war to break the log jam of party inhibition. Yet broken it was. Legislation deemed to be of considerable social consequence was enacted notwithstanding supposedly potent objections on divine, family, industrial and short-run party political and special interest grounds.

In that process much light was cast on the two political systems. The decentralized nature of American politics, the interaction between levels and the constraints on Presidency and Congress alike were all too visible. Visible also, however, were the forces making for a degree of 'unitariness' and cohesion so that a carefully orchestrated and timed campaign at local, state and federal levels produced a fairly rapid result as opposition within parties was outflanked or eroded. The deadlock resulting in Britain with its unitary system when the leadership of the governing party was split, and the Prime Minister in particular was opposed, is in obvious contrast. Less obvious, however, was the *inability* of Asquith to prevent the erosion of his position of strength so that by 1914 he was forced to hint at change.

In this must lie grounds for hope for feminists. The political systems of both countries, which have not changed in critical respects, showed themselves responsive to sustained pressure by feminists if these could find allies in society. Grounds, too, for some concern. The price of allies was a public muzzling of questions which had been deemed vital in nineteenth-century feminism, e.g. the place of women in the family and society. To win the vote required hierarchic organizations which worked best when directed towards a simple goal—the vote— and which were not friendly environments for feminists who questioned the fundamentals of society. 'Organization women' could win the right to vote but seemed less able to infuse women with enthusiasm for making feminist use of the vote.

In retrospect it may be possible to assert that political rights, anyway, may be easier to extract than social or economic rights. The assertions of the 'emptiness' of political rights is still not, thankfully, beyond argument and would certainly have struck early twentieth-century Americans and Britons as simply not true. Suffragists, then, were certainly women of their time in their over-estimation of the impact of narrowly defined political rights and privileges but they can hardly be faulted for that. What they did do was to lay the foundations for their feminist successors, and what they did demonstrate was that their political systems were responsive to changes which, at the time, were seen as far reaching.

The Suffrage campaign must give pause to those who assert the immutability of the Anglo-American *status quo*. The political consequences of voting women are nowadays seen by feminists as minimal. It may well be that this is so because those consequences are defined in terms of the *personnel* of politics, i.e. the failure of women to 'surface' politically. If, as with Almond and Verba,[23] we see the consequences in terms of party political agendas, for example in the steadily increasing emphasis on social policies, then the impact of women might be said to be considerable. Whether, of course, this is the proletarianization or modernization of politics, rather than its feminization, is a question which cannot be answered here.

## NOTES

1. In addition to the memoirs and biographical studies on the overall American movement and campaign see—more recently—Eleanor Flexner, *The Women's Rights Movement in the United States* (Boston,

1959); William O'Neill, *Everyone Was Brave: The Rise and Fall of American Feminism* (Chicago, 1969); Page Smith, *Daughters of the Promised Land. Women in American History* (Boston, 1970); and Andrew Sinclair, *The Better Half. The Emancipation of the American Woman* (New York, 1965). On the British side see Roger Fulford, *Votes for Women. The Story of a Struggle* (London, 1957); and David Mitchell, *The Fighting Pankhursts. A Study in Tenacity* (London, 1967).

2. On America see Aileen S. Kraditor, *The Ideas of the Woman Suffrage Movement 1890–1920* (New York, 1965). On Britain see Constance Rover, *Women's Suffrage and Party Politics in Britain 1866–1914* (London, 1967). This essay is based largely on my *Suffragists and Democrats. The Politics of Woman Suffrage in America* (East Lansing, 1972) and *Suffragists and Liberals. The Politics of Woman Suffrage in England* (Oxford, 1975) to which the reader is referred (cited hereafter as Morgan, *Dems*, or Morgan, *Libs*).

3. On this and the problems of Anglo-American comparisons see—*inter alia*—Louis Hartz, *The Founding of New Societies* (New York, 1964) and the essay, by Marcus Cunliffe, 'New World, Old World: The Historical Antithesis', in Richard Rose, ed., *Lessons From America. An Exploration* (New York, 1974), and Ross Evans Paulson, *Women's Suffrage and Prohibition* (Glenview, Illinois, 1973).

4. The term militant connoted principally a follower of the Pankhursts in the Women's Social and Political Union in England after 1906 and those of Alice Paul in the National Woman's Party in America after 1916. The label came to connote those who picketed, went to prison, hunger struck, etc. In both cases, as will be seen, the differences between militant and non-militant were not merely over tactics, but also over strategies for gaining and using the vote.

5. In her *Vindication of the Rights of Women* (London, 1891).

6. On this see, *inter alia*, Gerda Lerner, *The Grimke Sisters from South Carolina. Rebels Against Slavery* (New York, 1967).

7. Constance Rover, *Women's Suffrage*, chs. VI and VIII.

8. On this see Alan P. Grimes, *The Puritan Ethic and Woman Suffrage* (New York, 1967). See also J. A. Banks and Olive Banks, *Feminism and Family Planning in Victorian England* (Liverpool, 1964).

9. See H. Wiebe, *The Search for Order 1877–1920* (London, 1967).

10. For this very large and vital debate see C. C. Catt and Nettie Schuler, *Woman Suffrage and Politics—the Inside Story of the Suffrage Movement* (New York, 1926); also Wiebe, *Search for Order*, and Kraditor, *Woman Suffrage Movement*, and Morgan, *Dems*, chs. 5, 6 and 7.

11. Morgan, *Dems*, chs. 7–11.

12. See H. V. Emy, *Liberals, Radicals and Social Politics 1892–1914* (Cambridge, 1973).
13. See Morgan, *Libs*, chs. III–X.
14. See Morgan, *Dems*, pp. 73–77, 123–138.
15. See Morgan, *Libs*, pp. 50–56, 112–128.
16. Morgan, *Libs*, pp. 87–96.
17. Morgan, *Libs*, pp. 108–109 for the effects of Marconi.
18. The erosion of Wilson's position is discussed in Morgan, *Dems*, chs. 7 and 8.
19. By precedent enfranchising acts were followed by legislation redistributing seats and, more, by a general election as soon as the new register of voters was ready.
20. On Mrs Fawcett see her writings plus Ray Strachey, *Millicent Garrett Fawcett* (London, 1931). On Mrs Catt see Mary Ray Peck, *Carrie Chapman Catt* (New York, 1944).
21. On Alice Paul see Inez H. Irwin, *The Story of the Woman's Party* (New York, 1921). On Christabel Pankhurst see Mitchell, *The Fighting Pankhursts* and her own, *Unshackled. The Story of How We Won the Vote* (London, 1959) [ed. by Lord Pethick-Lawrence].
22. On Mrs Blatch see Harriett Stanton Blatch and Alma Lutz, *Challenging Years, The Memoirs of Harriett Stanton Blatch* (New York, 1940).
23. Gabriel Almond and Sidney Verba, *The Civic Culture. Political Attitudes and Democracy in Five Nations* (Princeton, 1963) pp. 397–400.

# 12

# The Atlantic Alliance, Eastern Europe and the Origins of the Cold War: From Pearl Harbor to Yalta

## ROBERT GARSON

During the Second World War the British and American governments converted their advantage in economic power and political influence into a handicap in their relations with the Soviet Union. The Russians had never equivocated about their fundamental war aim, namely the desire for territorial security along their southern and western frontiers. In time the Soviets would refine and even enlarge their ambitions. The Atlantic allies, however, were unable to formulate clearly a coherent policy that would either accommodate the Russians or seek to thwart their designs. This failure to develop a joint approach towards Soviet policy in Eastern Europe stemmed from two essential misunderstandings. First, throughout most of the war the Americans and the British differed fundamentally about the nature of Soviet diplomacy and the solidarity of the wartime alliance itself. Second, the Americans failed to define their basic interests in the disputed areas. For while they were concerned to create an effective system of collective security and to destroy economic nationalism in world trade, they never really examined the precise role which Eastern Europe and the Balkans would be required to play within this scheme. This basic fragility within the Atlantic alliance prevented the three allies from agreeing on boundary questions and so indirectly, and possibly directly, encouraged Stalin to inflate and extend his demands as the war progressed and deadlock continued. Furthermore, it will be argued, the tendency of the Americans to define their interests after Yalta as being inversely proportionate to the interests of Russia was the result of their earlier inability to delineate and measure the strategic and economic stakes involved in Eastern Europe.

From the very outset of its participation in the fighting, the United States had been careful to confine its articulated war aims to generalities. Franklin D. Roosevelt, like Winston S. Churchill, was anxious to win the war as rapidly as possible, and so was reluctant to confuse its prosecution with wider political and economic calculations. The President argued that publicized war aims, other than vague calls for international justice, would not only create the possibility of dissension within the alliance but also would encourage his advisers to formulate military strategy around the country's long-term interests, rather than immediate military exigency. So in 1942 Roosevelt agreed with Cordell Hull, Secretary of State, in his flat refusal to associate himself with the proposal for an Anglo-Soviet treaty, which would recognize Russia's 1941 frontiers along the Baltic, Poland and Romania. Roosevelt's stand was partly predicated on the view that a new international order after the war would be undermined if the grandiose principles of the Atlantic Charter were sacrificed to the winds prematurely. A projected security organization could be jeopardized by a disaffected and disillusioned American public and by the machinations of other nations which might seize opportunities to acquire new territory. The Americans also realized that frontier adjustments would have to be made at the peace conference anyway and premature cessions would deprive them of negotiating cards later. Cordell Hull commented that Britain and the United States would find it difficult to resist additional Soviet demands relating to frontiers 'which would almost certainly follow whenever the Soviet Government would find itself in a favourable bargaining position'.[1]

Yet it was not the specific fear of Russian ambitions that made Roosevelt reluctant to cede territory during the war. Despite his reservations about the Soviets' quest for security, the President remained convinced of his ability to gain Stalin's confidence. He felt that he was uniquely equipped, in economic, military and personal terms, to sustain the alliance and to create a system of collective security after the war. In particular, he believed his reputation in the Kremlin was good and that he did not carry Churchill's stigma as a die-hard opponent of bolshevism. In March 1942, he wrote to Churchill: 'I hope you will not mind my being brutally frank when I tell you that I think I can handle Stalin better than either your Foreign Office or my State Department.'[2] In similar vein, he tried to persuade

Stalin the following year to meet with him alone, without the British, to discuss mutual problems related to the conduct of the war. The President was sure that he could convince Stalin that no fundamental conflict of interest had arisen as a result of the vexing disagreements over frontiers, the timing of the invasion of France, and the furnishing of war material under lend–lease.[3]

Indeed, the initial formulations of American policy on a second front and lend–lease supplies had been drawn up and moulded by an overwhelming desire to draw the Soviet Union closer to the United States. In both cases Roosevelt had wanted to adopt policies which would diminish German pressure on Russia and consequently convince the Soviets of America's desire to share the burdens of war. Roosevelt believed with his close advisers that an early invasion of France would draw off sufficient German divisions from the Russian front, and so enable the Red Army to halt Germany's advances. Although Churchill finally convinced Roosevelt that landings in 1942 were premature and potentially disastrous, the President never lost sight of the diplomatic boost that the operation could offer. It would convince Stalin of America's good intentions and hopefully show him that territorial expansion was unnecessary since his allies were prepared to shed blood for Russian security. Harry Hopkins, one of Roosevelt's closest aides, believed that a second front would 'take the heat off Russia's diplomatic demands'.[4] Henry Stimson, Secretary of War, reported after a visit to London that Churchill's reluctance to commit troops to the continent was short-sighted and conducive to suspicion. 'To me, in the light of the post-war problems which we shall face, that attitude towards Russia seems terribly dangerous,' he commented.[5] And it was precisely this desire to guarantee the success of the Red Army that prompted Roosevelt to extend unconditional aid to the Soviet Union. He recognized that massive shipments of material to the Russians would yield two major benefits. It would enable the Red Army to inflict heavier losses on the Germans and so provide a breathing spell for the armies in the Western theatres. And, as an extra incentive, it would convince the Russians that there was no sinister plot afoot to exhaust their resources and thus prevent them from emerging as a major power after the war. 'I think that if I give him everything I possibly can,' said Roosevelt, 'and ask nothing from him in return, *noblesse oblige*, he won't try to annex anything and will work with me for a world of democracy and peace.'[6] He thus imposed no conditions on lend–lease—as he did with the British in the trade and tariff clauses—and often intervened personally to expedite shipments to the Soviet Union. He rejected advice to insist on detailed Soviet inventories of Russian supply needs as a condition for sending goods. He dismissed the assumption of William C. Bullitt, a former ambassador to Russia who continued to advise F.D.R. informally throughout the war, that 'By using the old technique of the donkey, the carrot and the club you might be able to make Stalin move in the direction in which we want him to move'. Trust, Roosevelt believed, could only be generated by placing trust in the Russians in the first place.[7] Stalin, he felt, might not want to create security zones in Eastern Europe once he realized that Russia faced no real danger from the capitalist nations of the West.

Thus American policy-makers revealed their Soviet perspectives in their military and foreign economic policies. They were not expressly worried about the effects of Soviet war aims on the security interests of the United States, since these interests were defined only in the broadest terms in the early years of the war anyway. Indeed, they subordinated economic and political concerns to the more pressing problem of winning the war. Military success on the Soviet front was perceived as a mutual and coincident goal. The Americans only shaped policy towards Eastern Europe and the Balkans as events and consequent realizations unfolded. They did not base it on any fixed, preconceived antagonism to Russia itself. Washington was concerned by the Soviets' territorial ambitions, but its concern was predicated on a wider preoccupation with political stability after the war. So while Americans would find themselves increasingly at variance with the Kremlin, their antipathy did not develop merely and naturally as a result of the Soviet occupation of Eastern Europe. Communism and unrestrained Soviet expansion only converged definitionally in the eyes of Americans in the final months of the war. In fact the United States grappled and agonized for a long time in its attempts to define its geopolitical interests. This uncertain groping, based upon an intrinsic optimism about Soviet intentions, underlines the fact that it was not inherent anti-bolshevism that finally moulded America's European policies.

The British, on the other hand, held a more sober, even sombre, view of the Soviet Union. Winston Churchill found it more difficult to forget the Molotov–Ribbentrop pact and throughout the war nurtured a profound mistrust of the Soviets, a suspicion that dated back to 1917. He believed, however, that it was vital not to threaten the new alliance, and so tempt Stalin to make a separate peace with Germany. He argued that the Soviet demands for the absorption of the Baltic states and for boundary adjustments in Poland, Finland and Romania should be accepted, on the grounds that this would allay Russian suspicions and inhibit further expansion. The postponement of territorial settlements, he believed, would place a premium on diplomatic connivance and politically motivated military strategy. The war aims of the allies should be declared and confronted so that military operations and political goals could, if possible, be co-ordinated. So while the Americans' penchant for vague declarations of principle was attractive psychologically, they could serve to undermine the national interests of the three allies. America's 'moral position' on frontiers could not be maintained, he wrote. 'In a deadly struggle it is not right to assume more burdens than those who are fighting for a great cause can bear.' The principles of the Atlantic Charter, he told Roosevelt, 'ought not to be construed so as to deny Russia the frontiers she occupied when Germany attacked her'.[8] Churchill essentially believed that Stalin would take territory by force if it were not conceded. So it made sense to obtain a *quid pro quo*. Britain wanted to keep its hold over communications in the Mediterranean in order to have access to the Middle East and India. Stalin would not try to undermine these aims if he were satisfied in Eastern Europe. Thus, according to Churchill, co-operation could be best secured by substantive agreement and concession, not by attempts to change the atmosphere of international relations.[9] He did not believe, as Roosevelt did, in Stalin's essential faith in the community of nations. He found it hard to forget Stalin's ruthless methods of eliminating his opponents at home, and had no reason to presume that he had changed.[10] While the Americans maintained that Stalin's dictatorship gave 'Soviet policy a degree of flexibility which is impossible in a democratic country', the British argued that it enabled the Russians to act without inhibitions.[11]

In short, the foreign policies of Britain and America stemmed from differing ideas about the nature of the Soviet regime. The Americans wished to nurture Russian friendship so that lasting international co-operation could be developed through a strong collective security organization. This would safeguard world peace and hopefully reinforce a new multilateral system of world trade, the principal keystone of Cordell Hull's foreign policy. The Russians were a vital element in this grand design and could, according to some officials, even become America's major trading partner. The Soviets, prophesied George Messersmith, U.S. Ambassador to Mexico and an ardent advocate of free trade, 'will be inclined more and more to work with us if we know how to handle that situation'. He was confident of a 'basis for understanding and collaboration'.[12] Thus Roosevelt always stalled on making firm territorial commitments, since he believed that Russia might alter its policies as the new era of co-operation unfolded. On the other hand, the British, while equally desirous of securing collaboration, believed that this could be only done by firmly establishing the ground rules and agreeing in so far as possible on territorial war aims and regional responsibilities.[13]

The areas most directly affected by territorial questions were, of course, Poland, the Baltic States and the Balkan countries. It is thus necessary to examine the interests of Britain and the United States in these areas, and to ascertain the extent to which these interests were shaped and determined by the obvious Soviet ambitions in those parts. As a first step, it would be useful to analyse the way in which military strategy itself was shaped by these separate understandings of Soviet foreign policy.

The decision taken in 1942 to delay an attack across the English Channel and to mount operations in North Africa instead immediately opened up the question of how to employ allied troops once the Axis forces had been expelled from the African coast. The British were tempted to undertake limited operations in the Balkans, as well as a general sweep through southern Italy. There were several incentives for some diversions in south-eastern Europe. The evisceration of the Axis armies in the Balkans would ease future allied landings in France, would deprive Germany of essential strategic materials extracted in the Balkans and also would pre-empt the need for Soviet operations there.[14]

Nevertheless, Britain's overriding concern was to knock Germany out of the war, not to shape strategy around their expectations of Soviet behaviour. The Foreign Office recognized that, despite the existence of active guerilla organizations in Yugoslavia and Greece, Hitler would try to hold on to the Balkans for as long as possible. The Germans could not afford to expose their south-eastern flanks, nor could they risk the loss of vital supplies of manganese, chrome and bauxite. The British Chiefs of Staff believed the Balkans constituted the economic and military pedestal of Germany's eastern campaign and that the Germans would shed much blood to keep them. The enemy would 'attempt to hold the whole of the Balkans and make the reinforcement of this area a primary charge on her available resources'.[15] Therefore a fully fledged invasion of south-eastern Europe would be too expensive. So, especially in the light of America's adamant refusal to commit troops to the Balkans, the British decided to concentrate on knocking Italy out of the war and to limit their activities in the Balkans to bombing and the dropping of supplies to the resistance groups.

The scope and type of military aid to the resistance raised several questions about British policy towards the spread of Soviet influence. The British had repeatedly declared that Greece and Yugoslavia were of direct interest to Britain, since their coastal areas lay on Britain's shipping routes to the East. Furthermore, according to the Foreign Office: 'Unrest in the Balkans may spread to adjacent areas which are of vital importance to the British Empire because of our lines of communication through the Mediterranean and the Red Sea and the oil supplies in Iraq and Persia, while the effective domination of south-eastern Europe by a rival Great Power would constitute a direct threat to these vital interests.'[16] So, the British undertook a complicated and somewhat ironic policy. In order to hold down the Germans, they decided to encourage and supply the resistance groups, the most effective of which were anti-monarchical and nationalist in persuasion. The British recognized that a large number of Greek and Yugoslav guerillas were also communists, who would probably not be sympathetic to British influence after the war. Yet they were indispensable. Only they could effectively harass the German forces and, possibly, prevent the entry of Russian troops later.

Britain's quandary was sharply focused in Yugoslavia where the resistance was split between the Chetnik forces of the Minister of War, General Draza Mihailović, and the Partisans under Josip Broz Tito. The schism was partly ideological, partly ethnic. Mihailović wanted to effect a return of the exiled Royalist government after the war and the continuing predominance of the more affluent Serbs. Tito, on the other hand, wanted a republican government which would change the basis of Yugoslav society. The British supported Mihailović who was unabashedly pro-Western. But when it became apparent that Tito enjoyed more popular support and was far more effective against the Axis than Mihailović (who had actually collaborated with the Italians in his attempts to quash the Partisans), the British realized that they could not maintain their military posture without aiding the Partisans.[17] They therefore had to formulate a policy which would still yield the desired military results, and at the same time preserve their interests in Yugoslavia. 'Our long-term political interests incline us to support of the Monarchies', wrote Anthony Eden, 'whereas our short-term military interests oblige us to support the most active elements of resistance, which happen to be Communist.'[18]

It was difficult, of course, to reconcile these two interests. Some of Churchill's advisers advocated only limited aid to the resistance. They wanted it to have enough supplies to hinder the Germans, but insufficient to overcome its domestic foes and so predominate after the war. Lord Selborne, Minister of Economic Warfare, welcomed the British missions to Yugoslavia as they would 'increase our personal influence'. By all means, he wrote, 'Supply all bands with the maximum amount of food and medical supplies . . . but only enough ammunition to enable them to fight this war'.[19] In a fascinating telegram to Churchill, Eden pointed out that 'our military policy (to exert the maximum possible pressure on the enemy) and our political policy (to do nothing to jeopardise the return of the monarchies) are fundamentally opposed'. This was because the resistance was 'Republican at best, and Communist at worst. To stimulate and increase guerilla effort in Greece and/or Yugoslavia we would have to arm and supply these Left Wing guerilla forces to an extent that would enable them to dominate their respective countries militarily and so politically as soon as the Germans are thrown out or go out.' The only solution, it seemed, was 'that we should *not* let up on our pressure on the enemy in the Balkans, but we should *not* increase it in the coming months to any substantial extent'.[20]

Churchill, however, was not entirely persuaded. He saw that this course could be followed in Greece, where Britain had more immediate political and military access. Indeed, when Greece was evacuated by the Germans, British troops were landed there to end domestic rivalry and disarm the People's Liberation Army, which was the most anti-monarchical (and anti-British) of all the resistance groups.[21] But Britain's ties with Yugoslavia were less close and allied landings there were unlikely. So Churchill decided to support Tito, who was anyway a more potent force in Yugoslav politics. Given the political ineptitude of the exiled King and Mihailović's reputation for collaboration, it seemed wise to cast Britain's lot with Tito in the hope of steering him on a neutral course after the war. Churchill believed that timely support from the West could temper Tito's presumed affinity for Russia and forestall a formal Slavic alignment. Furthermore, if the Partisans' considerable fighting strength could be maintained, the vacuum caused by a German evacuation would not necessarily be filled by the Red Army. The Partisans would thus perform a similar role to the much mooted but unrealizable Anglo-American invasion. There was no point, thought Churchill, in relying on the goodwill of the Soviets or the dream of internationally agreed rules of conduct. Military power alone would determine the shape of post-war regimes. As Britain was unable to furnish a presence in Yugoslavia, it was in her best interests to support Tito, who, despite his undisputed predilection for communism, was clearly not one of Stalin's standard bearers. So Churchill escalated Britain's support for Tito, withdrew the British mission from Mihailović's headquarters, and eventually drew up an agreement with the exiled government that would in reality place power in the hands of the Partisans.[22] Above all, he hoped that he could persuade the Russians to declare the extent of their interests in the area, so that any divisions that might emerge could be confronted and formally apportioned, thus preventing further crises in the Balkans. In short, Churchill saw the demarcation of authority as a more reliable method of containing communism than mechanisms of collective security that relied too heavily on cooperation.

Churchill's worries about Soviet interests in the Balkans were not really shared in the same way by Roosevelt and his close advisers. The President was never tempted to undertake military operations there because there were no overriding American interests. There were natural resources, such as oil in Romania and manganese in Yugoslavia, that did attract businessmen. The Balkans, too, could provide new, untapped export markets for American goods after the war.[23] But there is little evidence that American policy-makers before Yalta were particularly preoccupied with the economic potential of the area. Furthermore, south-eastern Europe seemed irrelevant to the defence of the United States. The Balkans only became strategically important at the end of the war when they fell under the influence of a Soviet Union deemed hostile to the West. Until the end of 1944, when the Red Army occupied Poland and Romania, Roosevelt was almost unshaken in his essential faith in Stalin. As long as he held this belief, the Balkans remained of peripheral interest.

Since America's perceived interests were relatively insignificant, there was no political incentive for direct military intervention. Indeed, the Americans believed that the most effective political capital could be obtained by demonstrating the Allies' goodwill to Russia. Harmony and restraint could be best achieved by personal diplomacy, vigorous prosecution of the war through France and unconditional aid. Furthermore, the Americans felt that there was not even a purely military justification for landings in Greece or Romania. George Marshall and the chiefs of staff maintained that the terrain was unsuitable and that incursions there would delay OVERLORD further. Marshall consistently argued that the most effective way of beating Germany was through an invasion of France. He feared the postponements and setbacks that a projected Balkan campaign would entail. Indeed, he said at Tehran, though possibly in a moment of pique, if the British insisted on a campaign in south-eastern Europe, 'we could say that . . . we will pull out and go into the Pacific with all our forces'. The Secretary of War, Henry Stimson, concurred in this view and saw that a Balkan campaign would infuriate the Russians and create the very problems that the British so eagerly wanted to forestall.[24]

There were few dissenters from this view among Roosevelt's advisers. There was one person, however, who did call for a military campaign in the Balkans, and that was William Bullitt. Bullitt's arguments are illuminating not only for their historical interest, but also because they paradoxically highlighted the nature of America's diplomatic calculations. Bullitt called for a major assault on the Axis through Turkey and the Balkans. His motive was, he admitted, largely political. Russia would try and extend its influence wherever possible after the war. If the Russians were permitted to invade the Balkans, they would not withdraw until they had acquired more territory and established puppet governments. The only way to prevent this, argued Bullitt, was through an Anglo-American occupation of the area. This would guarantee the establishment of 'progressive governments', presumably anti-communist. 'War', he counselled, 'is an attempt to achieve political objectives by fighting; and political objectives must be kept in mind in planning operations.' The United States could only secure its universalist aims if it stated them emphatically and worked to implement them. 'The strategic plan that promises political success is to be preferred to the strategic plan that promises political disaster', he said.[25] So, although Roosevelt rejected Bullitt's recommendation, namely an invasion of the Balkans, he did accept the fundamental premise that strategy should, if possible, parallel political interests. His principal aim, other than rapid victory, was to have a *rapprochement* with the Soviet Union and so prevent the division of Europe. While he had no precise plans for effecting this, he did believe that harmony could be best achieved by trust and communication. Bullitt's proposals were ignored, precisely because their fundamental premise—the expansionist nature of the Soviet regime—was held to be untrue or, at the very least, modifiable.

This fundamental belief in the need to foster cordial relations for their own sake was largely responsible for Roosevelt's ambivalent, often unrealistic, handling of Yugoslav affairs. He articulated only one aim in the Aegean countries, namely the desire to establish regimes that were democratically elected. Such regimes would, presumably, strengthen the new international order and, possibly, favour America's economic interests. But these direct interests always seemed secondary. Again, diplomats and officials concerned with Balkan affairs did not seem particularly concerned with their long-term strategic and economic potential. The re-evaluation of interests only seems to have come with the failure of the Allied *entente*. American policy in Yugoslavia, then, can only be understood in terms of its overall perception of the Soviet Union and its estimation of the future shape of international affairs.

The Americans had joined the British and Russians in recognizing the exiled government of King Peter II. As was the case with other allied governments, the Americans intended to continue to support them until free elections could be held after the war. However, the Yugoslav situation was confused by the fact that Tito had set up his own provisional government in November 1943, and had banned the King from returning until after the hostilities. The administration appreciated, furthermore, that Tito was very popular and that support for Mihailović and the pre-war factions had dissipated. Yet it was reluctant to confront the new realities. It hesitated to follow the British in withdrawing liaison officers from Mihailović's camp and to give Tito any form of political, as opposed to military, recognition.[26] This was not because, as Gabriel Kolko has suggested, the United States had a conscious economic interest in preventing the consolidation of a nationalist revolution.[27] Cavendish Cannon, of the State Department's south-east European desk, was probably honest when he said, 'We have no special interests to promote, and seek no special interests to promote, and seek no special privileges.'[28] What the United States did seek to do was to resolve the differences within a wider, international framework. This is not to suggest that America had *no* interests; its interests were merely not sufficiently substantial to warrant the unqualified support Churchill had given Tito. Roosevelt believed that if he supported British policy unequivocally, he would undermine his universalist blueprint for settling disputes. He straddled and in doing so lost the very influence he so eagerly sought. Roosevelt failed to see the paradox involved in his opposition to Tito and in continuing at the same time to criticize the British and the Soviets for fostering agreement at any price. The new Secretary of State, Edward Stettinius, underscored this contradictory absurdity when he, too, told the British of his opposition to the Tito–Subasić agreement (a staged plan for uniting the factions) on the grounds that 'the State Department feels that the exercise of its influence . . . would involve responsibilities which this Government considers it should not take in the circumstances'. In short, the United States was using its influence to kill any influence it might have in Yugoslav affairs.[29]

American policy towards the Axis nations in the Balkans, Bulgaria and Romania, revealed the same optimism and meandering plasticity. The Americans did not perceive any vital interests in those countries and, in common with Churchill, were prepared to concede predominant influence there to the Russians. Unlike Churchill, however, they were reluctant to make formal concessions in the area. They underestimated the Soviets' obsession with secure borders and were hopeful that Russia would change its posture once it realized America's determination to remove the danger of an anti-bolshevik crusade. They hoped to convince Stalin by creating effective international peace machinery and destroying Germany's industrial and military might. Thus, when Bulgaria and Romania sought an armistice, Roosevelt was prepared to offer terms that were both reasonably consistent with the doctrine of unconditional surrender and agreeable to the Russians, who had borne the entire burden of the war in Eastern Europe.

During the somewhat protracted armistice negotiations in Moscow, however, the Americans were anxious to secure a role in the control machinery that would be established after the surrender of Romania and Bulgaria. Although Washington's direct interest in the area was, on its own admission, relatively insignificant, the negotiators felt that participation would foster continued co-operation, an essential ingredient of post-war policy. The British, on the other hand, were less persistent, since they did not want the Russians to impose parallel obstacles to their pro-monarchical policies in Greece.[30] Indeed, the British would have been happy to hammer out occupation policies in the European Advisory Commission, based in London. But the State Department feared that individual deals could undermine its wider plan for collective security. John G. Winant, American ambassador in London and U.S. representative in the E.A.C., recognized that the British saw the Mediterranean 'as a life line of the British Empire'. They were thus prepared to concede formally to the Russians responsibility for the Black Sea area. 'A casual evaluation of the conversations in regard to Bulgarian armistice terms,' he informed Hull, 'might suggest that our friend Eden was having his pants traded off. But when you stop to realize the advance of Russian troops into Yugoslavia, it is clear that the primary British purpose was to continue their relationship with Greece and to maintain a sufficient degree of control in Yugoslavia to protect British Mediterranean interests.'[31] The former satellites only really assumed political importance to the Americans when the alliance crumbled. Before Yalta, the area was of symbolic significance only, just one element in the vast international mosaic that would somehow produce world peace. As a State Department memo declared bluntly in March 1944, 'we . . . acknowledge that distance and lack of important material considerations detach us somewhat from Rumanian affairs'.[32]

This absence of direct interest, combined with an appreciation of the wider ramifications of settling disputes outside an overall international framework, explains Roosevelt's attitude to Churchill's famous sphere of influence agreement with Stalin. When Churchill met Stalin in Moscow in October 1944, he agreed, as discussed in his earlier correspondence, to divide the Balkans into spheres of interest for a minimum period of three months. The Russians were to have predominant responsibility in Romania and Bulgaria, the British in Greece, and influence would be shared equally in Yugoslavia and Hungary. Roosevelt, as is well known, was very critical of this arrangement on the grounds that it placed a premium on bilateral bartering and a seal of approval on political blocs. Yet he did finally consent to a provisional agreement. His approval, therefore, was as revealing as his reservations. For although Roosevelt believed that an agreed division of interests 'would certainly result in the persistence of differences between you and the Soviets' and that it would undermine his programme for multilateral solutions to international conflict, he realized that it was futile to withhold consent. In the first place, as Churchill himself had pointed out, the Soviets would have a commanding authority in the eastern Balkans anyway; so an agreement would merely endorse an existing reality. If Stalin would agree formally to provide no encouragement to the Greek communists, then Britain could mould Greece's future in accordance with its 'direct interest as a Mediterranean power'.[33] However, a second reason for the President's assent can be conjectured. Washington had no major economic interests in that area. Its strategic interests, however hazy, would be temporarily safeguarded by the British and, it was hoped, permanently by the collective decisions of the major powers in a new world organization. So in the short term Roosevelt had little to lose by approving the arrangements.

It is something of an historical irony, therefore, that the United States broke with Russia after the war partly as a result of the latter's tightening hold over the Balkans. For while Soviet policy did indeed undermine the foundations of Roosevelt's vision of collective decision-making and multilateral trade, it did not threaten any perceived material interests in south-eastern Europe. During the war the United

States had eschewed major involvement in Balkan politics, since its direct interests there were minimal. Its preoccupation with equal economic opportunity and free elections was based on its wider desire to alter the basis of international relations and trade.[34] It was only when the dream floundered that the United States began to delineate its presumed interests in south-eastern Europe. In effect, the Americans created interests where none had existed before. These interests were primarily political, with all the imprecise and emotive connotations associated with that word.

The divergence between the British and American governments over the Soviets' territorial ambitions was particularly apparent in the case of Poland. The Polish question remained a source of contention throughout the war and would lead, more than any other issue, to the disintegration of the wartime alliance after Yalta. Simply stated, the fundamental issue at stake was Stalin's persistent demand that Poland's pre-war frontier with Russia be moved westwards to the Curzon line* in order to provide greater security from any future attack from the West. The Polish government in exile, located in London, rejected the Soviet claim and insisted that the 1939 frontiers should be continued, at least until the peace negotiations. This fundamental conflict, whose root lay in the historic antagonism between Poland and Russia, soon escalated. As a result of continued deadlock, the Soviets began to apply pressure. They made life exceptionally difficult for Polish officials still in Russia, altered the national status of Poles living in the disputed area, and rapidly came to the conclusion that its borders would only be secure if a government sympathetic to Russia was established in Warsaw. Thus the Soviets used all effective means at their disposal to obtain agreement on this central aim of their foreign policy.[35]

The United States and Britain found themselves in an invidiously circumscribed position over the vexing Soviet–Polish dispute. Churchill, and more particularly Eden, recognized the legitimacy of the Soviet claim on both historic and strategic grounds. Furthermore, they agreed that stability in Europe could be best achieved by recognizing, and so containing, the Soviets' desire for new frontiers. However, Churchill was always conscious of the fact that Britain had gone to

*A boundary to the west of the 1939 frontier that Britain had proposed at the end of the First World War.

war in 1939 over Germany's violation of Polish sovereignty. So, while Churchill wished to placate the Russians he could not, without impunity, repudiate the exiled government. Thus, many of his energies were devoted to finding a formula that would both satisfy the Soviets and simultaneously solder relations between the Poles and their neighbours. Eden was less concerned about the Poles. He reasoned that co-operation and the concomitant containment of Russia were more important than appeasing the London Poles. Temporary political embarrassment, he believed, was not too high a price for preserving harmony with Stalin.[36]

Eden's views were not universally shared in the Foreign Office, however. Sir Alexander Cadogan, Permanent Under-Secretary, felt that it was unwise to appease Stalin with such determination. Furthermore, he was worried that Eden's posture violated the Atlantic Charter and would consequently place a strain on Anglo-American relations.[37] For the Americans insisted, at least in 1942, that the question of Poland's frontiers should be deferred until after the war. Sumner Welles, Under-Secretary of State, was certain that discussions would 'accentuate various inherent differences' and would undermine the spirit of co-operation needed to solve post-war problems. The Americans projected their own perception of the world in believing that a cordial political climate between Russia and Poland would iron out substantive differences. Roosevelt himself wanted to concentrate on 'bringing about an improvement in these relations rather than citing too many specific problems'. He would soon realize, however, that it was the 'specific problems', and not abstract ambiance, that caused estrangement.[38]

Any hope for improved relations was shattered when the Soviet Union broke off diplomatic relations with Poland in April 1943. This breach followed the discovery of the murdered corpses of several thousand Polish officers in Katyn forest, near Smolensk, and the subsequent request of the London Poles for an independent investigation by the Red Cross to identify the perpetrators of the massacre.[39] After the Katyn crisis both Roosevelt and Churchill realized that there was little chance of cementing relations between Stalin and the Polish government. In fact their personal assessments of the dispute began to converge. Both leaders realized that the Polish question would finally have to be resolved irrespective of the worries of the London

L

Poles. But Roosevelt felt unable to articulate his position publicly and so formulate it into government policy. There were three main reasons for his dualistic stance. First, he was constrained by the possible electoral consequences of a deal on Poland amongst traditionally Democratic Polish–American voters. Secondly, Roosevelt found it politically difficult to reconcile his private inclination with his repeated pronouncements in favour of self-determination and the postponement of territorial settlements. He was aware that a reversal of policy could have serious repercussions in Congress. And thirdly, he clung to the hope that a tough peace with Germany and a fail-safe security organization would convince the Russians that they could afford magnanimity in their territorial demands.[40] Yet Roosevelt secretly confessed that the British position was reasonable and that the Poles should be ultimately forced to accept an agreement. Eden confirmed that F.D.R.'s 'mind about Russia's frontiers was almost exactly the same as mine'. However, Eden was not confident that American policy would actually reflect Roosevelt's views. Cordell Hull, according to Eden, 'is particularly likely to hold back on this issue', since it would undermine the credibility of his post-war vision. Hull was afraid that surrender to Russia's claims 'will inevitably be interpreted . . . as a significant step backward in the direction of power politics and spheres of influence'. This divorce between presidential preference and official policy, which was made very obvious at the Tehran conference in November 1943, only convinced Stalin that American policy was brittle and built on volatile foundations.[41]

British policy did not exhibit the same schizophrenia in the months leading up to the Tehran conference. Eden thought it essential to reach an agreement with the Soviets in order to quench any later thirst for additional territory in Eastern Europe or the Balkans. He warned Hull in August 1943 that America's refusal to endorse the Soviet claims would only make the Russians more suspicious and could actually undermine a post-war security organization. The Red Army, he said, would shortly enter the Balkans and cross the Polish frontier and 'it is our belief that a satisfactory solution would then be all the harder to obtain'.[42] Eden realized that Stalin would feel unconstrained in fostering a rival, communist government if he could not win a satisfactory settlement. In British eyes, territorial adjustments were ultimately preferable to communist influence in Eastern Europe.

In fact, the British position hardened at Tehran. Churchill realized that failure to alter the frontiers would result in the communisation of Poland, a prospect he would find intolerable. So he endorsed the Curzon line and received assurances that Poland would receive compensation in the West. He told Stalin that if the Poles refused the offer 'then Great Britain would be through with them and certainly would not oppose the Soviet Government under any condition at the peace table'.[43] He stuck to his word. He warned Eden afterwards that Britain would disown the Poles for their continual intransigence and let 'them make their own arrangements'. So when he met Polish leaders in London in January 1944, he told them acidly that Britain had discharged her duties and that 'it was useless to imagine we would embark on a conflict with Russia on that issue'.[44]

Although the British failed to persuade the Americans to endorse the frontier changes publicly, the two governments did agree that Poland should emerge from the war as an independent, democratic state. The Polish question was highly emotive, and neither government, on electoral grounds alone, could permit the introduction of pervasive Soviet influence in the newly constituted state. The British were prepared, therefore, to juggle with its frontiers, since they believed that adjustments would satisfy Stalin's concern for security. Furthermore, they realized that a large, independent Poland, wherever its final borders might be, would serve as a buffer between Russia and the West. The Americans, too, wanted to immunize Poland from Russian influence, but for different reasons. They believed that an independent Poland, bordered on the West by a weakened Germany, would convince the Russians of the improbability of any further invasions of Europe. So Roosevelt and Churchill were united in their determination, albeit for different reasons, to promote a government in Poland that was broadly reflective of public opinion within that country.

It is difficult to hazard, especially without adequate Soviet sources, whether or not the Russians intended to establish a communist government in Poland from the outset. Whatever the case may have been, the continued refusal of the Poles to agree to frontier adjustments, together with the reluctance of the allies to act independently of the London Poles, encouraged the Soviets to escalate their demands in Poland. When the Red Army crossed the Curzon line in July 1944, a rival administration, the Polish Committee of National Liberation, was created behind the Russian lines in Lublin. Shortly afterwards, the Soviets insisted that the committee should form the backbone of a new government on the grounds that it was friendly to the Russians and would not hinder peace. Soon the form of a post-war Polish government replaced the border question as a principal source of contention. For while the British, and to a less extent the Americans, were willing to adjust frontiers, they would not abandon completely the government of Stanislaw Mikolajczyk. The Atlantic partners reasoned that surrender to the Lublin Poles would jeopardize the bases of their foreign policies. Britain had calculated that agreed but limited adjustments would satisfy Soviet ambitions and so preserve its interests in Western Europe and the Mediterranean. The Americans, on the other hand, had argued that deferment and patience would convince the Russians that collective security would provide greater safety for them than spheres of influence or satellites. If the Soviets could be shown that their interests lay in political and economic co-operation with the West, Roosevelt believed, then the United States and Russia would prosper mutually. However, the President had underestimated Stalin's single-mindedness and had stalled too long. Just one month before the Yalta conference the Soviets defied their allies by recognizing the Lublin committee as the legitimate provisional government.[45]

The discussions on Poland and the Yalta conference in February 1945 proved to be a sobering experience. Both Churchill and Roosevelt finally realized that they were powerless to extract any real concessions from Stalin. The Russians were immovable in their determination to install a pro-Soviet government in the new Polish state and the West did not possess the military means and the political will to stop them. Indeed, the Marshal recognized the extent of his allies' impotence by their consuming preoccupation with political and symbolic satisfaction. While the Polish issue was probably the most emotive item on the agenda, it was obvious that neither Roosevelt nor Churchill would risk renewed hostilities or even an unrestrained scramble for territory in the closing months of the war. As Stalin persistently pointed out, Poland was a matter of security for Russia, while only a matter of honour for the West. He was also able to play off the two Atlantic leaders in their differing conceptions of diplomacy. To Roosevelt, he indicated that he would be more flexible on the detailed arrangements for a new collective security organization in return for a recognition of Soviet claims in Poland. Similarly, he delighted in reminding Churchill of Russia's aloofness from Greek and French affairs, in which the British had direct interests.

Churchill and Roosevelt admitted that Stalin was in a strong position. They consequently devoted most of their efforts at Yalta in finding face-saving formulae that simultaneously would comply with the Russian insistence on friendly governments and would appear to preserve the integrity and independence of Poland. The vague and ambiguous compromises agreed to at Yalta underscored to the West the fact that the Polish issue had become little more than an index or weather-vane of Russian intentions.[46]

In conclusion, therefore, the Atlantic partners themselves were largely responsible for the divisions and disillusionment over Eastern Europe which contributed so much to the disintegration of the wartime alliance. Their inability to agree on a fundamental posture towards Russia and to define the precise nature of their interests in the disputed areas effectively removed any inhibition on Stalin's desire to consolidate his hold in the East. The West's experiences of disillusionment were in many ways self-imposed, since its leaders constantly underestimated the very evident rigidity of the Russian position, especially in Poland. Churchill admittedly had a more sober and, in many ways, a more sophisticated understanding of Stalin's policy, but found it both personally and politically impossible to write off Poland. He was prepared to concede influence to Russia in the eastern Balkans, but President Roosevelt clung persistently to the belief that collective decision-making would both produce and be reinforced by democratic forms of government. Roosevelt's reluctance to dismiss Eastern Europe as a lost cause and to acknowledge publicly his circumscribed position only served to preserve hope where none could really flourish. Given the earlier decision to desist from military activity in the Balkans, Churchill and Roosevelt did not proceed to take the next logical step, namely a systematic assessment of what was really at stake materially there. Britain and the United States did, of course, believe that the political composition of Eastern Europe might influence the wider questions of collective security, liberalized trade, and access to the Middle and Far East. But they did not analyse the extent to which a communised Eastern Europe would undermine their articulated strategic and economic interests. Neither country, but especially the United States, ever seriously considered whether its post-war designs could survive without the full co-operation of the Eastern bloc. Indeed, the absence of focus, in conjunction with the reluctance to reinforce policy with either military occupation or parallel concession, enabled Stalin to increase Soviet influence in Eastern Europe without severe repercussions. It was only when Russia's expansionist intentions became completely clear that the Atlantic allies finally agreed on mutual criteria in defining their national interests—and these criteria were almost entirely political. By then it was too late to stop the Soviet domination of Eastern Europe. And in advocating purely political considerations, based on such nebulous concepts as the balance of ideology, they gave the cold war its manichean shape.

## NOTES

1. Cordell Hull, *Memoirs*, II (London, 1948) p. 1169; also, Herbert Feis, *Churchill, Roosevelt, Stalin: The War They Waged and the Peace They Sought* (Princeton, 1957) pp. 23–34, 57–80; John W. Wheeler-Bennett and Anthony Nicholls, *The Semblance of Peace: The Political Settlement After the Second World War* (London, 1972) pp. 44–50. Lynn E. Davis, *The Cold War begins: Soviet-American conflict over Eastern Europe* (Princeton, 1974) became available only after completion of this essay.
2. Winston S. Churchill, *The Second World War*, IV: *The Hinge of Fate* (London, 1951) p. 177.
3. *Stalin's Correspondence with Roosevelt and Truman* (New York, 1965) pp. 63–64; Diary, 29 April 1943, Box 13; 14 March 1943, Box 14, Joseph E. Davies Papers, Manuscripts Division, Library of Congress, Washington, D.C.
4. Robert E. Sherwood, *Roosevelt and Hopkins: An Intimate History* (New York, 1948) p. 528; Richard W. Steele, *The First Offensive, 1942: Roosevelt, Marshall, and the Making of American Strategy* (Bloomington, 1973) pp. 115–117.
5. Stimson to Roosevelt, 10 August 1943, U.S. Department of State, *Foreign Relations of the United States: The Conferences at Washington and Quebec, 1943* (Washington, D.C., 1970) p. 496 (hereafter cited as *F.R.*, relevant volume); Henry L. Stimson and McGeorge Bundy, *On Active Service in Peace and War* (New York, 1948) p. 436.

6. William C. Bullitt, 'How We Won the War and Lost the Peace', *Life*, XXV (30 August 1948) 94.

7. Harriman to Hopkins, 10 September 1944; Harriman to Hull, 20 September 1944; *F.R.*, *1944: IV, Europe* (Washington, D.C., 1966) pp. 988–990, 992–998. For detailed discussion of lend-lease policies, see George C. Herring, Jnr, *Aid to Russia, 1941–1946: Strategy, Diplomacy, The Origins of the Cold War* (New York and London, 1973). Bullitt to Roosevelt, 27 January 1943, Box 51, Cordell Hull Papers, Manuscripts Division, Library of Congress, Washington, D.C.

8. Churchill, *The Second World War*, IV, p. 293.

9. Not everybody in the Cabinet agreed. Lord Beaverbrook shared Roosevelt's desire to re-evaluate Western attitudes to Russia. He proclaimed in April 1942, that 'Communism under Stalin has won the applause and admiration of all the western nations'. He even defended the purges. It was apparently 'clear' that 'the men who were shot would have betrayed Russia to her German enemies'. See A. J. P. Taylor, *Beaverbrook* (Harmondsworth, 1974) p. 677.

10. Winston S. Churchill, *The Second World War*, III: *The Grand Alliance* (London, 1950) p. 615. See also Churchill's comments on the liquidation of the Kulaks in Churchill, *The Second World War*, IV, p. 448.

11. Memo, 'Current Problems in Relations with the Soviet Union', in Stettinius Mission File, 3, State Department Files, Group 740.0011, National Archives, Washington, D.C.

12. George Messersmith to Philip W. Bonsal, 13 December 1943, Box 53, Hull Papers.

13. Myron C. Taylor to Hull, 8 July 1943, Box 52, Hull Papers; Diary, 25 March 1943, Box 5, Breckinridge Long Papers, Manuscripts Division, Library of Congress, Washington, D.C.

14. Minutes of meeting, 10 August 1943, *F.R.: Conferences at Washington and Quebec, 1943*, pp. 498–503; Ronald Lewin, *Churchill as Warlord* (London, 1973) pp. 194–195.

15. Circular for Chiefs of Staff, 3 August 1943; unsigned memo, n.d., Prime Minister's Papers, Prem. 3, 66/1, Public Record Office, London.

16. F.O. memo, 'British Interests in South-Eastern Europe', 17 April 1944, *F.R.*, *1944: I, General* (Washington, D.C., 1966) pp. 596–599; Lord Ismay, *Memoirs* (London, 1960) p. 367; Winston S. Churchill, *The Second World War*, V: *Closing the Ring* (London, 1952) p. 475.

17. Hugh Seton-Watson, *The East European Revolution* (London, 1950) pp. 126–127; Walter R. Roberts, *Tito, Mihailović, and the Allies, 1941–1945* (Brunswick, N.J., 1973) pp. 90–91, 115–117.

18. Eden to Churchill, 9 October 1943, Prem. 3, 66/2.

19. Lord Selborne to Desmond Morton, 13 October 1943, Prem. 3, 66/2; also, Air Ministry to Britman, n.d., Prem. 3, 66/4.

20. Mideast to Air Ministry, 3 October 1943, Prem. 3, 66/2.

21. On the Greek question, see Edgar O'Ballance, *The Greek Civil War, 1944-1949* (London, 1966); Stephen G. Xydis, *Greece and The Great Powers, 1944-1947* (Thessaloniki, 1963); L. S. Stavrianos, *Greece: American Dilemma and Opportunity* (Chicago, 1952).

22. Churchill, *The Second World War*, V, p. 422; Matthews to Hull, 24 February 1943, *F.R., 1943: II, Europe* (Washington, D.C., 1964) pp. 975–977; British Embassy to Department of State, January 1944, *F.R., 1944: IV*, pp. 1331–33.

23. Gabriel Kolko has argued that extant investments and, more important, potential markets shaped American policy towards south-eastern Europe. See Gabriel Kolko, *The Politics of War: The World and United States Foreign Policy, 1943–1945* (New York, 1970), pp. 129–130, 156–160, 166–171. William A. Williams is less emphatic, but still believes that economic considerations were paramount. William A. Williams, *The Tragedy of American Diplomacy* (Delta Books edn., New York, 1962), pp. 211–243.

24. Minutes of President's Meeting with Joint Chiefs of Staff, 19 November 1943, *F.R.: The Conferences at Cairo and Tehran, 1943* (Washington, D.C., 1961) p. 258; minutes of meeting, Combined Chiefs of Staff, 19 May 1943; memo, U.S. Chiefs of Staff, 9 August 1943, *F.R.: Conferences at Washington and Quebec, 1943*, pp. 114–116, 472–482; Stimson and Bundy, *On Active Service*, pp. 436, 447.

25. Draft, Bullitt to Roosevelt, 6 August 1943; Bullitt to Roosevelt, 29 January 1943, Box 51, Hull Papers.

26. Roberts, *Tito, Mihailović, and the Allies*, pp. 90–99, 163–184.

27. Kolko, *The Politics of War*, pp. 131–138, 152–155, 432–436.

28. Memo by Cavendish W. Cannon, 19 May 1944, *F.R., 1944: IV*, pp. 1370–73; also, memo by Cannon, 17 May 1943, *F.R., 1943: II*, pp. 1009–10.

29. Draft, Roosevelt to Peter II, 12 May 1944, *F.R., 1944: IV*, pp. 1335–39; Stettinius to British Embassy, 23 December 1944, *F.R.: The Conferences at Malta and Yalta, 1945* (Washington, D.C., 1955) pp. 255–257; also, Briefing Book Paper, 'Principal Yugoslav Problems', *F.R.: Malta and Yalta, 1945*, pp. 262–265; memo, 'Yugoslavia', Stettinius Mission File, 3, State Department Files, Group 740.0011; David Dilks, ed., *The Diaries of Sir Alexander Cadogan, 1938–1945* (London, 1971) pp. 694–695; Roberts, *Tito, Mihailović, and the Allies*, pp. 288–289, 300.

30. See, for example, Hull to Winant, 5 July 1944; Winant to Hull,

12 October 1944; Winant to Hull, 22 October 1944, *F.R.*, *1944: III*, *British Commonwealth and Europe* (Washington, D.C., 1965) pp. 341–344, 450–451, 472–474; Harriman to Hull, 15 September 1944, *F.R.*, *1944: IV*, pp. 163–164, 234–237.

31. Winant to Hull, 12 October 1944, *F.R.*, *1944: III*, pp. 451–453; also, Hull to Winant, 9 January 1944; Winant to Hull, 14 April 1944, *F.R.*, *1944: I*, pp. 11, 28–30.

32. Memo, 'Rumania', in Stettinius Mission File, 3, State Department Files, Group 740.0011.

33. Winston S. Churchill, *The Second World War*, VI: *Triumph and Tragedy* (London, 1954) pp. 197–204; Feis, *Churchill, Roosevelt, Stalin*, pp. 447–453; Roosevelt to Churchill, 11 June 1944, *F.R.*, *1944: V, The Near East, South Asia and Africa; the Far East* (Washington, D.C., 1965) pp. 117–118; Roosevelt to Churchill, 22 June 1944; Churchill to Stalin, 11 October 1944; Churchill memo, 12 October 1944, Prem. 3, 66/7. The October memoranda are reproduced in Churchill, *The Second World War*, VI, pp. 197–204.

34. Briefing Book Papers, *F.R.: Conferences at Malta and Yalta, 1945*, pp. 234–240; Kolko, *The Politics of War*, pp. 166–171.

35. On the Polish dispute see Wheeler-Bennett and Nicholls, *The Semblance of Peace, passim*; Kolko, *The Politics of War*, pp. 99–122, 147–152, 389–427; Feis, *Churchill, Roosevelt, Stalin*, pp. 23–34, 191–199, 283–290, 373–392, 453–459; Jan M. Ciechanowski, *The Warsaw Rising of 1944* (Cambridge, 1974).

36. Biddle to Hull, 27 April 1942, *F.R. 1942: III*, *Europe* (Washington, D.C., 1961) pp. 142–143; Dilks, ed., *The Diaries of Sir Alexander Cadogan*, p. 437.

37. Cadogan to Churchill, 31 March 1943, Prem. 3, 354/8; Dilks, ed., *The Diaries of Sir Alexander Cadogan*, pp. 437, 442–443.

38. Welles to Biddle, 6 March 1942; Roosevelt to Biddle, 10 September 1942, *F.R.*, *1942: III*, pp. 116–117, 183–184.

39. On Katyn, see J. K. Zawodny, *Death in the Forest: The Story of the Katyn Forest Massacre* (London, 1971).

40. Halifax to Foreign Office, 16 March 1943, Prem. 3, 355/4; Diary, 13 June 1944, Box 5, Long Papers; Welles to Biddle, 16 June 1943; Hull to Standley, 29 June 1943, *F.R.*, *1943: III*, *British Commonwealth, Eastern Europe and the Far East* (Washington, D.C., 1963) pp. 431, 434–436.

41. Memo, Eden to War Cabinet, 'Western Frontiers of the U.S.S.R.', 5 October 1943, Prem. 3, 355/4; Hull to Harriman, 25 January 1944, *F.R.*, *1944: III*, pp. 1234–35; Bohlen minutes, Roosevelt–Stalin meeting,

1 December 1943, *F.R.: Conferences at Cairo and Tehran, 1943*, pp. 594–596.

42. Eden to Hull, 23 August 1943, *F.R.: Conferences at Washington and Quebec, 1943*, pp. 1113–16; also, Eden memo for War Cabinet, 22 November 1943, Prem. 3, 355/6.

43. Bohlen minutes, Tripartite meeting, 1 December 1943, *F.R.: Conferences at Cairo and Tehran, 1943*, p. 599; also, Churchill, *The Second World War*, V, 317–319; Dilks, ed., *The Diaries of Sir Alexander Cadogan*, p. 581.

44. Churchill to Eden, 7 January 1944, record of conversation, Churchill, Eden, Cadogan, Mikolajczyk, Romer and Raczynski, 20 January 1944, Prem. 3, 355/7.

45. Roosevelt to Stalin, 20 December 1944; Stalin to Roosevelt, 27 December 1944; Roosevelt to Stalin, 31 December 1944; Stalin to Roosevelt, 1 January 1945, *Stalin's Correspondence with Roosevelt and Truman*, pp. 175, 180–184; Hull to Harriman, 17 June 1944, *F.R., 1944: III*, pp. 1285–89; record of meeting, Churchill, Eden, Mikolajczyk, etc. 22 June 1944, Prem. 3, 352/14A; conversation, Churchill and Mikolajczyk, 14 October 1944, General Sikorski Historical Institute, *Documents on Polish–Soviet Relations, 1939–1945: II* (London, 1967) pp. 416–422.

46. On Yalta, see Diane S. Clemens, *Yalta* (New York, 1970); Feis, *Churchill, Roosevelt, Stalin*, pp. 497–558; Wheeler-Bennett and Nicholls, *The Semblance of Peace*, pp. 214–250; Kolko, *The Politics of War*, pp. 343–369; Nicholas Bethell, *Gomulka: His Poland and his Communism* (Harmondsworth, 1972) pp. 72–96.

# *13*

# *Anglo-American Images*

## HOWARD TEMPERLEY

In any conversation between two people, Oliver Wendell Holmes tells us, *six* people are involved: the two people as they actually are, the two as they see themselves and the two as they see one another. 'Of these,' adds Holmes, 'the least important, philosophically speaking, is the one we have called the real person. No wonder two disputants get angry when there are six of them talking and listening all at the same time.'[1]

Whatever its philosophical merits, Holmes's proposition accurately describes a phenomenon familiar to students of Anglo-American relations. In observing one another, Englishmen and Americans have frequently failed to pay adequate attention to what they saw. Often, indeed, the details have interested them very little. Usually this is because what they were looking for were non-visible concepts—ideas about the past and the future, about good and evil, or about their own relative positions in the world. Whatever the 'real' United States or the 'real' Britain—both complex societies with varied and often conflicting aspirations—what observers have tended to see, when they looked across the Atlantic, were simplified models, often illustrating particular vices or virtues—the perils of democracy, the errors of kingship, or the iniquities of unrestrained capitalism.

'Looking across the Atlantic' is perhaps a misleading metaphor. To be sure, many over the years made the pilgrimage. Some millions, in fact, transferred themselves permanently, often spurred on by the images they had already formed of life on the other continent. These had the opportunity of testing their beliefs against the realities they found on the other side. But a much larger number never travelled at all, relying for their impressions on what they gleaned from books, newspapers or, more recently, from the cinema, radio and television. ' "Have you ever been to England?" ' asks Martin Chuzzlewit, in

Dickens's novel, of one of his American interlocutors, who insists that Queen Victoria lives in the Tower of London; ' "In print I have, sir," said the General, "but not otherwise".' Many others would say the same, and with the General's utter confidence in the rightness of his judgement. How many Englishmen, one wonders, labour under the illusion that Washington State is located on the Potomac?

Ideas such as these can, of course, be easily refuted. Much harder to refute are ideas of a more general kind—the ideas that is to say about justice and injustice, vice and virtue, innocence and experience, which over the years have characterized the Anglo-American dialogue. To a degree, it is true, these can be 'disproved' to the extent that we can show how they failed adequately to reflect the true complexities of the situation. This is a legitimate and often necessary task.

But to achieve full understanding another kind of approach seems to be needed. This involves treating images not as reflections of some external reality but as expressions of the beliefs, values and aspirations of those who held them. Viewed in this light, what is interesting about Anglo-American images is not, primarily, whether they were true or false but what they reveal about the notions which over the years Americans and Englishmen have cherished about themselves and one another. As with other mythologies, these were partly self-generating. What Americans believed about Englishmen had much to do with what they believed about themselves. Often, too, they expressed not what people's senses told them but what they wished or needed to believe about one another. One consequence of this was that such images have often enjoyed remarkable longevity, far outlasting the particular circumstances which gave them birth. To this extent they are ahistorical. Yet in many cases such apparent continuity masks subtle internal changes in the nature of the myths themselves—for instance when what appeared at one stage to be an accurate representation of reality became in the course of time something else again, a caricature, a hypothesis, a convenient way of looking at things, or simply useful ammunition to have to hand in the event of an argument.

What concerns us, in other words, is a kind of international folklore, sometimes, as in the hands of caricaturists, a source of amusement, at other times, as when it impinged on the political policies of the two countries, capable of generating action. Calling it a folklore does not, of course, mean that it was in any sense static. For it was also, in a very literal sense, a *dialogue*; and just as with any other dialogue we would be ill-advised to look for objective truths, so with the Anglo-American dialogue we find ourselves dealing with much more subtle quantities. Call them half-truths if you wish, or embellished truths, or exaggerated truths, or poetic truths, although it might be safest to leave the word 'truth' out altogether. Essentially they are contributions to an ongoing debate which, beginning with the founding of the first colonies, has been carried on to the present and shows every sign of continuing into the future.

I

This phenomenon has given rise to so large a literature that it is as well to remind ourselves at the outset that the Anglo-American relationship has been far from exclusive. Mixed up with the images which Americans and Englishmen have held of one another have been images of other nations and peoples. The projection of foreign images is, after all, a common matter. If Englishmen and Americans have mythologized one another so also have Frenchmen and Germans, Russians and Poles, and Chinese and Japanese, not to mention Yorkshiremen and Londoners, Democrats and Republicans and blacks and whites. In a sense, what we observe when we look at the Anglo-American relationship is simply the familiar human spectacle of men seeking amusement, instruction and intellectual stimulation from observing the behaviour of others.

Viewed in this broader context it is plain that some features of the Anglo-American relationship and of the European–American relationship generally, are less remarkable than is often assumed. For example, the creation of the European Community has led many commentators to observe that Europeans themselves were at last coming around to a viewpoint that had long been held by Americans, who saw the nations of Europe as constituting a single cultural and geographic entity. Yet it is well to recognize that there is nothing specifically *American* about a view which has been held by non-European peoples from the beginning of history. What is perhaps remarkable in the American case is that, despite the fact of geographical separation, they were so long in adopting it and that it took a disenchanted Englishman, Thomas Paine, to spell out for them its implications.[2] And, again, the habit of 'homogenizing' the continent by blurring over its distinctive geographic and cultural features ('If it's Tuesday, this must be Belgium') is not an American but a non-European trait. Indeed, since large numbers of Americans have actually been to Belgium their discriminations on the matter are sometimes finer than those of other peoples, including, sometimes, those of the British themselves.

There is also the argument that, in the minds of Americans, the terms 'Europe' and 'America' have been used to designate not simply distinct geographical areas but utterly contrasting social and political systems. Here the antithetical character of much image-making comes into play. If America was one thing, then, by a process of pseudo-logic, Europe must be another. Yet here again we find that many Americans were sufficiently close to, and sufficiently affected by, the political and cultural experiences of Europe, often as a result of their subsequent impact on trade or immigration, to acquire a fair and dis-criminating knowledge. And within the broader framework the nature of the antithesis itself has been changeable, sometimes emphasizing one factor, sometimes another, and occasionally broadening out to include more than simply the two continents, as in the period after the Second World War when it was absorbed into the Free World–Communist antithesis.

But perhaps the most important element usually associated with the Europe–American antithesis is the familiar proposition that it has been persistently used, particularly by Americans, to establish their own sense of identity. One result of this, as Daniel Boorstin tells us, is that Americans have tended to '. . . define our national character negatively. The polar framework has thus served our need and our disposition to describe our national character in elusive, vague and shifting terms. It has required little precision and little agreement to assert that we stand for everything that Europe is *not*.'[3] There is much truth in this. What is doubtful is whether, as Boorstin goes on to argue, 'the antithesis of "Europe" was more or less adequate to the construction of our image of ourselves'—for certainly it would be remarkable if Americans had chosen to define their position in the world by reference to only one set of images associated with only one continent. That the reality was a good deal more complicated is suggested by the fact that virtually the same argument has been used with respect to American responses to Indians. According to Roy Harvey Pearce in

*The Savages of America*, civilized men could survive only if they believed in themselves, and in America before the 1850s, '. . . that belief was most often defined negatively—in terms of the savage Indians who, as stubborn obstacles to progress, forced Americans to consider and reconsider what it was to be civilized and what it took to build a civilization'.[4] The popularity of such antithetical modes of thought also emerges in descriptions of relations between whites and blacks. As Winthrop Jordan tells us in *White Over Black*, 'It seems almost as if the Negro had become a counter image for the European, a vivid reminder of the dangers facing transplanted Europeans, the living embodiment of what they must never allow themselves to become'.[5]

So without extending our enquiry to what Americans knew, or thought they knew, about Mexicans, Chinamen and South Sea Islanders (which, in each case, was not a little) it seems fair to conclude that they were in the habit of defining their own identity by means of essentially the same processes of cultural triangulation employed by other peoples at least since Aristotle's day, and presumably before. Aristotle himself attributed the virtues of the Greeks to the geographic chance which placed them between the energetic but anarchic peoples of Europe and the ingenious but servile Asiatics—which looks uncommonly like the Jeffersonian view which placed Americans between the 'artificial' Europeans on the one hand and 'primitive' Indians and blacks on the other.[6]

What can, of course, be urged is that, for clear historical reasons, Americans have felt a compelling need to engage in such acts of triangulation more frequently than most other peoples. As a nation of immigrants, founded in historical daylight and committed to the propagation of individualistic values, Americans have been much occupied with creating and identifying national characteristics. The British, whether because of deeper historical roots, a traditionally greater involvement in world affairs, a larger preoccupation with internal class distinctions, or characteristic reticence, have historically indulged in fewer overt attempts at self-definition. There are no British counterparts to the Declaration of Independence or the American Constitution, nor has there ever been a Parliamentary Committee on un-British Activities. Problems of national identity, however, are by no means unfamiliar to the British, although they have more often been associated with the Welsh, Scots and Irish than with the English themselves and have frequently been most marked in the case of recent immigrants and British groups overseas, both of which have experienced very much the same need as Americans to make nationality a matter of positive affirmation. Even the English, however, have never been reluctant to assign characters to others. When, in the late nineteenth century, this particular pastime briefly achieved the status of a 'science' thanks to the Social Darwinists, it enjoyed great popularity on both sides of the Atlantic, thereby revealing not only that Englishmen and Americans were given to thinking in similar ways, but that, to a remarkable degree, they shared the same prejudices.

## II

Granting, then, that Anglo-American image-making has been very much an open-ended process, and that mixed up with what each thought of the other will usually be found images of other groups, the fact remains that the relationship which produced it has been in many ways an unusual one. Here were two peoples, one originally an outgrowth of the other, sharing a common language, and retaining, in spite of two centuries of political separation, many striking affinities. One consequence of this is that British people have never fully adjusted their minds to the notion that Americans are 'foreigners'. Writing from London in 1863 Henry Adams noted that: 'In fact we are now one of the known and acknowledged units of the London and English world, and . . . the majority of people receive us much as they would Englishmen, and seem to consider us as such. I have been much struck by the way in which they affect to distinguish here between us and "foreigners"; that is, persons who won't speak English.'[7] The same view is expressed by British observers. Looking back on her first impressions of the United States in 1832 Frances Kemble recalled that 'the whole country was like some remote part of England that I had never seen before, the people were like *queer* English people'.[8] At international gatherings there is still the traditional banter about 'ex-colonials' and 'lousy redcoats'; while to those outside this charmed circle *les Anglo-Saxons* and *Angelsachsentum* remain familiar concepts. To all of which *Whitakers Almanac* adds the weight of its authority by steadfastly refusing to list the United States under the heading of foreign nations, placing it, along with the Republic of Ireland, in a separate unheaded category.

That America *was* a foreign nation was, of course, a point which Americans themselves, particularly during the early years of the Republic, were anxious to establish. This was an issue which played a significant part in the controversies leading up to the War of 1812. Yet in spite of this and although nowadays only a minority of Americans can claim to be of English descent there has remained on the American side too a lively awareness of America's cultural debt to Britain. 'Our civility', declared Emerson in 1844 in a speech commemorating Britain's emancipation of her West Indian slaves, 'England determines the style of, insomuch as England is the strongest of the family of existing nations and as we are an extension of that people.'[9] The same cultural debt was acknowledged, although in very different circumstances, in a *New Yorker* lead article of 31 December 1973, dealing with Britain's economic difficulties, which concluded with the declaration that 'For the United States, the collapse of England, the nation that gave us our law, our language, and much of our moral tradition, would be a tragic event of immeasurable import'.[10]

Such expressions of mutual concern do not, of course, adequately sum up a relationship which has, historically speaking, been as notable for expressions of enmity as of friendship. For many years Britain was America's traditional enemy, while the United States, in turn, posed a very real threat to Britain's remaining interests in North America. Even at such time of hostility, however, the sense of cultural affinity was not lacking. If Americans were transplanted Englishmen, the English were *un*transplanted Americans, in each case potent reminders of the effects of geographical separation and historical accident.

The ambiguities of this relationship have long teased the imagination of journalists, writers and politicians. How, without going into every factual detail, was the Anglo-American connection to be described? Plainly it was not like the Anglo-French connection which involved differences of language not to mention institutional and cultural distinctions. And, again, it was not quite like the Anglo-Canadian relationship which entailed no corresponding element of political rivalry and where links of a political nature remained in being much longer. Were Americans simply deracinated Europeans, whose English-

ness had been progressively diluted by immigration from elsewhere
and the vicissitudes of life in a new environment? Or were they, as
Americans themselves sometimes claimed, 'purer' English, realizing
on a rich and empty continent ideals which the English themselves,
on their cramped and cluttered little island, were incapable of
realizing?[11] Was America Uncle Sam, lean and benevolent, or Uncle
Shylock, clutching his profits, or the half-mad figure, brandishing
rockets, depicted on disarmament posters? Was England John Bull,
rotund and down-to-earth, or Perfidious Albion? Were England and
America two nations *joined* or *separated* by a common language? Was
Brave New World an expression to be taken literally, or ironically as
in Huxley's novel?

## III

One way of trying to make sense of these images is to sort them into
categories. At the simplest level, images occur as discrete units: the
bald eagle, a photograph of St Paul's during the blitz, or something
glimpsed on a television screen. Some are emblematic, some historic,
and some representative of events occurring at the present moment.
Depending on the temperament, nationality and political persuasion
of the observer, these can be more or less evocative. But what generally
concerns us when we talk about Anglo-American images are not
discrete units of this kind but composite images relating not just to
particular aspects of society or single events but to whole social
systems and extended chains of events. Moreover, what is immediately
evident when we examine these larger units is that they are composed
of the most heterogeneous elements, ranging from simple visual
images and straightforward statements of fact to elaborate metaphorical
structures.

Argument by analogy has, in fact, been one of the principal features
of Anglo-American image-making. Having much in common it was
natural for men in both societies to relate what they read or heard to
events in their own immediate lives. Thus the fact that the American
colonies originally developed under British authority and broke away
over an issue involving the exercise of that authority encouraged
observers to think in terms of *Familial Images*. The notion that the
relationship was like that between a father and a son was already in
common use in 1776 when Thomas Paine attacked it on the grounds

that Europe and not England was the parent country. Nevertheless, this belief has remained an important element in the Anglo-American discourse, mainly because it has seemed to explain a good deal about the subsequent behaviour of the two countries. As is the way with adolescents, the young Republic was unsure of itself, inclined to over-statement, and unduly prickly over issues affecting its pride, all of which, not surprisingly, led to further parental head-shaking, as well as to renewed family quarrels. But in due course, having shown that he could well stand on his own feet, the son became more self-assured and the father mellower, so that eventually amicable relations were restored.[12] At least this is one version, but within the broad analogical framework the details may be varied at will. The father may be shown as cruel and overbearing or kindly and longsuffering, the son's responses as natural and justified or unreasonable and excessive.

This malleability, as Marcus Cunliffe has shown, is characteristic of most of the archetypal images associated with America.[13] The image of America as the *Land of Liberty* can by judiciously altering the factual details (or simply by substituting new adjectives) be turned into the counter-image of America as the *Land of Libertinism*. The debate over whether America was, indeed, a land of freedom or licence is as old as the history of the European settlement itself, embracing, in the eighteenth century, the philosophical controversy between the champions of nature and civilization and, in the twentieth, that between the exponents of free enterprise and of the welfare state. It was of particular interest to Englishmen, however, in the years after 1783 when they were confronted with the unfamiliar spectacle of a large body of men and women very much like themselves making their way in the world free of the traditional restraints of European society. Here were Englishmen, or rather ex-Englishmen, set loose on a vast continent, with no established church, no monarch, no aristocracy, no squirearchy and very little in the way of a central government to exercise control over them. Whether any form of civilized society could survive in these circumstances seemed to many unlikely. 'Every Prognostic that can be formed from a Contemplation of their mutual Antipathies, and clashing Interests, their Differences of Governments, Habitudes and Manners,' wrote Josiah Tucker, a British clergyman, in 1781, 'plainly indicates that the Americans will have no . . . Common Interest to pursue, when the Power and

Government of England are finally removed.'[14] But whether they would or not it was natural for Americans and Englishmen to assume that what happened in the United States would have an important bearing on how Englishmen would in future regard the institutions of their own country.

Yet, as on so many other occasions, what Englishmen made of the American experiment had as much to do with their existing predilections as with what actually occurred in America. Had Americans immediately fallen to fighting among themselves or turned for salvation to a military dictator the response would no doubt have been different. But since the American Revolution did not go the way the French Revolution was to go and since what did happen was sufficiently varied to provide polemical ammunition for all parties, Englishmen were free to make of it pretty much what they wanted. To those of a conservative inclination, worried about incipient changes in England itself, the United States presented a distressing spectacle of social disharmony, greed and governmental ineffectiveness. Political radicals, on the other hand, strove to see in it a shining example of the economic and social benefits which Englishmen themselves would enjoy if only they were freed of the burdens of an oppressive governmental and class system. Not all succeeded. Many of the most vituperative attacks on the United States came, indeed, from those who saw in American realities a gross betrayal of American ideals.[15] But to most Englishmen the United States was not entirely one thing or the other but something in between, a mixture of good points and bad, from which, nevertheless, important lessons could be learned.

By and large this has remained the British attitude, allowing that the political orientation of the two countries has undergone continuous change and that over the years the Right has found as much praise as the Left. It has also been a common American attitude. Initially, as in the Boorstin argument, Britain was frequently regarded as an example of all that Americans should seek to avoid. Britain stood for aristocracy and tradition, America for democracy and freedom. Yet even in these early years British radicalism could be as alarming to some Americans as American radicalism was to some Englishmen. The abolition of slavery in the West Indies in 1834 appeared to Southerners every bit as threatening to their way of life as the notions of the Jeffersonians had appeared to conservative Englishmen, and no less hare-brained. As a committee of Southern senators reported in 1850, the British experiment had ruined the colonies economically without in any way improving the condition of the Negroes. Yet, blighting though its consequences were, they furnished only a faint image of the effects which a similar measure would have on the South, which would inevitably 'become the permanent abode of disorder, anarchy, poverty, misery and wretchedness'.[16] A century later similar claims were being made about 'socialized medicine'.

In judging one another, Americans and Englishmen have frequently had recourse to another archetypal image: that of America as the *Land of the Future*. Like the familial and libertarian images, this one was sufficiently elastic to permit an almost infinite variety of interpretations. As a statement about power it would be taken to mean that the United States would one day overtake the nations of the Old World in terms of population, wealth and influence, thus fulfilling Bishop Berkeley's famous prediction that 'Westward the course of Empire takes its way . . .'. American poets of the revolutionary generation, such as Timothy Dwight, elaborated boldly on this theme, albeit in rather antiquated verse:

> Thy fleets to all regions thy pow'r shall display,
> The nations admire, and the oceans obey;
> Each shore to thy glory its tribute unfold,
> And the east and the south yield their spices and gold. . . .[17]

Not all Americans, it is true, felt equally assured of so glorious a consummation. Nor did the British who, observing American society through more sober eyes, noted various tendencies which could lead to a quite different outcome. In 1811, Colonel Joseph Gubbins, recently arrived from England to take command of the New Brunswick militia, noted in his diary that 'The poor are not educated to respect the rich as in Europe. . . . The habits of the People are so averse to Subordination, the price of labour so high, and the facility for desertion so great, that it would require very extraordinary sacrifices to keep on foot a standing army even of ten thousand men. . . . Upon the whole, there never did exist a Government of such a numerous Population less capable of carrying on an offensive war than is that of the United States.'[18]

Events of the next two years were to prove this assessment largely correct. British observers were also quick to note the fissiparous tendencies of the United States. Nevertheless, it was plain simply from the extent of her territory and her growing population (which overtook that of Britain herself in the 1840s) that she was a power to be reckoned with. If only she held together, as by 1865 it was evident she would, she was clearly destined to become a major force in the world.

Implicit in the image of America as the Land of the Future, however, is also the notion that major new trends in the world would manifest themselves first in the United States. This has often, although by no means invariably, been the case. Much criticism of the United States has, in fact, been directed not at Americans personally but at aspects of modern life which happened to become visible there earlier than they did elsewhere. It was for precisely this reason that in the early years conservatives viewed America with such alarm. At that time the major new trend, as Americans and many Englishmen saw it, was democracy, a way of ordering society which Americans themselves, with their egalitarian traditions and ample territories, could adopt with relative ease, but which threatened to have cataclysmic consequences for the more geographically restricted and hierarchical societies of Europe—as in the case of the French it did. Appropriately, it was the ideologue of the American Revolution, Thomas Paine, who drew from Danton the famous remark 'Revolutions cannot be made with rosewater'.[19]

Underestimating the obstacles which stand in the way of other peoples achieving what Americans themselves have achieved has been a common American failing. Why should not others enjoy the good things of life on the same scale as Americans unless lack of ingenuity or moral turpitude prevented them from doing so? This attitude has also been evident with regard to what many observers believe has been the major development of the twentieth century: the harnessing together of technology and power to create societies dominated by the machine process, dependent on office and factory routines, and celebrating their success in acts of individual consumption. Here too America has led the field, an object of fascination and envy not only to the British but to the whole world. Where else was such technological ingenuity displayed, so much energy harnessed, so many goods made available for consumption? To the British traveller of the 1940s or 1950s, visiting the United States was like moving ahead two decades in time.[20] Coming out of San Francisco Terminal Airport and seeing the plain of parked cars, or observing the lights of Manhattan on a winter's evening from the steps of the Guggenheim, or lying in bed at night in someone's house and hearing the gadgets mysteriously switching themselves on and off, America seemed to represent not merely the future but something futuristic, a technological cornucopia whose products were being poured coruscating on a world accustomed to scrimping and saving but inevitably to be wiped away in the science fiction future for which we were all destined.

Today this image looks decidedly tarnished. Other countries have been increasing in wealth more rapidly than the United States. This has not been the experience of the British, but they too now have plains of parked cars and gadgets that (sometimes) switch themselves on and off and have discovered that both can be decided nuisances. Nevertheless, the fact that the United States has led the world in what have, quite possibly, been the two most important developments of modern times has encouraged the belief that she will do so again and that the wave of the future is already evident in the increasing fragmentation of American society and in the violence, decay and racial disharmony associated with America's great cities. According to *The Times*, 'The city of New York, with its contrast between the most exorbitant wealth and the most humiliating poverty within a few city blocks of each other, is a monument to the social failure of American capitalism'.[21] In more apocalyptic mood, a correspondent of the *Economist* who toured the United States concluded his series of articles by observing that 'I did feel that the most appropriate texts for a reporter on America in 1969 might be found in the story of the decline and fall of another mighty empire that Gibbon started as he wandered around another Capitol. The pertinent, though scattered, phrases seem to abound: *The decline of Rome was the natural and inevitable effect of immoderate greatness. Prosperity ripened the principle of decay. . . .*'[22]

The idea that after so much milk and honey the Four Horsemen must—not simply must but positively ought to—follow is not, of course, peculiar to the British. There are elements of suppressed puritanism in all of us. The notion that senescent capitalism is shaking itself apart—or, to use a current American image, that the machine has gone into self-destruct—is familiar enough in the United States, and has been a dominant theme in much recent American writing, achieving, in the works of William Burroughs, Saul Bellow and Thomas Pynchon, the dimensions of a nightmare vision.[23] On the whole, however, Americans have been better placed to judge the underlying realities of their society than the British, and to recognize hyperbole when they see it. At least they know that you can walk down Park Avenue *without* getting mugged.

So obsessed have the British been with the vision of America as the Land of the Future that they have often failed to note that similar notions have flourished in the United States with respect to themselves. As the nation which gave Americans the philosophical underpinnings for nineteenth-century democracy and which largely pioneered the industrial techniques from which twentieth-century American technology sprang, Britain has, in a sense, led the way for the United States. By and large Americans have recognized this, although there have been times when ideological preconceptions have obscured their vision. This was the case in the early nineteenth century when a well-developed chauvinism combined with an excessive preoccupation with democracy prevented them from perceiving the implications of the economic changes which were occurring in what they continued to regard as a backward-looking society. By mid-century Americans had begun to disabuse themselves of this idea and, by 1900, having caught up in industrial production, it became possible to imagine America and Britain together, an Anglo-Saxon partnership, leading the world in the twentieth century.[24]

Rightly or wrongly, Britain's increasing inability to play an effective role in such a partnership has been, for many Americans, a potent warning of the dangers which lay ahead for themselves. Having followed in Britain's footsteps so often in the past, the most dramatic illustration being her assumption of British world responsibilities since the Second World War, must she not, in the twenty-first century if not sooner, follow Britain into decline? Anxiously, Americans have scanned their society for signs that this might already be happening and, not infrequently, have found them. According to Senator Fulbright, 'Despite its dangerous and unproductive consequences, the idea of being responsible for the whole world seems to be flattering to

Americans and I am afraid it is turning our heads, just as the sense of universal responsibility turned the heads of ancient Romans and nineteenth-century British'.[25] The danger, in Fulbright's view, is that in taking on such responsibilities Americans, like the British before them, will weaken and corrupt their own society. Others, more concerned with strictly domestic trends, have used the British example to illustrate the perils of 'welfarism', 'creeping socialism' and other manifestations of the 'English Disease'. John Thomas Flynn's *The Road Ahead* (1949) painted a sufficiently gloomy picture of life in the Old Country to persuade the New York insurance tycoon, William Robertson Coe, the son of a Welsh gardener, to endow chairs in American Studies at Yale and Stanford as a means of counteracting such pernicious tendencies. But regardless of why they think Britain went wrong, if, indeed, she did go wrong, Americans have continued to find in Britain's decline ominous portents, reinforced by a growing awareness that they themselves no longer occupy the pinnacle of power they held in the immediate post-war years. After all, Britain's decline has been only relative.

Of late the British concern with America as an image of the future has largely obliterated from memory the fact that for many of their ancestors the New World also represented an *Older World* where time moved more slowly. Early accounts of Virginia emphasized its prelapsarian qualities—its sparkling streams, noble forests, and the abundance of its minerals, fruits and wildlife. Observations regarding its inhabitants, who were savage, untrustworthy and given to the worship of idols, did not, it is true, entirely fit into this picture. That they were different from Europeans was plain enough, although why they were different was not entirely clear. John White's watercolours, painted from the sketches he made on the 1587 Roanoke expedition, emphasized their noble qualities. White later used these pictures as the basis for his paintings of Picts and ancient Britons, showing, as his engraver, De Bry, noted, 'that the Inhabitants of the great Bretannie haue bin in times past as sauuage as those of Virginia'.[26] It was as a direct result of these early explorations that scholars began taking a serious interest in Europe's own primitive past, relics of which, they noted, closely resembled the Indian artifacts being brought home from North America.[27] John Locke was merely repeating a widely held view when he commented, a century later, that 'In the beginning all the world was America'.[28] To Englishmen of his day America was a vast continent which pre-dated civilization—wild, unformed, beckoning and yet threatening, inhabited by wild men, looking much as Europe itself must have looked thousands of years earlier. It was thus a continent to which men might go in search of a simpler life, as British farmers and their families were to continue doing right up to the end of the nineteenth century.[29]

To Americans, of course, the image of Britain as representing *The Past* is still very much alive. For some two million residents in the United States, Britain is the past in the sense that they were born there. To many others over the years, regardless of whether they were born there or not, it has been *Our Old Home*, with all the associations, favourable and unfavourable, that that implies. To some, as was the case with many immigrants and their children who went to America in search of a better life it meant misery, unemployment and poverty; to others, such as the American literary expatriates who in the nineteenth century flocked to Britain, it was a cultural homeland. 'If I were approaching the coast of Kamtschatka or New Holland,' wrote the Reverend Orville Dewey as he landed in England in 1833, 'it would be a different thing; it would be comparatively a commonplace occurrence; but here is the birthplace of my language, of my mind's nurture—the world where my thoughts have lived, my fatherland—and yet strange and mysterious, as if it were the land of some pre-existing being.'[30] John McPhee, who revisited his family home on the Scottish island of Colonsay in the 1960s, not only looked for but actually found the bones of his ancestors.[31] Yet anglophile sentiments have by no means been confined to Americans of British origin. Around the middle of the nineteenth century a number of American Negroes sought a home in Britain, on whose virtues they lavished praise in terms most flattering to their hosts. 'England is, indeed,' wrote William Wells Brown, 'the "land of the free and the home of the brave".'[32] White abolitionists, on the other hand, although they admired Britain's anti-slavery achievement, were often appalled at the contrast they observed between the wealth and privilege of the ruling class and the poverty of the masses, a contrast which reminded them not a little of their own backward-looking South.[33]

Travel firms continue to capitalize on American nostalgia by presenting an image of Britain as a nation of pageantry and historic tradition, scrupulously ignoring the effects which two hundred years of industrialization have had on its physical appearance and the habits of its people. Such pageantry as remains is, in fact, partly kept up for the benefit of American tourists, some one and a half million of whom visit Britain annually, and whose spending has become a significant factor in the nation's economic book-keeping. Many of these visitors continue to follow the well-worn trails of their ancestors from London to Oxford, Stratford-on-Avon and Edinburgh. In addition, there is a small but significantly growing number of Americans (35,000 in 1972)[34] who live and work in Britain. Some of these are here on assignment by American companies, others because they are married to British citizens. But many have simply chosen to live over here because particular jobs have attracted them or because there are aspects of life in Britain they prefer. Among those most commonly mentioned are the slower pace of life and the fact that England is 'civilized',[35] a comment which probably reflects less on the virtues of England than on the current problems of big American cities.

Attempting to classify such observations, hedged about as they usually are with elaborate qualifications, in terms of archetypal images is a rather pointless exercise. Essentially they are not different from the comments which Englishmen and Americans make about cities or regions of their own countries. Americans living in England—or, for that matter, tourists who, after all, see much more than the well-publicized attractions—are as well able to make discriminating judgements about what they see as the English themselves.

## IV

To a degree, of course, this has always been true. Attempting to equate what Americans and Englishmen thought of one another with the familiar archetypal images begs the question: 'How far did people take these images literally?'—to what extent, in other words, did they *believe* them? As with commercial advertising there is a distinction to be made between the image projected and the image received. Even in the early nineteenth century, when American views of England were peculiarly blinkered, the American sale of books by English authors about England indicates that Americans knew much more than is revealed by the popular rhetoric of the period. The enthusiasm for Dickens, Scott and other British novelists is an obvious case in point, but the same applied to other types of work as well. English and Scottish periodicals had a wider circulation in the United States than did any of their indigenous rivals. To suppose that American views of history are adequately summed up by the conventional pieties of George Bancroft is to ignore the fact that Americans were actually more apt to read Macaulay.[36]

These are appropriate matters for historical enquiry. Yet it must be admitted that this is not a field in which historians, by and large, feel at ease. Mainly this is because historians are happier dealing with actions than words. Even at the best of times relating images to beliefs and beliefs to actions is a tricky and often a pedantic business. What are historians to make of images which are simply playful or which have no ascertainable connection with actions—the world of national stereotypes and music hall humour, of cartoonists and caricaturists, of Hank Morgan and Mr La Fayette Kettle?

But if the historical mind is ill at ease in this world, the literary imagination is very much at home in it. Because of their relatively unstructured character Anglo-American images have provided a wealth of material for writers. One may speculate in this context on the frequent protestations of nineteenth-century American authors that there was less to write about in America than in Europe. The case was forcefully put early in the century by James Fenimore Cooper in *Notions of the Americans* (1828) in which he argued that a major 'obstacle against which American literature has to contend is in the poverty of materials. There is scarcely an ore which contributes to the wealth of the author that is found here in veins as rich as in Europe.' This may, indeed, have been the case, although it is hard to see why, particularly since much that was happening at the time has since become the material of legend. One possible explanation is that Americans actually believed their own rhetoric and that, like Soviet rhetoric a century later, it provided thin pickings for writers of genius. There is, however, another explanation which is that American writers and their audiences had not yet fully come to terms with their own society and so preferred to read about the, in a sense more familiar, history, manners, morals and follies of Englishmen.

How far literature can or should seek to reflect life is debatable. But if what America lacked were literary models and associations, as in part it was, this want was partially compensated for by the mythology which already attached to the transatlantic relationship and which American writers, from Washington Irving on, were to cultivate with profit. Here was a ready-made set of assumptions, beliefs, expectations and stereotypes upon which writers could elaborate at will. If Americans in America were, indeed, poor material for the novelists, this could be remedied by placing them in a European context, where their strengths and weaknesses would stand revealed. In Irving himself this approach is relatively straightforward, designed largely to satisfy the curiosity of his fellow-countrymen about life across the ocean and, in particular, about the more picturesque and whimsical aspects of the Old World. But in Cooper, Hawthorne and Melville the mythic qualities of the relationship are more fully exploited. In Melville's *Redburn* the hero's encounter with emigrants bound for America provokes the reflection that, 'The other world beyond this, which was longed for by the devout before Columbus' time, was found in the New; and the deep-sea-lead, that first struck these soundings, brought up the soil of Earth's Paradise. Not a Paradise then, or now; but to be made so at God's good pleasure, and in the fullness and mellowness of time. The seed is sown, and the harvest must come; and our children's children, on the world's jubilee morning, shall all go with their sickles to the reaping.'[37] Above all, in Henry James the transatlantic relationship provides a basis for elaborate allegories of good and evil, innocence and experience which exploit but far transcend the popular myths about the two continents.

There are obvious reasons why nineteenth-century British writers should have been less interested in America than American writers were in Britain. Even so, references to America in imaginative literature —as opposed to travellers' accounts—are remarkably few. Often it is no more than a convenient trapdoor for getting rid of characters or a device for explaining sudden changes in fortune, as in *Wuthering Heights* when Heathcliffe returns having possibly (although the fact is never fully established) made his fortune there. Among those who treated American themes more fully was the Irish poet, Thomas Moore, who toured the United States in 1805–06 and who contrasted American aspirations with what he saw as the realities of American life:

Who can, with patience, for a moment see
The medley mass of pride and misery,
Of whips and charters, manacles and rights,
Of slaving blacks and democratic whites,
And all the piebald polity that reigns
In free confusion o'er Columbia's plains?[38]

Dickens takes up the same theme in *Martin Chuzzlewit*, a novel which achieves its effect largely by inverting the familiar stereotypes: the plain democrats address one another by their military titles, namedrop, and ape British gentility. Martin pays over his savings to Scadder, a reptilian land agent, for a piece of land in the West. But Eden, as the settlement is called, turns out on arrival to be not Redburn's Paradise but a festering swamp 'on which the good growth of the earth seemed to have been wrecked and cast away, that from its ashes vile and ugly things might rise'.

In the twentieth century the shift in the cultural balance of power between the two nations has encouraged British writers to exploit the full range of transatlantic possibilities. That vile and ugly things have risen in America is a matter that has not escaped their attention, but the picture is too varied to allow of easy generalization. Nowadays, American characters of all sorts move freely in and out of the pages of British novels. We have also seen, in a succession of works, the Henry James theme reversed as aspiring Englishmen confront the confusions, misunderstandings and sheer bewilderment of the New World.[39]

More to the point, however, is the extent to which, in the realm of the arts at least, the two cultures have merged. Most films nowadays are international productions. American television westerns and comedy shows are watched eagerly by British viewers, as are British historical documentaries by American audiences. Top actors and entertainers commute regularly between the two countries. The process has gone furthest in the pop-music field which is nowadays almost totally international.

It may be objected that much of this is less novel than it seems. Even in the nineteenth century it was not uncommon for American novelists and poets to receive recognition first in England. (The reverse has, significantly, been the case with such British novelists as Le Carré, John Fowles and Richard Adams.) Nevertheless, the force and immediacy of the modern mass media make it difficult to talk about British images of America or American images of Britain since many of the actual images reaching audiences in the two countries are identical.

V

What these audiences make of such images is, of course, another matter. One way of throwing light on this problem is to employ what has recently been called image geography. Distorted maps of the world showing countries as larger or smaller in terms of their population, wealth, energy consumption or natural resources have long been a familiar feature of geography books. Producing similar maps to illustrate the images which men carry in their minds is, however, a recent development, although whimsical versions, like *A New Yorker's Idea of the United States of America* (which shows Hollywood and Reno as states and Texas as almost on the Pacific) have long been current. In *Mental Maps* (1974) Peter Gould and Rodney White make the point that such maps can tell us a great deal about the actual world in which we live and that, to the extent that men act on what they believe rather than on what is objectively true, they often tell us more about such things as population movement, the location of industries and the allocation of resources than do 'real' maps.

*Mental Maps* deals mainly with the images people have of their own countries. For example, a survey of the residential preferences of school-leavers in England, Wales and Scotland revealed, not surprisingly, that most felt strong ties to their own regions. But, once allowance had been made for this fact, there emerged a remarkably uniform picture of which parts of the United Kingdom were desirable to live in and which were not. Putting the results together produced a composite map in which the South Coast of England, the Cotswolds, East Anglia and the Lake District were rated highly while Central Wales, North East England and the whole of Scotland achieved overall low scores. A survey of American university students produced similar results, California and Colorado being thought residentially desirable (the American equivalents, evidently, of the South Coast of England and the Lake District) while North Dakota achieved the unique distinction of being the only area surveyed (North Dakota legislators please note!) whose residents did not express a local preference.

What results would be obtained from an Anglo-American survey of this kind remains to be seen, although a study conducted by Unesco in 1948–49, *How Nations See Each Other* (1953), offers some clues.[40] At that time 96 per cent of the Americans questioned as compared with only 51 per cent of the British believed that their own country offered the best opportunity for leading the kind of lives they wanted to lead. Moreover, while 9 per cent of the British believed they would lead better lives in the United States none of the Americans believed that they would be better off in Britain. On the other hand, both felt more friendly towards one another than they did towards any other nation. The survey also revealed that class and economic differences played an important part in determining people's views of other countries. Expressions of anglophilia were more often found in the responses of upper-class Americans (62 per cent) than in those of the poor (27 per cent) while pro-American sentiments were more characteristic of the British middle class (34 per cent) than of either the upper class or the working class (24 and 26 per cent, respectively). Another finding of the survey was that the British were generally less optimistic about changing human nature and more inclined to regard national characteristics as a matter of birth rather than upbringing.

There were, of course, special reasons why, in the late 1940s, Americans and Englishmen should have felt about one another the way they did—among them the recent wartime alliance, Marshall aid and the growing fear of Russia. A survey carried out ten years earlier or ten years later would almost certainly have produced different results. How different one can only guess. But one thing which a series of such surveys might be expected to reveal would be the general differences between the kinds of attitudes canvassed. Views on human nature and the origin of national characteristics, for example, are apt to be less volatile than those reflecting current political developments. Another likely conclusion would be that outside observers are less inclined to distinguish between nations and governments than are those who actually live in the countries concerned or who know them at first hand. It may even be that a useful way of testing the relative closeness of the Anglo-American relationship is to measure the frequency with which people make this important distinction.

These are matters on which image geographers may be able to throw some light. Analysing B.B.C. newscasts, for example, reveals that half the news is British news, much of it London news, but that of the remainder more is devoted to the United States than to any other nation.[41] Perceptual maps of the kind used to illustrate the way in which residents of different racial and ethnic groups view American cities could well be adapted to the broader context of international relations. Equally suggestive are the maps used to show patterns of ignorance and misinformation.[42] In a recent article, 'American Studies in British Classrooms', Roy Avery quotes, mainly as an illustration of the weight of ignorance with which British teachers have to contend, a series of impromptu impressions of America given by British school-children which reveal the extraordinary jumble of information and misinformation, beliefs and prejudices which British children (and presumably adults too) carry around in their heads.[43] Assuming that these are not essentially different from the ideas which these children have about other parts of their own country it is not altogether far-fetched to suppose, on the basis of the work already done by Gould and White, that an analysis of them might yield information of interest.

The real strength of this kind of approach, however, depends not on the drawing of maps and diagrams but on the framing of new questions and the systematic gathering of information. Questionnaires have their drawbacks, for which reason cultural anthropologists are sometimes reluctant to use them.[44] But if the object is to find out someone's views on a well-defined topic it makes more sense to ask him what they are than to try to deduce them from the editorial policies of the newspapers he reads—which is what, for want of any better method, historians are often reduced to doing.

How much light image geographers can throw on the past is not yet clear. Not all of them are quantitative in their approach. Recent articles by David Lowenthal and J. Wreford Watson are very much concerned with the past and the way in which the work of writers and painters may be used to illuminate it.[45] Although the questions they ask are different, the methods they use to answer them are very close to those traditionally used by historians and literary critics.

That image geographers should use such a variety of approaches is indicative of the fact that there is no simple, all-purpose method of dealing with images. As the comments of Oliver Wendell Holmes

M

show, images are essentially psychological phenomena. This is true of responses to immediate events no less than of the archetypal images which over the years have characterized the Anglo-American discourse. If any sense is to be made of either it will usually be by pursuing a variety of methods. Generally speaking, the mythic dimensions of the relationships are best described by writers. But even the most perceptive literary comments are unlikely to tell us how far these myths were *believed* or much about the way in which particular attitudes were distributed through the two societies.

That geographers, of all people, should have assumed the lead in this field will strike many as surprising. *Where* they will lead remains to be seen. In the meantime scholars in other disciplines may profit from observing their progress.

## NOTES

1. Oliver Wendell Holmes, *The Autocrat of the Breakfast Table* (1858, Everyman edn, 1906) p. 52.
2. Thomas Paine, *Common Sense* (1770), *The Writings of Thomas Paine*, ed. M. D. Conway (new edn, 4 Vols, New York, 1967), Vol. 1, pp. 84–111.
3. Daniel J. Boorstin, *America and the Image of Europe* (New York, 1960) p. 36.
4. Roy Harvey Pearce, *The Savages of America: A Study of the Indian and the Idea of Civilization* (revised edn, Baltimore, 1965) p. ix.
5. Winthrop D. Jordan, *White Over Black: American Attitudes Toward the Negro, 1550–1812* (Chapel Hill, 1968) p. 110.
6. Aristotle, *Politics* in *The Works of Aristotle* (11 Vols, Oxford, 1921), Vol. 10, pp. 1327–28; Thomas Jefferson, *Notes on the State of Virginia* (1781, Torchbook edn, 1964) pp. 56–66, 88–98 states that: 'Were it made a question, whether no law, as among the savage Americans, or too much law, as among the civilized Europeans, submits man to the greatest evil, one who has seen both conditions of existence would pronounce it to be the last; and that the sheep are happier of themselves, than under the care of wolves.' Ibid, p. 90. See also Cushing Strout, *The American Image of the Old World* (New York, 1963) pp. 25–34.
7. Henry Adams to Charles Francis Adams, Jr, London, 27 January 1863, in H. S. Commager, ed., *Britain Through American Eyes* (London, 1974) p. 371.

8. Margaret Armstrong, *Frances Kemble: A Passionate Victorian* (New York, 1938) p. 365.

9. Ralph Waldo Emerson, *Address Delivered in the Court House in Concord on the First of August 1844* (Concord, 1844) p. 18.

10. P. 17.

11. Lewis Mumford, *The Human Prospect* (Boston, 1955) pp. 191–201. The same argument, interestingly enough, was used by Noah Webster with respect to the English language, the American version of which he regarded as 'purer' than the English version. See Noah Webster, *Dissertations on the English Language* (Boston, 1789).

12. See, for example, H. C. Allen, *The Anglo-American Relationship Since 1783* (London, 1959) pp. 26–27.

13. Marcus Cunliffe, 'Europe and America: Transatlantic Images', *Encounter*, July (1961).

14. Josiah Tucker, *Cui Bono?* (Gloucester, 1781) p. 118.

15. The principal betrayal in these early years was, of course, the maintenance of slavery: see Joseph Sturge, *A Visit to the United States in 1841* (London, 1842); Charles Dickens, *American Notes* (London, 1842); Daniel O'Connell, *The Irish Patriot: Daniel O'Connell's Legacy to Irish Americans* (Philadelphia, 1863).

16. Quoted in Thomas Hart Benton, *Thirty Years' View* (2 Vols, New York, 1854), Vol. 2, pp. 734–735.

17. 'Columbia' (1777?) quoted in David M. Potter and Thomas G. Manning, *Nationalism and Sectionalism in America, 1775–1877* (New York, 1949) p. 25.

18. 'Journals of Colonel Joseph Gubbins, 1811–1813', manuscript in the possession of the author.

19. Alfred Owen Aldridge, *Man of Reason: The Life of Thomas Paine* (Philadelphia, 1959) p. 201.

20. The best account I know of the impact of American affluence on a British visitor in the 1950s is to be found in the early chapters of Dan Jacobson, *No Further West: California Visited* (London, 1959).

21. 'A Great Day for Europe', *The Times*, 1 January (1973). In this lead article, celebrating Britain's entry into the European Community, *The Times* contrasted the Russian system of 'totalitarian communism' with the American system of 'advanced capitalism with all its grotesque extremes'. 'Fortunately', it concluded, 'the Europe of the community has not adopted either ideology as its doctrine.'

22. Norman Macrea, *The Neurotic Trillionaire: A Survey of Mr. Nixon's America* (New York, 1970) p. 110.

23. See William Burroughs, *The Naked Lunch* (Paris, 1959); Saul Bellow,

*Mr. Sammler's Planet* (New York, 1970); Thomas Pynchon, *Gravity's Rainbow* (New York, 1973).

24. Cushing Strout, *The American Image of the Old World*, pp. 132–156.

25. J. William Fulbright, *The Arrogance of Power* (1966, Harmondsworth, 1970) p. 29.

26. Stefan Lorant, ed., *The New World: The First Pictures of America* (revised edn, New York, 1965) p. 183.

27. T. D. Kendrick, *British Antiquity* (London, 1950) pp. 121–125.

28. John Locke, *Two Treatises of Civil Government* (1690, Everyman edn, 1924) p. 140.

29. Charlotte Erickson, *Invisible Immigrants: The Adaptation of English and Scottish Immigrants in Nineteenth Century America* (London, 1972) pp. 16–25.

30. Quoted in Philip Rahv, ed., *Discovery of Europe: The Story of American Experience in the Old World* (1947, Anchor Book edn, 1960) p. xii.

31. John McPhee, *The Crofter and the Laird* (New York, 1970).

32. William Wells Brown, *Three Years in Europe* (London, 1852) p. 9.

33. Howard Temperley, *British Antislavery, 1833–1870* (London, 1972) pp. 214–215, 223.

34. Central Statistical Office, *Annual Abstract of Statistics, 1973* (London, 1973) p. 23. But very few of them (43 in 1972) choose to adopt British nationality, Ibid, p. 22.

35. Ludovic Kennedy, *Very Lovely People: A Personal Report on Some of the Two Million Americans who Live and Work Abroad* (London, 1969) p. 177.

36. John Higham, Leonard Krieger and Felix Gilbert, *History* (Englewood Cliffs, 1965) pp. 69, 156.

37. Herman Melville, *Redburn* (1849, New Library edn, 1924) p. 197.

38. Thomas Moore, 'From the City of Washington', *Irish Melodies* (4th edn, London, 1823) p. 463.

39. Kingsley Amis, *One Fat Englishman* (Harmondsworth, 1966); Malcolm Bradbury, *Stepping Westward* (London, 1965); Thomas Hinde, *High* (London, 1968); David Lodge, *Changing Places* (London, 1975).

40. William Buchanan and Hadley Cantril, *How Nations See Each Other: A Study in Public Opinion* (Urbana, 1953) pp. 5–7, 135–141, 211–216.

41. J. P. Cole, *Geography of World Affairs* (Harmondsworth, revised edn, 1972) p. 33.

42. Peter Gould and Rodney White, *Mental Maps* (Harmondsworth, 1974) pp. 119–156.

43. *The History Teacher*, VII (1974) 572–573.

44. Rhoda Métraux, 'Resonance in Imagery', in Margaret Mead and Rhoda Métraux, *The Study of Culture at a Distance* (Chicago, 1953) p. 347.

45. J. Wreford Watson, 'Image Geography: The Myth of America in the American Scene', *The Advancement of Science*, XXVII (1971–72); David Lowenthal, 'The American Scene', *The Geographical Review*, XVIII (1968) 61–88. I am also indebted to Professor Lowenthal for sending me a copy of his forthcoming article 'The Place of the Past in the American Landscape'.

# Index

Prepared by Brenda Hall, M.A.,
Registered Indexer of the Society of Indexers.

*Note:* This index contains references to footnotes (as well as text) where substantial information is contained therein. Purely bibliographical material is not indexed.